PERFORMANCE THROUGH LEARNING
KNOWLEDGE MANAGEMENT IN PRACTICE

PERFORMANCE THROUGH LEARNING

KNOWLEDGE MANAGEMENT IN PRACTICE

CAROL GORELICK

NICK MILTON

KURT APRIL

ELSEVIER
BUTTERWORTH
HEINEMANN

Amsterdam   Boston   Heidelberg   London   New York   Oxford   Paris   San Diego
San Francisco   Singapore   Sydney   Tokyo

Elsevier Butterworth–Heinemann
200 Wheeler Road, Burlington, MA 01803, USA
Linacre House, Jordan Hill, Oxford OX2 8DP, UK

Library of Congress Cataloging-in-Publication Data
Application submitted

British Library Cataloguing-in-Publication Data
A catalogue record for this book is available from the British Library.

ISBN: 0-7506-7582-9

For information on all Butterworth–Heinemann publications
visit our Web site at www.bh.com

04 05 06 07 08 09 10 10 9 8 7 6 5 4 3 2 1

Printed in the United States of America

Dedication

To our partners who actively participated:
Carter Crawford—C. G.
Tom Young, Paul Whiffen, and Walt Palen—N. M.
Amanda April—K. A.

Contents

8   Knowledge Management in the Aid and Development Sector: A Case Study in Implementation at Tearfund, 143

By Nick Milton in conversation with Paul Whiffen

9   Knowledge Management in Business Performance at BP Well Engineering, 163

By Nick Milton

Preface

In 1999, Ron Shevlin, a senior analyst at Forrester Research, told a conference audience that Knowledge Management (KM) was the hottest thing since reengineering. However, a Forrester Research study had just reported that six out of seven companies investing in Knowledge Management were doing so on faith—not even trying to measure the return. At the same time, British Petroleum's Knowledge Management team, led by Kent Greenes, published the fact that their Knowledge Management program had delivered documented savings of $260 million in a single year, and that $400 million more was possible but not yet delivered. Hearing this, Tom Stewart (*Fortune*, 1999)[1] asked, "Nearly $700 million. How'd they do it?" Stewart's question will be answered in this book.

We present a framework and model that any organization can adapt to increase performance through learning by using Knowledge Management tools and processes. We describe lessons from the application of this and similar frameworks in a variety of organizational settings, from large global financial and professional services firms to multinational oil and mining companies, to a small charity in the voluntary sector. We also describe lessons that the BP Knowledge Management team learned, and suggest a role for human resources (HR) professionals in implementing successful Knowledge Management initiatives.

The BP Knowledge Management team had several important advantages, one of them being commitment right from the very top of the organization. Lord John Browne, CEO of British Petroleum, recognized the need to improve performance by sharing good practices, reusing knowledge, and accelerating learning; and in 1997 he took a key step toward using learning to improve performance by commissioning the BP KM program. Since that time, companies all over the world in every industry have embarked on Knowledge Man-

---

[1] "Management at Work," Thomas A. Stewart in *Fortune*, June 7, 1999.

agement implementation projects. Few have had the benefit of support at the CEO level of Lord John Browne;[2] some have applied "stealth techniques" at the grassroots level. The intervening years have shown an upsurge in KM activity—innumerable books and Web sites have been published, a KM conference circuit is in place, and every major consulting firm has established a KM practice. But what are the measurable results? Stewart's question continues to be relevant: "How do you do it?" How do you deliver measurable performance improvement through the management of knowledge? And even more fundamentally, how can you manage knowledge in the first place?

What Is Knowledge Management?

At the beginning of a seminar, conference, or training session, when participants are asked to define Knowledge Management, they often respond that it is the "latest management fad." Many say that Knowledge Management is an oxymoron. Numerous people believe that knowledge, by definition, cannot be managed. On the other hand, most people agree that all work involves a knowledge component, and that any team uses knowledge, experience, and know-how as a resource in the process of completing any task or project. Students in an executive management program in 2002 at the Graduate School of Business (GSB) at the University of Cape Town in South Africa responded to the question "What does Knowledge Management mean to you?" Their answers are similar to statements heard in other programs in corporate and academic settings around the world.
Knowledge Management is

- What the company knows about competitors, processes.
- Learning from experience.
- Electronic libraries and databases.
- A systematic way of disseminating information and best practices.
- What we need to know, finding it, and using it to add value and get to a higher level of productivity.
- Energizing peoples' experiences and thoughts to make the organization grow.
- Formulating strategies and implementing them to integrate knowledge or information.

---

[2] Buckman Laboratories is an exception. Bob Buckman, CEO, personally initiated a Knowledge Management initiative called K'Netix in 1992 (Rifkin, G. "Buckman Labs Is Nothing but Net." *Fast Company*, June–July 1996).

- Effective use of skills and expertise in the organization.
- Exchanging new and old ideas for the growth of the company.
- An enabler to drive continuous improvement in the organization.
- Obtaining external information, customer information, and competitive information
- Communication technology.

It's clear that there is a range of perceptions about what Knowledge Management is and what it can deliver. What we would like to share with you in this book is our understanding, based on many years of working in this field, our perception of what is distinctive, and how and where it can add real business value. At its heart, Knowledge Management is the systems, procedures, approaches, and culture you put in place to manage one of your more valuable corporate assets—namely, your knowledge (and by knowledge we refer to the know-how, experience, insight, and capability that allow your teams and individuals to make correct and rapid decisions in support of strategy). Knowledge is a difficult asset to manage, being intangible, fluid, personal, elusive, invisible, immeasurable, and ever evolving. However, many of the other intangible corporate assets—such as safety, brand, reputation, customer loyalty, and so on—are already being actively managed, with positive results. Why not knowledge? Even if the intangible nature of knowledge means it cannot be directly controlled, you can at least manage the systems, cultures, and pathways through which knowledge flows around the organization.

Target Audience

The primary audience for this book is professionals and business managers who recognize that knowledge is an important resource and who want to unlock the value currently tied up in unmanaged know-how. People embarking on or supporting Knowledge Management initiatives will find this book particularly useful because it includes candid accounts of real stories—caveats as well as successes. Human resources, information technology, and business process or quality practitioners involved in organizational change efforts will use this book as a reference.

Structure of the Book

This book is divided into two parts that can be read separately. Part I is an overview of the field of Knowledge Management. It sets the context for Knowledge Management as a method for organizational learning. A practical framework and systematic approach to Knowledge Management is introduced as a starting point for creating a Knowledge Management strategy. Part II contains 11 cases expressed in the voices of participants in numerous KM initiatives. Each story highlights one or more elements in the Knowledge Management framework or systematic approach introduced in Part I. Woven through the book is the story of the British Petroleum Knowledge Management team. A Knowledge Management Toolbox is included in the appendices to list some of the approaches that practitioners can use in their organizations. The Toolbox includes a KM readiness instrument to assess your current state of Knowledge Management, described in Appendix A. Appendix B describes conversational techniques that facilitate sharing of knowledge. Tools to facilitate learning—before, during, and after a project or event—are also included.

The book is designed so that a reader can proceed sequentially or choose specific topics of interest. We are hopeful that people will read what is relevant and apply it to their own situation to demonstrate individual, team, and organizational learning.

CHAPTER DESCRIPTIONS

Part I: Setting the Context for Knowledge Management as a Method for Organizational Learning

Chapter 1, **The Knowledge Management Mandate: Performance Through Learning**, describes and defines Knowledge Management and provides the reader with a brief history of Knowledge Management as a discipline. It positions Knowledge Management as an opportunity for executives, business managers, and human resources professionals to play a critical role in organizational change efforts.

Chapter 2, **A Framework for Performance Through Learning to Produce Results**, presents the theoretical background and practical implications of organizational learning as a method to achieve sustained growth and competitive advantage. This chapter introduces the Organizational Learning Systems Model as the foundation for performance through learning using a Knowledge Management framework that integrates people, process, and technology functions to create a learning culture.

Chapter 3, **Going Deeper: Elements of Knowledge for Action to Produce Results**, explains the relationship between learning and performance to produce desired outcomes, identifying learning actions that contribute to organizational learning. The Knowledge Management approach developed by British Petroleum (and subsequently successfully implemented in many disparate organizations) is described in this chapter.

Chapter 4, **Creating a Culture for Learning,** introduces specific factors that can create a knowledge-friendly culture to support knowledge sharing and creation. Fundamentally, the challenge is to create and sustain an environment where employees believe that knowledge is a vital organizational resource and asset.

Chapter 5, **Structures That Support Learning,** presents observable and tangible structures that encourage collective learning. The challenge is to integrate people, process, and technology functions to capture, transfer, retrieve, and reuse information and knowledge to support performance goals through learning actions. The premise of this chapter is to introduce tools and processes that a knowledge manager can adapt for a specific situation.

Chapter 6, **The Bottom Line—Measuring Knowledge Management Initiatives: Return on Investment,** recognizes the requirement of a Knowledge Management initiative to report measurable results. The chapter presents a brief overview of intellectual capital and a description of an ROI process that has evolved since the 1970s that can be applied to Knowledge Management as a change initiative.

Part II: Voices of Experience: Applying Knowledge Management Tools

This part contains 11 cases written by practitioners from many industries, in disparate organizations located in North America, Europe, and South Africa. Each case describes a Knowledge Management initiative that took place over an extended period of time. The cases collectively address a Knowledge Management framework and approach, as well as the cultural and structural factors introduced in Part I.

Chapter 7, **British Petroleum's Knowledge Management Journey: A Decade of Change,** is the story of British Petroleum's Knowledge Management initiative. It begins by describing several change initiatives that were important precursors for Knowledge Management, and then details the genesis of the knowledge framework described in Part I. It is the foundation for the systematic approach to the management of knowledge that is referenced throughout the book.

Chapter 8, **Knowledge Management in the Aid and Development Sector: A Case Study in Implementation at Tearfund**, is an example of how a small organization in the charity sector successfully applied the systematic approach to Knowledge Management that had been developed by BP. The case is interesting in that the culture of the two organizations is very different, as is the level of technological infrastructure. However, the Knowledge Management approach itself proved to be entirely transferable.

Chapter 9, **Knowledge Management in Business Performance at BP Well Engineering**, looks at the community of well engineers dedicated to oil and gas drilling and completion within BP. This is a core area of business for BP and involves massive investment, where the performance improvements delivered through learning and KM can be immense. The case describes the evolution of the systematic approach to a level of high maturity, where the current focus is on assurance—assuring that knowledge is transferred systematically and strategically within and between all wells teams to achieve results estimated at hundreds of millions of dollars annually.

Chapter 10, **Implementing Knowledge Management Within De Beers: The Early Years**, describes the early stages of implementation of a Knowledge Management strategy in this major diamond mining and sales organization. The focus is on strategic implementation and the need to engage middle managers and business unit leaders in the development of a KM system to benefit the organization.

Chapter 11, **Knowledge Fuel for Fighting Fires: Knowledge Capture at Ukuvuka, a Four-Year Government, Business, and Community Partnership**, tells the story of an innovative project that used knowledge capture to meet a fundamental objective: to create a replicable role model for a partnership arrangement between business, government, and society. The project focused on the Knowledge Asset element of the KM approach. It tells the story from the leader's perspective of her journey in communicating the value of harvesting and capturing knowledge within her organization.

Chapter 12, **Where Did We Start? Building Our Own Knowledge Park at Old Mutual**, is written as a story, typical of the oral history of South Africa. This case describes the approach taken by Old Mutual, the largest financial services business in South Africa, to begin a Knowledge Management initiative later named "knowledge improvement." The initiative began in the corporate HR function with innovators creating the corporate university. The current approach is to apply the principle of "learn before," including the adaptation of selected KM tools and processes.

Chapter 13, **Generating Capabilities in Communities of Practice: The Clarica Story,** focuses on Clarica. Like BP, Clarica Life Insurance (now merged with Sun Life Financial) was a pioneer in developing and utilizing knowledge. This case focuses on Clarica's Agent Network, a community of practice. It outlines Clarica's approach for establishing a strategic community of independent financial planners and insurance agents to generate individual and organizational capabilities. The use of technology within this community of practice is an important enabler.

Chapter 14, **Building a Membership Firm Through Practice Communities at Arthur Andersen,** discusses the firm. In the early 1990s, Arthur Andersen recognized the need to implement a People Strategy that was aligned with their business strategy to achieve their objectives of being a high performing organization and an Employer of Choice. To create an Employer of Choice culture, the firm needed to create a membership feeling for employees. To accomplish this objective, Arthur Andersen established Practice Communities as a core component of building the membership culture. This was an early example of communities of practice without significant emphasis on technology.

Chapter 15, **Piloting Knowledge Management: Lessons Learned from the Small-Scale Approach to Design and Implementation at ETS,** focuses on the Educational Testing Service appointing a chief learning officer who understood the value of knowledge and wanted to advance the organization's management of knowledge. Recognizing the complexity of the domain of KM and the difficulties encountered in global approaches related to the need to obtain returns on investments, the chief learning officer developed a strategy of starting small. The case describes the approach taken to design, develop, implement, and evaluate several KM pilots.

Chapter 16, **Knowledge Management at Shell: Innovation and Integration,** focuses on the oil company. Within the exploration and production of the oil and gas business, Shell recognized barriers to the sharing of knowledge and best practices among Shell staff working in different operating units around the world and sometimes among different teams within the same operating unit. To address this issue, Shell needed to learn from previous experience by accessing the most relevant information. This case presents an approach to identify similar situations systematically through an artificial intelligence technique called case-based reasoning. The application is a customized KM solution using leading-edge technology.

Chapter 17, **Assessing Readiness to Successfully Implement a Knowledge Management Strategy: Back to Basics at Debswana,** describes the growing awareness of Knowledge Management concepts and how two M.B.A. students applied them in a large diamond mining company. The study assessed Debswana's capabilities, strengths, and weaknesses with respect to the KM processes of creation, capture, storage, sharing, and application of knowledge. As a result of the assessment, KM strategy and implementation plans were developed. This case is an example of applied theory within an action-learning experience.

APPENDICES—THE KNOWLEDGE MANAGEMENT TOOLBOX

Appendix A—Readiness Survey for a KM Initiative

The Readiness Survey is a diagnostic tool to administer to every level of employee as a starting point for management to claifiy the readiness of departments, business units, and divisions for embarking on a Knowledge Management initiative.

Appendix 2—Conversational Practices

Conversational Practices includes three tools that support conversations, which are critical for collaboration and knowledge capture, sharing, transfer, and creation: Dialogue, Open Space Technology, and the World Café.

Appendix 3—Knowledge Management Processes

Knowledge Management Processes describes tools that were developed and/or applied to implement BP's knowledge system: After Action Reviews, Knowledge Assets, Learning Histories, Peer Assists, and Retrospects.

Acknowledgments

A book that combines theory and practitioners' stories reflects the work of many people involved in the original projects as well as the authors, editors, and publishers of the book. We want to thank the British Petroleum Knowledge Management team as well as the people who participated in the Decade of Change and BP KM initiatives.

Core team members were Chris Collison, Catherine Day, Gareth Edwards, Kent Greenes, Tony Kuhel, Nick Milton, Walt Palen, Geoff Parcell, Keith Pearse, Barry Smale, Dave Wolstenholme, and Tom Young.

Among the participants in the BP KM initiatives were Neil Ashton, Phil Forth, Sharon Flynn, Nigel Gibbs, John Grundy, Ian Hamilton, Judith Howorth, Dave Jessel, Brad Meyer, Paul Monus, Sandy Petrie, and Argerie Vasillakes.

Without the enthusiasm and willingness of the people who shared their journeys as case projects, the book would not be rich with stories. We thank Stephen John—Arthur Andersen; Dave Evans—BP; Debra Wallace and Hubert Saint-Onge—Clarica; Ian Corbett—De Beers; Balisi Bonyongo and Nischal Sancho—Debswana; Felicia DeVincenzi and T. J. Elliott—Educational Testing Service; Antonia Gillham, Almur Killian, and Shireen Moodley—Old Mutual; Vikas Bhushan—Shell; Paul Whiffen—Tearfund; and Sandra Fowkes and Shanil Haricharan—Ukuvuka.

We are fortunate to be pioneers in the practice field of Knowledge Management. We want to acknowledge the work and support of our fellow travelers, clients, and thought leaders who contributed to our individual and collective understanding of Knowledge Management as a tool to enhance performance through learning.

In addition, we had continuous support from an incredible group of people as we wrote this book: Jack Phillips, series editor, Improving Human Performance; Joyce Alff, content editor; Debra Wallace, Anika Gakovic, and Andrea Honett, content editors;

Denyse Rodriquez, graphics designer; Karen Maloney, senior acquisitions editor (Butterworth-Heinemann); Ailsa Marks, commissioning editor (Butterworth-Heinemann); Dennis McGonagle, editorial coordinator; Simon Crump, publishing services manager; Marcy Barnes-Henrie, project manager; and Paul Gottehrer, senior project manager.

Writing this book was an exercise in remote collaboration for the authors. We were a virtual team, located on three continents. We created norms and used collaborative technology to produce the final product. We trust that people reading this book will have positive experiences and accept that it is not all uphill as they implement Knowledge Management initiatives. To everyone who participates in the conversations and projects that allow us to continue to learn, we are grateful.

Carol Gorelick—New York, New York
Nick Milton—Cheddar, United Kingdom
Kurt April—Cape Town, South Africa
September 9, 2003

PART I

Setting the Context for Knowledge Management as a Method for Organizational Learning

CHAPTER 1

The Knowledge Management Mandate: Performance Through Learning

WHAT IS KNOWLEDGE MANAGEMENT?

Knowledge Management is fundamentally a systematic approach for optimizing the access, for individuals and teams within an organization, to relevant actionable advice, knowledge and experience from elsewhere. Actionable is the critical element for the KM practice. If you cannot use the knowledge, it does not have measurable value. Organizations which are not yet applying Knowledge Management may be aware that they don't capture and reuse good or best practices, that they risk repeating the same mistakes, and that they are likely to lose what employees learn, but never share, about suppliers, customers, or competitors. The primary business problem that Knowledge Management is designed to solve is that teams and individuals are performing sub-optimally, because they do not have access to knowledge acquired through experience elsewhere. In addition, new endeavors and innovations may be impeded from lack of access to knowledge via Knowledge Management practices and tools.

Knowledge Management is a vehicle to systematically and routinely help individuals, groups, teams, and organizations to

- learn what the individual knows
- learn what others know (e.g., individuals and teams)
- learn what the organization knows
- learn what you need to learn
- organize and disseminate these learnings effectively and simply
- apply these learnings to new endeavors

This is simple and clear as a statement, but is difficult to accomplish. Although managing knowledge has been a human task for more than 5 million years, it has only recently gained attention as a business discipline.

GROWING INTEREST IN KM

Sandra, a managing director at a large financial services firm, is typical of managers who want to know more about KM. She was on a mission to implement a successful Knowledge Management initiative in her business unit. From experience, she knew that sharing knowledge and continuous learning were critical to meeting the constantly changing needs in her revenue-producing business. Her goal had been to isolate knowledge-related factors associated with revenue and bottom-line business results. Her focus was on return on investment (ROI) and the levers that affect organizational readiness for Knowledge Management tools. She wanted to know more about cost-effective tools that could support her efforts to make individual and collective learning an integral component of any project. She was determined to expand her success to the rest of the firm but knew that she could not meet her objective alone. She read voraciously and met with several consulting firms that were anxious to support her efforts, but Sandra was not convinced that the packaged methodologies described and proposed would work in her company.

Sandra is not alone. She grapples with issues that many managers have faced or are facing when they begin to identify knowledge as a critical resource and want to capture, disseminate, and use information and knowledge efficiently and effectively. Sandra wanted to increase the adoption rate of Knowledge Management in her firm.

Experience shows that she has common questions that anyone starting or involved in a Knowledge Management initiative might have. These questions include:

- Why should I implement or expand Knowledge Management initiatives in my firm now?
- Are there cultural prerequisites for Knowledge Management?
- What level of senior management support is required for KM to be implemented successfully in my firm?
- Are there structures that need to be in place before KM can be successful?
- How can I effectively implement Knowledge Management practices and tools?
- What is the role of information technology (IT) and human resources (HR) in Knowledge Management?
- How can I measure or assess the results of Knowledge Management initiatives?

These questions are answered in this book by presenting an organizational learning model, with a Knowledge Management framework and system that can be implemented in combination with any organization's strategy. The framework is designed to integrate learning with performance, and identifies factors and levers that contribute to improved performance, including several KM tools that help to create a system for continuous learning. Part II contains 11 cases told in the voice of, or from the point of view of, active participants in a KM initiative. Each case focuses on one or more elements of the framework. To ensure that we have a common starting point and language, this chapter begins by describing definitions and a framework for Knowledge Management. It sets the context for the rest of the book that will answer Sandra's questions, as well as those that someone starting a Knowledge Management initiative, wanting to encourage adoption or wanting to add to their tool kit, might ask.

DEFINITION OF TERMS

As in any new discipline, many KM terms are used inconsistently and have multiple meanings. Sharing common language is a critical factor for successful Knowledge Management initiatives. The following terms are frequently used within the book. Brief definitions, which will be expanded on later, are:

- Explicit knowledge—Knowledge contained within some artifact, such as a process, a document or a video, that has typically been created with the goal of communicating with another person. It is an intellectual asset of an organization.
- Intangible assets—Things owned by a company that have no physical existence but have value. As compared with tangible assets, they are predominantly invisible and may be difficult to track and quantify.
- Intellectual or knowledge capital—The intangible assets of an organization which are held by individuals. Relationships, customer loyalty, employees' know-how, culture, and values are elements of intellectual capital.
- Intellectual property—Legally protected knowledge components of a company. Inventions or patents, trademarks, industrial designs, copyrights are examples of intellectual property.
- Knowledge Assets—Compilations of the knowledge of an organization, structured in such a way as to provide guidance and to be a resource for future knowledge users. The compilations of knowledge are often stored electronically.
- Physical capital—Infrastructure and natural resources combined to be useful.
- Tacit knowledge—What the knower knows, that is not obvious to others and is derived from experience.
- Tangible assets—Physical capital that depreciates with use (e.g., plant and equipment).

Whereas tangible or physical assets usually depreciate with use, Knowledge Assets can grow when they are shared and transferred. For example knowledge about a customer leads to repeat business and loyalty, one employee's skill can be learned by others in the department, and so on. Knowledge Assets may be a source of competitive advantage because they can be unique. Saint-Onge (Saint-Onge and Wallace, 2003) categorized intellectual or knowledge related assets as follows:

- Knowing how—Human capital: individual capabilities
- Knowing what—Structural capital: organizational capabilities, including processes
- Knowing who—Relationship capital: knowledge of all stakeholders (people inside and outside the organization who have an interest in the organization; e.g., employees, stockholders, and customers)

In summary, Knowledge Management promotes a collaborative environment for identifying and accessing existing knowledge, creates opportunities to generate new knowledge, and provides the tools and approaches needed to apply what the organization knows in its efforts to meet its strategic goals.

KNOWLEDGE MANAGEMENT AND ORGANIZATIONAL LEARNING

The interest in Knowledge Management as a discipline is relatively new, beginning in the1990s.[1] The interest has been driven by a realization that Knowledge Management methods and tools can be instrumental in increasing performance. However, without continuous learning, sustainable increases in performance are not viable. This has been challenging in practice because Knowledge Management builds on and integrates several business and management disciplines: organizational learning, business management, anthropology, sociology, intellectual capital, virtual teams, and communities of practice. The solution provided in this book is to approach Knowledge Management by integrating people, process, and technology into a framework for implementation (see Figure 1-1).

The challenge is to design and implement a system that meets the needs of the organization. One source of debate about Knowledge Management is differentiating between knowledge as a stock (an asset) and as a flow or process. The Knowledge Management framework presented in this book addresses knowledge as an entity (stock) as well as a process (flow). Our framework eliminates the either/or dichotomy and, instead, uses both. Much as a plumbing system in a house includes stocks (tanks and reservoirs) and flows (pipes and pumps), so a Knowledge Management system in an organization also needs to include both stocks and flows.

HISTORY OF KNOWLEDGE MANAGEMENT

Moving from the industrial era to the knowledge era created a constant state of change. Peter Drucker identified a major trend in the 1970s when he coined the term "knowledge workers" and began to write about people whose minds and experience are more important to the organization than their physical skills. Change has become a constant. The pace of change is accelerating as we move further into the knowledge era. The change, in part, is a response to

---

[1] In 1992 there were 34 articles and 10 books categorized as Knowledge Management. In 2002 there were 3,138 articles and 393 books. In February 2004 there are 3,792 articles and 622 books based on a search of ABI/INFORM, a major business database, and Books in Print.

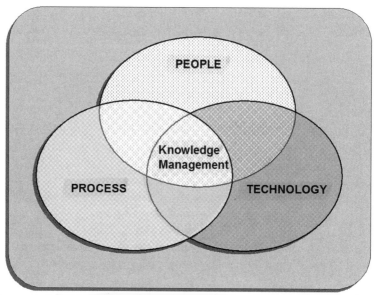

*Figure 1-1. Knowledge Management = people, process, technology
in a background of organizational culture.*

outdated organizational patterns that were built during the industrial era, when business decisions were primarily made to allocate scarce capital, specifically financial capital, to produce results. Whatever drives the change, companies need to learn to adapt if they are to survive. An organization that does not learn faster than the speed of change, is ultimately doomed. In the knowledge era, financial capital is more readily available through global resources than it was in the industrial era. The current challenge is to identify new sources and create new capabilities for organizations to grow. Financial capital is only one element. People and their associated knowledge as well as processes and technology have become major factors in organizational effectiveness. During the 1980s and '90s organizations embraced programs to improve productivity through quality initiatives—e.g., total quality management, business process reengineering, and Six Sigma. Now strategists recognize that the *intangible* assets of most enterprises are the key to the organization's ability to create competitive advantage and to grow at an accelerated pace. When these intangible assets are captured, stored, and shared, Knowledge Management is taking place.

When Knowledge Management became popular in the business press in the 1990s, many business practitioners initially considered it a fad. While KM gained credibility as conference programs and the press popularized the discipline, there is an ongoing debate about the role Knowledge Management plays in creating an organization's competitive advantage. The field of Knowledge Management has evolved over the last decade through contributions of academics from multiple disciplines, consultants, and a myriad of leading practitioners who were probably "doing" Knowledge Management well before the term was coined.

As with any new field of study, early KM efforts focused on establishing concepts and principles, identifying characteristics and elements, building a vocabulary with standardized definitions, and outlining successful applications of the underlying theory. Many discussions of Knowledge Management were and still are at a conceptual level. Using theoretical terms to talk about intangible things puts KM somewhat outside the realm of recognized and popular business language. Many discussions about Knowledge Management can be abstract, leading to a misunderstanding about the real value of "knowing what you know." This continues to fuel the debate about whether Knowledge Management makes a significant contribution to creating a competitive advantage. Even after a decade, the debate over Knowledge Management's value continues. Despite the debate, organizations have identified successful cases where they have developed and implemented an effective Knowledge Management strategy. Successful practices have been incorporated into standard business processes in the same way as accounting and IT have become integral to all business functions. Organizations such as British Petroleum (BP), Clarica, Hewlett-Packard, General Motors, Siemens, the United States Army, McKinsey, De Beers, and Buckman Laboratories lead a long list of Knowledge Management success stories—instances where concerted efforts to manage knowledge assets have resulted in significant competitive advantage through increased performance and learning.

Among the early adopters of Knowledge Management practices and tools were professional service organizations (e.g., McKinsey & Company, Ernst & Young, PricewaterhouseCoopers), whose core business relies on the expertise of its employees. These firms began by capturing, storing, and accessing their knowledge capital. Companies with distributed personnel working on similar problems, such as Xerox's service technicians, implemented systems to share "tricks of the trade" that practitioners had developed over time, thus reducing costs and increasing customer satisfaction. Global aid organizations, such as Tearfund and the World Bank, gathered examples of best practices in order to more rapidly deploy relief resources in human aid and disaster situations on the basis of past experience. Consulting firms collected proposals and client reports in electronic libraries to eliminate reinventing the wheel and to ensure that information was shared within the organization. Successful Knowledge Management initiatives applied existing knowledge or created new knowledge to innovate and collaborate for the purpose of solving existing problems or identifying new ways to do business.

Early KM proponents report these well-known published successes.

- Tom Davenport and Larry Prusak of IBM's Knowledge Management Institute suggest that "the only sustainable advantage a firm has comes from what it collectively knows, how efficiently it uses what it knows, and how readily it acquires and uses new knowledge" (Davenport and Prusak, 1998).
- Former Hewlett-Packard CEO Lew Platt states, "If HP knew what HP knows, we would be three times as profitable" (quoted in Davenport and Prusak, 1998).
- Lord John Browne, CEO of British Petroleum, operationalized the concepts of collecting knowledge and using it efficiently when he stated, "The wonderful thing about knowledge is that it is relatively inexpensive to replicate if you capture it. Most activities or tasks are not one-time events. Whether it's drilling a well or conducting a transaction at a service station, we do the same things repeatedly. Our philosophy is fairly simple: Every time we do something again, we should do it better than the last time (Prokesh, 1997).

THE FOUR PHASES OF KNOWLEDGE MANAGEMENT

The decade of Knowledge Management can be described as four phases. David Snowden (2000) summarizes the recent history of Knowledge Management as three phases. However, there is now evidence that a fourth phase is in progress. Phase 1 emphasized technology. Phase 2 moved the focus to tacit and explicit knowledge. Snowden's phase 3 recognizes the need to go beyond codified information by using stories in the form of narrative representation. The fourth phase integrates the previous three by using a systems approach to Knowledge Management, for the purpose of increasing performance through learning in an organization's internal culture within a specific external environment.

Phase 1: Information to Support Decision Makers

The first phase is considered to be prior to 1995. Here "knowledge" as a word was not problematic; it was used without conscious thought. The focus was on information flow to support decision makers. The term was most often associated with information technology and chief information officers (CIOs) who were responsible for Knowledge Management projects. Examples of Knowledge Management applications or systems that dominated the phase 1 period include

- Executive information systems—Providing easy-to-access, summary-level information to executives.
- Data warehousing—Large electronic libraries containing data that can be combined easily into information for multiple purposes.
- Process reengineering—Systems designed to improve quality by analyzing existing processes and implementing more efficient processes, most often for cost savings (e.g., staff reductions).

Phase 2: Tacit and Explicit Knowledge

In 1995 Nonaka and Takeuchi published *The Knowledge Creating Company*, triggering the second phase of Knowledge Management. For the first time, in common business language the words "tacit" and "explicit" were introduced (although Polyani had explored the subject in his 1962 Terry Lectures at Yale University). The popular success of *The Knowledge Creating Company* raised Knowledge Management to a practice in consulting firms and launched several software products to support collaboration. These technologies were labeled "groupware" or "collaborative technology" and were packaged with methods as well as tools. This second generation of Knowledge Management emphasized the conversion of tacit to explicit knowledge in order to translate individual knowledge into public or collective knowledge. Explicit knowledge is represented by some artifact, such as a document or a video, that has typically been created with the goal of communicating with another person. Tacit knowledge is primarily in the heads of people and is the most important basis for the generation of new knowledge. According to Nonaka and Takeuchi (1995), "the key to knowledge creation lies in the mobilization and conversion of tacit

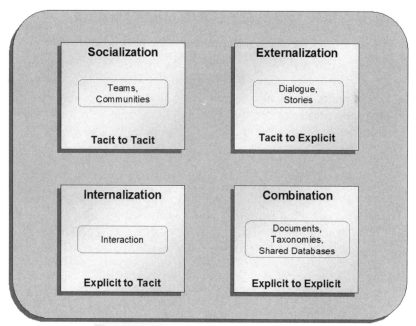

Figure 1-2. The SECI model (Nonaka and Takeuchi, 1995)

knowledge." Both forms of knowledge are important, however, for organizational effectiveness. Creation of new knowledge takes place through the social processes of combination and internalization. Figure 1-2 shows Nonaka and Takeuchi's SECI model, which includes the Socialization, Externalization, Combination, and Internalization processes by which knowledge is transformed within and between tacit and explicit knowledge forms. This model explains Knowledge Management as moving through four transition states (tacit to tacit, tacit to explicit, explicit to explicit, and explicit to tacit).

These SECI processes are as follows.

Socialization (tacit to tacit). Socialization includes the shared formation and communication of tacit knowledge between people (e.g., in meetings, or other forms of dialogue). Knowledge sharing is often done without ever producing explicit knowledge and, to be most effective, should take place between people who have a common culture and can work together effectively (see Davenport and Prusak, 1998). Thus, tacit knowledge sharing occurs in teams and communities.

Externalization (tacit to explicit). By its nature, tacit knowledge is difficult to convert into explicit knowledge. Through conceptualization, elicitation, and ultimately articulation (and typically in collaboration with others) some proportion of a person's tacit knowledge may be captured in explicit form. Activities that facilitate conversion include dialogue among team members, responding to questions, and elicitation of stories (narratives).

Combination (explicit to explicit). Explicit knowledge can be shared in meetings, via documents, e-mails, etc., or through education and training. The use of technology to manage and search collections of explicit knowledge is well established. However, there is a further opportunity to foster knowledge creation and enrich the collected information by reconfiguring it so that it is more usable. An example is to use text classification to assign documents automatically to a subject (e.g., taxonomies) to put a document into a shared database, or to create a Knowledge Asset.

Internalization (explicit to tacit). In order to act on information, individuals have to understand and internalize it. This process of internalizing or habituating the knowledge makes it tacit. By reading documents, individuals can to some extent re-experience what others previously learned. An internalization activity is to read and study documents from a number of different sources. By reading documents from many sources, people have the opportunity to create new knowledge by combining their existing tacit knowledge with the knowledge of others. The internalization process is becoming more challenging because individuals have to deal with ever-larger amounts of information.

In typical business situations, these processes outlined by Nonaka do not occur in isolation, but work together in different combinations. For example, knowledge creation results from the interaction of people and includes both tacit and explicit knowledge. Through interaction with others, tacit knowledge is externalized or codified and shared. The greatest business value occurs from process combination. In this way new knowledge is created, disseminated, and internalized by other employees who can act on it and form new experiences and tacit knowledge that can in turn be shared with others (Nonaka and Takeuchi, 1995). Since all the processes in Figure 1–2 are important, Knowledge Management needs to incorporate all four of them. However, the preferences and balance among the processes in a particular organization, department, or function for a specific project or task will depend on the Knowledge Management strategy used (Hansen, Nohria, and Tierney, 1999).

Codification and Personalization

Hansen, Nohria, and Tierney (1999) label the processes that make knowledge explicit "codification." This corresponds to Externalization and Combination in Nonaka and Takeuchi's model. In addition, Hansen and his colleagues use the label "personalization" to identify people who have the right knowledge, as a major component of Knowledge Management methods and tools. For second-generation thinkers and practitioners, most notably in central Europe (Probst, Raub, and Romhardt, 2000), the function of Knowledge Management was to convert individual or private assets into collective or public assets through the extraction of knowledge into codified form.

Snowden (2000) argues that the codification approach unnecessarily focuses on the container rather than the content. Increasingly, practitioners recognize that much tacit knowledge either cannot or should not be made explicit. Tacit to tacit sharing strategies can be powerful and add business value (e.g., job shadowing, mentoring and role modeling). Knowledge must be actionable to be useful and valuable to an individual, team or group, and organization. However, a strategy that does not incorporate codification is unable to address the problems associated with keeping knowledge in human heads. For example, heads grow old, they forget, they post-rationalize, and they can only be in one place at one time. The ideal solution is to balance codification with socialization, making sure that codification retains as much context and as much human dimension as possible. Each approach should be used for the knowledge it is most suited, as and when the business circumstances dictate.

Phase 3: The Use of Narrative in Organizations

> We always know more than we will say, and we will always say more than we will write down. (Snowden, 2000)

One of the basic operating principles of the third and fourth phases of Knowledge Management is that the process of moving from head (knowing) to mouth (saying) to hands (recording) inevitably involves some loss which may at times be massive. This raises the fundamental issue of the nature of Knowledge Management. Most second-phase KM approaches are *content* management. They focus on documents containing knowledge that is disconnected and separate from the knowledge holder, which diffuses easily and is formally structured. On the other hand, *context* management focuses on connecting and linking people through, for example, expertise location, social network stimulation, apprentice models of knowledge transfer, and retention strategies for key people. Managing context requires the recognition that knowledge cannot be easily separated from human beings either as givers or receivers of information. Context management takes control of what we know but are not able to completely say or write, while content management organizes what we can write. This has significant practical implications for Knowledge Management practitioners when they are designing KM systems. If the organization is relationship (context) centric, emphasis is placed on providing contact information (e.g., electronic yellow pages). In contrast, in content-centric organizations, emphasis is on designing standard and simple processes to capture and store material (e.g., electronic libraries). However in every case a balance of both approaches is needed.

Snowden labels "narrative management" the communication linking between context and content management. Narrative management is a tool to translate or act as a bridge in the knowledge-sharing process by managing the process of conversation and attempting to emulate the natural patterns of knowledge acquisition in organizations. This is done for two main reasons:

- It is easier to capture video stories than written knowledge, because one can record to a video camera in ten minutes what it can take two weeks to get around to writing up.
- It is a natural process. When we face a new task or encounter a problem, we find people to talk to, to ask questions, to narrate theirs stories so that they can provide context-sensitive answers and advice. This kind of knowledge cannot be provided by past project reviews and idealized statements of best practice.

This exemplifies the personalization process and connect strategy referred to earlier. According to Snowden (2000), the separation of context, narrative, and content management (in the third-phase Knowledge Management approaches) makes each sphere of KM more effective. When we understand the limitations and capabilities of each medium—head, mouth, and hands—each method is more effective and the whole is greater than the sum of its parts.

The Important Role of Stories in Organizations

For many people, narrative management is about telling stories that describe experiences and events that occur during organizational life. A common example is how a manager handles an event such as downsizing. The narrative includes the step-by-step process, the interactions between employees, as well as how the manager and the employees felt and reacted to the experience. KM and communication practitioners are increasingly adopting the practices of storytelling, conversation, and dialogue as vehicles for transmitting organizational culture. The management of narrative patterns is an old skill rediscovered in the context of the rapidly changing global environment. Stories that are integral to indigenous, collective cultures in the form of oral history (e.g., Native American, African) have the following attributes:

- They communicate a complex idea in a simple, memorable way
- They unravel their meaning over time and improve with repetition
- They resonate with the audience, to providing increased understanding and insight.

KM practitioners use oral history techniques to capture stories that are then codified and made available throughout the organization in the form of Knowledge Assets. To create Knowledge Assets, the process of capturing and presenting core stories needs to be a skill for Knowledge Management professionals. These stories should be real stories, from past experience, told in the words of the people who gained the experience. Traditionally, storytelling has not been a mandatory or even recognized management skill. In fact, good storytellers were unusual in most professional contexts. More recently, storytelling has been identified as an important management skill (Denning, 2001). External consultants have become mentors, advisers, and coaches providing tools for storytelling; but the stories of an organization belong to its people and must come from the members to be authentic and well received. Telling stories to communicate lessons or to make a point is one aspect of narrative. The most significant use of narrative in relation to Knowledge Management is as a knowledge repository that permits asynchronous conversations across time and space (Snowden, 2000).

Stories for Conversation Across Time and Space

When employees join an organization, it usually takes some time before they know enough to learn the ropes. Orientation courses and work-related training help in learning the new organization's culture.

Current employees understand "how things are done around here." Organizations or departments are a social network of people who have experience with how the organization was built, and have heard the historical stories. The new member relies on experienced employees and does not typically study a best practice database in advance of starting a new project. Most people will look for experienced individuals—friends or mentors whose opinions they respect or to whom they are referred by a trusted source. The problem with this approach to information seeking is that an individual is restricted to his social networks, and the organization is usually limited to its current employees. A solution is a KM system that encourages social interaction. In building a user-friendly narrative database, it is very important to replicate the natural conversational processes by which people both tell and seek out stories. This approach might be counterintuitive for managers who use the traditional deductive, analytic processes of scientific management, but it is intuitive for the end user, the new employee.

The narrative phase of Knowledge Management creates an opportunity for practitioners to adapt their approach to the specific circumstances within their culture. Functional groups such as finance, engineering, and business units often represent multiple cultures. In addition to fitting in to the overall culture, individuals are members of teams and communities of practice. These organizational units are significant contributors to knowledge use and creation. As organizations become geographically dispersed, it is mandatory to implement collaborative technologies to facilitate communication. Virtual teams, communities of practice, and collaborative technologies are building blocks for conversational practices described in the Knowledge Management Toolbox, Appendix B. These conversational practices are central to implementing the Knowledge Management architecture.

Phase 4: An Integrated Knowledge Management Framework

Phases 1, 2, and 3 can be seen as building blocks for an integrated model of Knowledge Management. The fourth phase is described as a framework that synthesizes the components introduced in Snowden's three phases of Knowledge Management.[2]

---

[2] A detailed explanation and critique of Snowden's three phases and a framework for second-generation Knowledge Management that corresponds to our fourth phase of KM has recently been published in McElroy's *The New Knowledge Management: Complexity, Learning, and Sustainable Innovation*, 2002.

KM is not a single thing, process, or a management slogan. Different authors and theorists define and explain KM differently. Each definition reflects the author's perspective and discipline. As a framework, KM can be seen as a collection of elements that work together in varying combinations to accomplish the goal of leveraging an organization's knowledge capital. The KM framework outlined in the next chapter addresses valuable knowledge within an organization that already exists as well as the knowledge created within the organization as a social system.

Chun Wei Choo bases his definition of Knowledge Management on the framework approach:

> Knowledge Management is a framework for designing an organization's goals, structures, and processes so that the organization can use what it knows to learn and to create value for its customers and community. (Choo, 1999)

The framework presented in this book expands Chun Wei Choo's definition by recognizing that, ultimately, the KM strategy drives the accomplishment of organizational goals by increasing performance through learning. A Knowledge Management strategy needs to address and integrate people, process, and technology as well as recognize the unique organizational culture and external environment. In other words, KM needs to drive organizational learning in order to continuously add value. Our definition is as follows:

Knowledge Management is a framework for applying, structures, and processes at the individual, group, team, and organizational levels so that the organization can learn from what it knows (and acquire new Knowledge if required) to create value for its customers and communities. The Knowledge Management framework integrates people, processes, and technology to ensure performance and learning for sustainable growth.

WHY KNOWLEDGE MANAGEMENT NOW?

Sharing knowledge has always been natural between individuals and teams and within organizations when people were co-located and had a common goal. For example, knowledge sharing was achieved through socializing at work and through informal and unofficial mentoring and apprenticeship systems. Because individual employees hold a wealth of experience and knowledge about their companies, profession, and practices, they are able to apply skills and knowledge in the specific organizational context. With the rapid pace of change, increased turnover, reduced loyalty to a company, and the increased use of free agents and subcontractors, the need to capture and disseminate information and knowledge move formally became critical. The need for knowledge sharing coincided with the acceleration of the *knowledge worker*, and the wide recognition that the *intangible* assets of an enterprise will be key to both its ability to create competitive advantage and to grow at an increased pace. As a result, more and more organizations are paying attention to the creation of value through leveraging knowledge. Companies recognize the rapid pace of change and increased level of complexity giving rise to the following challenges:

- competitive pressures for markets and talent
- increased globalization
- mandate to link resources to customer needs
- doubling of knowledge every two to three years
- failures of previous restructuring, reengineering programs
- desire to improve the organization's image
- imperatives to improve quality
- breakthroughs in new and advanced technologies
- the need to do more with fewer people
- a trend to become people-oriented
- the desire to encourage active experimentation

Everyone is searching for tools and techniques to address these issues. Knowledge Management offers a potential solution for dealing with this list of challenges. Organizations need to identify, increase, and utilize existing knowledge. An IDC Corporation study estimated that the global market for Knowledge Management software and services will increase from $1.4 billion in 1999 to $5.4 billion in 2004 (Wintrob, 2001). The projected increase in investment indicates that Knowledge Management initiatives will begin and expand in many organizations.

The investment in KM is driven by the move from the industrial era to the information and knowledge eras, evidenced by the explosion of easily available information. Easy access to information, combined with an increased understanding that intangible assets are essential for organizational growth, is contributing to the growing field of Knowledge Management. Because these issues are strategically imperature for executives and their partners in Human Resource (HR) departments, they have to partner and explore new roles for HR.

THE CHANGING ROLE OF HUMAN RESOURCES

The human resources function is often perceived as technophobic and slow to adapt to the new realities of the marketplace. Strategically HR often plays a secondary role in KM. This is because the classic definition of the HR mandate and traditional staff capabilities make it impossible to meet the fast paced expectations now in demand. When organizations changed the name of the Personnel Department to Human Resources, the intention was to move the department from a tactical or transaction processing environment to one having a strategic role. Successful organizations of the future will be able to quickly turn strategy into action by managing processes efficiently and intelligently (Ulrich, 1998). This requires maximizing employee contributions and commitment at the same time as the organization creates an environment that understands and supports constant change. Therefore, attracting, managing, and retaining talent becomes key to organizational effectiveness.

To meet these requirements, the human resources function has been changing. Human resources professionals participate in strategy development to ensure that the strategy can be successfully implemented. There is a direct link between employee motivation and behavior, the creation of value for customers, and increasing shareholder value. Once the organizational strategies have been developed and approved, human resources needs to create strategies, policies, and procedures that are aligned with the organizational strategies, to fulfill the organizational mission and vision (Holbeche, 2001). Since knowledge is a critical commodity, the knowledge strategy of an organization is central to the new mandate for HR management. However, these changing requirements are sometimes daunting to HR professionals.

HR can and should play an active role in KM. One indication of the changing role of human resources departments and professionals has been that organizations are creating new roles, often within the HR organization. Chief learning officers and chief knowledge officers have become popular functional titles (Bonner, 2000). Creating new roles is one tactic and sometimes a first step to implement new ways of working based on revised HR strategies, policies, and procedures. Linda Holbeche (2001) identifies the opportunity and changing focus for HR professionals as

- Encouraging cross-boundary working and innovation.
- Ensuring alignment between corporate and HR strategies by supporting line managers in moving from a short-term productivity focus to longer-term and cross-organizational issues.
- Overcoming the common perception about HR as passive, without the ability to take and cause action.
- Working with limited resources to improve operational effectiveness as well as focusing on individual development and growth.

The HR function and professionals will be more in demand and more valued going forward. HR can evolve to take on the key roles of formulating and implementing the organization's strategy for generating knowledge era capabilities and leveraging the knowledge of the organization. HR can play a key role in sustaining growth by integrating performance through learning using Knowledge Management tools and techniques. The key strategic issues that now face organizations revolve around scoping their limits, applying their knowledge in different ways, and building an environment where learning is the norm.

Human resources professionals should be included as members of the implementation team when a knowledge strategy is implemented and can be active participants in designing processes that change the way work is accomplished. HR people can function as subject matter experts and facilitators for programs involving people functions (e.g., training, rewards, recognition). HR can support the people circle in the integrated people, process, and technology model (Figure 1-1), for the purpose of creating value and sustainable growth within a unique environment and culture. The intersection of these functions presents an opportunity to create new knowledge-centric roles.

More and more organizations are paying increased attention to the creation of value through leveraging knowledge to increase performance. Historically, line managers addressed performance and measured results. Learning was the domain of a dedicated training department. It was either a staff function within a business unit or a function within a corporate or headquarters HR unit. These traditional industrial era structures are not appropriate for the new business challenges we face in the knowledge era. In this context,

HR can and should evolve to successfully take on a key role in formulating and implementing the organization's strategy for generating capabilities required to create new opportunities. A key element of this winning strategy is Knowledge Management.

FINAL THOUGHTS

Although there are many definitions, methodologies, and products using the label of Knowledge Management, it is clear that many organizations are attempting to address the issue of retaining and sharing and reusing knowledge. The concept is easy to understand. The challenge is in applying the concept effectively in unique environments. This book presents an opportunity for human resources professionals and other executives to play crucial roles in moving their organizations forward.

REFERENCES

Bonner, D. *In Action: Leading Knowledge Managment and Learning.* Alexandria, VA: American Society for Training and Development, 2000.

Choo, C. W. The FIS Knowledge Management Institute session presentations. Faculty of Information Studies, University of Toronto. www.choo.fis.utoronto.ca, 1999.

Davenport, T. H., and Prusak, L. *Working Knowledge: How Organizations Manage What They Know.* Boston, MA: Harvard Business School Press, 1998.

Denning, S. *The Springboard: How Storytelling Ignites Action in Knowledge Era Organizations.* Woburn, MA: Butterworth-Heinemann, 2001.

Hansen, M. T., Nohria, N., and Tierney, T. "What's Your Strategy for Managing Knowledge?" *Harvard Business Review*, March–April 1999.

Holbeche, L. *Aligning Human Resources and Business Strategy.* Oxford, UK: Butterworth-Heinemann, 2001.

McElroy, M. W. *The New Knowledge Management: Complexity, Learning, and Sustainable Innovation.* Boston, MA: Butterworth-Heinemann, 2002.

Nonaka, I., and Takeuchi, H. *The Knowledge Creating Company: How Japanese Companies Create the Dynamics of Innovation.* Oxford, UK: Oxford University Press, 1995.

Probst, G., Raub, S., and Romhardt, K. *Managing Knowledge: Building Blocks for Success.* Hoboken, NJ, John Wiley & Sons, 1999.

Prokesh, S. "Unleashing the Power of Learning: An Interview with British Petroleum's John Browne," *Harvard Business Review*, Volume 75, September–October 1997.

Saint-Onge, H., and Wallace, D. *Leveraging Communities of Practice for Strategic Advantage.* Boston, MA: Butterworth-Heinemann, 2003.

Snowden, D. J. "Organic Knowledge Management." *Knowledge Management*, Vol. 3, Nos. 7, 9, and 10, April–August 2000.

Ulrich, D., interviewed by MacLachland, R. (1998). "HR with attitude." *People Managment*, 13 August.

Wintrob, S. "Sharing Knowledge: The Smart Thing to Do." *Information Highways*, Vol. 8, No. 5, 2001, pp. 14–16.

CHAPTER 2

A Framework for Performance Through Learning to Produce Results

ORGANIZATIONAL LEARNING

Knowledge Management is not an end in itself. The goal of KM is to increase organizational performance through learning by ensuring that each operational decision is made with access to all relevant knowledge and experience. Historically, the prime purpose of business was to make a profit from a product. Today as products become increasingly knowledge intensive, the means of making profits and competing in the marketplace is to become an effective learning organization. Profit and product remain important, but it is continuous learning that enables growth. Harrison Owen (1991) concludes that "the business of business is learning—and all else will follow."

Achieving and sustaining competitive advantage requires organizations to learn better and faster from their successes and failures. In learning organizations, individuals, groups, and teams continuously engage in new processes to acquire, capture, store, disseminate, and reuse knowledge. Learning cannot be separated from performing and is a process that goes beyond time of entry into an organization or prescribed training sessions. "Learning is the heart of productive activity . . . the new form of labor" (Zuboff, 1988). Organizational learning represents a dynamic synergy between people, actions, symbols, and processes within an organization (Schwandt and Marquardt, 2000). Knowledge Management programs, processes, and tools support organizational learning and address more than the sum of the knowledge of each member of the organization or the sum of individual learnings. There is indeed a relationship between an individual's learning and the collective learning of the organization, but individual learning is not sufficient to produce the systematic knowledge required for organizational survival and growth. The following discussion presents the evolution of thought around organizational learning.

BACKGROUND

Peter Senge's book, *The Fifth Discipline* (1990), introduced the term learning organization to mainstream business describing five disciplines:

- Personal mastery—Continuously clarifying and deepening an individual's vision and ability to see reality objectively.
- Shared vision—The skills to build shared "pictures of the future" that generate individual and collective commitment and enrollment rather than compliance.
- Mental models—Deeply ingrained assumptions, generalizations, images that influence how an individual or collective understands the world and takes action.
- Team learning—Learning how to recognize the patterns and interaction in teams that detract from learning. Team learning uses dialogue, conversational techniques, to suspend individual assumptions and allow genuine "thinking" together.
- Systems thinking—A conceptual framework for understanding phenomena in terms of their total context and interrelationships of parts. Effort in one area can cause problems in another without an appreciation of the whole system.

Senge says that an organization that applies these five disciplines is a learning organization. Garvin (1993) defines the learning organization as "an organization skilled at creating, acquiring and transferring knowledge and at modifying its behavior to reflect new knowledge and insights." Therefore, a learning organization is an entity that increases collective capacity through learning. Emphasis is placed on the organization's behavior change because of increased knowledge and skills, as opposed to a focus on an individual's learning. There is, however, a relationship between individual and collective learning that is fundamental to the sustainability of any organization.

Many theorists have been studying organizational learning as a process for more than 35 years. Reg Revans (1966) was the first to identify learning explicitly as an organizational process. Later Chris Argyris and Donald Schon wrote the first book on the subject of organizational learning in 1978. Several themes emerge from these perspectives on organizational learning.

- Both individuals and organizations learn, using different methods, producing different outcomes.
- In order to grow, organizations need to learn.
- Information processing, knowledge storage, and sharing are important.
- Context (structure and culture) contributes to organizational learning.

These themes integrating knowledge and learning are a starting point for linking theories of organizational learning with Knowledge Management Practice. Because business performance must be integrated with systematic and systematized learning to sustain competitive advantage, Knowledge Management can be a means to achieve this goal.

Baird and Henderson (2001) state that strategy and execution have to be aligned, but it is a challenge to sustain the alignment in this fast-paced, rapidly changing environment. "Strategy must move into the world of real time, a constant interaction between what is done, what is learned, and what is planned." Competitive advantage comes from the insight based on knowledge and the speed with which that insight can be applied. Ultimately, the goal is to create organizational capability to extract learning and knowledge from interactions that lead to business decisions and action. This process becomes more complex when the interactions are facilitated through multiple technologies. Success is dependent on implementing the right learning (and KM) strategy efficiently to produce desired outcomes (e.g., standard processes, improved sharing of experience, accelerated acquisition of new competencies). An organization can determine if it is ready for a KM initiative by using the KM Readiness Instrument described in the KM Toolbox, Appendix A. The right strategy is not always evident, so the implementation is in actuality a pilot. The pilot can be an opportunity to both perform and learn for the purpose of innovating, serving customers better, cutting costs, increasing efficiency, and generally increasing performance.

While Senge popularized the term "learning organization," integrating the work of many people that preceded him. Talcott Parsons (1951), a sociologist, developed an organizational learning model, integrating performance and learning, that is the starting point for an organizational learning model with a KM framework.

PARSONS' ORGANIZATIONAL LEARNING MODEL

Parsons' General Theory of Action describes a combination of performance and learning processes that allow an organization to survive in a changing environment. Both performance and learning processes can produce changes in a social system—i.e., organizational culture. Parsons (1951) and Schein (1992) suggest that both performance and learning processes have the capacity to change the equilibrium in an organizational situation. An example of their thinking is the following. A human resources executive is asked to produce a succession plan for the CEO. Staff members in the HR department create a succession planning document. The document fulfilled the request and is an example of a production function. In the process of creating the document, team members recognized inefficiencies in the succession planning tasks as well as ways to improve the results. Learning took place and HR identified process changes. Organizational learning occurred in the actions performed to produce the succession plan for the CEO and should cause change to happen. Parsons' action theory includes four integrated elements for social action:

- An individual, a group or team, or an organization—An actor
- A situation—The physical or social objects the actor relates to
- Symbols—The means through which the actor relates to different situations and assigns meaning to them
- Rules, norms, and values—The guiding factors for the actor's relations with the social and nonsocial objects in his or her environment

Parsons also identified four functions (Figure 2-1) that create a dynamic system to categorize human actions:

- Adaptation to the external environment
- Goal attainment
- Integration of all parts of the organization

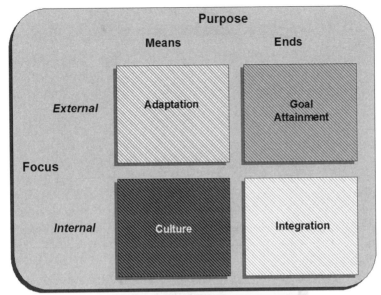

Figure 2-1. Parsons' four functions

- Pattern maintenance to reinforce the organization's cultural patterns and prevalent behaviors

These four functions can be applied at every level of analysis—the individual, team or group, organization, even society, which is beyond the scope of this book. Parsons' theory addresses how people integrate psychological, social, and cultural elements of organizational dynamics from three perspectives: actions associated only with performance, actions associated only with learning, and actions associated with both learning and performance simultaneously. Parsons' view is that information internalized as knowledge changes the conditions of the actions as well as the actions themselves.

SCHWANDT'S ADAPTATION OF PARSONS' MODEL— EMPHASIZING THE LEARNING SUBSYSTEM

Schwandt's adaptation of Parsons' (1951) Theory of Action is a lens to see how performance and learning actions can produce valued knowledge and organizational learning. The four functions of Schwandt's learning system (Figure 2-2) and the Parsons' (1968) performance equivalents (Figure 2-1) are as follows.

The *Environmental Interface Subsystem* (adaptation) is where information comes into and leaves the individual, team, or organization. Tools associated with the environmental interface capture and filter information. The tools are used to scan the environment and to choose and capture useful input for the organization. Examples of this in business include market research, competitive pay surveys, and benchmarking best-in-class.

The *Action-Reflection Subsystem* (goal attainment) creates valued knowledge from new actions in order for the organization to survive. Knowledge supports learning actions that include experimentation, research, evaluations, critical thinking, decision making, problem solving, and clarifying discussions. Examples of this in business include price changes, branding, and advertising.

The *Dissemination-Diffusion Subsystem* (integration) transfers information and knowledge within the organization. Dissemination techniques are formal procedures and policies. Diffusion techniques are informal communication, rumors, and more formal communications such as memos and official e-mails. This coordination function implements roles, leadership processes, structures, and communication techniques to enhance the movement of information and knowledge. In virtual teams, electronic tools are required. Examples of this function in business include expert locator systems, databases, policy manuals, and standard operating procedures.

The *Meaning and Memory Subsystem* (culture or pattern maintenance) creates, stores, and maintains processes for meaning or sense making. It establishes criteria for judgment, selection, focus, and control of the organizational learning system. It includes reasoning processes, comparisons, creating symbols that reflect beliefs, values, language, artifacts, and basic assumptions, and containers for storing and retrieving knowledge, including organizational memory systems. Examples of this function in business include orienting new employees to the story of the company's origins, annual reports, corporate museums, logos, and stories of legendary characters in the business.

Adapted from Schwandt and Marquardt (2000).

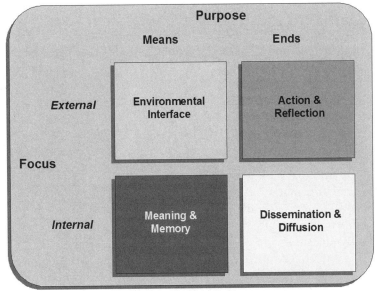

Figure 2-2. Schwandt learning subsystems

THEORETICAL BACKGROUND

Schwandt's four learning subsystems are interdependent. If they are all working well, like all cylinders in a vehicle, the organizational learning system is transforming new information into valued knowledge through actions. The result is the organization's long-term adaptation and survival, through the organization's high capacity for continuous learning. It is important to recognize that in practice all the subsystems do not function at full capacity or at the same capacity all the time. There are times when dissemination and diffusion are more active than action and reflection. For example, following a major organizational change such as a merger or an acquisition, dissemination and diffusion are central. A short-term requirement in a merger or an acquisition is to develop new processes and to make them quickly available to the original and new organizations. On the other hand, when a new product is in development, action and reflection will be strong. Scientists and product developers experiment, test, analyze (reflect), and revise the product. They do not transfer knowledge widely until the product is ready to go to market. Therefore, dissemination and diffusion functions are less significant than action and reflection during product development. To use the subsystems to help an organization learn, we need to understand how the subsystems interact. Schwandt proposes that we observe the inputs and outputs of the subsystems to understand mutual dependence and interaction among the four subsystems. Each subsystem depends on the others for critical input to perform its function and creates output that is required by the other subsystems. For example, the Dissemination-Diffusion Subsystem creates organizational roles as an output. If a research analyst role is created, then the person in that role scans the external environment for new information about the product (environmental interface). The research analyst then creates a summary of the information (action, reflection) and forwards the information to the appropriate people (dissemination and diffusion). Finally, the analyst adds the information to the database on the product (memory and meaning). It is a defined process and cycle. By identifying among these four functions specific interchange media that can be labeled and measured, we can design a tool to study an organization's capacity for learning. Such a tool allows the theory to be applied and evaluated in real work situations, and this is action learning.

Explanation of the Interchange Media

The interchange media represented by arrows in Figure 2-3 show the relationship between the four subsystems. These interchange mechanisms are the elements of input and output that Parsons (1968) defined as media of exchange. These are processes, procedures, and roles manipulated by the collective and by individual employees who produce formal and informal networks and communities. They can be seen as patterns of action that allow for mutual exchange among the subsystems. On a practical level, the media of interchange can be further defined as specific variables or levers that can be managed to produce performance and learning at the individual, group or team, and organizational levels. For purposes of analysis, the performance and learning subsystems are separated (see Figures 2-1 and 2-2). In practice, they are inseparable. The media of interchange are as follows.

New information is an output of the Environmental Interface Subsystem. The learning system accesses new information from the external environment and from within the organization. New information comes into the system from outside and leaves the organizational learning system through the adaptation function.

Goal-referenced knowledge is an output of the Action-Reflection Subsystem. The goals of the learning system are to adapt through learning. This is different from the goal of the performance system, which adapts through performance. Both contribute to the organization's ability to change to ensure survival of the organization.

Structuring is an output of the Dissemination-Diffusion Subsystem. The integration of organizational structures, information technology, roles, policies, procedures, and processes produces a dynamic result. Structuring mechanisms allow for information and knowledge to move within the learning system and the organization.

Sense making is an output of the Meaning and Memory Subsystem. Sense making functions to create a culture. Language and symbols represent the sense making produced and transferred by the Meaning and Memory Subsystem. This medium makes sense of actions through reflection and moves into memory classifications of goal-referenced knowledge. The meaning and memory subsystem is required by the Dissemination-Diffusion Subsystem to generate appropriate structuring. In this way, language and symbols, defined as words and signals, develop to communicate with the other subsystems to create meaning.

(Source: Schwandt et al., 1998)

These four interchange media operate together but, for analysis purposes, can be separated and measured as specific organizational factors such as industry conferences (new information), strategy formation processes (goal-referenced knowledge), roles and norms (structuring), and language and values (sense making). These factors are considered levers that individuals, groups and teams, or organizations can develop, implement, and manipulate to increase learning

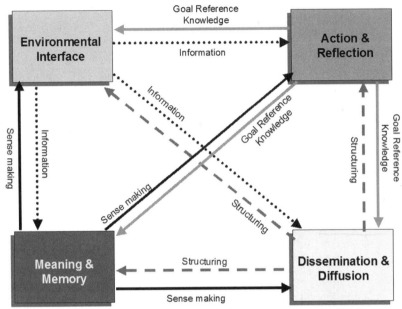

Figure 2-3. Media of interchange in Schwandt's learning subsystems

and performance by developing a strategy that uses appropriate levers within the context or culture.

THE SCHWANDT ORGANIZATIONAL LEARNING SYSTEMS MODEL

An organization consists of a collective of individuals who need to learn to react to the external environment and question processes and procedures in order to sustain growth (Schwandt and Marquardt, 2000). The Organizational Learning Systems Model (OLSM; see Figure 2-4) makes the assumption that organizations are dynamic social entities that exist within a complex environment and combine the two interdependent subsystems: performance and learning. The OLSM is used to analyze performance and learning in relation to organizational and knowledge strategies.

The OLSM expansion on Parsons' work as it relates to the learning subsystem is the focus of the Knowledge Management framework that is central to this book.

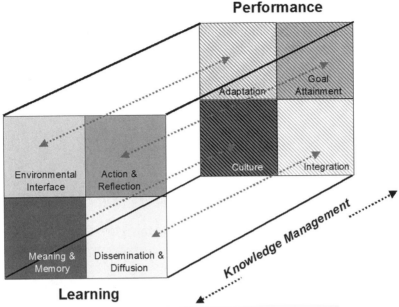

Figure 2-4. Performance through learning

Our Knowledge Management Framework

The foundation of the Knowledge Management framework is the integration of people, process, and technology within the organizational culture (see Figure 2-5).

In traditional organizations, individuals and departments usually specialize in one of the three functions: People issues are addressed in human resources departments, process is often related to quality, business process reengineering, and/or project management, and technology resides in the information systems department. Often staff specialists within these functions are highly capable and competent within their discipline. The challenge to business in general and the opportunity provided for Knowledge Management practitioners, is to integrate people, process, and technology functions to support continuous learning for the purpose of increasing organizational performance. Knowledge management tools that contribute to organizational learning take advantage of the unique culture, resources, and capabilities of the organization.

The OLSM (performance through learning) combined with the Knowledge Management framework (integrate people, process, and

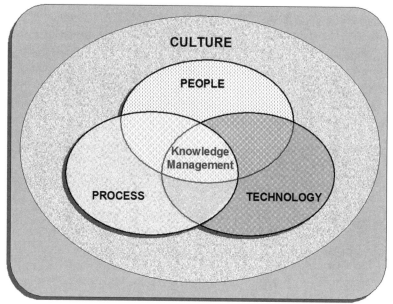

Figure 2-5. KM framework—people, process, and technology integrated through KM

technology using KM tools) can guide implementation initiatives dependent on knowledge or intellectual capital.

Changes in the social system are the result of learning processes that Schein (1992) describes as cultural patterns and basic assumptions. The OLSM model focuses on the learning aspect of an organization as a social system to explain learning and survival in a changing environment. The model suggests that looking at specific behaviors within an organization will reveal how people collectively engage in the learning process. In this context, organizational learning is defined as "a system of actions, actors, symbols, and processes that enables an organization to transform information into valued knowledge, which in turn increases its long-run adaptive capacity" (Schwandt, 1993) and "dynamic human processes required to increase the cognitive capacity of the total organization linked to performance" (Schwandt and Marquardt, 2000).

An important tenet of this model is that there is no moral value associated with knowledge: It is neither good nor bad. However there is positive value for learning because the model assumes that learning is critical for long-term survival.

HOW ORGANIZATIONS LEARN

Prior to entering the workforce, every employee has had experience with formal learning in school and with participating in training sessions designed to enhance knowledge and skills. Organizational learning, however, is more than the sum of individuals' formal learning. It is the result of employees' experiences at the individual, group or team, and company or community levels. Organizations are social units represented by mutually dependent and interdependent actions. The organization develops and transmits a unique culture through the use of symbols and language. This is an important foundation for the emphasis on conversation and narrative that are central to ongoing organizational learning (described as phase 3 of the Knowledge Management cycle; see Chapter 1).

This OLSM model is presented as a means to analyze the relationship between actions of people and their individual and collective ability to adapt to their environments. The model raises the following questions:

- What do we know as an organization?
- How can we apply what we know faster and more efficiently?
- How can we generate more and better knowledge faster?

The OLSM and Knowledge Management framework are a practical way to answer these questions.

A DYNAMIC LEARNING PROCESS

The direct relationship between knowledge and action is an imperative for an organization's sustained ability to continuously learn and grow (Baird and Henderson, 2001; Schwandt and Marquardt, 2000). OLSM represents a dynamic learning process that integrates strategy and performance. There are examples of how the model has been applied in a member of organizations including Andersen Worldwide, Canadian Bank of International Commerce, Federal Express, Hewlett-Packard, Matsushita, McKinsey & Company, NASA, National Semiconductor, PricewaterhouseCoopers, Royal Dutch Shell, and Whirlpool (Schwandt and Marquardt, 2000).

Two assumptions are inherent in the Knowledge Management framework and in the Schwandt Organizational Learning Systems Model. The first assumption is that the model and practices apply at the individual, group or team, and organizational levels. Organizations, groups and teams, as well as individuals can have knowledge and take action. However, most of what is known about the knowledge-action relationship is derived from studies of individuals rather than organizations (Baird and Henderson, 2001). Although we recognize that, in practice, organizations and individuals both know and act, it is nevertheless important to distinguish more clearly between them to identify what organizations can do to build stronger linkages between knowledge and action. The second assumption is that knowledge is concrete, an entity. This is true; knowledge can be seen as a container for explicit content e.g., a database of patents or stock or a website with standard operating procedures. Knowledge Management strategies that focus on creating a container are labeled collect or codification strategies (Hansen, Nohria, and Tierney, 1999). An example is a consulting firm that creates a library of templates to facilitate production of standardized reports that "brand" the firm. However, as discussed in Chapter 1, knowledge is also a process and flow. Knowledge strategies that focus on knowledge flows are labeled connect or personalization strategies. If the emphasis is on people through interactions, relationships, and communities of practice, knowledge will flow through human interaction. In a connect firm, the focus is to connect knowledge seekers with knowledge owners so that the emphasis is on tools that identify people whom others can contact for expert knowledge based on experience.

In summary, "knowledge" is dynamic and highly complex and includes both explicit knowledge, which is highly specific, tangible, and codified (e.g., patents, processes and routines, names and addresses), and tacit knowledge, a less concrete concept of what should be done (e.g., know-how, experience, culture). Although there is recognition of the importance of both explicit and tacit knowledge, most organizations have implemented KM initiatives to capture explicit knowledge—a collect strategy—using information technology, described in Chapter 1. The assumption is that once explicit knowledge is available (often in the form of databases or knowledge bases), it will be used efficiently and effectively. Success depends on a deep understanding of the knowledge that helps people do their work and leads to specific actions, creating a culture where asking for help and learning is expected. Unfortunately, the "If You Build It, They Will Come" philosophy is very unlikely to work.

FINAL THOUGHTS

Organizational learning is critical to an organization's growth and survival. The ability to learn at the individual, group or team, and organizational levels is a recognized competitive advantage. A Knowledge Management strategy that integrates people, process, and technology contributes to organizational learning through the performance and learning subsystems. The Knowledge Management framework provided here includes processes, tools, and techniques that increase performance through learning, creating a learning culture. Learning should be an integral component of every project and activity. In a learning organization, Knowledge Management is a core discipline analogous to finance and safety.

REFERENCES

Argyris, C., and Schon, D. *Organizational Learning: A Theory of Action Perspective*. Reading, MA: Addison-Wesley, 1978.

Baird, L., and Henderson, J. C. *The Knowledge Engine: How to Create Fast Cycles of Knowledge-to-Performance and Performance-to-Knowledge*. San Francisco, CA: Barrett-Koehler, 2001.

Garvin, D. A. "Building a Learning Organization." *Harvard Business Review*, 1993.

Hansen, M., Nohria, N., and Tierney, T. "What's Your Strategy for Managing Knowledge?" *Harvard Business Review*, March–April 1999.

Owen, H. *Riding the Tiger: Business in a Transforming World*. Potomac, MD: Abbott Publishing, 1991.

Parsons, T. *A Sociological Approach to the Theory of Organizations: The Social System*. New York: The Free Press, 1951.

Parsons, T. *The Structure of Social Action*. New York: The Free Press, 1968.

Revans, R. *The Theory of Practice in Management*. London: Macdonald & Co., 1966.

Schein, E. H. "On Dialogue, Culture and Organizational Learning." *Organizational Dynamics*, 1992.

Schwandt, D. R. Organizational Learning: A Dynamic Integrative Construct. Unpublished manuscript. The George Washington University Executive Leadership in Human Resource Development Program, 1993.

Schwandt, D. R., Casey, A., and Gorman, M. Dynamic Role of Collective Memory in Knowledge Systems: A Human Action Theory Perspective, 1998.

Schwandt, D. R., and Marquardt, M. J. *Organizational Learning: From World-Class Theories to Global Best Practices*. Boca Raton, FL: St. Lucie Press, 2000.

Senge, P. M. *The Fifth Discipline: The Art and Practice of the Learning Organization*. New York: Doubleday, 1990.

Zuboff, S. *In the Age of the Smart Machine*. New York: Basic Books, 1988.

CHAPTER 3

Going Deeper: Elements of Knowledge for Action to Produce Results

Many organizations have implemented culture change and process improvement initiatives, supported by popular and proven approaches. Examples include performance management for people functions, "total quality management" and Six Sigma for process improvement, and "case-based reasoning" technology to make help desks more effective and efficient. Measures are required to assess the results of these initiatives, which have led to the widespread development and use of balanced scorecards and traditional return-on-investment calculations.

THE KNOWLEDGE-PERFORMANCE RELATIONSHIP

By focusing on results, the knowledge manager can create a successful track record for an effective link between knowledge and performance, which is fundamental to institutionalizing KM. In practice, performance requires action, beginning with defined tasks and ending with measurable results. Ideally, there should be no gap between action and knowledge as knowledge is the "know-how" that allows you to know how to act). In a small enterprise, where action and knowledge are linked in a single individual or a small team, this is easy. Examples are found in professional services firms that work with apprenticeship systems, where junior people learn from experts. In large and diverse organizations, people with particular knowledge may be widely separated from those who could effectively use that knowledge. Recognizing this, many organizations have created a Knowledge Management system to make the appropriate connections between knowledge providers and knowledge seekers. KM can be a link between knowledge providers and knowledge seekers in the same way that a bridge enables easy movement between two islands. However, just as a bridge would be relatively ineffective if it only enabled one-way traffic, KM must facilitate movement both ways between knowledge and action and between knowledge owners and knowledge seekers (see Figure 3-1). The challenge for an organization's KM function is to stimulate performance and enable correct action by getting the right knowledge to the right people at the right time. Further, an effective KM system identifies where performance is already high, and seeks to learn from this high performance to develop an even greater level of organizational knowledge. Therefore, the knowledge-performance relationship is a two-way connection, with both utilization and learning directions to support performance goals.

The key to delivering useful knowledge for improving performance is developing the links between a direct action in a specific setting and the knowledge that will allow that action to be performed effectively. Therefore, the challenge for knowledge managers is to

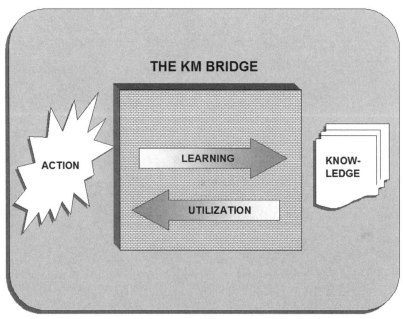

Figure 3-1. The KM performance connection-knowledge bridge

build a bridge backward from a specific goal toward the acquisition and packaging of structured, targeted, actionable knowledge that will clearly provide improved performance to a specific team or group, in ways that the team or group finds useful. The two-way linkage between knowledge and performance is one that can ideally spiral upward in the organization, creating new levels of knowledge and new levels of performance at both the tactical and strategic levels. Strategic knowledge is aligned with business strategy for long-term results, while tactical knowledge impacts operational performance. Many KM initiatives expect KM to help others in the organization learn from existing knowledge, rather than helping KM practitioners learn from action to create totally new knowledge However, successful KM projects that produce measurable results evolve out of a clear and detailed understanding of the actions and results that can be facilitated by knowledge directly related to performance, and analyse action and performance to create new knowledge. Therefore knowledge about action must be continually assessed to develop knowledge for future action. Closing the loop between action and knowledge means paying careful attention to knowledge content and packaging as well as monitoring how it is utilized in the organizational context, including the culture within which it resides. This requires integrating people, process, and technology initiatives within the organizational culture to create a successful KM system (Figure 1-1). In essence, Knowledge Management efforts are directly related to managing change to sustain and increase performance.

Two Equations for Change

To sustain performance improvements and growth, an organization must continuously learn. Ultimately, in a learning organization, performance and learning are so closely intertwined that they are inseparable. This is not current reality in most organizations and teams. Institutionalizing learning is a goal for any change management function. Historically, individuals and organizations separated performance and learning. The equation was

$$Change = Performance + Learning$$

implying that one can exist without the other. For example, perhaps an organization was sued for sexual harassment. The organization's response was to create a policy and a compliance procedure. The HR department sent the policy to every employee annually, reminding each employee of the definition of sexual harassment and the serious consequences of behaving in an unacceptable way. The number of complaints was reduced dramatically. The organization was pleased and prided itself on high performance and taking action to overcome the problem of sexual harassment. Several years later, the executives were surprised when the company was sued again. The earlier solution was nearsighted because the company had implemented a policy and created a compliance procedure but had not developed and offered a mandatory training program, as many other companies had done. A training program with follow-up is a form of learning that educates employees with the goal of eliminating the unacceptable and illegal behavior. Implementing a new policy and compliance procedure alone did not embed or institutionalize the learning. The change program to eliminate sexual harassment only addressed the performance element in the Change = Performance + Learning equation.

When learning is integral to change, the equation becomes

$$\text{Change} = \text{Performance} \times \text{Learning}$$

Therefore, if either performance or learning does not take place, there is *no* sustainable change. This view of change is essential to address learning to sustain performance increases. In addition, it is likely that effort spent on increasing learning will have an exponential impact on sustainable change. If additional learning programs are implemented and a culture of ongoing learning is created, the learning factor within the equation will be multiplied, increasing the overall change significantly (see Table 3-1).

Mechanisms for Learning

The Organizational Learning Systems Model (OLSM) described in Chapter 2 recognizes the need for an organization to adapt and learn simultaneously in order to sustain performance. This requires internal mechanisms for the acquisition, distribution, and interpretation of knowledge as well as creating organizational memory. With the rapid pace of change, these mechanisms give organizations the ability to cope with dynamic environments and the complexity of external and internal environments. Schwandt suggests that we look at patterns of actions rather than causal relationships between individual factors. Organizational learning is primarily "a system's

Table 3-1
The Impact of Learning on Change

Situation	Performance + Learning	Performance × Learning	Interpretation
Performance without learning	$2 + 0 = 2$	$2 \times 0 = 0$	In the short term you can achieve results with no learning.
Performance with learning	$2 + 1 = 3$	$2 \times 1 = 2$	When you first introduce learning the results may not be clearly evident.
Performance with increased learning	$2 + 2 = 4$	$2 \times 2 = 4$	Over time learning activities are offered for newbusiness processes.
Performance with focused learning	$2 + 4 = 6$ $2 + 8 = 10$ $2 + 5 = 7$	$2 \times 4 = 8$ $2 \times 8 = 16$ $2 \times 5 = 10$	When direct attention is paid to learning initiatives, institutionalizing the way business is done, the results exceed those when learning is separated from performance.

ability to adapt to its environment, which has a performance orientation; however, it represents a creative learning capacity through the transformation of information into knowledge" (Schwandt and Marquardt, 2000). The conditions that encourage and sustain learning for action can be isolated as levers that can impact learning and performance within a specific culture. This is important for knowledge managers who are often asked to show direct correlations between their initiatives and business results using traditional ROI calculations. This measurement issue is addressed in detail in Chapter 6.

A knowledge manager can begin by focusing on factors that executives or managers can build on to achieve desired results. The previous chapter discussed Parsons' four exchange media as well as Schwandt's performance and learning subsystems. Although the functions and exchange media are interrelated, and impact performance and learning results, this book addresses them from the Knowledge Management perspective, focusing on the learning sub-

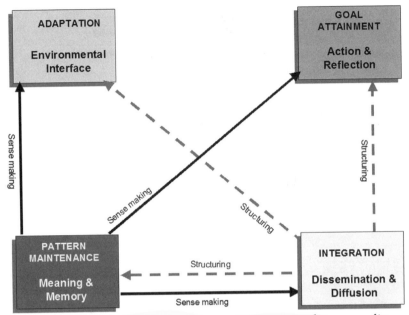

Figure 3-2. Structuring and sense-making interchange media

system. It looks at the internal functions of culture and integration as well as the structuring and sense-making media of exchange described in Chapter 2. Structuring tools ensure the movement of information and knowledge within the system. Sense making creates the culture of "how we do things here." The book also presents levers with their associated tools and processes that can be applied in practical ways. Actions need to be understood at the individual, group or team, and organizational levels as they contribute to the processes of performing and learning. The structuring and sense-making exchange media in Figure 3.2 represent the patterns of inter-related actions that transform information into knowledge, creating an organization's capacity to learn. The ultimate goal is to integrate learning into the culture of the organization at all levels: the individual, team or group, and organizational levels.

MOVING TOWARD PRACTICE

Table 3-2 provides examples of the structuring and sense-making interchange media derived from the experience of participants in Knowledge Management initiatives. Understanding the interdependence of these levers is as much art as science and a significant

Table 3-2
Levers that Contribute to Organizational Learning

Interchange Media	Levers or Variables
Structuring	• Organizational structure
	• Norms (policies, procedures)
	• Roles
	• Technology
	• Leadership
	• Education/Training/Development
	• Rewards & Recognition
Sensemaking	• Shared Context; mission, objectives, goals
	• Language and symbols
	• Values and assumptions
	• Schema, scripts (stories)

(Adapted from Schwandt, *Organization Learning: Advances in Strategic Management*)

tool in a knowledge manager's tool kit. Detailed explanations and examples of the specific levers and tools are included in Chapters 4 and 5.

The levers can be assessed for a specific KM initiative to determine the value of each action. The Knowledge Management system presented in Figure 3-3, emphasizes learning as a means to increase performance and can be used to understand the intent and effect of specific levers.

THE KNOWLEDGE MANAGEMENT SYSTEM

The Knowledge Management system shown in Figure 3-3 has proven to be an effective blueprint for implementing Knowledge Management in several organizations (see Part II, Case Studies).

The system begins with the assumption that business units and teams in the organization work on specific projects with associated goals. Processes to learn before, during, and after the project can capture and apply knowledge to increase performance. These codified processes are designed to capture and maintain content that is easily accessible and dynamic, as opposed to static data or information.

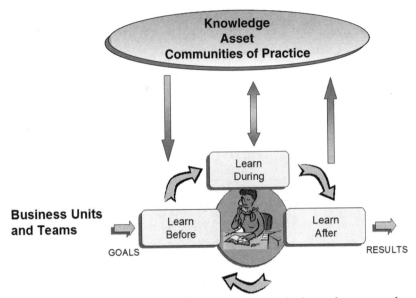

Figure 3-3. Knowledge Architecture: Learn before, during, and after a project or event

To improve organizational performance, the goal is to systematically capture and re-use knowledge. Sometimes this knowledge can be transferred face-to-face, and thereby kept in tacit form. Often, though, it needs to be stored for publication and re-use, somewhere where it can be accessed by future users. It also needs to be "packaged" in a form which makes it easily usable and understandable by the knowledge re-user. This packaged and stored knowledge is labeled a "Knowledge Asset."

The Knowledge Management system described here was developed by British Petroleum's Knowledge Management team and has been applied in disparate organizations like the Tearfund, DeBeers, and Old Mutual (cases are included in Part II) as well as many others. The application of this system begins with the assumption that a knowledge initiative is related to a project or event for specific goals and expected results. Once the project or event is clearly defined and the project team is assembled, a "Learn Before" process should take place. The objective is to identify knowledge from people, documents, and Knowledge Assets which can improve the way the project will be delivered. Knowledge can be accessed by reading from published sources, and speaking to knowedgeable people (for example, as a Peer Assist). During the "Learn Before" stage, knowledge is acquired so that the project team can begin their work at a higher point on the learning curve than they would have if they had not embarked on the learning process. As the project or event takes place, multiple tools are available to ensure that the team "Learns During" the project. An example is to stop and assess results against plans at the end of a shift, (or day, or week), in order to identify (and make explicit) any learning points that can be applied during the next shift (or day, or week). The After Action Renew is a suitable process. Finally, when the project or event is complete, a process is required for "Learning After" the project, to ensure that any knowledge that could be useful to a subsequent team working on a similar is identified project.

The knowledge, advice and experience thus gained is packaged into a Knowledge Asset. Knowledge Assets are useful tools for teams to access previous knowledge and experience during the "Learn Before" process, and a Knowledge Asset is the place that information, knowledge, and lessons learned are stored as a result of the "Learn After" process. Knowledge Assets should be easy to navigate and contain advice experience and recommendations that the reader can use as a basis for planning and decision making.

This cycle repeats itself when a related project or event is initiated and the team uses the Knowledge Asset created earlier to acquire relevant information and to identify people who are knowledgeable about the new content or processes required.

A Knowledge Asset is ideally owned by a group of people who share professional interests and responsibilities, defined as a community of practice. Communities of practice refer to "groups of people in an organization who share a concern, a set of problems, or a passion about a topic, and who deepen their understanding and knowledge of this area by interacting on an ongoing basis" (Wenger, McDermott, and Synder, 2002). The Arthur Andersen and Clarica cases in Part II contain examples of communities of practice in organizational settings. The communities of practice form the interface between the Knowledge Assets and the business projects.

The Knowledge Management system requires that accountability for knowledge management be assigned within each project. A "knowledge manager" needs to be appointed, to make sure the learning processes (Learning Before, During and After) are applied.

FINAL THOUGHTS

Performance and learning are interconnected and must be integrated in learning organizations, to ensure sustained performance and growth. Recognizing the dynamic nature of the two performance and learning functions creates a large opportunity for action using the Knowledge Management system described in this chapter. For practitioners, the questions become these: What should I do? What can I do? What actions should I take? or Where can I intervene to get the largest return for my organization? Chapter 4 describes the cultural issues that need to be considered by a knowledge manager assessing the barriers and enablers associated with influencing performance through learning in a particular organization.

REFERENCES

Schwandt, D. R., Advances in Strategic Management: Organizational Learning and Strategic Management (Vol 14), (J.P. Walsh, A. Huff, P. Shrivastava eds.) Stamford, CT, JAI Press, 1997.

Schwandt, D. R., and Marquardt, M. J. *Organizational Learning: From World-Class Theories to Global Best Practices.* Boca Raton, FL: St. Lucie Press, 2000.

Wenger, E., McDermott, R., and Synder, W. M. *Cultivating Communities of Practice: A Guide to Managing Knowledge.* Cambridge, MA: Harvard Business School Press, 2002.

CHAPTER 4

Creating a Culture for Learning

Understanding organizational and knowledge strategies is essential before we plan Knowledge Management initiatives. It is also important to recognize that systematically managing knowledge requires a cultural transition. New technologies, processes, and roles will be needed, but a more fundamental requirement is a cultural shift in the way that knowledge is perceived. If employees really believe that knowledge is a vital resource to the organization, and truly behave as if it is important, then they will use every available process or technology to share and learn. Most organizations have access to the required processes and technologies, but often employees do not yet understand the value of using them. Exceptions to this statement are informal networks such as the grapevine, the gossip circle, and the rumor mill. These are highly effective knowledge-sharing mechanisms, which often work better than officially sanctioned practices for knowledge exchange. They work precisely because the rumor culture is alive and well in all organizations. If it were possible to develop a culture where individuals saw operational knowledge as being as important and interesting as rumor and gossip, Knowledge Management would be integrated into every action, interconnecting performance with learning.

The nature of the unique organizational culture will make the implementation of Knowledge Management either easier or more difficult, depending on whether the culture is aligned or unaligned with the values of knowledge sharing. In an unaligned culture, Knowledge Management will be a real struggle, while in the right culture, it can be comparatively straightforward. Therefore, part of the challenge in implementing Knowledge Management may be to change the culture. Paradoxically, Knowledge Management itself may be one of the main tools for changing a culture. Knowledge

51

Management is by nature reflective because of the focus on learning and performance improvement. It can also lead to cultural improvements. If culture is a barrier to performance improvement, then Knowledge Management efforts will inevitably raise the issue of necessary cultural changes. An example of a common barrier to Knowledge Management implementation is a culture that sees knowledge as individual power and discourages knowledge sharing. Success can be anticipated when KM and cultural changes are approached simultaneously. Kent Greenes (1999), the leader of the British Petroleum Knowledge Management team, said, "If you wait for the right conditions, the right time, and the right place, you will never begin." The successful approach the BP KM team took is described in the "Decade of Change" case in Part II, Chapter 7. Similarly the Educational Testing Service (described in Part II, Chapter 15), recognized that the organization was not ready for a KM strategy, so they began with one focused initiative to capture knowledge concerned with a core business process.

There is a parallel between a KM system and a system for the management of money. At one time financial management was a specialized function in most organizations, while now every manager is responsible for managing his or her budgets and often profit and loss. A financial management system consists of a holistic blend of people, processes, and technology—not only formulas and spreadsheets. Financial management roles in organizations include financial planners, accountants, and auditors as well as budgeting and accounting processes. SAP, Quicken, and many other software solutions are technologies used in financial management functions.

However, none of these roles and technologies would be brought into a culture where the management of money was considered unimportant. The majority of people in most organizations now work in a financially aware culture. Employees know they need to manage money, they need to look after it, and they need to not waste it. Similarly, a Knowledge Management system needs a knowledge-aware culture, where people know that the knowledge they work with is not just their personal knowledge, it is company knowledge. Employees know they need to manage knowledge, they need to look after it, and they need to not waste it. Changing the culture of the organization to become knowledge-aware will not be easy and it will not be quick; however, it is possible, as illustrated by the cases in Part II.

To begin, a knowledge manager needs to examine cultural barriers that may exist in his or her organization.

Cultural Barriers

Some of the main cultural barriers are embedded in the beliefs of individuals, teams, and the organization. People are attracted to organizations that support their beliefs and values, and managers tend to hire employees that share their beliefs and values. This in itself is a significant barrier to changing a culture. Here are some other common barriers and suggested solutions.

Knowledge is power. This belief is prevalent in an organization with lots of internal competition, where knowledge is currently being managed by leaving it in the heads of experts as tacit knowledge. People need to see that sharing knowledge actually delivers greater power when it comes to competing against major competitors.

Drive to innovate. Some company cultures are built so strongly around the principle of innovation (or pioneering, inventing, and creativity) that there is a strong cultural barrier when it comes to reuse of knowledge. This culture can be so powerful that even when a successful solution exists, people will still seek to do things differently just so they can be more creative. They need to realize that while invention is good, reinvention is a waste of time. Although pioneering and discovery are good, rediscovery is a waste of time. Even the great pioneering voyages of discovery to the New World started from a full knowledge base of what had already been discovered. The explorers began their voyage with explicit knowledge in the form of maps of new lands and intended to fill in the gaps in the current knowledge base.

Individual work bias. Cultures where employees work as individuals, with individual objectives and rewards are difficult places to successfully implement Knowledge Management. Knowledge Management will flourish in a culture where collaboration and co-operation are the norm and where employees work in teams and communities and are rewarded for collective performance. When employees are rewarded only for individual performance, anything that compromises that individual performance (such as spending time sharing knowledge with others) tends not to get done. A goal for a knowledge manager is to move the culture toward having a team or community orientation.

Local focus. In cultures where employees are focused purely on their own team or business unit, Knowledge Management can be difficult. Introducing some form of cross–business unit structure, such as a peer groupings or communities of practice, and providing tools for knowledge to flow in and out of the local teams or departments, is essential to generate more of a network focus.

"Not invented here." This is one of the biggest cultural barriers to knowledge sharing. Individuals prefer their own solutions to anybody else's solution because they trust something they have created themselves. This barrier is largely a lack of familiarity with the people who offer knowledge, and therefore as mistrust of the knowledge they offer. Managers need to look for ways to bring individuals together and to build trust. Their goal should be to help build relationships and trust so that "invented in the community" is as trustworthy as "invented here." At the same time, management can support the trust by sending the message that "invented here" is not good enough. Any solutions based purely on local knowledge will not be as good as a solution based on community knowledge, and so will not be acceptable to management.

"It won't work here." Employees may need to be convinced that knowledge can be managed in their own cultural and organizational context. There are always instances in every organization where knowledge is already being managed to some extent. A knowledge manager needs to demonstrate existing examples, using stories or case histories, as evidence of value being delivered through knowledge sharing. This "showcasing" of success is very powerful for changing the culture by reinforcing a new mind-set of "it does work here."

Don't see the value. This is a barrier that is similar to "it won't work here." A knowledge manager can address this barrier by telling success stories of where knowledge has added value by being managed. An alternative is to share horror stories of where value has been lost when knowledge was not managed. Eventually, the mind-set and the culture should change to "knowledge is one of our key resources."

Making mistakes is wrong. This can be a very powerful barrier when it comes to capturing knowledge from projects that have gone badly or are not successful. The "blame culture" is a powerful disincentive to honest and open knowledge sharing. It is potentially even more of a barrier to knowledge reuse, since people can mistrust knowledge as being "a whitewash." Publicizing some high-profile knowledge capture from disastrous projects most easily breaks this barrier. When employees can see that managers are not afraid to learn from failures, and that learning from failures is not punished, they may in time become more comfortable with the idea of learning from mistakes. In fact, the message from management needs to be that the really unforgivable crime is *failing* to learn from mistakes and thus causing mistakes to be repeated.

Information overload. Employees often complain about being overwhelmed by information, and seem to think that Knowledge Management will just add to this overload. The response to this is the reassurance that Knowledge Management is not about bombarding employees with information but rather providing them with the tailored knowledge they need, at the time they need it.

Knowledge underload. A barrier may occur at the start of a Knowledge Management program, when employees start to look in the "knowledge bank" and find there is nothing in there. There may be nothing for employees to go to, browse, and then learn from. A knowledge manager should start with the exchange of tacit knowledge, using a "connect" (personalization) rather than "collect" (codification) strategy, and at the same time, begin to put material in the bank. To begin, a knowledge manager may perform some knowledge capture and packaging to demonstrate the principle and to begin to build a stock of knowledge capital.

No time to share. The time barrier is a difficult one. Although Knowledge Management will ultimately save time for the organization, it requires a time investment at the beginning. Knowledge Management should start with knowledge processes that save time for the team in the short term. The project should ensure that the new knowledge processes that are introduced have a minimum time burden. The knowledge manager should teach short, focused processes that are quick and easy and will save time over the life of the project. If technology is introduced, it must be easy to use.

Not paid to share. Knowledge Management needs to be embedded into other management processes, such as project management, so that it becomes part of the job rather than an add-on. When Knowledge Management becomes part of the job, integrating learning and performance, it is no longer seen as an alternative to the job. Managing knowledge is part of being paid to do the job. No manager says, "I am not paid to do budgets," or "I am not paid to ensure a safe work environment," or "I am not paid to manage my direct reports," because all of these activities are seen as just "part of the job." As soon as Knowledge Management is seen as "part of the job," it becomes part of the reward structure too.

KNOWLEDGE-FRIENDLY CULTURES

Performance cultures based around teamwork are the most knowledge-friendly cultures. Organizations that work in teams on projects toward performance goals are a good fit for Knowledge Management. In this environment, there are usually processes for goal setting and for review and measurement. There is often a focus on performance improvement when teamwork is common, collaboration and sharing are valued, and the team is project oriented. Performance measurement allows good practices and less effective practices to be identified. It is much more difficult to introduce Knowledge Management and to achieve desired results in organizations where employees still work individually, where there is no performance management system, or where work is not organized into projects with goals, objectives, and deadlines. Internal competition is one of the key enemies of Knowledge Management. Where business units are in competition for money, time, or resources, there is less of an incentive to help the other business units perform better. In fact, it may be advantageous for a particular business unit to keep knowledge to itself in order to win the internal competition. Similarly, if individuals are competing with each other for results (e.g., performance bonuses), there is no incentive for them to help each other perform better. In extreme cases, employees deliberately keep important knowledge to themselves so that a rival team will be unsuccessful, and will then reveal the nugget of essential knowledge at a crucial moment in order to "save the day" and enhance their internal reputation.

Knowledge-friendly cultures are created and nurtured; they cannot be dictated or imposed. The simple tools and processes of knowledge sharing and dialogue that were introduced in Chapter 3 can be a means for developing and sustaining a collaborative and knowledge-friendly culture.

SENSE MAKING AND CULTURE

Sense making is the mechanism that links the meaning and memory, or culture, function to the others functions in the OLSM (see Figure 4-1).

The sense-making actions can be characterized as levers that are available to a person, a team, or an organization to develop and maintain some sense of order or culture. An example is the commitment to learning which team or organization has before a project

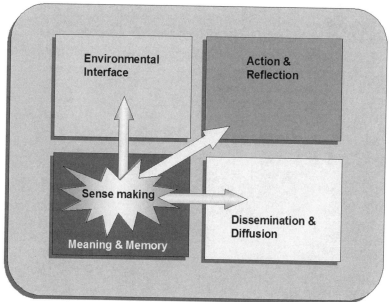

Figure 4-1. Sensemaking, and meaning and memory function

begins. There is a shared value that learning is important, and there may be a common process. (For example, British Petroleum's peer assist tool.) Sense-making actions include:

- Policies
- Procedures
- Creating symbols
- Reflecting beliefs, values
- Common language, artifacts
- Basic assumptions and containers for storing and retrieving knowledge

The sense-making actions are often invisible, as compared with the structuring actions that will be discussed in Chapter 5. The sense-making actions are important to understand because they represent the culture. Specific sense-making levers that have been identified as impacting Knowledge Management initiatives and contributing to organizational learning are:

- Shared context, mission, objectives, goals
- Language and symbols

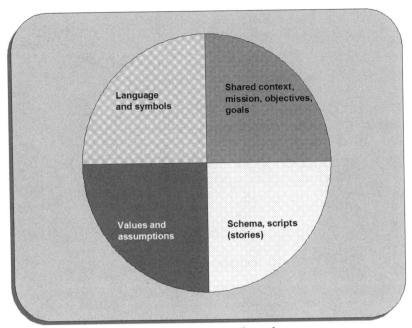

Figure 4-2. Sense-making levers

- Values and assumptions
- Schema, scripts (stories)

These levers are interconnected. An individual, a team, or an organization needs to be aware of the possible effect of each lever, and to integrate the approach for a unique Knowledge Management initiative that fits the project, work unit, and organizational context. Figure 4-2 illustrates the sense-making levers of organizational learning.

SHARED CONTEXT, MISSION, OBJECTIVES, GOALS

The first requirement for aligned action to support learning is an understanding of what is being done, or what is desired, and why. Assuming that leadership has created a vision, an essential activity is to make the vision meaningful and doable for the employees who will implement the vision. Shared context, mission, objectives, and goals are required. In a knowledge-friendly culture, there is a collective awareness of what the organization stands for, what it is trying to do (mission and goals), why the organization is trying to do what it is doing, the purpose and how it will be accomplished. In high-performance Knowledge Management organizations, teams are passionately aligned on mission and objectives that include ongoing learning processes. However, goals and tactics might be individual and situational or context-specific. Cohesion and alignment within the team abound. The mission and objectives are considered a critical success factor. Within a professional team, there needs to be recognition of expertise and autonomy of each team member as well as freedom for each individual to develop his or her own process based on context. In a knowledge-friendly culture, there is an individual and collective commitment to capture and share knowledge at the conclusion of every significant project or event. A standard process will be available for learning after the project or event that assesses performance against goals and contributes significant learnings.

LANGUAGE AND SYMBOLS

Language and symbols are the building blocks of sense making. Language consists of words, combined into sentences and transmitted as conversation about something meaningful based on individual experiences. Weick (1995) states that "people only know what they think when they see what they say." In other words, thought is based on language. This applies to teams and communities as well as to individuals. Language is the way that communities and teams define themselves. For example, in professional communities, outsiders often consider the language to be jargon, while it provides the community with a unique identity. Therefore, alignment requires a team, a group, or an organization to have a common message, with the same words carrying the same meaning. To reinforce an emphasis on learning, a knowledge-friendly culture needs to consciously develop a common language.

VALUES AND ASSUMPTIONS

Values represent an understanding of the operative culture. An organization's value system is a large component of its culture. Shared values and assumptions are significant for creating a knowledge-friendly culture. Value alignment is arguably the most difficult sense-making element to achieve. In order to create alignment, organizational values need to be explicit. This is particularly true for successful Knowledge Management efforts, because of the need to continuously learn and to share learnings, and to integrate learning into performance tasks. The effectiveness of reward and recognition systems is directly related to the values of the staff. For example, a professional might not enter knowledge into a database for a relatively small monetary reward but would gladly share his or her knowledge in exchange for receiving recognition of expertise from colleagues. High-performance Knowledge Management teams share values that guide their conversations and are evident in their stories, leading to positive connections and caring relationships.

Schema, Scripts, and Stories

Scripts and schemas are frameworks within which meaning is created. Schemas represent shared meanings, mental models, or frames of reference, which Senge (1990) defined as "deeply ingrained assumptions, generalizations, or even pictures or images that influence how we understand the world and how we take action." A mental model in Knowledge Management, for example, is that learning is a mandatory and valuable component of every project. Scripts are a special type of schema. They contain context-specific knowledge about events and event sequences. For example, meetings and activities may end with an After Action Review (described in the KM Toolbox, Appendix C). Stories communicate knowledge derived from experience, by presenting that experience in a personal, emotional and context-rich way, which makes it far easier for the listener to identify with. This element of sense making is central to Snowden's third phase of Knowledge Management—the narrative, described in Chapter 1.

In a knowledge-friendly culture, there are shared meanings central to the organization's and group's, or team's, work. Many successful Knowledge Management initiatives are rich with stories of the team's or group's journey. There are often several important events that are universally referred to, thus building the story and creating organizational memory.

Final Thoughts

Together, the sense-making levers are critical to an organization because they play a significant role in knowledge creation. Since teams and groups can learn and store knowledge that derives from positive as well as negative results, it is essential that knowledge managers pay attention to the knowledge capture and storage processes that link learning and performance and ultimately create a knowledge-friendly culture.

An effective way for a knowledge manager to begin to implement KM is to choose a small area, transform a project or a work unit, and use it as a showcase example and success story for the rest of the organization. For practitioners, the question becomes, What actions should I take to get the largest return for my organization? Chapter 5 introduces specific tools for learning that can be used within a particular organization.

REFERENCES

Greenes, K. Personal communication with Carol Gorelick. February 12, 1999, Sunbury, UK.

Senge, P. *The Fifth Discipline.* New York, NY: Doubleday, 1990.

Weick, K. E. *Sensemaking in Organizations.* Thousand Oaks, CA: Sage Publications, 1995.

CHAPTER 5

Structures That Support Learning

Once a learning culture is established and knowledge is recognized as a critical resource, it is necessary to address the people, process, and technology issues that support performance goals through learning actions. Identifying specific enablers that enhance community and team learning is the first step in developing an action plan. Examples are reward systems and electronic community or team spaces. Structuring is the process that moves, transfers, retrieves, and captures information and knowledge. The dissemination and diffusion function of the organizational learning system integrates the requirements of the environmental interface, action and reflection, and memory and meaning functions (see Figure 5-1). Dissemination and diffusion are the most tangible and observable of the four organizational learning functions.

Structuring levers, also referred to as enablers or tools are related to communication, networking, management, coordination, and implementing processes and norms that move (disseminate and diffuse) information and knowledge. An example is a center of excellence that establishes a norm that everyone in the community actively participates by posting their status at least once a week. Another example is a community of practice that designs an electronic discussion forum to support its disparate members. Although use is sporadic, members report that they are dependent on the discussion forum for answers to specific questions related to performance. Dissemination involves formal policies and procedures, while diffusion is accomplished through informal communication networks such as grapevines. Knowledge Management initiatives often focus on specific actions that are observable and tangible, such as technology (electronic communication tools and multimedia knowledge containers) and knowledge-sharing processes. The KM Toolbox in

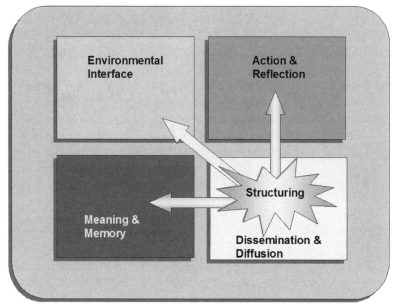

Figure 5-1. Structuring output is dissemination and diffusion

Appendix C includes structuring levers that support KM processes—e.g., tools and techniques for learning before, during, and after a project or event.

STRUCTURE VERSUS STRUCTURING

There is a significant distinction between *structure* and *structuring*. The term "structuring" is used in this context to indicate that this element goes beyond the organizational structure—e.g., hierarchical, flat, or matrixed. The dissemination and diffusion function dynamically integrates organizational structure, roles, norms, objects (such as Knowledge Assets), and processes. It is labeled "structuring" to indicate the process or flow rather than the entity or stock characteristics of these variables. These structuring mechanisms focus on information and knowledge and its movement within the learning system as it integrates with the performance subsystem to meet organizational goals (Schwandt and Marquardt, 2000). Structuring is central to Knowledge Management because it facilitates the learning of the organization. Institutionalized actions move to the meaning and memory or culture subsystem through the sense-making media of interchange process described in Chapter 4, becoming "the way we do things here."

Structuring Actions

The structuring actions are levers that are available to a person, a team, or an organization to encourage the development of formal processes that capture, store, and disseminate valuable learnings from successes and failures. A structuring action is appointing a knowledge manager for a community of practice. Structuring actions are more visible and explicit than the sense-making actions and are important to understand. Specific structuring levers that are key for Knowledge Management initiatives and contribute to organizational learning are:

- Organizational structure
- Norms (policies, procedures)
- Roles
- Technology
- Leadership
- Education/training/development
- Rewards and recognition

A knowledge manager, a team, or an organization can choose from these structuring levers those that fit the project, work unit, and organizational context. The challenge is to integrate the appropriate levers in a specific culture for a unique Knowledge Management initiative. This is the art of Knowledge Management. Figure 5-2 illustrates the structural levers that support the learning process.

Implementation

It is not good practice to implement a change initiative, such as Knowledge Management, simultaneously across an organization. KM implementations have been most effective when they begin with one or more pilots in small areas, work with those pilot groups, adjust and adapt the process, and use successful pilots as showcase examples for the rest of the organization. Once several effective pilots are complete, approaches such as education and training can be deployed to embed Knowledge Management into ever expanding parts of the organization. For practitioners, the question becomes, What levers can I pull or deploy to get the largest return for my

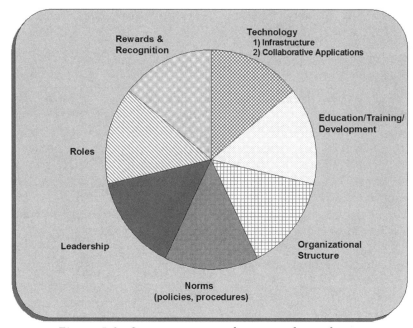

Figure 5-2. Structuring interchange media or levers

organization? Each lever and its supporting actions is described in this chapter. Appendix C in the KM Toolbox contains detailed descriptions of practical methods and tools. Part II—Voices from Experience contains stories that describe implementation efforts from the point of view of participants who have deployed one or more of the structuring levers.

STRUCTURING LEVERS

Organizational Structure

How a company is organized, especially if it is consciously a knowledge-based company, directly influences the strategy and tactics for knowledge sharing. A hierarchical, siloed organization is less likely to share knowledge across people, teams, and the entire organization than a highly matrixed organization where cross-functional work in teams is a way of life. Consulting companies have put considerable effort into organizing to encourage learning, and are good examples of environments where there is a high awareness that information and knowledge are integral to the business. One example is professional services firms like McKinsey, which are organized into practice centers devoted to industries and functions as well as being organized on a geographical basis. Practice Centers within McKinsey include banking and securities, media and entertainment, and transportation. Representative functional practices are corporate finance and strategy, innovation and technology management, and organizational effectiveness. Temporary project teams include members from appropriate industry and functional practices based on the individual client's requirements. Being organized into practice groups facilitates gathering knowledge and developing expertise that can be applied to supporting clients.

A completely different example is British Petroleum, which reorganized itself into a federation of self-standing businesses to achieve performance results (see the "Decade of Change" case study in Part II, Chapter 7). To prevent losing know-how across businesses in the process of becoming a federation, BP responded by creating peer groups as a formal structure for senior managers to share performance goals and resource allocations. Peer groups consist of the leaders of separate business units that face similar challenges (e.g., the peer group of offshore oil fields or the peer group of chemical refinery business units). Peer groups encourage networking, cooperation, and communication across the business units. This structural change contributed to the organization's desire and ability to share knowledge. In addition to the peer groups, BP encourages and supports networks of people and communities of practice that share professional interests. Lord John Browne (Collison and Parcell, 2001) sees peer groups and networks as vehicles to support his belief that "outstanding business performance comes from liberating our staff, creating a culture where they feel comfortable asking for help." The organizational structure of a federation consisting of business units and peer groups within the BP culture (sense making) encourages performance through learning.

Communities of Practice

As companies move away from functional organizations, where people are colocated, they put specialist professionals, e.g., engineers and process experts, into disparate businesses to work on cross-functional teams. Especially in global organizations, these practitioners may be dispersed around the world and probably do not know each other. New processes, tools, and techniques need to replace the traditional methods to encourage knowledge sharing and learning. One method that has been adopted by many organizations is to establish and support communities of practice or networks of professionals.

One of the early definitions for a community of practice was developed from early work within Xerox Corporation: "a group of professionals within a corporation who are informally bound to one another through their exposure to a common class of problems and common pursuit of solutions. Members within the community of practice freely exchange knowledge that creates an even greater resource base of knowledge" (Lave and Wenger, 1991). The community members share common issues and seek common solutions as they share knowledge with each other to improve performance. People must be highly motivated and share a common purpose to participate actively in a community of practice. It is not effective to mandate communities of practice.

In a community of practice, the members deliver individual objectives as members of separate business teams, but cooperate in sharing knowledge to improve their individual performance. If a community member doesn't benefit from being a member, then the community is not working for them and they should be free to leave. Successful communities have voluntary membership. The purpose is a free, and usually informal exchange of knowledge to increase the resource base of knowledge and experience available to the members both individually and as a group.

An individual in the community might have 10 years of industry experience, but collectively the community might have 5,000 years of industry experience. Even more experienced practitioners have found that they increase their resource base by joining and participating in communities of practice. Communities of practice are explicitly supported and recognized as a key element within a KM strategy, because of their ability to respond to the rapid pace of change, and because of the movement toward distributing expertise.

Virtual Teams

Another organizational form, virtual teams, is relatively new but is an important emerging structure for accomplishing work. A virtual team is defined as a team that has members dispersed across distance and time who are linked together by some form of electronic communication technology and who are able to physically interact as a team only on a limited basis (Sessa et al., 1999). People working in virtual teams have been a driver for raising the awareness of the need to institutionalize Knowledge Management tools and practices, because virtual teams by definition require mechanisms for knowledge sharing. At the most basic level, virtual teams are not different from colocated teams. Members of the team have to communicate, coordinate, and collaborate to complete tasks and/or to produce a product or result. Many issues are more obvious and significant in a virtual team than in a traditional colocated team because members cross distance, time, and often organizational boundaries. Therefore technology is a primary means of communicating. Lipnack and Stamps (1997) state that virtual teams are the basic working unit of organizations in the information age and face new challenges because, "It is harder for virtual teams to be successful than for traditional face-to-face teams. Misunderstandings are more likely to arise and more things are likely to go wrong than in colocated teams." The transition from colocated teams, with everyone working in the same location at the same time, to virtual teams, where people can work at any time and in any place, has created the explicit need for collaboration tools and explicit Knowledge Management.

NORMS

Norms are policies, procedures, and rules for accepted behavior within a team or an organization. Best practices are tools and techniques associated with improving and optimizing norms. However, "best practices" is a misleading term because a KM principle is that every practice can be improved. Therefore, "better" or "proven" practice is a more descriptive label than "best practice." Over time, norms evolve into standard and formal tools. For example, having clear and simple rules for communication (e.g., meeting frequency and document storage) is even more critical for virtual teams than for colocated groups. In addition to team standards, individuals have different needs for connection. A team should explicitly address these differences. For example, use e-mail for information updates on a schedule or on an as-needed basis. In summary, explicit norms are critical for a team's interactions that lead to performance results, actions leading to improvement. The Knowledge Management system described in Chapter 3 (Figure 5-3) includes several norms.

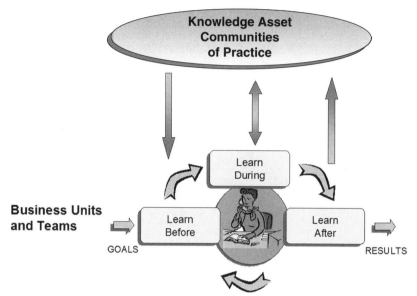

Figure 5-3. Knowledge Management System

Successful teams learn before, during, and after a project or event. The procedures and tools listed in Table 5-1 enable the learning process.

Technology tools can be used during each phase of a project. Examples are virtual teamworking (VT), a PC videoconference technology with coaching, Webcasts, and database search tools. Each of these tools can be made available as part of the technology infrastructure and used when appropriate. For example, PC videoconferences can replace or augment face-to-face meetings. Webcasts are a methodology to include people in many locations in a large-scale meeting or conference that otherwise would have limited reach. Communication tools and expectations, as well as structures for team meetings that include knowledge acquisition, creation, and storage, are significant norms in Knowledge Management practices and are essential components of a KM tool kit. Processes and conversational tools include After Action Reviews, dialogue, expertise finders or yellow pages, Knowledge Assets, Learning Histories, Open Space Technology, Peer Assists, Retrospects, and the World Café. The KM Toolbox in Appendices B and C provides brief descriptions of each process and tool as well as references for detailed information.

Table 5-1
Norms-Learning Tools

Function	Tool
Learn Before	Peer Assist
Learn During	After Action Review
Learn After	Retrospect and Learning Histories

TECHNOLOGY

Technology is a critical enabler for teams in general and virtual teams in particular. Team and/or communication technology can be separated into two categories: infrastructure and collaborative applications. Infrastructure is the hardware and software that allow anyone to communicate with anyone else from any place at any time. Without the technical infrastructure that supports communication and information sharing, virtual teams cannot function. Components of the infrastructure are standardized hardware and software as well as networks that provide fast, reliable, consistent access. Many companies have established standards and created organizational structures to support a Common Operating Environment. If a robust infrastructure is available, people are often unconscious of the capability. They see it as a utility analogous to electricity that is always available. When was the last time that you called an electric company to say thank you for continued service? If your service is interrupted, how quickly do you call to complain? When the technology infrastructure is not built or elements are unavailable or there are multiple incompatible systems across an organization, then there is a significant barrier to knowledge sharing. Once the infrastructure is in place, collaborative technology (or groupware) applications can be effectively implemented to address communication across time and space. The three categories of collaborative technology (Dalton, 1992) include group communications, group memory, and group process support. *Group communications* involves teleconferencing, screen sharing, group scheduling, meetings support, and group writing. *Group memory* refers to existing databases, group filing, filtering, and refining. *Group process support* involves managing groups and workflow. Each element can be separated, but for optimum efficiency and effectiveness, the components form a

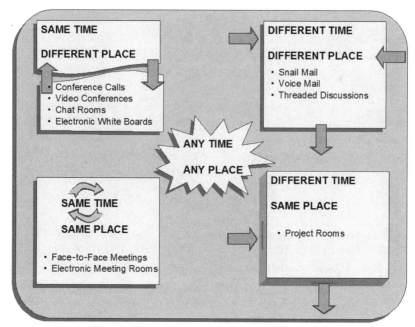

Figure 5-4. Johansen's Four Box Model

"system" that combines the core groupware functionality of communication, coordination, and collaboration. Johansen's (1992) Four Box Model (Figure 5-4) is a tool that categorizes applications for business team needs: same time, same place (meeting room support); same time, different place (videoconferencing); different time, same place (group workspace for document creation); and different time, different place (computer conferencing, e-mail, knowledge sharing).

Underlying the use of collaborative technologies is the basic premise that virtual work requires increased shared efforts, cooperation, and collaboration. Schrage (1995) states that the goal of groupware is to create value through human interaction, not just better information. Computer mediation can help distributed teams increase interaction by providing communication, coordination, and collaboration tools.

Although a virtual team cannot function efficiently without some collaborative technology, without other structuring and sensemaking variables that include information practices, resources, and capabilities, performance and learning cannot be sustained.

> If *All* You Do Is Build It, They Will *Not* Come.[1]

In addition to having technology available, team members need to gather, analyze, share, and utilize key management information. Their challenge is to develop suitable processes, such as those described in Appendix B in the KM Toolbox, and to allocate resources to continuously collect and codify knowledge and to facilitate communications among individuals within the team, across the organization, and sometimes with external people or organizations.

Roles

Formal and informal roles are assigned or assumed in every team. In addition to the traditional team roles such as Belbin's team new roles (see Table 5-2), knowledge managers and knowledge brokers have been identified as part of the Knowledge Architecture that contributes to organizational learning.

These roles support performance through learning for the employee, business project, and organization. The overarching purpose of people who assume these roles is to help workers share their learnings and to demonstrate different approaches to sharing information. Team members typically play multiple roles and recognize that outside perspectives and expertise can add value to a project. Although the appointed leader is accountable for results, many people perform leadership roles in different KM contexts. There are separate and integrated role categories that can be internal or external to a project team. Within each category, there can be functional and behavioral roles assigned and assumed that facilitate a Knowledge Management team's work. The five categories are

- Internal or intragroup:
  - ▽ Supporting socio-emotional issues—Evident as behaviors (e.g., conflict resolution)
  - ▽ Supporting task issues—Measurable results (e.g., status reports)
- External or cross-boundary:
  - ▽ Supporting client projects—Measurable results (e.g., strategy)

---

[1] This expression was first used in a SOLUTIONS electronic team room project report at a major consulting firm in 1996.

Table 5-2
Belbin's Team Roles

Role	Description
Action-Oriented Roles	
Shaper	Challenging, dynamic, thrives on pressure. The drive and courage to overcome obstacles.
Implementer	Disciplined, reliable, conservative, and efficient. Turns ideas into practical actions.
Completer Finisher	Painstaking, conscientious, anxious. Searches out errors and omissions. Delivers on time.
People-Oriented Roles	
Coordinator	Mature, confident, a good chairperson. Clarifies goals, promotes decision making, delegates well.
Teamworker	Cooperative, mild, perceptive, and diplomatic. Listens, builds, averts friction.
Resource Investigator	Extrovert, enthusiastic, communicative. Explores opportunities. Develops contacts.
Cerebral Roles	
Plant	Creative, imaginative, unorthodox. Solves difficult problems.
Monitor Evaluator	Sober, strategic, and discerning. Sees all options. Judges accurately.
Specialist	Single-minded, self-starting, dedicated. Provides knowledge and skills in rare supply.

Source: http://www.belbin.com

▽ Supporting and participating in communities of practice—Evident in knowledge sharing (e.g., IT or HR professionals)
▽ Gaining recognition for the discipline of Knowledge Management to increase performance through learning—Institutionalized practices (e.g., participation in industry conferences)

An example of an internal role is a subject matter expert leading a subtask to collect background information and knowledge in the Learn-Before phase of the project. The role of a knowledge manager is another internal role, which is critical when a business or team is committed to managing its key operational knowledge. Knowledge managers need to be technically skilled and business aware, but even more significant is their attitude and their softer skills. Nick Milton (2002) in an interview said it well: "You know, the really important thing is that Knowledge Managers need to be people who like people."

Observing people working in Knowledge Management for years seems to indicate that "liking people" is a characteristic of people who are really doing this well. In addition, they love what they do. The conclusion is that the competencies that knowledge managers need in terms of tools and technology, and how they do it, are very important, but the thing that makes knowledge managers most effective is their ability to deal with people, their ability to be connectors, and (most of all, maybe) their ability to be self-effacing and to get pleasure out of doing things for other people and helping them to be successful, rather than getting the glory themselves.

Over time, some of the capabilities and activities that are now performed by a designated knowledge manager will become skills that every manager is expected to demonstrate, in the same way as knowledge of finance and information technology have become required management skills.

LEADERSHIP

Leadership in teams in general and for knowledge functions is particular, is not limited to formally appointed leaders. Although the appointed leader is most often the one with accountability, many people perform leadership functions based on the given context. Tissen, Andriessen, and Deprez (2000) identify four leadership functions within a Knowledge Management initiative: (1) expertise in a content area so that the individual and/or team can *sense and respond to*, *combine and connect with*, and *create and produce* unstructured knowledge; (2) the ability to *direct and guide*, *coordinate and control*, *participate and develop* high potential in team members; (3) the capability to be involved in talent management to *detect and develop* team members with requisite knowledge and skills; and (4) the ability and willingness to become involved in self-management and self-development by applying *refresh and refocus skills* at regular intervals in their career. Table 5-3 is an example of leadership functions that were performed by team members during the British Petroleum Knowledge Management initiative (see the "Decade of Change" case in Part II, Chapter 7). A leader with a strong passion for Knowledge Management as a tool to increase performance is critical for success.

The leader allocates resources, including time required for the initiative. Another significant role for the leader is to communicate and

Table 5-3
Leadership Functions Performed by BP Knowledge Management Team Members

Leadership Action	Primary Team Member(s)	Secondary Team Member(s)
Door opener-engager	Leader	All except support staff
Official spokesperson for team	Leader	No one
Traveling ambassador	Leader	All
Representative of BP Group level support	Leader	No one
One who keeps sponsor happy	Leader	No one
Goal setter	Leader	All
Ultimate decision maker	Leader	No one
Leader of strategy development	Leader	No one
Creator of a culture of trust, respect, and friendship	Leader	All
Backup Leader		No one

Leader is the positional leader.

model basic values associated with the importance of knowledge capture and sharing. In many respects, the leader's strong passion for the Knowledge Management discipline, and the will to make it succeed, can drive a team and an organization's accomplishments. Waiting for the right conditions to exist at the right time leads to never accomplishing anything. Passion and motivation can overcome barriers such as unavailable structures and lack of resources. In BP's case, the team leader, Kent Greenes (1999), explained, "We were able to accelerate the impact across the organization because of the pre-existing conditions, but we could have found ways to make things happen without them."

Values that are evident in successful Knowledge Management initiatives include recognition and rewards, ongoing professional development through learning, and providing time to accomplish change. Although values are an explicit element in the sense-making and culture components of learning organizations, values are inextricably linked to the structuring element of successful leadership. In addition to positional leadership and functions, the importance of the personality of the leader is a universal theme in successful Knowledge Management initiatives. The most successful leaders are appointed by senior executives and are described as charismatic, powerful, a presence, strong, and effective. The best leaders are commended for not having an "I know what is best" attitude and for acting as a facilitator by favoring consensus and collaboration as decision-making methods whenever possible. Exemplary leaders are committed to creating and providing learning opportunities for individuals on the team. Kent Greenes, the BP Knowledge Management team leader, stated his philosophy: "As a leader you should provide a framework, then build people's confidence and trust enough to allow them to push against the boundaries and framework that you've created" (Gorelick, 2000).

Some of the cases in Part II, Voices from Experience, are stories of leaders with exceptional knowledge of the organization and with considerable influencing skills. They gained high visibility within and outside the organization, participating in Knowledge Management conferences and sharing their experiences with colleagues in other organizations. In addition to being valuable resources for knowledge acquisition for internal projects, these activities raised awareness of KM's role within the organization. An example is when Chase Manhattan Bank hosted a KM conference in New York for employees and invited people from professional services firms, including financial services and consulting, to attend a presentation and panel discussion titled British Petroleum's Knowledge Management Journey: A Decade of Change.

EDUCATION AND TRAINING

Education and training are elements of any change management function, and Knowledge Management is no exception. Initiatives need to include formal as well as informal training programs. An early requirement in most organizations is to raise awareness of the strategy and benefits of embracing a Knowledge Management program. Experience shows that following awareness programs where the concept of KM is "sold" to business leaders, specific training workshops that introduce and apply recommended tools and techniques are critical for the process of embedding the KM concepts and processes into an organization. BP's Knowledge Management team did *not* develop a formal training program until late in their implementation program. Training wasn't the priority because the main focus was delivering projects with results. Within projects there was always informal, "on the job" training and skills transfer, which was well received. At BP, "We just never gave training the time, effort, and focus that it was due" (Gorelick, 2000). The KM team created exercises that were used during working sessions with internal teams. In retrospect, team members were very aware that not developing a formal course was a mistake and limited the uptake of the team's work. The reason that training was neglected was that it did not come high on the list of priorities determined by the steering group. However the development of a formal KM training program is a way to embed and institutionalize Knowledge Management tools, processes, and behaviors. The challenge is to include an education process as an integral component of the Knowledge Management program as a deliverable; a practical example of integrating learning with performing. For example, two workshops (The KM Primer [Figure 5-5] and The Knowledge Management Master Class [Figure 5-6]) have since been developed by Nick Milton and other members of the BP KM team and are now being provided within BP and other companies (including some of the other organizations described in Part II).

If we consider Knowledge Management a new system that needs to be learned, we can accelerate diffusion and increase the adoption rate for the system through formal training programs. The programs do not have to be in the traditional instructor-led format but can combine online modules and just-in-time learning with stand-up training. To be effective, creating and delivering education to support professional development in the new discipline of Knowledge Management requires accountability. A leader or knowledge manager must be assigned to the task and evaluated on her performance.

REWARDS AND RECOGNITION

Experience has shown that extrinsic rewards, specifically financial ones—e.g., $100 for entering a lesson into a Knowledge Management system—are not very effective in a knowledge-centric professional environment. Recognition, expectation, cultural and peer pressure, and individual personal motivation are more effective to promote and encourage knowledge sharing. What is clear is that established motivational theories, such as those of Maslow and Herzberg, although successful for industrial bureaucracies, will not necessarily work for the establishment of new cultural behaviors. The structuring components of rewards and recognition in the form of compensation policies and procedures are less significant as a means of promoting knowledge sharing. There is an exception when a decision is made about allocating team bonuses. Should everyone be rewarded equally, or should people be rewarded differently based on results, effort, etc.? Duarte and Snyder (1999) predict that equally

Purpose   **The KM Primer**

The aim of this course is to transfer an awareness of the principles and practice of

Knowledge Management. Through a mixture of tutorial and exercise work, the participant

will develop an understanding of the people, process, cultural, and technological aspects

of knowledge management, and will be aware of how knowledge management can be

implemented within a company for measurable business benefit. The course will be

illustrated throughout with practical examples and detailed case studies. The course is

designed for those who are interested in knowledge management and wish to have a

deeper appreciation of what is involved and how it can be implemented.

Audience

This course is designed for the novice who is either interested in understanding KM or

has been selected for a KM project or role. Class size is 10–20 people. No prior

knowledge, skills, or experience is required.

Content

* The tools and techniques of knowledge capture and transfer

* Knowledge management as an organizational change process

* Introductory case studies

* Communities of practice and knowledge roles

* Business implementation

Time

2 days

Source: **Knoco Ltd** http://www.Knoco.cn.uk

Figure 5-5. The KM Primer

Knowledge Management Master Class

Purpose

The aim of this course is to transfer some of the skills and techniques of Knowledge Management to your employees. Through a mixture of tutorial and exercise work, the participant will develop skills in the capture, packaging, and transfer of knowledge, and will develop implementation plans for business pilots. Techniques and strategies or cultural change will also be covered.

The course will be illustrated throughout with practical examples, detailed case studies, and hands-on exercises.

Audience

The Master Class is designed for those who are already working in the field of knowledge management and who wish to develop and practice their skills, or for people assigned to Knowledge Management roles. Class size is 12–15 people.

Content

- The principles of knowledge management
- Knowledge capture tools and techniques
- Advanced case studies
- Knowledge packaging tools and techniques
- Initiating and working with communities of practice
- Cultural blockers and enablers
- Ranking and selecting knowledge management projects
- Enabling technologies
- Implementing knowledge management and measuring the benefit

Timing

3–4 days

Source: **Knoco Ltd** http://www.knoco.cn.uk

Figure 5-6. Knowledge Management Master Class

distributed rewards will become standard as team-based structures are implemented. This is because the new work processes, with teams using technology, create interdependencies between tasks and between people, making one person's contributions almost indistinguishable from those of the next person. As new technology creates a sense of shared work and purpose, collaboration becomes intrinsic to the team's work, and virtual teams become more common. Team-based rewards will consequently become more acceptable. However, knowledge sharing primarily operates at a team or community level (processes such as Peer Assist and Retrospect are team processes), and you could argue that teams with better knowledge-sharing behaviors should be the ones to get team bonuses. On the other hand, Knowledge Management is implemented as a tool to improve performance, so a team that manages knowledge will improve its performance and may well be eligible for performance-related bonuses. Successful Knowledge Management initiatives will be dependent on motivating participants. In general, motivation for learning and performance is directly related to personal, organizational, and societal values that go beyond extrinsic rewards such as money and promotions. For the British Petroleum Knowledge Management Team (KMT), individuals reported the highest motivation when the following circumstances and norms were met and valued.

- A team member believed that what he or she was doing would lead to certain outcomes.
- A team member felt that he or she was playing a meaningful role at the start of something significant to the organization.
- A team member believed that he or she would be recognized (with little or no financial rewards), both within the team and in the organization, for his or her contribution.
- A team member was made aware of articles, books, and conferences citing the BP KMT as a world-class leader in Knowledge Management (external recognition).
- The team member believed that his or her own personal learning was of value and could contribute to the KMT learning.
- A team member believed that his or her colleagues were committed to the goals and objectives of the KMT.
- A team member believed that the desired levels of learning and performance were possible, given the resources, competencies, and skills he or she possessed.

- The team member believed that he or she was seen to be assisting and developing others.
- A team member communicated his or her desire to sustain the team effort of the KMT through agreeing to the equal distribution of performance bonuses.
- A team member witnessed his or her colleagues choosing to continue to work in Knowledge Management rather than return to their original disciplines.
- A team member believed that he or she would be continuously learning something new, since Knowledge Management is a relatively underdeveloped discipline (Gorelick, 2000).

These conditions exist in many high-performing Knowledge Management communities and teams where all the members are committed to both acquiring and sharing information and knowledge. Such motivators create a culture of "openness" for the purpose of successful learning as a collective (the team or organization). Ultimately, personal satisfaction derived from the work is a potent motivator. The absolute monetary value of a salary increase or bonus has less significance than the recognition demonstrated by an increase in salary. As one BP team member stated:

> It's like a relationship between effort and value. How valuable was my effort to you, and how important is it that I repeat that effort? It's easy to say "Great job, well done." Some of my colleagues say that management recognition/peer recognition is the thing that motivates them. I disagree with that. If I do a good job and the leader says "great job," what do I get for that? For me it's very easy to say well done. For the leader to give me a $1 pay rise is extremely difficult. He has to get HR agreement. He has to get HR to process it, and then the Peer Group [another organizational level] has to approve it. Then because it's a change in my salary, my pension has to be reforecast. So to actually change a salary requires significant effort on the part of your line manager. Therefore, if I get a monetary pay rise, I know that he was pleased [with my effort] and went to bat [for me]. (Gorelick, 2000)

MEANINGFUL RESULTS-ORIENTED WORK

Since KM is a relatively new discipline, successful practitioners report that they value the experience of starting at the beginning of a significant change effort more than the financial reward. There is excitement about doing something new. For many Knowledge Management professionals, an important reward is recognition that they are helping other people and their organizations. This is a critical success factor in establishing a learning culture.

RECOGNITION OUTSIDE ONE'S OWN ORGANIZATION

Recognition is important for professionals and is a strong motivator (Schein, 1992; Maister, 1993). Doing meaningful work that makes a difference (self-actualization in Maslow's hierarchy) can motivate Knowledge Management professionals. Several people who contributed cases in Part II have spoken at industry conferences and have published related articles to further the field of Knowledge Management. The knowledge managers have represented their companies as thought leaders. BP, Clarica, and Shell (see the cases in Part II) have been recognized in the Teleos Most Admired Knowledge Enterprises survey, www.destinationkm.com. Being identified as a world-class leader in Knowledge Management is significant recognition for the participants. Organizational awards and recognition also may lead to inquiries from other companies. In fact, sometimes people in knowledge champion roles feel that they get more recognition outside the company than inside, where they continually have to "sell" their services.

RECOGNITION FROM PEERS

Knowledge managers are motivated when they receive recognition from "kindred spirits." One practitioner said this:

> I need to have my own reasons before I'll use my own ways to contribute to a growing repository of knowledge. It's not automatic. . . . It is something I do for passion, for interest, to some extent for survival, but it is not what I'm measured on. No one asks "How much have you contributed to a public folder?" I need to find my own ways, based on my own reasons to share. Sharing is often seen as idle chat. (Gorelick, 2000)

An implicit reward for many of the case writers is the understanding that they, as individuals within a team, were forging new ground within their companies. The case writers who played the role of Knowledge Management champions in their organizations focused on learning with a willingness to share and propagate information and experiences related to knowledge transfer and learning. There was awareness that embedding Knowledge Management in the culture is a long-term change process, and each case writer was committed to the long-term success of his or her work. In the early stages of implementation, KM team members often have to act almost as evangelists as they seek to change the way people think and behave. The development of a growing band of KM disciples is also a strong motivator for those with evangelistic fervor!

FINAL THOUGHTS

Structuring levers are observable and tangible tools that knowledge managers have to support a KM initiative. The group, team, or organizational context determines which levers will produce the largest results. Leadership is essential to integrate the KM strategy with the business strategy. A common technology infrastructure is an enabler. Norms that include tools and techniques that support learning are critical success factors. Ongoing training and education are required to embed KM in an organization.

Together, the sense-making and structuring variables contribute to creating a culture that integrates performance through learning, leading to measurable results. Chapter 6 introduces a methodology for assessing and reporting the effectiveness Knowledge Management initiatives.

REFERENCES

Collison, C., and Parcell, G. *Learning to Fly: Practical Lessons from One of the World's Leading Knowledge Companies.* CT: Capstone Publishing Inc., 2001.

Dalton, R. *Integrating Yesterday, Today and Tomorrow.* Menlo Park, CA: Institute for the Future, 1992.

Duarte, D. L., and Snyder, N. T. *Mastering Virtual Teams: Strategies, Tools, and Techniques That Succeed.* San Francisco, CA: Jossey-Bass, 1999.

Gorelick, C. K. Toward an Understanding of Organizational Learning and Collaborative Technology: A Case Study of Structuration and Sensemaking in a Virtual Project Team. Unpublished doctoral dissertation, The George Washington University, 2000.

Greenes, K. Personal communication with Carol Gorelick. February 12, 1999, Sunbury, UK.

Johansen, R. "An Introduction to Computer Augmented Teamwork." In *Computer Augmented Teamwork: A Guided Tour* (R.

Bostrom, R. Watson, and S. Kinney, eds.). New York: Van Nostrand Rheinhold, 1992.

Lave, J., and Wenger, E. *Situated Practice Learning: Legitimate Peripheral Participation.* Cambridge, UK: University of Cambridge Press, 1991.

Lipnack, J., and Stamps, J. *Virtual Teams: Reaching Across Space, Time, and Organizations with Technology.* New York: John Wiley & Sons, 1997.

Maister, D. *Managing the Professional Service Firm.* New York: The Free Press, 1993.

Milton, N. Interview by Carol Gorelick, March 16, 2002, New York.

Saint-Onge, H., and Wallace, D. *Leveraging Communities of Practice for Strategic Advantage.* Boston, MA: Butterworth-Heinemann, 2003.

Schein, E. H. "On Dialogue, Culture and Organizational Learning." *Organizational Dynamics,* 1992.

Schrage, M. *No More Teams! Mastering the Dynamics of Creative Collaboration.* New York: Doubleday, 1995.

Schwandt, D. R., and Marquardt, M. J. *Organizational Learning: From World-Class Theories to Global Best Practices.* Boca Raton, FL: St. Lucie Press, 2000.

Sessa, V., Hansen, M., Prestridge, S., and Kossler, M. *Geographically Dispersed Reams: An Annotated Bibliography.* Greensboro, NC: Center for Creative Leadership, 1999.

Tissen, R., Andriessen, D., and Deprez, F. L. *The Knowledge Dividend: Creating High-Performance Companies Through Value-Based Knowledge Management.* London, UK: Financial Times-Prentice Hall, 2000.

CHAPTER 6

The Bottom Line—
Measuring Knowledge
Management Initiatives:
Return on Investment

Knowledge Management and organizational learning have been evolving concurrently with intellectual capital (IC), a closely related discipline. Intellectual capital refers to:

> The possession of the knowledge, applied experience, organizational technology, customer relationships, and professional skills that provide a company with a competitive edge in the market. The value of Intellectual Capital is the extent to which these intangible assets can be converted into financial returns for the company. (Edvinsson and Malone, 1997)

Interest in intellectual capital began with the widening gap between companies' market capitalizations (the stock market value) and book values (accounting statements). IC is the difference between book value and tangible assets, which is attributed to "intangibles" and appears on the balance sheet as "goodwill." Although traditional accounting measures do not show real prospects and future opportunities for companies because they are lag indicators based on historical data, intellectual capital represents future earnings expectations (April, Bosma, and Deglan, 2003).

To date, the accounting profession has not established Generally Accepted Accounting Principles (GAAP) to provide for measurement and reporting of intellectual or intangible capital. Although reporting results of KM initiatives in accounting terms is beyond the scope of knowledge managers' responsibility and this book, it is important to demonstrate the impact of KM programs. The ability of a company to learn and adapt is a component of IC (Edvinsson and Malone, 1997). April, Bosma, and Deglan (2003) identify the quest to develop better enabling technological and infrastructure systems as crucial for creating, capturing, and disseminating "know-how." Examples of these systems are described in Chapter 5. The challenge is that "what most, if not all, of the competing views on how to measure and report intellectual capital have failed to do is to reflect the enormous value of a firm's capacity to produce and integrate its knowledge" (McElroy, 2002). Despite this reality, KM practitioners are expected to demonstrate value, measurable results, and return on investment. A solution is applying ROI measurements such as those that have been successfully implemented in human resources functions and training and development.

WHY MEASURE THE RETURN ON INVESTMENT?

Return on investment (ROI) answers the question "What's in it for my business," and answers it in monetary terms. According to Jack Phillips (1997), a recognized authority in ROI, ROI has become one of the most challenging and intriguing issues facing the human resources development and performance improvement field. This is driven by senior managers' requirement to demonstrate value for expenditures. Examples of programs that have developed ROI calculations are HR programs, reengineering initiatives, and technology implementation situations, as well as changes of procedures, practices, and policies. Any change process, including Knowledge Management, can use the ROI process to capture and calculate ROI and bottom-line measures such as productivity improvements, quality enhancements, cost reductions, and time savings. The challenge is to isolate the effects of the specific initiative and to develop strategies for converting data to monetary values.

ROI FOR KNOWLEDGE MANAGEMENT

Demonstrating return on investment is crucial in the early stages of a Knowledge Management program. The early stages of KM are all about evangelism—firing up the company to rethink old paradigms and embrace a new way of working. Nothing supports evangelism like a miracle: If KM can work financial miracles, then the company will support the initiative.

In the later stages, once the management of knowledge has become established as "the way we work," ROI is less important. Does anyone bother to calculate the ROI on safety management? Financial management? Or the accounting department? No, because safety or financial management is established as "good business practice." Once Knowledge Management becomes established as "good business practice," ROI becomes less of an issue.

Because Knowledge Management is still a new discipline, very few, if any, organizations have reached the later stages of Knowledge Management being embedded to the same extent as safety or financial management. A method for calculating ROI is an essential component of a successful and sustainable Knowledge Management strategy.

THE ROI PROCESS

The foundation of the ROI calculation is a comprehensive measurement and evaluation process. The puzzle in Figure 6-1 illustrates the ROI process and reporting system.

EVALUATION FRAMEWORK—STEP ONE

The first step is an **evaluation framework** for categorizing different types of data at different times from different sources. Several different types of instruments can be used to collect meaningful data. Some examples are:

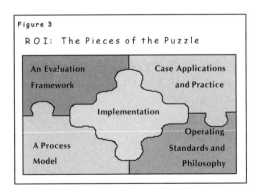

Figure 6-1. The Major Elements of ROI (Source: Corporate University Scorecard; Phillips and Phillips, 2001)

	Figure 4	
	Evaluation Levels	
	Level	*Measurement Focus*
1.	Reaction and Planned Action	Measures participant satisfaction with the program and captures planned actions.
2.	Learning	Measures changes in knowledge, skills, and attitudes.
3.	Job Application	Measures changes in on-the-job behavior.
4.	Business Impact	Measures changes in business impact variables.
5.	Return on Investment	Compares program benefits with the costs.

Figure 6-2. Levels of evaluation (Figure 4, Balanced Scorecard)

- Surveys
- Questionnaires
- Interviews
- Focus groups
- Observation
- Performance records

The five evaluation levels in Figure 6-2 are used to capture data at different times—before, during, and after an initiative. The first four evaluation levels are based on Kirkpatrick's Model (1975), while Jack Phillips (1994) added the fifth level.

THE PROCESS MODEL—STEP TWO

The second step and element is a **process model** (Figure 6-3) used to plan and implement the evaluation with a focus on postimplementation time frames (long term). The process model is designed to ensure that data is collected, analyzed, and reported following logical and sequential steps.

This process has been used by thousands of organizations to develop impact studies on different types of learning solutions. Over a hundred case studies have been published on the process, and 2,000 individuals have been certified to implement this process within their organizations. Knowledge Management is a learning solution that is

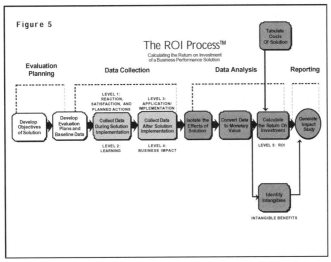

Figure 6-3. The ROI methodology (Figure 5, Balanced Scorecard)

directly integrated with performance and affects bottom-line results. An important feature of this model is the number of techniques available to isolate the effect of the learning solution from other solutions. The goal is to pinpoint the amount of improvement directly related to the Knowledge Management initiative, which adds accuracy and credibility to the ROI calculation. The level of improvement is often a subjective assessment, unless a control group is used to compare the performance of a group that has applied KM tools and techniques with the performance of a group that has not. When subjective measures are used, participants, supervisors of participants, senior managers, subordinates of participants, and experts can be asked to estimate the amount of improvement related to the initiative and to indicate the percent of the improvement attributable to the KM initiative. If this is not feasible, other factors that influenced the results can be identified and their impact estimated, while anything that is not explained can be attributed to the KM initiative.

OPERATING STANDARDS

The third step is the **operating standards** (i.e., guiding principles) used to ensure consistency in the approach to measurement. The standards ensure that the results of an impact study conducted by one individual, one team, or one business unit can be replicated and compared with a study done by another individual, team, or busi-

---

Figure 6

Guiding Principles

1. When a higher-level evaluation is conducted, data must be collected at lower levels.

2. When an evaluation is planned for a higher level, the previous level of evaluation does not have to be comprehensive.

3. When collecting and analyzing data, use only the most credible sources.

4. When analyzing data, select the most conservative alternative for calculations.

5. At least one method must be used to isolate the effects of the project/initiative.

6. If no improvement data is available for a population or from a specific source, it is assumed that little or no improvement has occurred.

7. Estimates of improvement should be adjusted for the potential error of the estimate.

8. Extreme data items and unsupported claims should not be used in ROI calculations.

9. Only the first year of benefits (annual) should be used in the ROI analysis of short-term projects/initiatives.

10. Project/program costs should be fully loaded for ROI analysis.

Figure 6-4. Guiding principles (Figure 6, Balanced Scorecard)

ness unit. The guiding principles (Figure 6-4) provide operating rules, and a basic philosophy ensures consistency and a conservative approach to the analysis.

IMPLEMENTATION

The fourth puzzle piece is **implementation**. This essential step integrates the framework and process model into the routine of a KM program. Implementation requires a deliberate and methodical approach to evaluation and measurement. The implementation issues in Figure 6-5 must be addressed for measurement and evaluation to be embedded in the organization. When organizations are developing a comprehensive system, implementation often presents a challenge, which, if ignored or minimized, leads to disappointment and reactive, sporadic evaluations that do not support ongoing investment in the initiative.

```
┌─────────────────────────────────────────────┐
│ Figure 7                                      │
│           Implementation Issues               │
│                                               │
│  ✳ Resources (staffing/budget)               │
│                                               │
│  ✳ Leadership (individual, group, cross-      │
│     functional team)                          │
│                                               │
│  ✳ Timing (urgency, activities)              │
│                                               │
│  ✳ Communication (various audiences)         │
│                                               │
│  ✳ Commitment (staff, managers, top          │
│     executives)                               │
└─────────────────────────────────────────────┘
```

Figure 6-5. Implementation Issues (Figure 7, Balanced Scorecard)

APPLICATION

The last puzzle piece is **application**—that is, showing results from impact studies in the organization. This requires assessment at the fourth and fifth levels: business impact and return on investment, comparing program benefits with costs. Wherever possible, one should report results in monetary terms.

ASSESSING MONETARY VALUES

Another important part of the process model is the multiple ways to convert data to monetary values. To do this, each unit of data is connected to the initiative being valued.

Strategies to convert data into value include:

- Output data—Use profit contribution or cost savings.
- Cost of quality—Convert quality improvements to cost savings.
- Participants' wages and benefits—Convert the value of time to monetary equivalents.
- Historical costs—Use organizational cost data to establish a value for an improvement.
- Internal and external experts—Estimate the value of an improvement based on experience.
- External databases—Use research, government, and industry information sources.
- Participants, supervisors of participants, senior managers, and Knowledge Management professionals—Estimate the value.

Once a value is established, the impact of the KM initiative costs can be tabulated. Cost components include:

- Design and development of the specific initiative
- Materials provided to participants
- Knowledge Management professionals' time (salary and benefits)
- Facilities
- Travel, lodging, and meal costs

The conservative approach suggests that all costs are included for the ROI calculation.

Finally, the return on investment is calculated using program benefits and costs. The benefit/cost ratio (BCR) is the program benefits divided by the costs:

$$\text{BCR} = \text{Program Benefits} \div \text{Program Costs}$$

The return on investment uses the net benefits divided by program costs. Net benefits are the program benefits minus the costs:

$$\text{ROI (\%)} = (\text{Program Benefits} - \text{Program Costs} \times 100) \div \text{Program Costs}$$

INTANGIBLE MEASURES

Many KM initiatives report nonmonetary, intangible benefits. These benefits *cannot* be converted into a monetary value but are very important in the evaluation process. Examples are:

- Increased employee satisfaction
- Increased organizational commitment
- Improved teamwork
- Improved customer service
- Reduced complaints
- Reduced conflicts

Intangible measures can be identified at the beginning of an initiative. For example, employees who actively participate in a community of practice may experience increased job satisfaction. However, job satisfaction is not equated to a monetary benefit. Intangibles are often identified directly when clients discuss the impact of the initiative. Another way to identify intangible measures is when it becomes impossible to establish a monetary value for an aspect of a program (e.g., employee satisfaction). Sometimes participants recognize intangible benefits during a follow-up evaluation (e.g., using KM tools improved every business meeting) and not only during events directly associated with a KM program.

THE ROI PROCESS IN PRACTICE

Demonstrating ROI is relatively easy when organizations are applying KM at a project level. The first step is to establish the predicted cost/revenue of the project, apply KM tools and practices, and then evaluate what the actual cost/revenue is at the end of the day. A baseline figure is necessary to demonstrate improvement. The baseline can be the predicted revenue, or how much the project cost last time, or a benchmark against similar projects. For example, BP applied KM practices and processes to the 1998 maintenance shutdown of the Nerefco refinery. Compared with the previous shutdown, four years earlier, Nerefco cut costs by 20%, reduced the time of the shutdown by nine days, and increased the time to next shutdown by half a year (with no safety incidents and no environmental breaches). Those improvements were worth nearly $10 million.

How much of that savings can be assigned to KM? Is it all due to KM efforts, or are there other factors involved as well? It's hard to know. Often KM is a key component of a number of different approaches, an integral part of the recipe but not the only ingredient. As one BP business unit leader said, "You are in there with the spaghetti. We can't isolate the KM component on its own." But without KM, the recipe would not have worked.

The greatest measurable ROI for KM is in areas of repetitive high spending, such as releasing a series of new products or, as in the BP case, drilling a series of wells. These are the areas where KM can enable cutting the learning curve and releasing a lot of value. In a repetitive series of projects, maybe 20% to 30% of the cost is related to the learning curve. Therefore, a $100 million operation has the potential to save $20 million and is worth a $2 million investment in KM. Tom Young, a member of the original BP KM team says, "I wouldn't get out of bed in the morning if I didn't think you couldn't achieve an ROI of at least 10." The scale of the enterprise and the scale of the cost determine the scale of investment. Bill Kirton, on BP's Schiehallion project, saw the potential to save up to $100 million in cost through management of knowledge. Bill invested in three full-time learning engineers, plus consultancy support, to access that cost, and achieved an ROI of twentyfold or more. The BP KM team had a two-year budget of $5 million, and Kent Greenes quotes savings of $260 million from KM-enabled projects in 1998 for a fifty-fold ROI. There was no heavy IT spending as part of the program. The company already had a good common operating platform with intranet and e-mail. There was no need for major cultural change. The company had a good culture of cooperation and networking (see Chapter 7, the "Decade of Change" case). All that was needed was application of the principles and introduction of the practices, and this made it possible to deliver such a high return on investment.

If the KM program does not depend on massive IT purchases, then the investment can be relatively small. Knowledge Management is a catalyst—a little investment goes a long way. KM is not asking people to do extra things, but rather asking them to do different things or do things in a different way. A KM initiative requires an investment in coaching, training, facilitation, and mentoring, but ultimately the initiative needs to belong to the business. The work is done by the business, as part of normal business, and the incremental investment becomes minor.

Part of the challenge with KM is that the benefits go way beyond the measurable, in bottom-line terms. Experience says, "What you get back will depend on the quality of the soil in which you are planting the seeds" (Milton, 2003). The behaviors and culture of knowledge sharing—of seeking help and providing help—will have massive payoffs across an entire organization. Costs will fall, efficiencies will rise, innovations will start to emerge, and new attitudes will be created. A word of caution from Tom Young (2000): Once the KM program achieves critical mass, the benefits will just start to roll in. It is necessary to have faith in this, but faith will not be enough to get the organization started. The key is a couple of early wins with significant demonstrable ROI to get the ball rolling.

FINAL THOUGHTS

Business initiatives require measurable results; Knowledge Management is no exception. Significant progress has been made and major efforts are underway to establish KM programs with measurable results in organizations that recognize the need to harness knowledge to ensure increased performance through learning. Simultaneously, a more difficult effort is being made to evaluate intellectual capital by establishing values for knowledge as intangible assets.

TRANSITION TO CASES

Part II provides the stories of practitioners who are Knowledge Management professionals. Each story emphasizes a different element in the KM framework and architecture discussed in the preceding chapters. Time is a significant component in each case. Knowledge Management, as does all change initiatives, takes time to plan, implement, embed, and evaluate. Together, the cases support Benjamin Franklin's belief that "an investment in knowledge always pays the best interest" and "the beauty of an investment in knowledge and learning is that it can continue to pay dividends each and every year."

REFERENCES

April, K., Bosma, P., and Deglan, D. A. "IC Measurement and Reporting: Establishing a Practice in SA Mining." *Journal of Intellectual Capital*, Vol. 4, No. 2, 2003.

Edvinsson, L., and Malone, M. S. *Intellectual Capital: Realizing Your Company's True Value by Finding Its Hidden Roots.* New York: HarperBusiness, 1997.

Kirkpatrick, D. L. "Techniques for Evaluating Training Programs." *Evaluating Training Programs.* Alexandria, VA: American Society for Training and Development, 1975, pp. 1–17.

McElroy, M. W. *The New Knowledge Management: Complexity, Learning and Sustainable Innovation.* Woburn, MA: Butterworth-Heinemann, 2002.

Milton, N. (2003) Personal e-mail communication 4/23/2003.

Phillips, J. J. (ed.). *In Action: Measuring Return on Investment.* Alexandria, VA: American Society for Training and Development, 1994.

Phillips, J. J. *Return on Investment in Training and Performance Improvement Programs.* Woburn, MA: Butterworth-Heinemann, 2nd Edition 2003.

Phillips, Jack J., and Phillips, Patricia P. The Corporate University Scorecard: A Tool to Measure the Contribution of the Corporate University. 2001.

Young, Tom. 2000.

PART II

Voices of Experience: Applying Knowledge Management Tools

CHAPTER 7

British Petroleum's Knowledge Management Journey: A Decade of Change

By Nick Milton and Carol Gorelick in conversation with Kent Greenes

This case is the story of British Petroleum's (BP) journey that took place over a decade that retrospectively was labeled "The Decade of Change" by Kent Greenes, the leader of British Petroleum's original Knowledge Management team. Lord John Browne, CEO of British Petroleum, was an early adopter and frequently quoted proponent of knowledge as a critical element in BP's strategy. The three-year story of the successful implementation of Knowledge Management in BP, through 1997–2000 is told by Nick Milton, the team's knowledge manager, and Kent Greenes, the team leader. The story describes the Knowledge-Enhanced Performance model that is used by BP and other organizations as a systematic approach to the management of knowledge. It closes with lessons learned as advice for KM practitioners.

THE BP JOURNEY

BP is known as a world-class leader in Knowledge Management, having developed a robust and systematic framework for performance through learning. BP has appeared in the winner's listing of the global Most Admired Knowledge Enterprises award (see http://www.knowledgebusiness.com) for each of the five years the award has been given. Internally, BP recognizes that "knowledge is one of its most important assets and potentially our greatest source of sustainable competitive advantage" (Prokesh, 1997). BP initiated a Knowledge Management implementation program in 1997 as a catalyst to accelerate and strengthen BP's continuous change efforts that began in 1990. Toward the end of this decade of radical change, BP had a flat organization, entrepreneurial business units, and a web of alliances that positioned BP to face the challenge common to all companies battling it out in the global information age: using knowledge more effectively than their competitors. Lord John Browne, the CEO, had recognized very early the need to align a knowledge strategy with the overall business strategy and drove BP's Knowledge Management program.

In 1997, BP set up a central Knowledge Management team (KMT) with a budget, objectives, and vision and with a remit to develop a Knowledge Management solution for the organization. The KMT developed a three-stage implementation program to (1) raise awareness, (2) demonstrate success through pilots, and (3) embed the methodology in the organization. The team's duration and success were determined by their accomplishment against these objectives and were evaluated year by year by the managing directors. Kent Greenes and Nick Milton were KM pioneers as members of the central Knowledge Management team.

Precursors to Success—Change Efforts Preceding Knowledge Management

In 1990, BP understood that a program of both continuous and radical change was required in order for the company to survive in the competitive energy industry. The fundamental goal was to change the way individuals and teams within BP behaved in order to increase performance and distinguish them from the competition. The philosophy for implementing this program was not to tell anyone how to change, but instead to ask each major business to develop its own way of implementing a continuous change program. BP used a myriad of tools to learn how to manage change, shown in timeline form in Figure 7.1.

Performance and Teamwork

The first level of change was an emphasis on performance results and teamwork, encouraging open behavior. The tools were a potpourri of change initiatives—total quality management (TQM), busi-

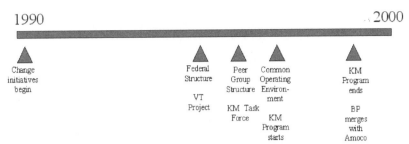

Figure 7-1. The Decade of Change timeline

ness process reengineering, breakthrough thinking, and teamwork—supported by numerous consultants. As a leader of a business developing the Endicott Oil Field, Kent was directly involved in a teamworking change effort in Alaska. Over time, a small group of people involved in various change initiatives got together to create a community of interest. The group started to meet informally. Three of the members of this community were selected to be trained to become facilitators for the BP Management Conference (an event for the top 60 managers held three or four times a year). Facilitation skills were highly valued in BP. Many managers and employees were trained in the "art of facilitation" for running effective meetings. Admitting that you needed help running meetings was an early sign of openness within the changing BP organization. In hindsight, Kent's work as a BP Management Conference facilitator was the starting point for the KMT that was formed in 1997.

In 1991, two teams from the community of interest, one from Aberdeen, Scotland, and Kent's from Alaska, recognized they had common objectives—if not the same approach—to managing change. They planned a one-week meeting. At the end of that week, it was clear that there was an opportunity to share knowledge and help each other while helping their own teams. The Change Management Network was born. This network produced the report "Good Practices in Managing Change Toolkit: What BP Knows about Managing Change." Looking back, this was an early Knowledge Asset (knowledge that is packaged in context and is valuable to the business). Change was accelerating, and in a short amount of time a Coaching Network was formed to support change initiatives.

THE FEDERAL ORGANIZATION

In 1995, a significant organizational change occurred in BP's structure. It went from a traditional hierarchy to a federal organization.

The federal structure has a small central core with large semi-autonomous business units outside the core. The leadership in the central core provides enterprise-wide vision, and everyone is expected to consider themselves as being under the "same flag." However, for each unit in the federation, separate performance contracts are negotiated that drive strategy and operating tactics. The performance contract is a commitment and is seen as a promise not to be broken. The performance contracts include stretch targets designed to continuously challenge people to improve, without being burned out or failing. A crucial path to success is asking for help and reusing knowledge from elsewhere in the federation.

VIRTUAL TEAMWORKING

To encourage the cross–business unit teamwork and open communication essential to the federal structure, the virtual teamworking (VT) project was initiated. This project aimed to facilitate the creation of virtual teams, with geographically separated members, brought together by desktop videoconferencing. The model for this initiative was to address people, process, and technology issues simultaneously. Thus the project deliverables were a technological solution plus a coaching process that facilitated people connecting from disparate locations using PC videoconferencing. Kent was selected to lead this initiative. An important message that "the VT project was more than technology" was sent when the VT project did not report to the information technology organization, but rather to the BP Group chief executive, part of the small central core of the federal structure. VT was expected to create a more enabling technology in the new flattened organization. The VT project has been written about elsewhere and won a Computerworld Smithsonian Award. The successful VT project helped influence the establishment of a Common Operating Environment (COE) initiative that created a standard technology platform and set of tools. It paved the road for standard PC functionality and the intranet at BP. This allowed any employee to access information anytime from anywhere, a major enabling factor in the BP KM story.

In addition to the federal structure and the technology platform already implemented, BP modified the federal structure in 1996 to add Peer Groups. Peer Groups are a structure for encouraging networking, cooperation, and communication across the business units. Peer Groups are groupings of the leaders of separate business units that face similar challenges (for example, the Peer Group of offshore oil fields or the Peer Group of chemical refinery business units). Although the business units have individual performance contracts, the Peer Groups were required to accept additional challenges (performance contract items) from the BP Group corporate center. These items would be difficult or impossible to deliver without collaboration and sharing knowledge across business units.

As the VT project rolled out, the team told stories about successful implementations. A concrete measure of the VT project's success was Peer Groups paying for VT capability (equipment and coaching) from their budgets. The added value of the VT project was confirmed at a meeting Kent had with Lord John Browne to report the results of the VT initiative. Lord John Browne observed that VT created a level of alignment and engagement between people and teams that could not be accomplished through traditional means. It encouraged transferring of experience that led to commitment, and from commitment came delivered results. It was in this meeting that Kent realized VT was working as a mechanism to deploy know-how throughout the company.

Team members began telling the VT success story at conferences. They were being introduced as the first team to make the "virtual stuff" work. Team members were unanimous that the people and coaching (process) elements were the critical success factors (as much as 50% of the budget had been spent on coaching). They used every opportunity to demonstrate how to use the VT system to teach people how to do work differently. For the VT team, the real goal was to create relationships between people and to allow honest, open conversations. Learning to use the technology was only the first step in the process.

Information to Knowledge

In February 1996, the VT team realized that the "real value" of what they had implemented was sharing know-how and experience—tacit knowledge. The team invited a group of 40 fellow travelers from all over the company, plus several academics, industry experts, and external consultants, to join them to plan what was needed to understand the interactions about knowledge. The team was aware that good interaction requires handling conflict, and the outcome is measurable results and relationships. Having raised awareness and implemented pilots, the VT project team moved from pilot mode to production mode during 1996. The installed technology base went from 150 to 1,000 units. The major activity for the team was engaging people to use VT—spreading the word and embedding the methodology in the business.

In the third quarter of 1996, the Technology Advisory Board of BP senior scientists, R&D, and so on met with external professors and industry experts for one of the two or three colloquia BP delivers annually. This colloquium was focused on the enabling use of IT. A memorable event was Dr. John Henderson's (Boston University) rousing speech to the group on knowledge and leadership. He got people to think about this statement: "If you become part of a team or organization that learns and reuses learning, you can be ready for anything." Among the stories Henderson told was the following story, from the U.S. Army—a compelling story that provided BP with a vision of what KM could make possible.

"I interviewed a colonel. Now this colonel was a colonel in one of the elite groups in the U.S. Army. He had gotten a call, 8 O'clock on Saturday morning, reminding him that a hurricane had just hit outside a U.S. city, and was told that because the current administration had very strong ties to the area, they believed that this should not be left to the reserve group, because they wanted no mess-ups. The orders to the colonel were clear—go down there, provide any help and support necessary to the state of Louisiana after this hurricane, and *don't mess up*. Clear orders—the Army calls it 'intent,' 'strategic intent.' The strategic intent was clear. Now this particular colonel was in fact a highly decorated combat soldier; he had never done this in his life. He had never actually commanded any type of civilian-related activity; he had always been right on the front lines in hot action."

"It turns out, though, that as part of his executive education in the Army, he had been exposed to this thing called the Center for Army Lessons Learned. So he got on his laptop computer, dialed into Army Net, hooked into the Center for Army Lessons Learned, and asked the following question (he actually showed me the type): 'What does the Army know about Hurricane Support Clean-up?'"

"And within four hours, he had a profile of the deployment of troops from the last three hurricanes in North America that the Army had been sent to support and clean up, including types of staff, types of skills, numbers of skills; he had a pro forma budget, both what budget was requested and what the actual budget was, and where the cost overruns were; he had the 10 questions you will be asked by CNN in the first 30 minutes after your arrival; he had a list of every state agency and federal agency that had to be contacted and coordinated with, and the name of the person that he had to contact, and the Army liaison person who was currently working with that group, someplace in North America. And he had established a Lotus Notes advisory team of the three commanders, two of whom were currently generals, one was still a colonel, who agreed to be his advisory group in this command structure. Four hours later."

"Is that relevant for British Petroleum?"

An "Aha!" Moment

Kent remembers instantly learning from this event that (a) it's important to relate to the customer—if this worked for the Army, an organization in a similar situation to BP, it should work within BP; and (b) there is very strong power in storytelling. In retrospect, the IT Colloquium ignited the KM fire at BP by legitimizing Knowledge Management.

The Genesis of the KM Team

After the IT Colloquium, a task force was formed with 5 to 10 executives, members from each business stream and thought leaders from business units as well as central functions such as HR, IT, and organizational learning. This task force was charged with assessing the state of Knowledge Management in BP and making recommendations. Kent was one of the three core members of the task force. A first step for the task force was to study other organizations. They found that VT was seen as a leading-edge concept by outsiders and that many companies learned better (or accepted learnings better) from outsiders than insiders. The hope in researching other organizations was to find a methodology that could act as a silver bullet for KM within BP. They were not successful. They found that their own VT experience could be applied to KM. The team believed that the VT principle of integrating people, process, and technology could become the framework for effective Knowledge Management.

The task force concluded that the BP environment had many factors conducive for Knowledge Management, such as a team structure, the IT infrastructure with the Common Operating Environment, and results-based behavior orientation. BP was an action-oriented company, and people were encouraged to talk. However, there was a lack of ability to capture what had worked, and teams were not routinely learning before, during, and after their work. The task force concluded that there were good things happening, but that a major knowledge effort was needed. This effort should have the following objective: to accelerate the pace and benefits of BP's transformation to a learning organization, and to maintain the momentum of existing knowledge efforts.

The team recommended that a dedicated Knowledge Management team be sanctioned, containing core team members from the existing VT team. The task force presented its recommendations to the managing directors.

The presentation was very persuasive. Half a billion dollars in annual savings was the anticipated "big prize" for BP if they found a way to better leverage know-how. The KM initiative did not have to be built from the ground up. The new team would build on what had been developed in the VT project. They would focus on raising awareness and piloting to leverage the "good stuff" happening within BP. The goal was to embed Knowledge Management within the businesses. The steering committee approved all the task force recommendations, with one exception. One member raised a concern about the KM effort being a central function. Keeping with the principles of the federal structure, he believed that the business streams should own the Knowledge Management function. Kent agreed that ultimately it should not be a corporate unit or be organized to live forever. He vividly remembers saying, "I won't let it become a corporate thing. We will revisit the existence of a KM team year by year." Within a week, a decision was made to establish a central KM team with Kent leading it, reporting to a corporate managing director. Kent believed that this was a way to "join VT and KM at the hip," to keep going with what had started to change the business and provide a lever for further improving performance.

GETTING STARTED BY CREATING AWARENESS

Once the KMT was formally announced, the next step was to quickly create the right team and then to develop a vision, mission,

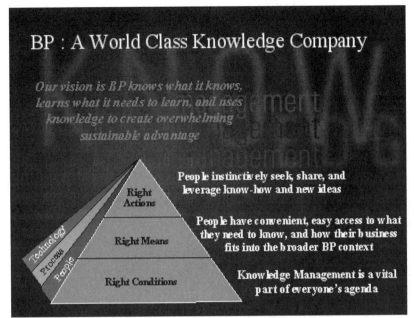

Figure 7-2. The what-it-takes pyramid

and objectives. Figure 7-2 represents the vision and strategy to achieve the objectives.

The new team was conscious that committing to this vision, this mission, and these objectives without insights from people outside the core team would be a first step in creating the unwanted fiefdom. Many people had been instrumental in getting to this point, and the team wanted them all to "own" the KM vision together.

THE WORK BEGAN IN EARNEST

The team planned an "away day" meeting at Shepperton (UK) in January 1997 for the purpose of enrolling others and creating a shared vision and plan for early deliverables. Attendees included internal and external fellow travelers. Many different business processes and backgrounds were represented. External people who came were offered the opportunity to "get in on the ground floor." The offer was to help develop a realistic plan that in all likelihood would provide opportunities for external participants during implementation (e.g., as facilitators and coaches).

The fundamental objective of this event was for all attendees to share what they were doing in Knowledge Management and what they thought needed to be done. The team identified a common interest. The collective outcome of the meeting was the beginning of a community of practice about Knowledge Management, an awareness that there was lots of learning going on in BP but it was not being captured or routinely applied, a plan to meet quarterly, a focus on doing (not only saying), and shared ownership of a Knowledge Management vision.

The preliminary KMT objectives for 1997 were modified to include input from the Shepperton meeting. These objectives were presented to and approved by a KM steering committee of high-level corporate leaders. The KMT members were adamant that one of Kent's major roles as KMT leader was to maintain a link to the managing directors and senior executives, to keep KM on the corporate agenda and ensure that "the KMT had a seat at the table."

The culture of BP recognizes that the key decision makers are the business leaders. An early success, which Kent called a "small win," was getting agreement to add pivotal business leaders to the steering committee. The larger steering committee guided the team to "simplify" the original objectives, reducing the key efforts from six to three.

THE KM FRAMEWORK

The team continued the efforts begun by the KM task force of looking outside BP for KM tools and practices. They developed a concrete, but simple, framework to tie together everything they knew at that time about Knowledge Management. It was a real challenge to take a fuzzy concept and make it into something with demonstrable value. BP prides itself on value and emphasizes "walking the talk" more than "talking the talk." So the team adopted the term "Knowledge Asset" to indicate knowledge that had been made accessible to add value to the business. They narrowed the focus to a three-element framework, with an emphasis on reuse of knowledge to deliver today's performance. This focus quickly became the KMT doctrine. The three-element framework was:

1. Getting the organization ready for KM—raising awareness, learning, and engagement
2. Managing knowledge in the form of assets
3. Leveraging knowledge and expertise

The team monitored their progress with quarterly progress reviews. By mid-1997 some progress was already evident. Awareness of the value of reusing knowledge—by demonstrating that if you reused knowledge, you could deliver today's performance better, cheaper, and faster—had been firmly created There was awareness that you can't really separate knowledge creation from reuse. The team believed that "reusing knowledge fuels innovation," and they had seen this in operation in KM processes across the business (as an example see the sidebar The Retail Peer Assist Project).

The Retail Peer Assist Project
Richard Appleyard, BP

"We had a challenge from the business to improve capital productivity by 30%; otherwise, we would not have enough Capex to realize all of our ambitions in Retail. There was a Peer Assist organized for Retail Engineering, and it brought in people from Exploration, from refineries, etc. We had a talk at that Peer Assist from Brown & Root, who explained to us what alliances were. So we formed a little syndicate and asked, 'Why don't we form an alliance for Retail Engineering?' People at first said, 'No, that would be impossible,' but we developed an action plan, and out of that action plan came the Bovis Alliance— purely as a result of cross-business knowledge sharing. And that Bovis Alliance has saved a fortune for BP. I think it is thought to be the most successful alliance BP has had."

The team also recognized that people responded when it was obvious that they would gain personally by participating in a knowledge effort. For example, the shift workers in a refinery turnaround became keen advocates when they realized that sharing and reusing knowledge would make their job easier and safer. Once people were convinced of relevance to them, the goal was to encourage relationships and trust to develop. It became apparent that many people were ready to share their knowledge but were holding back because of the lack of both a codified inventory of explicit knowledge and a method for finding and connecting to the right people. There was also a sense that sharing knowledge was not a legitimate use of time. All these barriers could be resolved if results were seen to be delivered through

KM tools and techniques. Spending time on sharing could become highly desirable, expected behavior. Capturing and codifying information could become a common process. Finding out who had relevant knowledge, and getting to know that person, could be accomplished using technology.

RAISING AWARENESS

The team's message to raise awareness was, "If you are not learning before, during, and after an event, you are not optimizing performance. You should consider our KM tools for yourself and your team because it is likely that any mistakes or inefficiencies made this time will happen again. The KM systems have been made available to all BP employees, so it will not add costs to try them." Outsiders presenting relevant examples at the right time added credibility.

The team worked diligently to develop a three-step process for capturing, transferring, and embedding knowledge gained in one business or project to another business or project. The first step was to capture knowledge by reflecting on an experience, distilling knowledge from that experience, and packaging the knowledge. The second step required finding a customer for the knowledge and transferring the knowledge. Finally, the knowledge was embedded in people and work processes at the right place at the right time.

ENGAGEMENT

With awareness raised and the three-step process available, the team focused on engaging the organization, with the intent of identifying pilot projects. Engagement involved motivating someone to do something as a result of a conversation; it was not the same as a traditional "show and tell" presentation for the KMT. In the case of the KMT, the message was, "We have used KM tools successfully and we offer to share our experiences with you. We are not coming as experts." The team developed a method to create possibilities for the future by harvesting learning through real conversation and stories. The outcome of an ideal session was action, in the form of a pilot project. At a minimum, the conversation created a new level of awareness of the possibilities of KM.

Kent spent a month engaging 10 local business teams. This forced the team itself to get clear on the message they wanted to give and the best way to give that message. It was the team's own pilot process. They created a powerful way to engage people in the possibilities of Knowledge Management to impact business performance using the tools we had developed. Then Barry Smale, Phil Forth, and Kent spent three weeks in Southeast Asia engaging businesses in Chemicals joint ventures in China, Japan, Korea, Indonesia, and Singapore. During this time, Kent learned the value of leveraging presentation styles. It was often effective for another team member with a different style to present the material and for Kent to intervene with his emotion and stories. A turning point for the team came when Barry, Phil, and Kent returned from the Southeast Asia trip and enthusiastically reported their successful experiences engaging people. It was obvious that other team members did not share their enthusiasm. Geoff Parcell challenged Kent, asking, "Why are you the only one doing the engaging?" Kent was not convinced and confident that other team members would deliver the same message as he did, and believed there is only one chance to engage business leaders. He had not been willing to risk not doing his best to accomplish the task at hand. Kent offered to go through the presentation with the whole team to show them why he believed that the presentations were best done by him. He found himself presenting the engagement material to the team as if they were a business unit. He says, "I was not pretending!" To everyone's surprise, Kent was pleased with the confrontation. The entire team had started to understand and learn about themselves. It helped make the individuals become a cohesive team. Kent says:

> We all learned together. I taught them what I thought was important, and they taught me by asking many levels of "Why?" questions. The result was the first formal KM engagement presentation. It encouraged the team to think about what we needed to do and where we needed to focus. We generated three areas of focus with deliverables that steered us through the rest of the year. At the end of that intense engagement session, I believed everyone on the team had "got it." Engagement was not giving a talk, but creating something that motivates someone as a result of your conversation. Everyone had the master script to work from. Most of the team members decided to do one or more engagements with me.

This continued the practice of partnering on engagements that Barry, Phil, and Kent had started in Southeast Asia. It was very effective. Everyone had his or her own style of presenting the standard material, but the content was the same. At this point, the individuals were functioning as a team with one message, despite having individual styles and implementation techniques.

The getting-started phase created the three-step process and initiated the team's approach of creating awareness through engagement sessions that continued throughout the life of the team.

Building the Framework—Pilots

By the middle of 1997, the massive exercise of engaging the business units was beginning to pay off. The team had spoken to nearly half the organization, and the conversation was beginning to shift from "What is Knowledge Management?" to "How can we do this?" Many of the business unit leaders, such as Steve Ainger in Vietnam and Ronnie Forbes in Japan, had really grasped what a huge difference KM could make to them. The pressure was now for the KM team to shift into action and deliver some business results. The team needed to set up some pilot projects, where they could start to develop and implement some tools and techniques and where they could build, on the job, a working KM system.

The Toolkit

A good KM principle is never to reinvent if an adequate solution already exists. So the team was already looking for existing KM tools and processes both within BP and from outside. One of these was the Peer Assist process: a simple procedure that had been implemented in the Exploration sector[1] of the company in 1994 as a means of spreading good practice around the federation of business units. By using Peer Assists, a business unit could ask other business units for help and advice, and so there was no longer the need for central pools of expertise or centers of excellence. Andrew Mackenzie, a firm believer in KM and a member of the KM steering team, had been one of the implementers of Peer Assists in BP Exploration, and had coordinated the first 20 or 30 of these knowledge-sharing meetings until they developed a life of their own. By 1997, hundreds, if not thousands, of Peer Assists had been held in Exploration. Here was a proven tool the team could adopt for importing learning at the start of a piece of work.

---

[1] Exploration is one of BP's four business sectors, the others being Chemicals, Retail, and Gas and Power.

From John Henderson's rousing speech at the IT Colloquium, the team had become aware of the U.S. Army's reputation as a knowledge-managing company. They got in touch with Colonel Ed Guthrie, a retired soldier, who had helped develop the U.S. Army system and who was now working as an organizational consultant. Colonel Guthrie flew over and spent a lot of time with the team, particularly with Keith Pearse, as the team endeavored to find out just how the U.S. Army model for KM worked. Colonel Guthrie explained the After Action Review (AAR), a team-based learning exercise that was at the heart of the Army system of KM. The KMT picked up on AARs and began to use them in their team meetings as a sort of trial run before using them in the business.

A third learning tool was a type of team knowledge-capture meeting, which Nick had developed and used extensively in BP Norway over a number of years. This was the Retrospect, a process suited to end-of-project review that was more formal and more rigorous than the AAR and that benefited from a skilled facilitator. Nick had been facilitating these for several years, often running several in a week. He was confident that this was an effective and robust system for capturing and packaging knowledge. Here was a third tool for knowledge work, and the Norway system was another possible model we could learn from.

So existing KM tools could be exploited. Previous KM models were there to learn from. But the team needed to come up with a simple, robust and integrated system for managing knowledge that could be road tested in the business, would deliver results, and could become the BP default standard. The team members had all been busy engaging the business and learning from as many people as they could. It was now time to sit down as a team and thrash out a practical approach. The team set aside four days in June 1997 and traveled down to the South Coast to stay at the Powder Mills Hotel, a quiet country hotel not far from Hastings.

Nick says:

Looking back on it, those four days at Powder Mills were a turning point for the rest of the team and me. We were finally getting a handle on KM—what it might mean, how it might work. We all felt the need to crystallize a model, commit to an objective, and build a strategy. We also felt the need to meet again. As a virtual team, we were seeing relatively little of each other. It was easy to lose touch, particularly during the long engagement visits. I (and I believe the other team members) really appreciated the opportunity to get together again in a relaxed location, with a loose agenda, to just sit down and talk. Nigel Gibbs (an outside consultant familiar with BP and the team) was the facilitator and kept us on track. We invited Phil Forth, an old friend from the VT days, to be an observer and to bring an outside perspective. The time went quickly in a mixture of intense discussion and relaxation, and the ideas began to take shape, which formed the foundation for all our later success.

The Knowledge Management Model

The model that emerged from Powder Mills had the following elements:

- Knowledge bank—"What BP knows" should be formalized and stored in a way that allows access by everyone in the BP Group.
- Knowledge Assets—Bodies of knowledge need to be created for topics critical to BP's future, which can be applied to enhance business value. These should go beyond the knowledge databases Nick had built as a knowledge manager in Norway.
- Knowledge toolbox—We needed a standard set of tools, techniques, and processes for handling knowledge, with supporting manuals.
- Knowledge environment—We needed a cultural and technology infrastructure to support the management of knowledge.
- Knowledge roles—We needed to introduce skills and competencies into the organization and create knowledge jobs (posts).
- Systematized approach—This should cover innovation, capture, embedding, transfer, validation, distillation, and use of knowledge.
- Communities of practice—We needed the full involvement of the people who do the work.

Some of these elements were in place, but most of them needed much more definition and formalization before the team could be comfortable that they had a stable solution for BP. One of the next steps was to take this concept to a wider audience and to dialogue with others. It was great being able to decide on a framework ourselves, but it had to "feel right" to the organization as well. The team believed they could introduce the concept at a large KM meeting they were planning in early September, in Milan, Italy (see the sidebar Quark Hotel, Milan!).

Quark Hotel, Milan!

Quark Hotel, Milan—Jim Shannon onstage

The room was too small for the number of tables, and the pillars made it difficult to see the stage. People needed to crane their heads to get a clear view, and the air was stifling from the heat of the video lights (the whole event was being captured on video and Webcast live on the BP intranet). And yet there was a tremendous buzz in the room. The three days had been an intense experience, as KM enthusiasts from around the BP Group had stood up on stage and described the approaches they were applying to managing knowledge. Ray King had told us of his online community of computer modelers, Tony Kuhel told us about the Olympus system in BP Oil, John Minge beamed in by videoconference to talk about knowledge sharing on Texas drilling rigs, and many others shared their successes and plans. Then there were the outside experts: Colonel Guthrie with his "war stories" from the Army, Larry Prusak talking animatedly and powerfully for an hour without notes, John Henderson with his view of the future knowledge economies. Finally, there was the input from the rest of the company, as people used the Knowledge Management Web site to raise issues and ask questions, which Chris Collison read out loud to the assembled delegates in Milan every morning.

It was now the afternoon on the third day. The buzz was still high. We had spent the late morning in breakout groups, working some of the critical issues that needed to be overcome if KM was ever to be a way of life for BP. Jim Shannon, a video producer from the Alaska office, was standing onstage reporting the results from his group's discussion.

Jim explained how the top levels of BP need to articulate the scale of the challenge and the potential benefits, and then cascade the KM ideals down to the production floor. People need to be involved, and the Knowledge Management community, exemplified by the attendees at this meeting, needs to identify and understand those people they will depend on for success. "How many of you people attending the meeting," Jim asked, "are willing to go back and become champions within your businesses, to evangelize and lead Knowledge Management? Stand up if you are willing to be an evangelist for KM." There was a moment's pause, and then chairs began scraping back all around the room as every delegate rose to their feet in a silent movement of commitment to the cause.

After the meeting was over, the KM team traveled to a restaurant on the shores of Lake Como, where Nick led the group in our own Retrospect of the conference. Each of us could identify our personal success factor. For Nigel Gibbs, it was "the sense, level, and quality of community that we developed. Transforming 80 individual learners into a community of learners was the biggest shift I've encountered in such a session. The challenge now, for me, is to shift the community of learners to be a learning community." Barry Smale noted that we avoided the event being a "show and tell" of KM team presentations. "This was an objective in the organization of the event and worked extremely well since the delegates got ownership." Georgie Dicker recalled the continual buzz of enthusiasm in the room and how she ended up in a nightclub with a bunch of the delegates, where they were still talking about Knowledge Management at 3 in the morning.

All of us agreed that Milan had been the right event at the right time and had sparked an excitement and commitment that would form the foundation of BP's move toward a fully knowledge-enabled company.

The KM Community of Practice

One of the strategic elements that had been identified at Powder Mills was the role of communities of practice in Knowledge Management. The team had already begun to operate a KM community (a community of Knowledge Management practitioners). The Powder Mills endorsement plus the excitement generated by Milan caused the team to look again at this community as a means of focusing the KM effort across the company. BP had already recognized the need for strong formal networks in a federal organization, and many people around the BP Group had been running knowledge-sharing networks for a year or more. Nick became the coordinator or facilitator for the Knowledge Management community of practice (kmcop). People in the kmcop shared their knowledge in an electronic workspace that has proven to be a robust model for a virtual community of practice, with an e-mail discussion forum, a facilitator, and a Web site for storing collective knowledge. The conversation within the community ebbed and flowed (Figure 7-3 is a graph of the frequency of participation in the kmcop), but was proven to be an invaluable way to keep alive a sense of purpose around the topic of Knowledge Management. One major disappointment for the rest of the team and Nick was that there was never a repeat of Milan to keep the community spirit alive. The team had

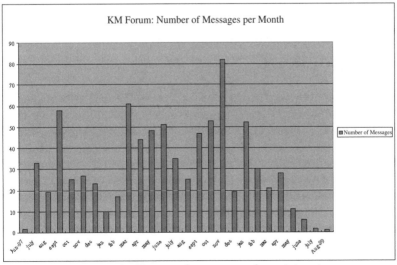

Figure 7-3. Kmcop frequency of participation

always planned to hold a second meeting in early to mid-1998, but the collapse of the oil price brought a strong focus on costs and reluctance for anyone to travel by air. In a cost-centered climate such as this, the team could not make a business case for a second face-to-face meeting.

CONNECTING PEOPLE

Ironically, the team's deep conviction that Knowledge Management is a people issue led to the one piece of technology investment the team made. Although BP relies heavily on networking between individuals, it is a huge organization, and it was hard to find "who knows what." However, a small initiative by one of the technical service groups in the company looked as if it might be the solution for finding people with specific knowledge. This solution was a piece of software called Connect, which linked the e-mail directory with the BP intranet, making it possible for people to create and maintain their own Web pages—a sort of knowledge index (or yellow pages) for the company. The team took over the funding of Connect and started the process toward making it a company-wide knowledge directory.[2] By the autumn of 1998, most of the elements of the KM model were in place. The Powder Mills vision was coming together. The KM initiative had the support of a community, and the KMT was developing and road testing a number of tools. The hoped for knowledge-sharing environment was becoming a reality. The team was beginning to support the development of specific knowledge roles in places as far apart as London, Vietnam, Alaska, and Australia. There was only one gap in the system: the concept of the Knowledge Asset, the packaged bundle of knowledge with shelf life, which could be reused and reapplied for business success. Various members of the team had experimented with some early versions, covering topics such as shift handover and joint ventures in SE Asia, but collectively they were not sure that they had fully exploited the potential of packaging explicit knowledge. Then, in October, came a call from Colombia (see the sidebar Bogotá, Colombia—1997) that led to the development of a stable and effective Knowledge Asset format.

---

[2] A full description of Connect is in Collison, Chris, "Connecting the New Organization: How BP Amoco Encourages Post-Merger Collaboration," *Knowledge Management Review*, March–April 1999.

Bogotá, Colombia—1997

When Kent and Neil Ashton visited Colombia in April 1997, Kent spoke with an old colleague from Alaska, Mike Davidson. Kent asked Mike if he could showcase some of the good practice they had been applying in the field of drilling technology. Mike's answer was a short one: "Sorry, Kent, we're too busy." Now Mike was faced with a challenge, and he was on the phone asking for help.

At the end of 1997, BP Exploration Colombia was facing a transition point as it moved from the exploration phase (investment, growth) to development (production focus, cost control). In addition to the business transition, the rapid fall in the global oil price was forcing a critical appraisal of the cost structure of the business unit. It was obvious that a major reorganization was needed—to simplify the organization, reduce complexity, and cut costs. Such reorganization carries a risk of major distraction to employees, with possible inefficiencies, poor decisions, accidents, and environmental damage. A small team was set up to implement the restructuring, and Mike was in charge. When Mike called Kent and asked, "Can you compile a Knowledge Asset on 'What BP knows about business restructuring'?" Kent was glad to help and gave Nick the task of assembling and packaging the relevant knowledge of the company.

After a Web search resulted in nothing useful, Nick started calling people, collecting past reports and conducting interviews. Pretty soon he had compiled a first-pass Knowledge Asset for Mike. Nick put it on the Web and e-mailed Mike the link. He liked it, and so Nick continued to refine the Knowledge Asset with additional input over the next few weeks. Mike recalls the use he made of the Knowledge Asset in the planning stages of his project. "Getting that collective experience was very valuable in that it allowed us to consider our options. In the end we tried to pick up elements from the experience that had happened across the company. We very consciously used that experience in terms of our design—how we would go about doing things in Colombia. There is great value in having the collective experience of the company gathered in this rather simple way before we embark on tasks such as these, which fundamentally change the lives of many of our employees."

After the exercise was over and the new Colombia model was implemented, Mike called again and asked if Nick would like to help him collect the knowledge from the Colombia restructuring. He had found the Knowledge Asset so useful that he felt the need to reciprocate. Nick flew to Bogotá for a week to interview the key players and capture what Colombia had learned, so that the asset could be updated. This added another layer of richness to the Knowledge Asset, which has since been used (and updated) by Venezuela, New Zealand, and other business units around the BP Group, as well as providing vital guidance after the BP-Amoco merger.

At the end of 1998, the team was very confident that they were on the right track. All components of the model had been road tested and could now be refined by applying them out in the business, on important, risky business projects, with real money at stake. The team knew that they were on the verge of a winning combination of committed people, first-class technology, and an effective, tailored business process. They felt ready for any challenge the company might throw them. At that stage they did not realize just how big those challenges would be!

BIG BUSINESS: DELIVERING NOTICEABLE RESULTS THROUGH PROJECT WORK

The Knowledge Management team started 1998 in a confident mood. They were happy that they had a robust model for managing knowledge. They had an active community of practice. They had much of their knowledge about KM captured and codified on a Web site. Lastly, there was a growing demand from the business for the KMT's support and services. The year 1998 was going to be the year of the mass rollout. The slogan "99 in '99" was used to refer to the team's intention to have nearly a hundred trained knowledge managers working in the business by the end of the year. They had developed a list of people who understood the philosophy and framework to work with. They had developed a set of service lines that could be offered, and they had a detailed action list from the fourth quarter of 1997. All that was needed was guidance from the BP Group chief executives at the steering committee meeting on the 23rd of January.

The guidance received at the steering committee meeting really sharpened the team's focus. What they needed to do, the steering committee said, was to work at great depth in a small number of selected business projects and to deliver real monetary value back to the BP Group. There were two reasons why this needed to be done: First, hard business results would overcome any remaining skepticism about the value of Knowledge Management; second, the falling oil price made it imperative to deliver short-term value to the BP Group. The team needed to pick five or six of the most promising business projects, devote most of their attention to these (at least 80% of the team's effort), and deliver to the business $100 million in enhanced value. This was quite a challenge!

Goals and Project 1998

The team called another time-out and sat down to work out how they could deliver against this target. They needed to select the projects carefully. They needed a rigorous way of measuring the value, and they needed the Knowledge Management framework, tools, and processes packaged for their own use in the first quarter and for group-wide use in the second half of the year. A substantial proportion of the population would need to be on BP Connect to facilitate identification of expertise by year-end. They needed to transfer the awareness and the skills of Knowledge Management into the selected project teams at great depth. In addition, they still needed to service at least some of the demand that was coming from the rest of the organization. This would stretch the team's resources to the fullest. The team decided that Chris Collison would work Connect; Catherine Day and Nick would act as a hub for the team, collating and packaging what the organization knew and was learning about Knowledge Management; and the rest of the team would work the projects identified as having a potentially high return.

Which projects should the team do? This was the first question to be answered. They needed projects that had good support from the business, where the business unit leader was a strong advocate and was prepared to assign some good people from their own team. Also, the projects should cover areas of significant investment,

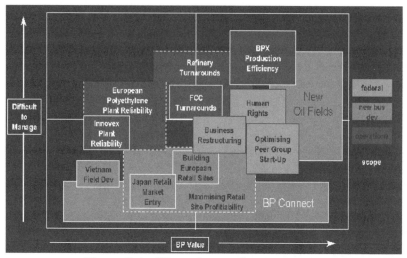

Figure 7-4. BP project evaluation matrix

and therefore have the potential of large savings (performance improvement through Knowledge Management delivers maximum value for high-cost repetitive activity, where the repeat savings are large). In addition, the knowledge generated, captured, and reused should be applicable elsewhere for added business gain. The team quickly reviewed their portfolio of opportunities and ranked them against these criteria, plotting them on a matrix of potential value versus deliverability (Figure 7-4). The projects that seemed most promising included field development in Vietnam, gas station construction in Japan, improving the reliability of BP's polyethylene plant in Scotland, building service stations in Europe, improving the efficiency of maintenance shutdown of oil refineries, improving the efficiency and effectiveness of business restructuring, optimizing the start-up of Peer Groups in BP Oil, and developing the way in which BP worked with nongovernmental organizations (NGOs) in the field of human rights.

JAPAN RETAIL MARKET ENTRY PROJECT

Entering the Japanese retail market was chosen as a pilot project because it was relatively easy to manage but could impact an area of strategic importance, namely New-Market Entry. BP was a new entrant to the field of fuel retail in Japan (in fact BP built the first-ever western-style gas station in Japan), and BP was finding it quite a learning experience. The culture was different, the buying habits were different, and the whole approach BP needed to take was different. BP needed to learn very quickly, if they were to make inroads into the Japanese market. Keith Pearse was the KMT "man in Japan." He spent a long time on regular visits to the office, helping them conduct Retrospects and introducing After Action Reviews. Together with the Tokyo staff, Keith built Knowledge Assets on topics such as self-service (self-service gas stations were a novelty to the Japanese), co-branding, and gala openings of new service stations. According to the business unit leader, Ronnie Forbes:

> I don't think it would have been possible to have moved forward as we have done from the time we started the project, with the improvements that we are going to have for the second site, unless we had learned quickly, both from the first site experience and from the experience of people around the world. We will open the second site with a quick-serve restaurant, and to do this with the second site in a new market is, I think, probably unique. Without being able to systematically draw on what folks have done in other markets, that just wouldn't have been possible.

The Retrospects were the first tools that helped BP Japan find a way of learning from the construction of the first site. The team learned a lot from this experience, and the Retrospects provided the framework to enable the team to learn more quickly for the second site. The After Action Reviews probably had the widest impact in the Tokyo office. They helped Ronnie and the team have quicker, sharper, more focused meetings and a much more efficient way of doing business, at an operational level as well as within the project team.

EUROPEAN RETAIL PROJECT

Building gas stations was also the focus of another major project (see the sidebar Retail Engagement, Madrid—1997), for which Tom Young was the primary KMT contact. BP builds gas stations throughout Europe, in 11 different countries, in a joint venture partnership with Bovis. Looking at the results from the different countries made it obvious that there was a spread of practices. Some countries built their gas stations quickly, some countries were able to obtain permits for sites very rapidly, and some countries were able to maximize profitability from individual service stations. There was great value to be gained by exchanging best practices and bringing all the countries up to the standard of the best. The initial focus was on construction costs, where there was a wide range of performance across the continent. At the beginning of 1998, management set a target to reduce the building costs of retail gas stations in Europe by 10%. Knowledge Management was chosen as a crucial component in delivering this reduction. By the end of the project, the business had achieved a 26% cost reduction—way beyond the initial target.

Because of the huge geography involved, it was not practical for Tom to do everything on his own, so he decided he had to train local people to become conversant in the technology and techniques of Knowledge Management. Tom identified the project engineers to do this—the people who build the sites. The KMT held a training session for the project engineers and combined this with a series of Retrospects to capture the knowledge they had acquired in 1997. Tom decided to hold this session at the offices of British Telecom (the national telecommunications provider). Tom explains, "The reason we held the session at the BT office rather than a BP office was to bring home to everyone that if you are a partner with someone they will help you whenever they can. BT had better facilities for this type of session and they offered them freely." This meeting was the start of the knowledge community and construction of the Knowledge Asset. Because the knowledge needed to be shared between the two companies (BP and Bovis), an extranet was built to house the Knowledge Asset. The project engineers created and sent back (to the central KMT team) Retrospects for each retail site. A community of practice assessed the Retrospects for techniques and best practices to be adopted across the alliance. The KMT built a detailed Knowledge Asset containing site plans and drawings and other documents. Peer Assists had tremendous impact as well. These have really become a way of life in BP Oil retail.

Retail Engagement, Madrid—1997

Implementing a Knowledge Management project in the European retail business in BP Oil was an extra challenge. Retail covers many countries, many languages, and many different cultures. All of these issues needed to be addressed before knowledge could start to flow freely, and the language barrier is a big one. One of the early challenges was engaging the country's managers and engineers. Tom Young held a meeting in Madrid and started off by running through the standard Knowledge Management presentation (the engagement presentation mentioned in the Engagement section). However, he followed this up with something different and tailored to the audience. Tom explains:

> Engineers are visual people; they think in terms of drawings and charts. This makes the language barrier less of an issue. So I needed to engage them in the language they knew best, the language of images. For the second part of the meeting, I went into a scenario. I said, "You are going to build 12 retail sites. You have just finished the first one. Here is what happens next."
>
> I had discussed the meeting with Ian Hamilton of British Telecom, who had worked very closely with me on the VT project. Our mutually beneficial relationship had extended into many other areas and I was sure it would deliver value here as well.
>
> We had set up a videoconference link, and shared photographs across the network, pretending that this was being used for sharing between the field office and the head-office planner. The images were projected onto a large screen. We showed examples where litter bins had been positioned behind the signage so that people could not use them. We showed examples where the lighting had been arranged at the site so that it shone in people's eyes as they drove up, dazzling the motorists. We showed several other examples of design faults and errors in the site construction.
>
> By the time we got to the fifth picture, the audience was "living this"; it was no longer a scenario for them. Accusations began to fly around the room: "That sort of thing should not have been allowed to happen." I said to them,

> "Traditionally, those mistakes at the first site would have been repeated at the next station, and the next station, and the next station after that. By learning before, during, and after, the mistakes are picked up at the first site and eliminated from all the others." At the end, they all got up and started clapping. When the applause had died down, the guy in charge said, "We are going to do this. Go ahead and arrange the training." So we had buy-in from the management team. We had reinforced the idea of learning from the first site, by using pictures and images that helped them "live through it." Only afterward did we add the "Knowledge Management" label.

Actions like those taken for the Japanese and European retail projects generated a lot of value for their respective business units. However, there was a lot more value to be realized if these projects could be linked, and the knowledge could begin to be shared and applied globally. In the case of retail, this was addressed by holding a three-day meeting in Singapore where representatives from Europe, Venezuela, the Far East, and the former Soviet Union were invited. The purpose of the meeting was to exchange knowledge and best practices about entering and growing new retail markets such as in the Far East and South America. The KM team held a whole series of Peer Assists and Retrospects and built several Knowledge Assets. They also laid the foundation for a global community of practice on the topic of entering new retail markets. By the end of the meeting, there was a commitment to the management of BP Oil that the knowledge exchanged at the meeting would save $6 million in 1998 and a further potential $50 million in 1999.

REFINERY TURNAROUNDS PROJECT

One of the other major projects the KMT was involved in covered the topic of turnarounds in BP refineries. These are major refurbishment projects undertaken every four or five years at each refinery, where the refinery is shut down for maintenance. Each turnaround can require budgets of tens of millions of dollars, and up to a thousand people can be working at the plant for several weeks. Because turnarounds have a significant impact on the profitability of the plant, they need to be done quickly, cheaply, safely, and effectively. A network of people involved in turnarounds was already in existence (the Turnarounds Improvements Network), and they had already set for themselves tough performance goals, aimed at putting all of BP's refineries in the top quartile of oil industry performers. Kent and Gareth Edwards engaged the refinery managers in this opportunity at one of their quarterly network meetings. In this session, they were able to convince the managers that KM would not disrupt their planned operational activities, but rather support and enhance them. Since Gareth came from the refinery business, he was accepted in their culture and became the KMT leader for this project. The five refineries that had major turnarounds coming up that year agreed to participate in the project. Kent and Gareth visited each one to deeply engage their local management and operations teams and codevelop the expected performance improvement targets.

What the KMT needed to do was arm these people with the tools, techniques, and technologies of Knowledge Management. The team introduced a structured set of Peer Assists for each turnaround. The first Peer Assist was a strategy review 16 months ahead of site work. The last Peer Assist was two months ahead of the site work, to assess if the site was prepared. The team used Retrospects and in-depth interviews to capture lessons learned after the turnaround was over, and then developed a Knowledge Asset to capture and make visible the global knowledge of the network. The team also introduced After Action Reviews to learn day by day as the turnaround progressed. These had maximum impact at the Toledo refinery, where they were used on a daily basis by the shift teams (see the sidebar After Action Reviews—Feedback on Their Use at the Toledo Refinery). The KM tools and techniques were used at refineries in the Netherlands, Australia, Singapore, and the United States. Record-breaking results were achieved at Kwinana and Nerefco, and the other refineries showed improvements attributable to Knowledge Management. The Turnaround Improvement Network aimed to beat the original tough performance targets by generating $60 million of extra value by the year 2000. Knowledge Management tools and techniques were a key enabler of this performance improvement.

After Action Reviews—Feedback on Their Use at the Toledo Refinery

"I first thought AARs would be a waste of time, but it was good because it slowed things down to get good ideas and discuss them."—Supervisor

"When I first heard about it, I didn't think it would work; I was extremely skeptical. The way the team works together convinced me it works."—Lead supervisor

"I was skeptical as to what this was going to do, but the payout was immediate."—Boilermaker

"Before the AARs, they didn't feel like they were a team. After a few AARs, they became one."—Lead supervisor

"I thought I needed to be the expert and felt threatened at first. After a few AARs, I felt comfortable that the guys appreciated using their ideas, and we became a team."—Supervisor

"The crew was as skeptical as I was—what was this! Now they look forward to it and wouldn't miss it."—Lead supervisor

"Most of it is just common sense, but reviewing everyday allows us to use our common sense."—Boilermaker

"There are times when you think, 'We don't have time to do this'; then you do it and you think, 'We don't have time not to do this.' "—Supervisor

"When people saw it being taken seriously, they took it seriously."—Boilermaker

"If you can't take 15 minutes to do the AAR, you have bigger problems than you realize."—Supervisor

"I have been doing this work for 20 years, and no one asked me what I thought before, so it was a change."—Boilermaker

As the end of 1998 approached, the team was feeling pretty tired. It had been a hard year, but very successful. When the team started to add up the business results that had been achieved through Knowledge Management projects, they could see hard, unarguable results of $84 million, a likely figure of $260 million, and a possible upside of $700 million. The team had met, and surpassed, their targets. They had proved the business value of Knowledge Management and provided valuable income to the BP Group. Now it was time to roll out the tools and techniques across the entire organization.

Developing Organizational Capacity

One of the key success factors in the BP KM program was that it was not something the KMT did *to* the business, but something that they did *with* the business. In all their business-focused activity, the aim was to keep Kent's promise to the management committee by transferring the capability for Knowledge Management to the business, rather than retaining it as a central function. As Kent likes to put it, "Knowledge is very personal, and you can't make someone share what they know. So, you can't 'do KM to them.' Just like you can't learn for someone else. It's their knowledge and their decision to apply it. We just helped."

In all the projects that the team did in 1998, they made sure that they were working alongside people drawn from the business. These were the people who would make KM live on after the central team had withdrawn. The team saw and understood that building organizational capacity was key to their success. However, this had to be capacity not just in the five to six key projects they had selected to focus on, but in the rest of the organization as well. Somehow, by the end of 1998, the team had to be in a position to start to withdraw central team support.

This was a challenge. The team members were already very busy with project work and had very little time to spare for coaching and training people. The plan had been to spend 80% of the time on the key projects and 20% on building capacity. But that 20% was not enough. Sometimes it felt as if it were 80% on the projects, with another 80% needed to build capacity!

Sustaining the Community

The engagement sessions had been run, and the early results coming out of the projects meant that there was a huge groundswell of interest in KM in early 1998. People all over the company had come to see the value in Knowledge Management and wanted to try it themselves, whether they were part of a major KM project or not. The community forum was busy. A steady stream of questions was coming in from around the world, asking for advice or help. Some examples: Tim Blandon, the knowledge manager for BP Oil in Australia, wrote in, saying he was finalizing his performance contract and objectives, and asking if anybody could assist by describing KM performance indicators. John Morton raised a question about virtual meetings: Did anybody have any experience or guidance to offer? Greg Clark told us about the system that he had derived for recording, publishing, and distributing After Action Reviews. Vasso Tsatsami asked for help in sharing large documents across the world. And many other similar queries were raised and, invariably, quickly answered by others in the community. The conversation within the community ebbed and flowed (see Figure 7-3), but it proved an invaluable way to keep alive a sense of purpose around the topic of Knowledge Management. However, the inability to hold a follow-up to Milan was still bothering Nick. In the absence of a second meeting, what steps could the team take to sustain and increase the sense of community?

A catalyst to one of the steps was a visit by George Por. George was a consultant living in California and a founder of the Community Intelligence Labs, a network of consultants specializing in developing Web-based enterprise intelligence systems. George had met Kent at a conference, and Kent had asked him to come out and speak with the team about communities of practice. The team had a lively morning with George. One of the things Nick picked up from him was the need to build "community purpose" in the Knowledge Management community of practice. The community needed to work out some charter. Nick sent an e-mail to the forum titled "KM Community: What Is It For? Your input needed!" which sparked one of the liveliest debates ever held in the forum. All the key questions, like "Why are we here?" and "How do we operate?" were discussed. Slowly the community thrashed out their aims, objectives, principles, and procedures (see the sidebar Charter for the BP Knowledge Management Community). This was a great discussion, and long overdue. For over a year, the community had been operating as a forum, without ever actually agreeing what they were there for!

Charter for the BP Knowledge Management Community

The aim of the KM community is to deliver value to the business by increasing the effectiveness of KM practitioners around the BP Group.

The objectives of the KM community are:

• To realize value by embedding KM practice/process and behavior in the business
• To provide linkages between the KM practitioners across the group, thereby increasing effectiveness
• To create a relationship between these practitioners to encourage/promote communication
• To provide and maintain a mechanism so that people will seek and exchange operational knowledge about the application of KM for business benefit

- To provide ownership, guardianship, and leadership concerning the principles of KM, as applied within the group.

The KM community will operate with a minimum of formality. It will be operationally focused, facilitated with membership by self-selection. Wherever possible, community members will be free and open with their questions and answers, sharing them through the community forum.

The KM community will be supported by:

- A membership list on BP Connect
- A discussion forum linked to e-mail
- A Web site representing the current state of knowledge of KM
- A facilitator whose responsibilities will include moderating activities and discussion within this community

THE KM KNOWLEDGE ASSET

The community and the e-mail forum gave the Knowledge Management practitioners around the company a way of asking questions and a way of giving each other mutual support. This was a great way of exchanging tacit knowledge. At the same time, the KMT was building their own practical experience within the team in the tools and techniques of Knowledge Management—mostly from the project work that was in process. There had to be a way to make this experience available to the people out there in the business units trying to do Knowledge Management. The answer, of course, was to use the same processes and systems that the team had been recommending and to build a Knowledge Asset: "What BP knows about Knowledge Management." One of the first things the team had done together in 1997 had been to build a Web site: the Knowledge Management home page. To start with, this had been an information page about the team, with a few additional resources like how-to guides, PowerPoint presentations, and copies of the team's key documents. Now was the time to evolve this into a Knowledge Asset that the practitioners could use, a distillation of all the practical experience of the KMT presented in such a way that others could use it as a guideline or recipe for repeating success. Like other Knowledge Assets, it needed to contain advice, stories, video clips, people to contact, and all the artifacts and documents that someone would need to do Knowledge Management.

With the help of a KMT member, Catherine Day, Nick started this major upgrade at the beginning of 1998, aiming to put together a resource pack for the KM practitioners at the end of the first quarter. This resource pack would be a complete Knowledge Asset on managing knowledge. It would be made available via the intranet or on CD, together with copies of all the presentation and engagement material that the team had been using. This was a major step toward alleviating some of the concerns of the people who had been engaged, who didn't become one of the key pilot projects, but who still wanted to do something. The premise was that anyone in the business could run his or her own KM program armed with this resource pack. The team members spent time codifying what they knew, holding Retrospects on the projects, collating material from After Action Reviews, and building a whole set of guidelines and examples on topics like capturing knowledge, packaging knowledge, setting up e-mail discussion groups, building Knowledge Assets—everything a Knowledge Manager needed to know to do his or her job. All this material would just about fit on a CD. In April, Catherine had a whole stack of CDs on her desk, ready to send out to KM community members worldwide. Together with the CDs were printed glossy brochures covering the key tools of Knowledge Management: Peer Assists, Retrospects, After Action Reviews, Learning Histories, communities of practice, and BP Connect. Kent recorded an introductory video, and it was bundled into an attractive folder as the KMT's Easter present to the community.

Response to the resource pack was varied. Some people used it immediately, running engagement meetings for their business and trying out the tools and technologies. Other people were not ready. They put it up on their shelves, next to the telephone directory, for reference in the future. Clearly, there was work to be done to increase the state of readiness in the organization. In the meantime, the team could get some feedback on the Web site and the resource pack, aiming for rerelease in the third quarter of the year.

Assessment and Feedback

There are many ways to get feedback on a Web site. The team collected usage statistics. They built feedback buttons. They asked people what they thought. By the time the autumn came around, Nick decided it was time to run a major survey of the community. Once again the Knowledge Management forum was a great mechanism. Nick fired off a set of questions, and one of the characteristically lively debates followed. Nick says:

Perhaps we could have predicted some of the responses: "We need more content," "easier navigation," "fewer clicks to reach the real stuff," "simpler language." We decided to set ourselves some targets—links to all areas from a front page, only two clicks to reach all material, simple overviews as well as detail for each topic—and we built a good-looking design modeled from a successful Internet site.

At the same time, the team was upgrading the material to include all the learning that had been derived from the major KM projects in 1998: knowledge and experience about how to manage knowledge and also how to implement a KM change program in the business. Not only was everyone learning very fast about how to do KM, there was a requirement to capture the learning, distill it, package it, and share it with the community worldwide, in real time.

Knowledge Asset Version 2

The revamped Web site (Figure 7-5) and the second resource pack received a great reception. But these materials were still not enough to transfer the capability to manage knowledge. The practitioners out there in the business had been given a recipe book for doing Knowledge Management, which gave them all the knowledge they needed to be proficient managers of knowledge, but it did not provide them with the confidence to make a start.

Because Nick's name was at the bottom of most of the Web pages, he was getting calls from people saying things like, "I'm planning to hold a Retrospect for my project. I've read your Web site, but could you just talk me through it please." So the Web site by itself was not enough. Perhaps they had the procedures for "doing" Knowledge Management, but they did not feel they had the skills and experience. They wanted to speak to somebody who had done it before, to reassure themselves that they would be able to deliver. Keryn Smart called from Melbourne about a Retrospect she wanted to hold on IT projects. Tamara Oldham called from Caracas about a series of Retrospects at gas stations. Paul Whiffen came to see Nick about the Retrospect he wanted to hold on the Euro program in Europe. For Keryn and Tamara, Nick spent an hour on a videoconference where he transferred his tips and tricks, hints and stories on Retrospects. He also planned a strategy with them for the meeting. Paul's case was a little different. This was a major project involving much of BP Oil Europe, and Nick and Paul decided to run the meeting together. Paul would do the organizing. Nick would do the facili-

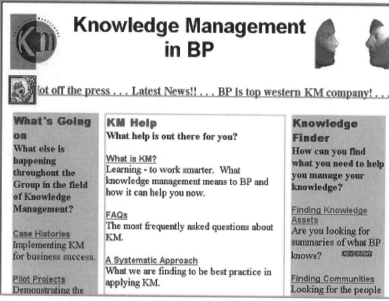

Figure 7-5. Snapshot from the new Web site

tating. Paul would learn by watching Nick, and Paul would build the Knowledge Asset. This worked like a dream; the combination of personal coaching and backup from the Knowledge Asset was just what people needed to try the tools. The tools are simple, certainly, but people needed to see them in action before they could be really confident of their simplicity. (Paul has since left BP Amoco and worked as the knowledge manager for Tearfund, a charitable organization. A case study on Paul's work is included in Chapter 8.)

If BP wanted Knowledge Management to survive long after the KM team had moved on, then they couldn't rely on the central team to permanently coach the knowledge managers in the business. The team had to find some alternative support mechanism where knowledge managers in the business could help each other gain the confidence they needed to implement the tools. The Knowledge Management community was too large, too diffuse, and too global to fulfill this role. People needed to be able to meet together face-to-face to exchange ideas and reinforce each other's activities. One of the best mechanisms the team found for this was "Knowledge Management pools," small subcommunities that could meet in a single location to support each other's Knowledge Management activities.

Two of these pools were particularly successful: the KM pool for BP Oil Europe, based in Brussels (see the sidebar The Brussels KM Pool—Late 1998) and the KM pool for BP Exploration Alaska, based in Anchorage.

The Brussels KM Pool—Late 1998

It was a mixed group sitting around the small meeting table in Brussels—mixed not only in terms of nationality but also in terms of understanding of, and commitment to, Knowledge Management. Some were enthusiastic converts, already driving forward their own initiatives in the business. Some were new to the topic but had heard enough to know there was some potential. Others were still trying to come to grips with the topic. These were the members of the Knowledge Management pool for BP Oil Europe—the major part of BP's fuels and lubricants marketing business—and this was one of the monthly pool meetings.

We had spent the first hour discussing the level of service provided by an outsourced vendor who managed the intranet site for BP in Europe. Now we were going around the table reviewing what we were doing in our parts of the business to deliver value through management of knowledge. Clyde had been sitting quietly in the corner, looking rather puzzled. When we got to him, he spoke up. "Look, I'm still not really sure what value there is in this Knowledge Management stuff. I mean, if my manager asks me to justify to him the time I spend here with you, what can I reply? Where is the real business benefit here?"

Nick took a deep breath, ready to trot out the examples and success stories that he had used so many times to justify expense on Knowledge Management, but before he could start to speak, the others had already begun to reply. Richard explained the value that had been generated by reducing the cost of service station construction in Europe. Sath talked about how much value could be generated if the different call centers that we were implementing around Europe could learn from each other. Someone else mentioned the Peer Assist on leaky storage tanks. Clyde nodded thoughtfully; yes, he could see the value. He would try a Peer Assist for himself. Nick thought to himself, "These people do not need support from the KMT anymore, they have each other for support."

TRAINING PROGRAMS

Eventually the team realized that if they were ever going to build the organizational capacity to the level needed for KM to be self-sustaining, they would have to move on from individual coaching to more wide-scale training. Nick says:

> In fact, if I look back at the two years we spent on the Knowledge Management program in BP, one of my greatest regrets is that we didn't introduce formal training earlier. Perhaps we should have set up a program of training courses as soon as the KM system was stable and had proven business results. At that time, we were so busy delivering value through the projects that we had little time to spare for developing training courses. Eventually, however, we had to get down to it and build a training course. This would be a third mechanism (together with the community and the Web site) for delivering the skills, competencies, and confidence to those practitioners in the business: the people who would keep Knowledge Management alive after central support was withdrawn.

The first few courses were run in early 1999 and attracted Knowledge Management enthusiasts from around the company. People in BP were busy with the merger with Amoco during that period, and time was at a premium. By using preparatory reading and a combination of early mornings and late nights, the team was able to cram what was probably four days of training into two days.

WHAT DID WE LEARN FROM THIS JOURNEY?

The team completed what they had set out to do. There was a real sense of accomplishment, but also a feeling of loss as the individual KMT members went off to do other things. The team had established real relationships and friendships. It had taken hard work and time. Kent said, "I believe that we have learned that, with available technology, the world is a small place, and I expect to keep in touch."

A few of the major lessons Kent learned are as follows.

- It is amazing how easy the process of learning is if there is a need. People are able to learn quickly and apply the learning so that it has a significant impact, provided they stop to think and ask for help.

- It is simple, but not easy, to "do Knowledge Management." Kent learned over time to live it himself, and he preached it. People need to see you doing what you are striving to deliver and learn. Be a role model. Take the risk of not being perfect.
- Support is necessary because people are already doing "the business" and they need help making the change. There are new processes (Peer Assists, After Action Reviews, and Retrospects) and new roles (knowledge owner and manager). Start with small, focused initiatives, and then grow the initiatives based on pull and business demand.
- Our principle of learning before, during, and after an event has been powerful and produced results. Learning after is the most difficult component; once something is over, making time to assess what happened must become habitual.
- Reciprocity guides interaction, as our experience in Colombia showed. Sharing knowledge can be leveraged to your advantage.
- Technology is necessary but not sufficient. We took the availability of basic technology for granted. Technology can minimize the key barrier to sharing knowledge or information. Lack of technology and connectivity can become a positive barrier for people who don't want to share information. With or without the right technology, learning in order to deliver results is possible if the use of time for knowledge-based activities is legitimized, and when the right people and right information are easily accessible.

FINAL THOUGHTS FROM KENT

"Often we hear there are prerequisites to a Knowledge Management project. Technology needs to be in place, senior management support is essential, you have to have your data and information management together first, etc. We were fortunate. BP had many pre-existing conditions that we took for granted: a technology infrastructure, a federal organization, familiarity with facilitation, and support from the CEO. Nonetheless, in individual locations the conditions were still not always right, but motivated people overcame the barriers. I believe that you don't have to, and cannot, wait for the conditions to be right. We were able to accelerate the impact across the organization because of the preexisting conditions, but we could have found ways to make things happen without them.

"I've learned that you can get where you want to be not just by doing but by learning while doing. And if you adopt a process of learning and doing together, you get there better, faster, and cheaper. We learned that if you are not learning before, during, and after, you are not optimizing performance.

"For me, the KMT and business customers were codevelopers. The KMT's starting point was 'We don't know everything, but we'll share what we know.' For the businesses, the knowledge that was created and reused had local value and thus did not need to be validated or policed. Voluntary participation was a principle of the KMT. The local knowledge had credibility and was a link to people. Once a business unit knew what it knew, they were part of the process of creating what BP knows. KM should become part of everyone's job, as opposed to something separate. This principle is evident in the KMT's message to every individual, team, and business within BP: Performance Through Learning and Learning Through Performance. There was momentum. BP's ability to leverage knowledge continued to grow. People became more confident as they found it easier to reuse knowledge. We have found it possible, if not easy, to change behavior and deliver results. We don't know if we have reached critical mass. We know we have planted seeds and they are growing.

"The concepts of Knowledge Management are universal and simple. Everyone has knowledge. It is a common ground for people to relate to. The journey continues for BP, the members of the KMT, and me. There is no end."

POSTSCRIPT—WHAT HAPPENED NEXT

The KMT disbanded in 1999, with the majority of the team leaving the organization, their mission completed. Kent went to head up KM at SAIC, while Nick, Tom and others set up business as Knoco Ltd. (www.knoco.co.uk) offering Knowledge Management consultancy services. Two team members were left in BP to act as central stewards for KM, but the bulk of activity was devolved to the business. Knowledge Management now takes place in the business units and the communities of practice within BP, particularly the legal community, the green operations community, operations excellence, major projects, and health and safety. Knowledge Management has been particularly successfully embedded within the well engineering community, as described in Chapter 9. Most important, people routinely learn before, during, and after the work they do. In this way, KM has become part of the way people work. It doesn't get much better than that!

Kent Greenes is chief knowledge officer and senior vice president of Science Applications International Corporation (SAIC). He has worked internationally in a variety of executive, operations, technology, and business renewal roles in the energy and engineering industries. He is recognized as one of the world's leading pioneers and practitioners of Knowledge Management, and won a Computerworld Smithsonian Award for his groundbreaking work in virtual teamworking.

Fortune magazine recognized Greenes in 1999 as the world's leading moneymaker in KM as a result of his track record in leading KM for British Petroleum. He is listed as one of the top 20 Most Admired Knowledge Leaders in the Global Teleos 2000 Most Admired Knowledge Leaders (MAKL) survey. His experience and insights have been documented in many articles and publications, including some highly acclaimed books such as *Simplicity, Learning to Fly, The Knowledge Engine,* and *Knowledge Capital.* He is on the editorial board of the *Journal of Knowledge Management,* and a founding member of several KM consortiums and communities, including the latest round of the Harvard Learning and Innovation Laboratory.

Greenes is sought after worldwide to deliver keynote speeches at symposiums, conferences, universities, and organizations in the public and private sectors. In addition to applying KM inside SAIC, Greenes runs a successful KM consultancy practice that provides services for Johnson & Johnson, Entergy, Saudi Aramco, Unocal, Amerada Hess, British American Tobacco, the U.S. Army, the U.S. Navy, the Department of Defense, the Defense Threat Reduction Agency, and, most recently, Iraqi Reconstruction.

Reference

Prokesh, S. "Leveraging the Power of Learning: An Interview with Sir John Browne of British Petroleum." *Harvard Business Review,* 1997.

CHAPTER 8

Knowledge Management in the Aid and Development Sector: A Case Study in Implementation at Tearfund

By Nick Milton in conversation with Paul Whiffen

The case study for Tearfund is an example of the transfer of Knowledge Management processes and systems from a large industrial corporation into a smaller organization within the charity sector. The case study is interesting in that the cultures of the two organizations are very different, as are the levels of technological enablement. However, the Knowledge Management processes themselves have proved entirely transferable.

Knowledge Management was introduced into Tearfund when a Knowledge Management champion from BP, Paul Whiffen, was appointed to lead one of the internal teams. Paul arrived at a time when the organization was asking how it could encourage more reflection around the action-reflection cycle. Paul and his manager, Ian Wallace, both recognized that knowledge was not flowing freely within Tearfund but was remaining trapped within the organizational units, and, as a result, the organization was repeating mistakes and reinventing wheels. By working with those who recognized the problem and were anxious to find a solution, Paul managed to demonstrate the value of Knowledge Management, to gain high-level support, and to establish a Knowledge Management implementation program, which he led.

The processes adopted by the organization are largely based on the capture and transfer of lessons learned, through Retrospects (which Tearfund called Learning Reviews) and through the collation of lessons in the in-house computer system. Roles and accountabilities for the management of knowledge were designated. Tearfund is an Evangelical Christian organization, and individual members of the staff are highly motivated, with a strong personal sense of the need to do "what is right." This can sometimes lead to a culture of individualism, which can make Knowledge Management difficult to deploy, and there were many cultural barriers to overcome. However, Paul's vision and passion led to a gradual but pervasive culture change, and Tearfund is now recognized by some as a leader in Knowledge Management within the aid and development sector.

Paul has now left the organization, since he feels that the initiation/launch phase of Knowledge Management is now over. Astrid Foxen is the new Knowledge Management champion for the next phase of implementation within Tearfund.

BACKGROUND

Tearfund is an Evangelical Christian relief and development organization working in partnership with other organizations in the third world to bring help and support to the world's poor. It currently works in three main areas:

- Public health—Supporting communities in managing their own health care, particularly, addressing HIV/AIDS and water and sanitation issues
- Children at risk—Working with high-risk children from poor communities
- Disaster response—Helping vulnerable communities prepare for natural disasters, such as earthquakes, floods, and hurricanes, and aiding them in recovery from such disasters

Tearfund grew out of World Refugee Year in 1960, as a way of coordinating donations for refugee programs from the Evangelical Alliance. Tearfund itself developed as an organization in 1968, when the relief programs were extended to address the underlying causes of poverty through longer-term development work. Over the decades, the organization has grown and now has an annual income through donations in excess of £35 million.

Tearfund operates in over 70 countries around the globe, mostly in the poor South and in the third world. It supports skilled expatriates who work on location with over 400 local partner organizations that, in turn, work with the local population to deal with the causes of poverty in their area. Approximately 37 staff work in the international development area, 360 national and expatriate staff within disaster response, and another 87 people within Tearfund's UK headquarters, acting to coordinate global activity. It was within this UK office that the Knowledge Management initiative was first begun.

You can learn more about Tearfund on their website at www.tearfund.org or on their information sharing website, "The Tearfund International Learning Zone," at www.tilz.info, which they have recently established as a means of sharing information and best practices.

Making a Start

The vision for Tearfund's transition to a knowledge-enabled organization was largely driven by one person: Paul Whiffen. Paul had worked at BP in the late 1990s, the time of Knowledge Management implementation within the major British oil company, and had seen firsthand the value that the systematic approach to managing knowledge could bring. He had worked in European procurement in Brussels and had personally applied Knowledge Management to the "Euro-readiness" project, which was set up to ensure that BP was fully ready for transition to the Euro currency. Paul was making a lifestyle choice, leaving big business to work in the charity sector, and had applied to Tearfund for the role of team leader for the Program Development team, a team with responsibility for promoting good practice within Tearfund. Paul explains what happened at the interview.

> I had no development experience of any sort, so I could not talk about this during the interview, but the turning point in the interview came when the interviewer said, "We keep losing knowledge and information. We know we are bad at this; do you have any ideas of how we can address this issue?" So then I started to talk about Knowledge Management as I understood

it, and about the learning before, during, and after model, and communities of practice, and from then I sensed a change in the interview. I think that was what got me the original team leader job.

So Paul was not appointed as a knowledge manager, but as team leader for the team driving organizational change. However, he was given the mandate by the organization to think about how to help Tearfund manage its knowledge and become a learning organization. Once he had his feet under the desk, he contacted BP for permission to use their KM approach and began on a small scale to introduce some of the Knowledge Management processes.

The BP KM system is well described in the literature and is a six-component model for managing knowledge (see Figure 8-1), involving:

- Learning before
- Learning during
- Learning after
- Knowledge roles
- Communities of practice
- Knowledge Assets

Because this system is process-led, rather than being technology-led, it is applicable to all sorts of organizations at all sorts of scales.

Figure 8-1. The Tearfund/BP learning cycle

Paul felt that it would be equally applicable to small, informal, capital-constrained Tearfund as it was in large, structured, capital-rich BP.

Paul's approach at Tearfund was to start with some small-scale trials of components of this model. This approach itself was countercultural to Tearfund, which had a tradition of careful planning and consultation and was unfamiliar with a piloting, "try it and see and learn" approach. Paul now had to decide on suitable activities to pilot test the first Knowledge Management processes.

One of the key activities of Tearfund, and one that is critical to its success and to delivery of its vision and mission, is disaster response (supporting the indigenous population at times of natural disaster such as floods, hurricanes or earthquakes). Disaster response is a prime candidate for Knowledge Management in that disaster response activities are intermittent and time-limited; have a start, middle, and end; and occur all over the globe. Learning would not be transferred automatically from one disaster response project to another, because disasters in different parts of the world may well be attended by different staff. However, there was huge potential benefit for increasing the effectiveness of response and therefore saving human lives if knowledge could be captured, saved, and reused. So, Paul's initial pilot was to hold a Retrospect on Tearfund's response to the floods in Bangladesh. Paul reports as follows:

> There is no doubt that demonstrating the Bangladesh Retrospect in the summer of 1999 was a great thing. It is much better to just demonstrate success, just to do stuff. Don't worry about getting all sorts of plans and strategies in place; just do something and demonstrate to people how simple and yet how powerful these processes are. Do it on a well-defined, specific project with a start and an end—ideally on one that was itself successful, so that some of that success rubs off on you and on Knowledge Management. Certainly, the Learning Review of the Bangladesh floods response was a well-defined, clear-start-and-end project.

The Bangladesh Retrospect was well received by people who attended, and several lessons were identified and recorded, which could be used in future flood response programs. However, this turned out not to be just an academic exercise, because shortly after the Retrospect had been completed, the Orissa cyclone hit India, and flooding started there. Although the Orissa cyclone was a sudden-onset disaster, unlike the floods in Bangladesh, which had developed over a period of weeks, Tearfund found that many of the lessons from Bangladesh were immediately applicable to Orissa. The first thing that the Asia team leader did was to look for the Bangladesh lessons, because they were fresh and applicable. He was impressed by the process and became an effective advocate at the management level.

THE ORGANIC DEVELOPMENT OF THE KNOWLEDGE MANAGEMENT PROGRAM

After the initial success of the Bangladesh Retrospect, Paul was looking to build awareness and understanding of Knowledge Management within Tearfund. He addressed this on three fronts: at a management level, at a staff level, and externally to the organization. Figure 8-2 shows the timeline of the developing Knowledge Management program in Tearfund.

Externally, Paul was looking to talk with other organizations about Knowledge Management, to help sell the idea that Knowledge Management was a good thing, and to ask for their thoughts about how it should be done. He was doing this for two reasons: first, to start the process of knowledge sharing between Tearfund and other organizations, and also to use external contacts as the way of raising awareness within Tearfund itself. He chose organizations that were influential to Tearfund and that were significant presences in

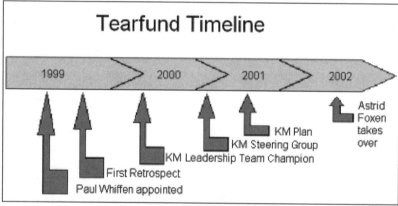

Figure 8-2. Tearfund timeline

the development sector, in order to be able to say to Tearfund, "Knowledge Management is not just something that Paul Whiffen is keen on; look, these other big organizations think it is a good idea too."

He spoke with the Department for International Development (DFID), a government department dedicated to addressing the promotion of development and the reduction of poverty, which is highly influential in the UK development sector. The director of DFID's Knowledge Policy Unit was highly supportive. He also spoke with British Overseas NGOs for Development (BOND), a network of more than 270 UK-based voluntary organizations working in international development and development education. BOND has a coordinating and educational role to play in the development sector, and Paul was able to get Knowledge Management firmly on BOND's agenda, resulting in a series of Knowledge Management workshops for charities and NGOs.

He also found himself being asked to talk to other organizations, workshops, and conferences, and to write articles for magazines. All of these profile-raising activities had an impact within Tearfund and reinforced the message that Knowledge Management was a valuable and accepted methodology that needed to be taken seriously.

Within Tearfund, at the staff level, Paul was still being determinedly opportunistic in introducing Knowledge Management processes and concepts wherever possible. This was not only on discrete projects. One manager was interested in the concepts but had no specific project on which to apply Knowledge Management, so Paul conducted a Retrospect on his previous 12 months' activity, just in time to influence the next 12 months' planning process. Again, this manager was delighted with the outcome and was happy to talk about the success in the leadership team meetings. In addition, Paul and Nick Milton set up an internal seminar for Tearfund staff in order to import some ideas and case histories on the management of knowledge (Nick was acting as Paul's coach and mentor throughout the Tearfund implementation).

Paul also gave some thought as to what were the main stakeholder groups within the organization, and realized that the field staff were very influential in whether new ideas would be adopted. Buy-in from the field staff was important. During a week-long visit to Africa, Paul met with a local Tanzanian consultant to speak with him about Knowledge Management. He was very supportive of the learning before, during, and after model, and endorsed Paul's approach, as Paul explains:

What was going on in my [Paul's] mind when I was speaking to this man was that this particular model of Knowledge Management started off in the U.S. Army and then went from the military sector to the corporate sector. It went to Tearfund head office and went down very well there, but I know what some of the purists might be thinking: "It only works in military and corporate environments. What we are really interested in is our partners and the difference it makes to them." This was an early interaction with somebody from the partner stakeholders group, and it was important to get his endorsement.

At a high level, Paul spoke with the general director of Tearfund, Doug Balfour. Since it was a relatively small organization, it was fairly easy to get access to him, and Paul outlined what he planned to do. Doug was supportive and offered a quote that Paul could use internally to frame the context of Knowledge Management. This quote asserted that it will only be organizations that learn, and treat their knowledge successfully and proactively, that will survive in the future. This simple concept gave focus to the Knowledge Management initiative and also demonstrated top-level commitment and belief.

Paul also had an informal champion at the leadership level, Ian Wallace, who had recognized that Knowledge Management could solve Tearfund's issues of "trapped knowledge and information." However, during Paul's first nine months, there was no official or explicit Knowledge Management program; it was all being driven by spare-time personal belief in addition to Paul's "day job" as team leader. At the beginning of 2000, this was about to change.

Developing a Formal Knowledge Management Program

By early 2000, Tearfund had pretty much been through the "proof of concept" phase of Knowledge Management, thanks to Paul's informal awareness raising and thanks to the success of the Retrospect process. The organization decided that it was time to approach Knowledge Management implementation in a systematic way, and a semiofficial leadership team champion for Knowledge Management was identified. There was a lot more serious talk across the leadership team of Knowledge Management as something they wanted to do. There was no Knowledge Management strategy written down at this point, but the official wheels had begun to turn, and the beginnings of a strategic intent were starting to appear.

Paul started to ramp up his awareness campaign, producing, for example, a briefing slide set for team meetings. He was still talking externally, especially to BOND, and continuing to conduct internal Knowledge Management processes (such as Retrospects) at an increasing rate. After a while, the organization began to realize that collecting lessons was not enough and that there needed to be a systematic way of reapplying the lessons. Paul explains:

> During the summer of 2000 and into the early autumn, we had done lots of Retrospects on various disasters responses, but we had never had the time to take these lessons and consolidate and disseminate them to find out what was going on. There was a person in the disaster response area called Tony who was frustrated with this, because he had never had time to assimilate the lessons, and I remember saying to him that eventually these disasters will stop, and we will find a quiet period and then we will do it. And sure enough, a quiet period came, by which time we had held eight Retrospects in various different forms, and he went home with lots of lessons and lots of yellow Post-it notes, and wrote them all up, and discovered that there were lots of lessons that had been learned and relearned over the year. It was a case of focusing on the ones we had learned many times. He focused on the 25 lessons that had come up three times out of the eight Retrospects. One of the lessons had come out every single time! Tony focused on embedding those lessons in the processes, procedures, guidelines, etc. for future disaster responses.

The simple process of comparing the outcomes, and demonstrating that many lessons had come many times, allowed Paul to go to the organization and say, "This is documented proof that Tearfund keeps on learning the same lessons, and reinventing the same wheel, on our most strategic activity." This was a very powerful exercise to go through, to demonstrate the need for the systematic management of knowledge.

Such continued success elicited a management response, and on September 1, 2000, a corporate project was initiated to embed good Knowledge Management practice within Tearfund on a day-to-day basis. Paul was appointed full-time knowledge manager and put together an implementation project plan. Until then, he had been doing Knowledge Management on top of his "day job" as a team leader. A small project team was formed, consisting of himself; an information management (IM) professional, Astrid Foxen; Ian Wallace and his personal assistant; and a member of the Training and Development team. The team met every two or three weeks to discuss knowledge and information management, and the cultural and organizational issues associated with that. Involving information management was a key step. There is a long and illustrious tradition of librarianship and professional information management in the development sector, and in some other organizations in the sector Knowledge Management and information management were involved in "turf wars" over who should do what. To avoid this, Paul worked with the information manager to decide how knowledge and information would be kept distinct but would work together, and, therefore, how KM and IM would work together.

Paul ran a check on the suitability of the BP Knowledge Management model, comparing it with how Knowledge Management is applied at other leading organizations, such as Microsoft, the World Bank, and Buckman Laboratories, and became convinced that the approach applied to Tearfund, was robust and fit for the purpose.

In early 2001, the Knowledge Management implementation project was further strengthened by the appointment of a steering team within Tearfund, comprising 12 representatives from different parts of the business. The purpose of the team was to support the program, to give creative ideas, to challenge, and also to advocate for Knowledge Management across the organization. The project team met with the steering team every couple of months in order to sense check what they were doing and, if necessary, to gain endorsement. After the first couple of meetings, Paul was able to put together a formal three-year project plan. This was endorsed by the steering team, and the plan contained the following three major objectives:

- To deliver a Knowledge Management system that enhances organizational effectiveness
- To develop user-friendly processes that reward the desire to learn and stimulate a learning culture, and can easily be integrated into normal working practices
- To pilot Web-based interactive learning as a means of combating poverty

These objectives had been initially applied within the Tearfund corporate head office in the UK, but the plan was to extend the Knowledge Management system to include partner organizations, and ultimately to include Tearfund's donors and Tearfund's clients, the world's poor.

Taking the first step to extending the system, Tearfund held a workshop for partner organizations from all over the world. Such meetings have happened before, but only on a regional basis. This time it involved global partners, so in the same room were people from Africa, Latin America, Central Europe, the Far East, and so on. This was a great opportunity to introduce the concept of Knowledge Management to the partner community. Paul led a session within the meeting to talk about Knowledge Management. He recalls:

Some of the reactions were incredible. One chap said it had been a life-changing experience. Partners recognized that if they could just connect up like one big family, they could help each other, rather than all dealing individually with Tearfund. There is such a vast body of knowledge amongst them all, if they could just access it.

Dealing with issues such as the exchange of knowledge directly between partner organizations will be part of the future focus for Knowledge Management within Tearfund.

Paul left Tearfund in 2002. By this time, the initial evangelistic phase of Knowledge Management implementation—raising awareness, proving the concept, winning the hearts and minds of the stakeholders—was over. It was time to hand over the reins to somebody who would systematically apply and grow the program. Astrid Foxen, the former information management professional and key member of the Knowledge Management project team, has now taken over as knowledge manager within Tearfund, while Paul has left to take up a career in consultancy. Since then Tearfund has worked to "embed" Knowledge Management throughout the organization by working with and training all team leaders to ensure both that they recognize their responsibility to promote and reward learning and that they know how to create a learning environment within their teams. In addition, the organization has adopted a KM measure as one of its key performance indicators.

Program Methodology and Results

The methodology for the management of knowledge applied within Tearfund is based on the BP KM system shown earlier in Figure 8-1:

• Learning before
• Learning during
• Learning after
• Knowledge roles
• Communities of practice
• Knowledge Assets

The Tearfund system seeks to apply these as follows:

• Learning before—Team and project plans should include a section of identified lessons learned from past experience that will be included in the new activities, and all key new activities and projects will include a Peer Assist process near the start.
• Learning during—Project managers and team leaders will make sure that learning is captured as activity goes on.
• Learning after—All projects and activities will end with a Learning Review (Retrospect) where lessons are identified and captured. These Retrospects are facilitated by trained members of staff with facilitation skills. In addition, when key staff leave the organization, they go through a knowledge debriefing to make sure that important knowledge is captured before they go. Similarly, staff returning from overseas assignments are debriefed, and their knowledge is stored for briefing other staff going to the same country.
• Knowledge roles—"Knowledge champions" are identified in the organization to promote Knowledge Management. Similarly, staff are identified to look after (maintain and manage) the knowledge associated with each of the key activities of the organization. Each of these key activities is championed by a senior staff member, who makes sure that learning captured within the activity is embedded into policies, processes, and procedures.
• Communities of practice—There are identified communities of practice in the organization, covering the key subject areas, and these communities are represented on the organizational intranet.

- Knowledge Assets—Knowledge and information pertaining to the key activities of the organization, and the main countries in which Tearfund operates, are stored on Tearfund's shared information drive, and each Knowledge Asset is owned and managed by identified staff members. The whole information structure within Tearfund has now been reorganized around the key activities and communities of practice.

These six components fit together to make a systematic and holistic approach to Knowledge Management within the organization. Knowledge gained through activity, or through time in country, or as part of a career within Tearfund, is systematically gathered by trained facilitators. This knowledge is stored on the intranet, according to the activity that was involved or according to the country in question. The knowledge stores are owned and managed by identified individuals. Project teams addressing similar activities in the future, or staff going to similar countries in the future, can access the knowledge store to learn before they start. Activity-based communities are being developed, many of which go beyond the Tearfund head office and include members of partner organizations worldwide, and these provide an instant forum for tapping into the knowledge and experience of peers.

This system was not yet fully in place as of the end of 2003 and is still being rolled out across the organization with the intention of being fully embedded by the end of 2004.

The Issue of Culture

The cultural aspect was a particularly interesting issue within Tearfund. As stated earlier, Tearfund is an Evangelical Christian organization, and people are motivated to work there through the strengths of their personal beliefs and commitment. They feel very strongly that they are individually called to work in the sector, and have a strong sense of right and wrong. This individual motivation needs to be transformed into a team motivation. Also, the evangelical background of Tearfund staff can sometimes lead to a suspicion of big business and of management strategies that may have been linked to a profit motive. This reluctance extends to Knowledge Management and also to performance management. Performance is difficult to measure in the aid and development sector anyway, and if it is difficult to measure, it is difficult to manage. Also, staff in such organizations are driven and motivated more by personal conviction than adherence to corporate targets and measures. However, Knowledge Management prefers a performance management culture; without measuring results, it is difficult to know which practices are best practices and which are not; which practices improve performance and which do not; what knowledge is valid and useful and what is not.

Changing the culture within Tearfund was a slow business. The general director, Doug Balfour, had already begun a process to establish performance measures across the organization. Even so, Paul had to reassure people that just because a process or practice such as After Action Review had been imported, via big business from the military sector, did not mean that it was necessarily inapplicable to a (more morally conscious) Christian organization. Tearfund also had at the time a traditional silo management structure, and the silo-crossing philosophy of KM was a further cultural change. The early opportunistic Retrospects were very helpful here, as were a high-level champion on the leadership team.

Paul's advice in dealing with cultural change is as follows:

First, make sure that you are mentally and emotionally well prepared. You will be, according to some, treading on other people's feet if they are not used to this way of working. If the culture is one of working in organizational silos, then challenging this will upset people. It is good to be well connected to a senior person who can champion your cause. Also, be aware of what the culture is. It helps if you know that you are going to have a hard time, and why you are going to have a hard time. So [have] some sense of knowing what the culture is first and then be able to see where the challenges might come. That makes it a logical thing rather than an emotional thing.

In addition, the constant awareness campaign, described earlier, working at staff level, leadership level, and outside the organization, helped to chip away at the old ways of working, until KM became accepted almost by stealth as "something Tearfund does."

Tearfund Now and in the Future

Implementation of Knowledge Management is now well under way within corporate Tearfund in the UK. It has gone through the proof-of-concept phase and is now in the rollout phase, well beyond the point of no return. Tearfund has been recognized as a leader in KM within the aid and development sector in the UK and by external organizations as well. For example, Paul was recently asked by the British Army to come and talk with them about KM, a concept that Tearfund had adopted from BP, which in turn had partly adopted it from the military sector.

However, the operations and activities of Tearfund extend well beyond the head office, to encompass the partner companies, the donors and supporters, and ultimately the poor. Could the KM system also be extended to include these communities, as in Figure 8-3?

The first steps have been taken to involve the partner organizations, with workshops and the first steps toward communities of practice. There are, however, extreme challenges in sharing knowledge among the partner organizations, such as the small size of many of the partners, their lack of technology, and the fact that many operate from war zones or disaster areas. An e-mail exchange has been set up between the partners, which were introduced to KM at the workshop mentioned earlier (which the head of an NGO in Kazakhstan had said was a "life-changing experience"). In addition, Tearfund provides guidance, through their Web site, on how the partner organizations can manage their own knowledge.

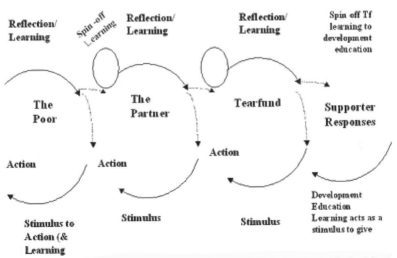

Figure 8-3. Interlocking learning loops among the stakeholder communities

No steps have as yet been taken toward extending the Knowledge Management system to the donors and sponsors. It is, however, very intriguing to consider how Knowledge Management can be extended to Tearfund's ultimate user population, the poor of the developing world. The old model of the rich North providing money and food to the poor South has already been superseded by a new model where the rich North provides knowledge and resources to allow the poor South to develop a sustainable future—knowledge that is often gathered from experience of previous development projects. But do Western organizations really need to gather knowledge from poor communities and provide it to other poor communities? Could the poor communities exchange knowledge with each other without the need of an intermediary? Can Knowledge Management help at a more fundamental level to address world poverty and hunger? Paul Whiffen thinks so:

What is clear, is that, to the poor, KM is more than something to increase corporate performance—it improves their lives. Connecting people up is giving people access to help, confidence, and the esteem to challenge the status quo. Because of this, there are powerful and effective communities setting themselves up to make things better—one mountain community in Asia is so pleased with what it has done in this area (including using an intranet) that they wish to export their ideas and experiences to other mountain communities, including those of the first world! I have heard (secondhand) that Western companies are beginning to look at such sites as best practice because they are the product of more energy/commitment and therefore work very well.

PROBLEMS AND CONCERNS

The challenge areas for Knowledge Management implementation within Tearfund have primarily been cultural. We have discussed previously how the unique characteristics of the development sector make it difficult to introduce good practices from the business world. We have also discussed how Knowledge Management sits most easily with a performance measurement and performance management culture, a culture that is not yet fully developed within the aid and development sector. We have also discussed how these problems were overcome by a strategy of proving the concept first and then raising awareness through a number of parallel approaches over a period of a year or more.

One story that illustrates how countercultural Knowledge Management can be goes back to a time when Tearfund was conducting a review of staff posts. They called in an external organization with experience in staff review, and everybody within Tearfund was asked to fill out a form describing their roles, responsibilities, budget, reports, pressure, and so on. They then went through a regrading and reranking exercise, which was primarily biased toward giving high grades to people with large budgets and big staff. The result was that the knowledge manager role, which had no budget and no staff, despite being hugely influential and a very powerful agent for cultural change and performance improvement, received a very low-grade rank. In fact, the knowledge manager was ranked at the same level as the chef in the canteen. Given the degree of influence that Paul had within Tearfund, within the partner organizations, and within the sector, this was obviously ridiculous and represented an old approach struggling to fit in a new idea.

Paul refused to take this personally, got help and support from senior people, spoke with external agencies and knowledge managers in other organizations, and used the opportunity not only to reestablish the Knowledge Management role at an appropriate grade, but also to continue educating the organization about the importance of Knowledge Management.

Lessons Learned

Start your strategy by balancing *connecting* with *collecting*. Paul started proving the concept of Knowledge Management within Tearfund by collecting lessons—first from the Bangladesh floods, but then from most of the activities within the Teddington office (he conducted over 100 Retrospects during his two years). Were he starting again, he would try to also address the other end of the value chain, with the clients, implementing communities of practice in parallel with collecting lessons.

Make sure you have a management champion. Unless you have access on a daily basis to the general director, Paul feels that you should have a senior manager who supports you and to whom you do have access. Keep that relationship strong.

Plan for a proof-of-concept phase. If you are introducing something radically new to an organization, you always need to prove that concept before you can have a strategy. Otherwise, it will be very difficult to get budgets, to get a team, or to persuade people that it's a good idea. Until the concept is proven locally, the act of formalizing a strategy may actually make it more difficult to implement. Be opportunistic; look for all opportunities to prove the concept.

Look for a good place to demonstrate the concept. Find a project or activity that is important to the organization. It should be well defined, with a clear start and end, and the activity should happen quite often (even if the context of what is happening changes). Ideally, choose a project that was itself successful so that some of that success rubs off on you. Hold a Retrospect, and clearly show how knowledge from the project can be applied in the future. Then get other people to talk about how successful it has been.

Make sure that Knowledge Management and information management are well aligned. Be very clear in your own mind about the difference between knowledge and information, and sit down with the information managers and help them come to the same sort of understanding.

Work to raise awareness and understanding with the key stakeholders. Decide who the stakeholders are—not just the key corporate players but also the customers, the beneficiaries, and other stakeholders. Look to raise the profile of Knowledge Management in all of these groups, and ideally gain endorsement from within each group. Look for multiple avenues for raising awareness: informal talks, formal talks, bringing in experts, speaking to external organizations, speaking to academic institutions, and general word-of-mouth promotion.

Be aware of the cultural issues. Implementing Knowledge Management is a culture change process, and if the culture is well aligned, it can be a slow and painful process. Be aware of the culture, be aware of the barriers, and, if necessary, be personally prepared for some long-term work.

Paul Whiffen, having acquired KM awareness and expertise at BP, has experience in KM design and implementation in both the NGO and corporate sectors. He has taken the theory and applied it to make a difference in organizational delivery while influencing management thinking, culture change, information management, and technology systems. He has had an influence on the NGO sector, helping many organizations to see and value what KM can do and the benefits it can bring. He continues to be a strong networker with effective skills in communication and inspiring people in what KM can do for them and their world. He was also a member of a small team providing facilitation, culture change, and KM support and advice to the Stakeholder Implementation Conference, which was an immediate prelude to the Earth Summit in Johannesburg in 2002. Whiffen has been appointed a director of Aid Workers Network (www.aidworkers.net), which is an NGO concerned with using KM principles to connect aid workers worldwide so that they can share and exchange their experience. He has a First Class Honours Degree from Newcastle University, England, and is working as a lead associate for Knoco Ltd. (www.knoco.co.uk).

CHAPTER 9

Knowledge Management in Business Performance at BP Well Engineering

By Nick Milton

This case study looks at an organization, or rather a community within an organization, where Knowledge Management (KM) was first introduced several years ago, and where the use of the tools and processes is well advanced. The focus is now on assuring the use of Knowledge Management in service of business delivery.

Well engineering—the drilling of oil and gas wells—is an area of massive strategic focus for BP. Much of BP's upstream expenditure is spent on drilling wells, often in new, demanding, or sensitive locations. There are constantly lessons to be learned and knowledge to be gained if wells are to be drilled more quickly, safely, and cost-effectively. The transfer of knowledge within and between well teams is worth hundreds of millions of dollars annually to the organization. BP well engineering has developed a practical and robust system for Knowledge Management and is now making sure that this is applied systematically and strategically by all well teams (a process known in BP as "assurance").

This assurance is coordinated by Dave Evans,[1] a well engineer based in the Upstream Technology group. Dave supports and maintains the Knowledge Management technologies and develops Knowledge Management practices used by the organization. These practices are promoted through publications, lectures, and a tailored training course for the well teams. The assurance system is further

---

[1] Since this chapter was written, Dave has been replaced in this role by Emma Frost.

strengthened by the appointment of knowledge managers in individual well teams, and the requirement for each team to conduct self-assessments and develop a Knowledge Management plan.

These plans are linked with other performance management systems to provide a comprehensive program that ensures all resources are managed in this critical area of business performance.

Background

BP is one of the world's leading companies, in terms of size and market capitalization, with an annual profit and revenue in the region of $80 billion and $175 billion, respectively. It ranks number three in the global oil and gas sector, producing almost 3 million barrels of oil equivalent production per year. The company employs 110,000 people, working in over 100 countries, with well-established operations in Europe, North and South America, Asia, Australasia, and much of Africa.

The company is divided into four main business streams:

- Exploration and Production
- Gas, Power, Renewables, and Alternatives
- Refining and Marketing
- Chemicals

The Exploration and Production stream, often referred to as the "upstream" business, is concerned with finding new oil and gas fields, developing them through drilling wells, installing infrastructure such as platforms and pipelines, and then producing the oil and gas. This is a highly capital-intensive business, requiring billion-dollar expenditures to develop relatively uncertain resources. New technologies and techniques are constantly being developed and applied to aid exploration and production, and a willingness to learn and to share new knowledge is a fundamental business need. Exploration and Production activity takes place all over the world, in a variety of environments (desert, deep seas, arctic tundra), and this sharing of knowledge needs to be global.

The process of exploring for, and producing, oil and gas is as follows.

Oil companies apply to host governments for an exploration license on a particular tract of land or seabed, on a speculative basis. The decision to apply for acreage is based on reconnaissance seismic data, and an understanding of the regional geology of the area that leads the geologists to suspect that the conditions are right for generating and accumulating oil and gas in the subsurface. The companies often work in partnership with each other as a way of spreading the risk.

Once the acreage has been acquired, further seismic data are acquired to try to delineate the possible presence and extent of any oil and gas fields. The geologists and geophysicists need to assess whether there is a reasonable chance of commercial volumes being present—a good enough chance to make it worth investing in a well. Oil wells, particularly those offshore, can be very expensive to drill, costing in the order of tens of millions of dollars. Wells need to be drilled only when the chance of success outweighs the cost, and they need to be drilled in the right place.

If the well finds oil and gas in (potentially) commercial quantities, then the companies need to make a decision on whether to develop the field and produce and sell the hydrocarbons. Production requires huge investment. An offshore platform may need to be built, or a pipeline, or a gas-gathering station, or a liquid petroleum gas plant. This could be a multi-billion-dollar investment, and the companies need to be sure that the investment is justified. Perhaps some more wells are needed first, but eventually the decision needs to be made.

Once the companies have decided to develop, then the pressure on the drillers and geologists becomes even greater. A series of development wells needs to be drilled, ready to produce oil once the platform is in place. They need to be drilled safely, quickly, cheaply, in the right place, and in such a way as to maximize production rates. Each well is a new data point, and the teams will be learning very rapidly as each well is drilled.

When the platform is in place, development drilling will continue for a while, but the attention of the organization will shift toward optimizing the throughput of hydrocarbons from the reservoir to the pipeline and extending the life of the field for as long as possible.

Three main groups of technical specialists are employed in Exploration and Production: those who deal with understanding the subsurface, such as geologists, geophysicists, and reservoir engineers; those who deal with surface facilities such as manifolds, separators, platforms, and pipelines; and those who deal with designing and drilling wells. Each of these groups of specialists handles huge investment decisions, is responsible for very significant parts of the company cash flow and income stream, and works intensely with knowledge and know-how. Each group needs Knowledge Management, and this article discusses the approach the third group, the well engineers, take toward using KM to optimize their performance.

There are around 50 separate teams in BP involved with planning and drilling wells. These teams are spread around the globe and work in a variety of settings: desert, tundra, mountains, shallow seas, and deep seas. About 500 people are parented to the drilling engineering function, although the total number of people working on wells projects exceeds 1,200.

THE EARLY STAGES—DEVELOPING THE SYSTEM

When the Knowledge Management program was initiated in BP in 1997, it was already clear that well engineering was going to be one of the key areas where KM could deliver a huge return. This is an area where major investment was being made on a regular basis and where learning demonstrably could add value. Each field development project was familiar with the idea of the learning curve. As more wells are drilled on a field, the crews get to know the local conditions and understand the technology they are using, and get better at their job. They drill successive wells faster and more cheaply, and finally reach a technical limit, beyond which it is very difficult to progress without a change in technology. The only things the crews have at the end of the program that they did not have before are knowledge and experience. The area below the learning curve and above the technical limit in Figure 9-1 represents the cost of learning. This cost can easily run into hundreds of millions of dollars on a big multiwell program. Knowledge Management can help reduce this cost, and it can do this in two ways.

First, the team can accelerate their own learning through the conscious identification, capture, and reuse of lessons learned during operations. If they can steepen the learning curve, they can drive costs down faster and can reduce the area under the curve (see Figure 9-2).

Second, if a team can prelearn from the experiences of other teams working with similar technology or on nearby fields, then they need not start at the top of the learning curve at all—they can start part of the way down (see Figure 9-3). Obviously, this needs some investment in prelearning, and it needs much of the knowledge to already be available, but if the potential benefit is in the order of hundreds of millions of dollars, then investing a couple of million in

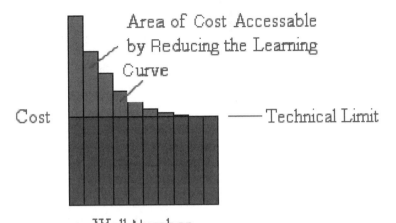

Figure 9-1 *The value under the learning curve*

Figure 9-2 *Reducing the area under the curve*

Figure 9-3 *Transferring learning to start halfway down the curve*

prelearning makes a lot of sense. This is known is BP as "front-end loading."

Given that the well engineering area was such a potentially rich practice ground for KM, BP decided to ensure that the KM implementation program described in Chapter 7 worked closely with the drilling function, and BP set up the "Drilling Learning project" to work in alliance with Knowledge Management. This project was initiated in 1997 and still continues in BP more than six years later. It has taken KM through the full cycle of awareness, engagement, definition, rollout, embedding, and assurance.

Initially, the Drilling Learning project team concentrated on the identification and development of tools and processes that the well engineers could use to capture, store, and exchange knowledge. Some of these processes, such as the Peer Assist and Retrospect, were already locally in place within BP but needed to be rolled out to the well engineers. Other processes and technologies needed to be developed or brought in from elsewhere. The Drilling Learning team used the same basic model—learning before, during, and after—as that chosen by the central KM team (see Figure 9-4).

Once this model was robust, and once all necessary technologies were in place, the drilling learning team set about rolling out a systematic approach to teams worldwide. KM was embedded into the standard company methodology for managing drilling programs, an approach known as Drilling Value Assurance. This took place within the context of a company-wide initiative to improve performance. At the same time, the author of this chapter codeveloped and delivered a training and induction course that could be rolled out globally to individual well teams. The course involves:

- An introduction to KM
- A self-assessment of the current state of KM in the team

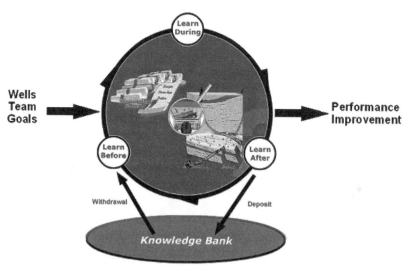

Figure 9-4 The KM model used by well engineering in BP

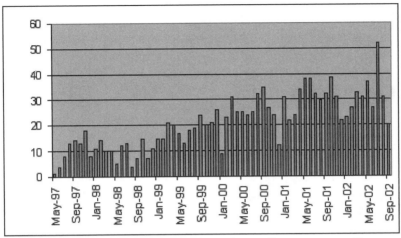

Figure 9-5 Questions per month in the Well Engineering Forum

- A series of success stories and cautionary tales
- A practical hands-on experience of the value of KM
- An identification of the key knowledge needs and outputs
- An introduction to, and demonstration of, the approved KM processes
- An introduction to, and hands-on experience of, the approved KM technologies
- Development of Knowledge Management plan for the team

This course has been held 20 times over the past three years, in many locations around the globe, and is one factor in rolling out the use and application of KM. The steady growth of knowledge sharing can be seen from the graph in Figure 9-5, which charts the growth of use of the Well Engineering Forum (WEF), an e-mail-based Q&A forum used by the well engineering community as a quick and easy way of accessing know-how and experience from around the world.

How the Well Engineers Manage Knowledge

The well engineers within BP use a variety of processes and technologies for sharing, storing, and accessing knowledge. The most commonly used ones follow in alphabetical order.

After Action Review—An After Action Review (AAR) is a short meeting focused on identifying and capturing learning, which can be held on a daily basis, or at the end of a shift, during well operations. The purpose of the AAR is for the team to look at the activity just completed, compare what was planned against what actually happened, and understand why it happened and what could be done differently next time to improve performance.

Basis of Design—The Basis of Design (BoD) acts as a local knowledge bank for well teams, containing knowledge about the well design for their local area. Well design is a crucial area of know-how, and a competently designed well can be drilled safely, cheaply, and effectively. Every team retains its well design documents, but the BoD holds the thought processes and assumptions on which the design was based. The well design documents explain *how* a well should be designed for that field; the BoD records *why* they are designed that way. The BoD is updated at the end of each well as new local knowledge is gained.

Connect—This online database of skills and experience acts as a yellow pages for BP. It is an easy way for people to find expertise and experience from across the full range of BP's operations. If the team identifies a knowledge need, they can use Connect to find others in the organization who can help fill that need. There are currently about 32,000 people voluntarily registered on Connect.

Knowledge Bundle—The Knowledge Bundles are collations of knowledge covering key topics to do with well engineering. They contain current best practice plus case studies and reference material. The Knowledge Bundles focus primarily on well planning and the earlier stages of a well program. Some business units have developed their own Knowledge Bundles, such as the bundle on Extended Reach Drilling developed by the Wytch Farm field in the United Kingdom.

LINK—Standing for "Lessons and Incidents Networked = Knowledge," LINK is the lessons-learned database for the global well engineering community. It acts as a repository for lessons learned during well planning and drilling operations and as a broadcast mechanism for the lessons. Lessons that have been identified at an After Action Review (see the definition earlier) or Retrospect (see the definition later) are entered into LINK via a form-based input screen. LINK then performs a matching run to see which other teams would be interested in this lesson (based on interest profiles that have been registered by the teams), forwarding it by e-mail to relevant team administrators. LINK is very heavily used, with a new lesson being added every day, on average.[2]

---

[2] Figures representative of 2002.

Peer Assist—A Peer Assist is a face-to-face meeting where knowledge is brought in at the planning stage of a well or well program. People (peers) with experience in similar operations in other parts of the world come and share their experience with the team to help them devise the optimum well design. There may be an element of challenge in a Peer Assist meeting, but it is designed as a knowledge-sharing event.

Peer Review—A Peer Review is a meeting to review the well plans before they are approved. This is part of the approval process rather than a knowledge-sharing meeting, and is often attended by senior staff and technical experts.

Retrospect—Retrospects are face-to-face meetings that take place as soon as possible after the well project is completed. The duration of the meeting varies depending on number of people, length, and complexity of the well, but typically lasts half a day to a day. The Retrospect focuses on what has been learned during the well planning and execution, and works through a structured process to draw out lessons for future wells and for other well teams. Lessons identified during the Retrospect are stored in LINK or in one of the Knowledge Bundles.

Well Connected—This is a newsletter for the well community, produced in the traditional paper format and distributed to all members of the community on a monthly basis. It offers a way of showcasing successes, techniques, achievements, and new approaches.

Well Engineering Forum—This is a question-and-answer forum used to rapidly access advice and recommendations from the well engineering community. Approximately 1,400 people are signed up to the forum, which runs primarily within the Microsoft Outlook e-mail system (though it can also be accessed through the intranet). It allows any engineer anywhere in the world to send a query to a central point, which is then broadcast to the community members, who receive it through their e-mail in-box. Anyone who can answer the query replies to the message, and the replies are forwarded to the originator. A copy of the question and all replies is kept in a searchable public folder as a threaded discussion. The forum is generally used just for questions and answers. The forum is extensively used, with 30 or 40 questions per month,[3] each receiving several replies, typically within a few hours of the question being asked.

---

[3] Figures representative of 2002.

Wells Online—The Wells Online site is a Yahoo-like taxonomy of well-related information and Web sites. It provides a way through the "information jungle."

Worldwide Drilling Conference—This is a biannual meeting where a subset of the well engineering community can meet face-to-face, share ideas and best practices, and reinforce the relationships and trust that are needed for the community to function.

These tools constitute the basic toolbox for Knowledge Management within the well engineering discipline in BP. If each well team were to apply these tools properly and effectively to the key strategic knowledge areas of each well, the organization would reap huge benefits through cost savings and performance improvement. In fact, the potential prize here was so great that BP could not just leave it up to the individual teams to decide whether or not to implement KM—they needed to *make sure* that the knowledge was managed. They needed what they called an "assurance system" that would ensure the systematic application of Knowledge Management.

THE ASSURANCE SYSTEM

The BP well engineering KM assurance system is set within a wider system of assurance, called Drilling Value Assurance. This ensures that all wells are drilled using management systems and approaches that meet corporate conditions of satisfaction. There are three KM-specific conditions of satisfaction within this wider system, which all need to be in place: a self-assessment or self-audit known as the PTL (Performance Through Learning) Assessment, the appointment of a knowledge manager to own the KM process, and the development of a Knowledge Management plan.

Self-assessment—The PTL Assessment is completed by the well team in a meeting, generally within the two-day training course mentioned earlier, that combines self-assessment, training in the tools, and production of the outline KM plan. The teams run through a series of questions that assess whether the tools are in place, whether the leadership is aligned, whether the KM processes are understood and applied, whether the culture is conducive to KM, and so on. The team assesses whether they receive a green light (all is in place), a yellow light (progress is being made), or a red light (action is needed). They then work through the actions that need to be taken to ensure they have the conditions they need to manage knowledge.

Knowledge managers—Someone needs to "own" the management of knowledge within any one particular team. Someone needs to make sure that the correct processes are applied—that Peer Assists are held when needed, that Retrospects are scheduled, that everyone has access to all the tools they need, and so on. Other people may be assigned to own particular areas of knowledge. For example, if the well is to be drilled from an artificial island accessed by an ice road, the knowledge manager might appoint one person to look after (i.e., gather in advance and capture afterward) knowledge about artificial island construction, and someone else to look after knowledge about ice roads. Obviously, it makes sense that these people should be the island manager and the road constructor, and the knowledge manager makes sure that they access all relevant knowledge and update the knowledge base after the work is complete.

Knowledge Management plan—The Knowledge Management plan is one of the fundamental planning documents of the well, together with the risk management plan, the project plan, the well plan, etc. The KM plan covers the following items:

• What knowledge is needed to deliver the well objectives? What are the areas about which the team needs to learn? Where might this knowledge be found? Who is accountable for going to find it?
• What knowledge will be created during the operations? What are the areas where this well will deliver new knowledge, which needs to be captured for organizational benefit? How will this knowledge be captured and shared? Who is accountable for monitoring the capture?
• What tools and processes will be applied? When will they be applied? Who will facilitate, or administer, the processes and technologies? Where is the reference material?
• What are the roles associated with Knowledge Management? What roles do the different team members have within the KM process? What training do they need to bring them up to speed?

Different teams take different approaches to the KM plan and to KM assurance, depending on the complexity of their well program, the extent to which it is breaking new ground, and the cost and number of the individual wells—in other words, depending on the dollar value of the area under the learning curve. A well program with $100 million in value under the learning curve will give a lot more attention to the KM plan than a well program with $1 million in value under the curve. However, the elements mentioned previously all need to be addressed in order to meet the minimum conditions of satisfaction.

Knowledge Management within the well engineering function is coordinated by the Drilling Learning team mentioned earlier, led by Dave Evans. Dave comes from an information management background within drilling and has been leading the Drilling Learning team since 2001. Now that the KM tools have been chosen, are robust, and are available to all, Dave's main focus is on rolling out the assurance process described earlier. Dave has the full-time support of a couple of individuals working in the major operating centers, and the part-time support of a network of 25 enthusiastic champions.

Knowledge Management is linked with other aspects of performance management within the well engineering function. Risk management, for example, is an accepted routine discipline for well planning, and most teams develop a "risk register." This should link closely with the KM plan because knowledge can be a key factor in mitigating risk. Also, all wells go through a process known as Technical Limit, where the rig crews are involved in developing targets for how quickly the drilling activities can be completed. These activities are reviewed during operations using the After Action Review process, where the actual result is compared with the Technical Limit target. Where the actual result deviates from the target, learnings are generated.

Knowledge Management also links with a component of drilling activity known as "no drilling surprises," where the geoscientists work closely with the drilling engineers to identify any hazards or drilling challenges in the geological succession that the well will pass through. Knowledge is shared between these disciplines using visualization technology, often in a high-resolution immersive environment with big screens. Engineers and geologists use 3-D visualization technology as a background for holding conversations and sharing knowledge about the difficulties the well might encounter.

VALUE DELIVERY

It is very difficult to measure precisely the total value delivered by Knowledge Management within the well engineering discipline. It can, however, be addressed in a few ways.

Often, individual knowledge transactions can be shown to have value. Individual requests to the Well Engineering Forum can deliver knowledge of immediate benefit. As an example, one team was facing a major problem, with a broken two-inch drillpipe full of cement lost down the hole. Unless they could retrieve this, the well would need to be redrilled at a cost of $5 million. They wanted to try a particular retrieval tool called a Snipper Overshot to recover this drillpipe, but had no local experience. A request to the Well Engineering Forum resulted in a wealth of advice on suitable procedures, and, as a result, the team started an eight-day program that successfully recovered over 2 km of drillpipe and salvaged the well. One could claim that the KM system helped avoid a $5 million loss, but it would be difficult to put an absolute dollar figure on this knowledge without knowing by *how much* the risk of loss was reduced.

Sometimes, individual well programs can demonstrate the value of knowledge by reducing or eliminating their learning curve. One of the earliest demonstrations of this within BP was a field west of the Shetland Islands called Schiehallion. Schiehallion was discovered adjacent to a very similar field called Foinaven, which was developed without specific attention to Knowledge Management. The drilling costs for Foinaven demonstrate a normal learning curve, with well costs generally declining to the final well, which was drilled at a record rate of 20 days per 10,000 feet. Schiehallion, in response to performance improvement targets, embarked on a major Knowledge Management initiative as part of their drilling program, including paying attention to learning before the drilling program (by learning from Foinaven and other similar developments) and during and after each well (by learning from their own activity). The first seven wells on the field were drilled very close to the record of 20 days per 10,000 feet established by Foinaven, thus showing that the learning curve could be eliminated by prelearning. This saved Schiehallion in the order of $83 million. The well team leader from Schiehallion (Bill Kirton) has now transferred the same KM approach to a deep-water field in the Gulf of Mexico, called Thunder Horse, and is already demonstrating huge savings.

Well programs can also demonstrate the power of learning by coming in substantially under budget. In Venezuela, BP undertook a reactivation program on the Pedernales field, an old field underneath the swamps and rivers of the northern reaches of the Orinoco. This field contained a number of old wells, some of them dating back as far as 1930. A decision was made to abandon 40 of these wells, abandonment involving cementing in the wells and capping them to permanently close them. BP contracted a well control consultancy to help with this program, and also set in place a KM system, involving After Action Reviews, collation of lessons learned, management of change procedures, and risk management. Although each well took perhaps four or five days to abandon, when you are working with 70-year old wells, there is a need to update knowledge on a daily basis, so the AARs were run at the end of each day's activity. The Knowledge Management system was responsible for saving 30% of the well program costs, compared with the budgeted figure.

The sharing and reuse of new operational methods can also demonstrate cost savings. A well-known example within BP involves the exchange of knowledge between Norway and Trinidad. On the Valhall platform in the Norwegian North Sea, the wells team had developed an innovative method of widening the wellbore on extended reach wells by running a tool called a Near Bit Reamer behind the rotary steerable drilling assembly. Where previously they would have pulled out the drillstring, put on a new bottom hole assembly, and drilled a "hole opening run" to widen the hole, they were now able to do this in one operation, thus saving between three and five days' rig time. At the end-of-well Retrospect, this was identified as new knowledge, and Marton Haga, the drilling engineer, was tasked with entering this into the LINK database (see the earlier discussion). LINK automatically forwarded the lesson to other teams working on extended reach wells, one of which was the team working in Trinidad. The Trinidad team were intrigued by the approach and contacted Marton for more information. He was more than happy to help and sent off details of procedures and reference runs. Trinidad assessed the possibilities, decided this was a valuable approach for them, and invited Marton to a Peer Assist to share his operational knowledge. The technique was applied during the 2000 drilling season in Trinidad, resulting in a $900,000 cost saving. The Trinidad team refined the process slightly and have shared their new knowledge with the rest of the community through articles in the *Well Connected* newsletter (as well as through lessons in LINK).

The LINK system tries to assign value to the transfer of knowledge, and in fact every lesson entered into LINK is assigned a monetary value and a frequency value. The monetary value of a lesson learned through something that went wrong is linked to the cost of the incident (a product of the daily cost of the rig and the time lost through the incident). Alternatively, the monetary value of a process improvement lesson is a product of the daily cost of the rig and the time saved through process improvement. LINK also requires a value to be estimated for the *potential* value—i.e., the time that might be

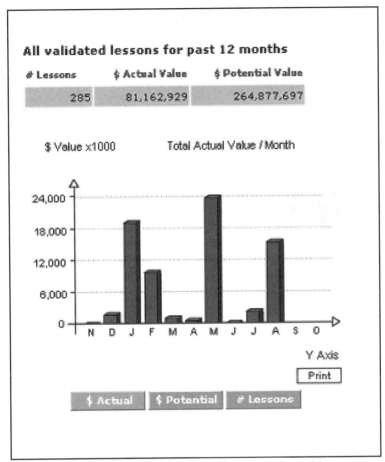

Figure 9-6 LINK screen shot showing value of lessons

lost or gained, in an extreme case. LINK also requires an estimate of the frequency of occurrence of that particular process. Although the value of the lessons is not realized until the lesson is reapplied, it is still interesting to track the value assigned to the lessons. At the moment, the lessons entered into LINK each year have a total assigned value of $81 million and a potential value of $265 million (see Figure 9-6).[4]

---

[4] Figures representation of 2002.

Problems and Concerns

There are still a few problems and concerns with the Knowledge Management system for the BP well engineers. Even though the system is one of the most comprehensive and fully embedded Knowledge Management systems this author has seen, there is always room for improvement.

The two most widely used components of the system are the LINK database and the Well Engineering Forum. The forum is particularly highly used, and most well engineers in BP would cite it as the most valuable mechanism they have for accessing knowledge. LINK, however, suffers from the same problem as any database: garbage in, garbage out. It takes care and attention to write a really useful lesson, and the degree of attention varies considerably. At best, LINK lessons are succinct summaries of real use to the reader. At worst, they are uninformative. BP addresses this by introducing a validation step to LINK lessons. The lesson is entered directly by the well engineers involved in planning and operating a particular well, but the lessons are not forwarded to other teams until they have been validated by a designated expert (usually a senior drilling engineer). This step should ideally ensure that the lessons are useful, helpful, relevant to other teams, and well written. That said, the LINK system is often not itself the means of transferring knowledge but is a means of putting people in touch with people so that they can contact each other for knowledge transfer. For example, if one team enters a lesson into LINK, which is then forwarded to another team, the name of the originator is attached to the lesson, and anyone who wants to know more will pick up the phone or send an e-mail. At a recent training course, we heard an example of this, where LINK forwarded a lesson from one team in Houston, Texas, to another team working on a different floor of the same Houston building; they were unaware of the details of the first team's operations. In this case, a short trip down in the elevator led to a detailed face-to-face exchange of knowledge.

Another concern is the ownership of the Knowledge Bundles, and the resource the organization invests in keeping best practices up to date. Tools such as the Well Engineering Forum and LINK are operated by the users in the teams and tend to cover short-term knowledge—knowledge that is needed in the short term, or a lesson that has just been learned. At the moment, anyone interested in a particular technical issue, such as conductor jetting, sand screens, or Near Bit Reamers, needs to search through LINK, the forum, and the intranet. They may find masses of material and need to sift through to find what is useful, what is not helpful, and what is out of date and misleading. The ideal next step for the organization would be to distill and sort this knowledge into new Knowledge Bundles. This step requires resourcing, but would add huge value to the KM system. When the current Knowledge Bundles become outdated, resources are applied to refresh them as necessary (for instance, the information on Peer Assists may be old, but it is as relevant today as it was when it was written). Several of the technical Knowledge Bundles were refreshed in 2001/2002, and BP has identified new owners for updates in 2003, so the process of refreshing and updating is being addressed.

Lessons Learned

A KM system needs a variety of tools. Part of the success of the well engineering system in BP is that tools are provided to the teams, which cover all aspects of the movement and storage of knowledge. There are process tools for knowledge capture (AARs, Retrospects), there are technologies for knowledge push and pull (LINK, the WEF, *Well Connected*), there are systems and formats for knowledge storage (BoD, Knowledge Bundles, LINK), there is technology for knowledge search and retrieval (Wells Online), and there are processes and mechanisms for face-to-face knowledge exchange (Peer Assist, Peer Review, and the Worldwide Drilling Conference). No single tool can cover all the aspects of Knowledge Management. The well engineers in BP are provided with a toolbox that covers all their needs.

A KM system needs to be rolled out. Even though the tools provided to the well engineering community are mostly simple and intuitive, people do not use them until they are shown how and until it is explained why they should use them. The two-day "Knowledge Management for Well Teams" course is a very effective mechanism for rollout. Combining this with a self-assessment and construction of a KM plan enables tailoring the whole experience to the needs of the individual teams. Where there are strong KM champions already in a team, the course is important, but for teams in remote locations, or teams new to BP, the course has proved to be vital in bringing these teams into the company-wide knowledge system (as shown by the sudden increase in use of LINK and the WEF after a course has been held).

To fully embed a KM system, you need some sort of assurance process. Just providing the tools is not enough—if KM is a really important means of value delivery, the company needs to make sure that knowledge is managed properly. The threefold system described here is an excellent and effective assurance mechanism. The KM plans, in particular, are being used to direct Knowledge Management toward organizational goals.

Address the validation step. Any KM system will suffer from garbage in, garbage out. Make sure there is some validation of lessons entered into the system, and look for a way to regularly compile lessons into best practices documents. A lessons-learned database becomes a liability if the lessons are of variable quality and out of date.

Make sure there is ownership at the local and the organizational level. The KM system in the well engineering discipline at BP would not survive without the presence of someone like Dave Evans and a network of champions in the business. Similarly, the KM systems within individual well teams would not be applied if they were not owned, and if local knowledge managers were not appointed.

Track the value as best you can. Although this is easier said than done, you still need to make some attempt at tracking value. BP does this through collecting anecdotal evidence and through assigning value to lessons entered into LINK (even though that value is not delivered until the lesson is reused).

CHAPTER 10

Implementing Knowledge Management Within De Beers: The Early Years

By Nick Milton and Ian Corbett

The De Beers case study looks at the selection and the early stages of implementation of a Knowledge Management (KM) strategy within a large multinational organization. It derives lessons on strategic implementation, and, in particular, it throws light on the need to engage the middle managers and business unit leaders when an organization is developing the components of a KM system.

Knowledge Management within De Beers arose out of a project looking at the intellectual capital of the organization. This project was led by Ian Corbett, a geologist, who was at the time also working within the Mineral Resources Management group. In his reading and research on the subject, Ian came to realize that studying intellectual capital was one thing, but that increasing the value of that capital through Knowledge Management could yield even more benefit to the organization.

Ian gained an understanding of the internal KM initiatives already underway within De Beers, and invited about 20 of the internal pioneers in this area to a four-day Knowledge Management workshop. This workshop proved to be the launching pad for the KM program within the organization, leading to development of the vision, objectives, strategy, and a number of potential pilot projects.

Armed with a strategic approach, Ian set about proving the concept of KM through a number of business-focused pilot activities. These were successful not only in delivering value, but also in providing excellent stories and case histories with which to influence and educate management. With business management on his side, Ian was able to select and deliver even more pilot projects, and to test various tools and processes for the management of knowledge.

Gradually, a holistic KM system, with components of people, process, and technology, was developed and road tested. Ian is now in the process of developing in-house capacity and capability in order to roll out this system across the entire organization with the assistance of Rene Walsh, the recently appointed knowledge manager for the Operations and Exploration Division (OPEX).

BACKGROUND

The De Beers Group is the world's leading producer and marketer of diamonds, producing almost half of the annual global production of diamonds. Operating in South Africa and in partnership with the government of Botswana and Namibia, De Beers owns a number of diamond mines, some of them open pits, some underground, some alluvial (dredge) operations, and some submarine. De Beers also operates an extensive exploration program looking for new diamond-bearing deposits across practically the entire globe. In addition to exploration, De Beers markets the majority of the world supply of rough diamonds through its selling arm, the Diamond Trading Company, based in London. The group has a turnover in the region of $5 billion and on the order of 23,500 staff, mostly located in southern Africa.

De Beers was founded in Kimberley, South Africa, in 1888, arising from the "Diamond Rush" of the late 1800s under the chairmanship of Cecil John Rhodes. The company has a long history of investment and involvement in South Africa, with the Oppenheimer family at the helm since the 1920s. The establishment of diamonds as an affordable luxury, led by the slogan "A diamond is forever," established an expanding market that continues to grow today. However, a luxury market like this is not without risks, and the slump in 1981, the growth of diamond production from Russia, plus the political developments in South Africa, alerted De Beers to the need to rethink its business model, to develop a more competitive footing, and to become a learning organization. These changes were put in place, highlighted by the leveraged buyout of De Beers in 2001, ending its 112-year history as a publicly held company.

De Beers operates eight major diamond mines within South Africa and is involved in three mines within Botswana, six extraction areas in Namibia, and two projects in Canada. Despite the great variety of operational settings, these operations have many issues in common, and there is great value in sharing learning. In addition, De Beers in South Africa has made a commitment to Employment Equity—redressing the balance of workforce diversity to reflect the diversity in the South African population. This also is a Knowledge Management issue, since operational knowledge will need to be transferred quickly and effectively to the many new staff from previously disadvantaged groups who will be joining the De Beers structure, and on whom the future success of the South African operations will depend.

You can read more details about De Beers from the company Web site at http://www.debeersgroup.com.

MAKING A START

As part of the structural and strategic changes the De Beers Group was going through at the beginning of the 21st century, the issue of Knowledge Management and intellectual capital management was beginning to gain more prominence within the Operations and Exploration Division. Both components of the division relied to a large extent on knowledge, technology, and intellect. Exploring for diamondiferous deposits is a highly skilled task requiring experience, expertise, and sound judgment. Similarly, extracting diamonds, particularly from the challenging environments in which they occur, requires high levels of expertise and judgment. In both of these fields, the intellectual capability and know-how of the organization were beginning to be seen as a key asset. Ian Corbett, a senior geologist working in the mineral resources management area of exploration, was given responsibility for developing an intellectual capital management system within De Beers. Knowledge Management, it soon became apparent, would be a key component of this system. Ian began discussions with Janine Nahapiet, of Templeton College, Oxford, and developed a keen interest in the role that conversation plays in creating and transferring knowledge and ideas. Through the assistance of Thea Rutherford in De Beers Marine's Information Centre, Ian began investigating approaches to KM.

Help and guidance were immediately available from business schools, universities, books, and magazines, and Ian started to assess and compare the various approaches to KM that had been taken at other companies in other industries. This process was accelerated when the company took the unprecedented step of granting Ian a sabbatical, following the conclusion of the Templeton Advanced Management Programme in Oxford, England. He recognized a significant similarity between De Beers and BP: a correspondence in the challenge that both organizations hope to address through Knowledge Management—the challenge of removing the wast and inefficiency that can be caused by repeating mistakes, reinventing wheels, and failing to apply better practice systematically. There was also a correspondence in culture; both companies are rich in technology and tend to focus on technological solutions, spending less time on the softer issues. The Knowledge Management program at BP went against the corporate trend, in very consciously addressing the cultural and people issues, and thus presented a fascinating opportunity to Ian, given the spectrum of diversity and the many softer issues that De Beers was learning to work through in its southern African context. Also, both companies had a similar value-chain business model in that they were exploring for resource, developing resource, and then marketing it (even though one was marketing petroleum products, and the other, gemstones).

Ian decided to bring together the information professionals and other interested parties in Knowledge Management within De Beers, to develop a more coherent and systematic approach to the management of knowledge. He could see Retrospects and After Action Reviews, among other processes, as having huge potential for unearthing the knowledge that was developed during projects but often did not "see the light of day." It would be good for staff within De Beers to meet each other through the development of skills in this area, and then to address the challenge of working with the diverse cultural groups across the operational teams. Through Paul Bosma and Thea Rutherford, Ian got in touch with Nick Milton, formerly of the BP Knowledge Management team, to provide guidance and training. Plans began to form for a significant workshop at the end of 2001, to introduce skills and processes into De Beers, to develop the start of a Knowledge Management community of practice, and to begin to work on an implementation strategy. The timeline of the events described here is shown in Figure 10-1.

KICKING OFF THE KM PROGRAM

December 2001 was the date for the De Beers Knowledge Management Workshop in Kimberley. This was a four-day event, held in

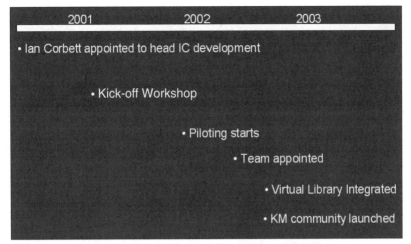

Figure 10-1. Timeline for KM at De Beers

a rustic-style conference facility in the middle of the game park, adjacent to the De Beers Kimberley mine. Twenty people were present—representatives from all parts of the exploration and operations side of the business, people who had an interest in KM, or who were already working in KM or information management. The intention was to stimulate people spanning a diverse group of the division's activities to explore how the application of systematic Knowledge Management would not only complement existing initiatives, such as the "Knowledge Exchange" being piloted by the metallurgists' community of practice, but also create new and exciting opportunities. An important consideration was to ensure that the people invited already had or could win senior management support for trial processes discussed and also to bring together people from the "Central Mines" (consisting of the Kimberley, Koffiefontein, and Finsch mines, which had many issues in common).

The workshop was designed to introduce people to ways in which systematic KM can deliver tremendous value across an organization, by packaging the product of structured conversation and dialogue and disseminating knowledge effectively. The objective was that the participants would not only understand and internalize the practical application of KM, but also realize that it can be simple to apply effectively. Practicality was the key here; De Beers needed to move from theory to practical application, to get some KM activities actually working in the business, and to start to develop the strategy.

During the first two days of the workshop, Ian and Nick concentrated on the transfer of skills, looking to give the participants practice in capturing knowledge and packaging it for reuse, and insights into the formation and operation of communities of practice. A blend of presentations, case histories, exercises, and practical work proved to be a very successful format for engaging the attendees, and by the end of the two days, everybody had developed a common understanding of KM and how it could add value to their part of De Beers. The third day was therefore spent looking in more detail at the implementation aspects, such as the creation of knowledge roles, identification and ranking of pilot projects, and implementation planning for those projects. A whole range of potential possibilities were identified for taking Knowledge Management forward, and then on the fourth day, participants from Central Mines, Metallurgy, and De Beers Marine stayed behind to do some focused work on strategy planning. They worked together on creating a vision and then on developing objectives for each of the three areas. Finally, they used stakeholder analysis as the first step toward developing a strategy and an implementation plan for the various areas. This planning day was a critical step in developing momentum for Knowledge Management that would live beyond the workshop and take De Beers to a point where it could apply KM on a small-scale success and hopefully prove the concept.

THE EARLY PROOF-OF-CONCEPT PHASE

Coincidently with the workshop, Ian and Nick began working on a high-level strategy for De Beers. One of the earliest stages of the strategy would be to try some simple KM processes on some of the key activities or projects within the organization—to see if they worked, to see if they generated value, to come up with some early wins, and to create some success stories that could be used for marketing. Ian had already identified one or two possibilities, and more had come up during the workshop. There was one very interesting and challenging possibility, though, that would be a real test of the power of Knowledge Management—the !Gariep project.

!Gariep had been a blue-sky technology project for De Beers Marine. The De Beers Marine team had plans to build a piece of mining technology beyond anything that currently existed. The project had been an ambitious challenge, and many, many learnings had been generated—so many learnings that the organization had been unsure how to harvest them for reuse. Some of the key players were still in the organization; others had left. Ian saw the possibility of using the Retrospect process as a powerful and non-confrontational way of harnessing some of that knowledge.

The !Gariep Retrospect took place over two days in Cape Town, involving 25 members of the project team, with up to four years' history with the project. The project was divided into four stages and spent half a day on each stage. With the benefit of hindsight, we can see that we invited too many managers and not enough "workers" to the Retrospect, because many of the most valuable insights came from some of the more junior members of the project team. However, some very interesting and powerful lessons were captured, and we took the opportunity to record some video advice from the participants as well as some feedback on the Retrospect process itself.

Although the lessons from !Gariep were extremely valuable and have already been carried forward to future projects to great effect, those video clips were an even more powerful demonstration of the value of Knowledge Management. Shortly after the Retrospect had been completed, Ian attended a meeting of the senior management team of the De Beers Group to talk to them about KM. He had recorded one of the engineers at the Retrospect, a young, credible, and eloquent contributor with some excellent knowledge and advice to offer, and he embedded this video in his presentations. This was the turning point for some of the senior managers; it transformed the whole presentation and got them on the edge of their seats. It was a real-life, highly relevant demonstration of KM within the De Beers context and from a complex and high-profile project as well. And then, when the senior managers asked, "And how did the participants feel about the Retrospect process?" Ian was able to show them a second video clip of enthusiastic feedback.

Central Mines was one of the areas identified before the workshop as a potential pilot area for De Beers. Dieter Haage, the general manager at one of the larger mines, Finsch mine, already saw the potential of Knowledge Management but at that point did not have a clear idea of how he would implement it. That was partly why the December workshop had been so powerful; it had provided the mines with a tool kit and an implementation plan. Bruce Emerton had been identified as the potential knowledge manager for Finsch, and Bruce had attended the workshop. Bruce identified a couple of options for the application of KM, one of which was to hold a Peer Assist on the subject of earth-moving equipment. Finsch was about to invest heavily in earth-moving equipment, and wanted to draw on the knowledge and experience of the other mines first, also to evolve the relationship with the chosen supplier through sharing knowledge to improve the outcome for mutual benefit. In some ways, the Peer Assist was held later than would have been ideal, but the level of sharing was still very high, and some crucial knowledge and insights were exchanged during the breakout groups within the Peer Assist. The facilitator calculated that there were over 240 man-years of knowledge and experience present in the room, all of which could be brought to bear on Finsch's issues. Bruce believes that this knowledge has helped deliver R80 million rand (the currency of South Africa) in added value for Finsch mine. Again, this was a crucial early win for De Beers, and particularly valuable in that it delivered a hard monetary benefit in an area of strategic focus: underground mining. A similar Peer Assist for Premier mine proved equally successful in providing the Premier team with collective insight into how to improve current and future operational performance.

At the same time that Ian was trying out face-to-face KM processes such as Retrospects and Peer Assists, the De Beers eBusiness team, led by James Campbell, was experimenting with the concept of communities of practice and how these could be enabled by the use of technology. A community portal known as Knowledge-Xchange (K_{Ex}) was commissioned from Accenture, which allowed the members of the community to post challenges to knowledgeable colleagues, to seek guidance, and to have questions answered. Some soft issues were highlighted by the project, such as credibility of knowledge sources, trust, readiness for technology, and methods of working virtually as a team or community. This has been an interesting pilot technology for communities of practice.

PROGRAM METHODOLOGY AND RESULTS

After the December workshop, Ian was beginning to develop a strategic approach for De Beers. Presentation of the results from !Gariep had created a lot of interest at the senior management level and developed some high-level supporters on the De Beers executive committee, which resulted in the creation of a full-time knowledge manager post within the Operations and Exploration Division of De Beers based in Johannesburg, at a time when increases in staff were difficult to win approval for. Further changes occurred in the senior management team in January 2002, which resulted in Ian being given the opportunity to focus on the Knowledge Management implementation program as the first full-time intellectual capital manager to be appointed in the De Beers Group. After an extensive period of recruitment, Rene Walsh was appointed as the OPEX knowledge manager and commenced work for De Beers in April 2002.

The initial stage of Ian's strategy focused on proving the concept, trying out the processes and technologies, and building a holistic KM system. Some of the early proof-of-concept work, such as that done at !Gariep and Finsch, was useful in demonstrating value, and Ian began on a systematic campaign of engaging the key players in the organization. His stated objective was to have secured the support of the senior team by mid-2002. Although there was no shortage of opportunities to apply Knowledge Management, it proved more difficult to actually generate the momentum to get things moving. Ian found that carry-through on KM projects was entirely a factor of senior management commitment, and even when managers were committed, Ian or Rene still needed continually to drive things forward and maintain a presence. The central team needed to assist people within the operations and business units to seek out the opportunities, and then hang in there until the work was complete and benefit could be identified by the internal client to inject additional momentum and embed belief in the process. Implementing Knowledge Management, Ian was beginning to discover, requires full-time hands-on management and a significant amount of engagement to both identify and support enthusiastic managerial support. However, significant progress had been made, and the majority of general managers committed to embedding KM into their Balanced Scorecards and identifying and appointing a permanent Knowledge Management resource within their teams in the form of knowledge champions.

During the first half of 2002, Knowledge Management implementation within De Beers was focused on road testing the components of the KM model. The model they were using was very much based on the learning before, during, and after model applied within BP and discussed in Chapter 8 in the context of Tearfund. Given the project nature of much of De Beers' work, and given that its work was becoming increasingly managed using the common project management framework, this systematic approach of learning before, during, and after works extremely well within the De Beers corporate culture. In particular, the engineering function led by Dave Porter was keen to investigate ways by which KM could be embedded into the team structurally, as well as into processes and procedures. This commitment by leadership testified to the success of the December 2001 workshop in engaging key engineering personnel such as Michael Goodson and George Eddey, who were involved in developing new systems for the engineering function and could see the potential offered by more effective Knowledge Management.

Ian also needed to define and formalize the structure of the KM implementation project. He himself was the project manager, reporting to an internal client within the operations division, and with sponsorship at the board level. He needed to appoint the right person who could work in detail and depth within the business. This was successfully achieved in early 2002 with the appointment of Rene Walsh as OPEX knowledge manager. Rene had a background in KM within the financial sector, and has tremendous energy and enthusiasm. She was able to take much of the hands-on load from Ian, leaving him free to work at a higher level within the organization. With the successful track record of trialing processes to draw on, a high-level steering team from within the business is currently being appointed, to make sure that the implementation program and the Knowledge Management model are fully aligned with De Beers' business strategy. Also, consultancy support was secured from external Knowledge Management consultants, to make sure that the De Beers implementation program was based on proven good practices from other similar organizations. Finally, Ian and Rene needed to build a KM community of practice, involving the knowledge champions from across the organization (see Figure 10-

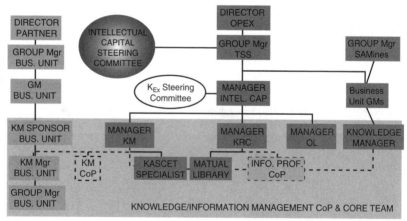

Figure 10-2. Organizational structure of the DeBeers Knowledge Management program (TSS = Technical Services, KRC = Knowledge Resource Centre, OL = Organizational Learning, Info Prot Cop = Information Professionals Community of Practice)

2), in order to build and mobilize internal resources and support to create the capacity to derive benefit as widely as possible.

The first face-to-face meeting of the core Knowledge Management community came in August 2002, when 35 knowledge "activists" from within De Beers came together in Kimberley. This time it was a two-day agenda, focusing partly on skills development but also on the creation and operation of the community, and the further identification of potential for pilot work within the business beyond the technical and operational base. Initially, there seemed to be a split in the meeting between those who had volunteered to become champions and those who had been appointed by their managers. Knowledge Management implementation certainly seemed to be driven with more energy by those who are personally committed to the concept, but as the course went on, the attendees became fully engaged, and some great discussions were held on the potential for using this approach in the workplace. One of the most exciting pilot projects was to capture knowledge from De Beers' involvement in the 2002 Earth Summit on Sustainable Development in Johannesburg, which would provide an opportunity for feedback to the chairman, Nicky Oppenheimer. This would be Knowledge Management going right to the very top of the organization—a unique opportunity to show that the whole of De Beers could be committed to the management of knowledge. This pilot project is now complete and was extremely successful in identifying further opportunities to enhance the positive contribution made through the efforts of the team to De Beers' corporate reputation internationally.

In fact, the majority of pilot projects within De Beers have been successful, reflecting the willingness of "De Beers people" at all levels to participate and share experience and knowledge. Knowledge has been transferred from !Gariep to the follow-up project, from Snap Lake mine in Canada to the Victor mine, to Finsch mine and to Premier mine from the other South African mines, from the Kimberley acid lab to future acid labs, from the Earth Summit, and so on. Tangible savings in the order of tens of millions of U.S. dollars have already been demonstrated. Communities of practice are underway within the Metallurgy, Engineering and Exploration, and Mineral Resource Services functions, and approaches are being developed to further catalyze the establishment of more communities in 2003 and beyond. De Beers now has the internal target of a KM presence, with evidence of repeatable KM capability and activity, in 90% of the OPEX business units by the end of 2003.

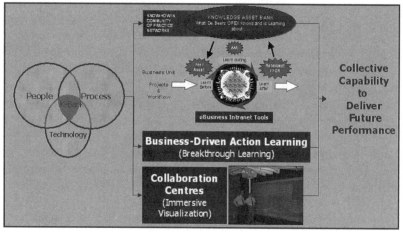

Figure 10-3. De Beers Knowledge Management model

BUILDING ORGANIZATIONAL CAPACITY AND PREPARING FOR ROLLOUT

Achieving 90% penetration within a year means that Ian will need to roll out a robust systematic Knowledge Management approach across the majority of the OPEX business units, but will need to have a framework in place to support the future KM activity. Knowledge champions have already been identified, and the workshop described earlier created the nucleus of a Knowledge Management community of practice. The focus for De Beers over the next few months is going to be one of building organizational capacity, skills, and awareness.

PROBLEMS AND CONCERNS

The main challenge for implementing Knowledge Management within De Beers, as explained earlier, was gaining the attention of the business management. Managers of business units in a performance-driven operation have very many demands on their time, and although they can often see the importance of KM, it may not have the degree of urgency that other tasks have. And yet these are the people you most need to have on your side. They are the ones who set the agendas for their parts of the business, and they are the ones who make the difficult decisions about resourcing. One of the big learnings from the first year of implementation in De Beers has been the need to keep engaging and re-engaging the business management, to continue to be high on their agenda wherever possible—either directly or through more senior managers and executives inquiring about levels of activity.

The second major challenge is providing resources for follow-through, which ideally has to be the responsibility of the people seeking to receive the benefit. If it is true that Knowledge Management needs to be driven enthusiastically from the center, there need to be enough resources to do that driving. This became much easier for Ian once Rene was appointed, and Ian is now looking at ways of building up the implementation team still further. Provision of resources has to be a major focus of the next stage of implementation.

One area of concern within De Beers, which may be a positive or a negative factor, depending on how it is handled, is the number of initiatives that are taking place simultaneously across the organization. Because of the nature of the changes that took place within De Beers in 2000 and 2001, there are very many initiatives all happening simultaneously, which creates the risk of initiative overload or of initiative conflict. Ian has been very careful to analyze the boundaries between KM and the other initiatives, to make sure there are no conflicts of interest or no areas left uncovered. In particular, there are some major eBusiness activities underway, which need to be carefully coordinated with Knowledge Management, to ensure that the cultural aspects and the process aspects link together with the new technology so that the two are complementary and consistently support each other. Experience within De Beers has already shown that a technological solution for KM will not be effective without addressing the culture, the processes, and the rules that support it. Ian's governance structure, involving a steering team with representation from the major parts of the business and the major initiatives, is one mechanism for making sure that everything is aligned.

It has been found that people feel good about learning, even when it occurs under difficult circumstances, and the cultural aspect within De Beers has proved to not be a major issue. The company already has a strong culture of focusing on performance and safety, and is happy to embrace any new approach that will enhance either of these. Knowledge Management has been presented within De Beers as a tool to enable better performance, and consequently it has been welcomed in most instances. In particular, people derive a lot of benefit from meeting other people to share experience, develop personal networks, and create space to pause and reflect on what they are learning. The organization is also focused on building a robust, systematic approach to the management of projects, which Knowledge Management can be embedded within very easily. The engineering department within De Beers has taken to Knowledge Management very well because of the appeal of a practical, systematic, and structured approach, which fits well with the other management systems. This also reflects the open approach taken by the leadership, which is actively seeking new ways to improve performance and build strong capability in the project environment.

LESSONS LEARNED

You have to work, in the early stages, with the managers who show enthusiasm. The early stages of implementation are all about trial, piloting, and proof of concept. The early successes within De Beers were where the management had already seen the need to address systematic learning and the reuse of lessons learned, and were looking to the KM team to provide a practical solution and an approach. This was certainly the case with the "early wins" of !Gariep and Finsch.

Knowledge champions need to be volunteers, not press-ganged. Although it was very powerful for the senior managers to request that every unit should appoint a knowledge champion, there were downsides to this process as well. The people who accepted knowledge champion posts because they believe in the possibilities that this might create were very motivated and energized. Those who were appointed with the approach of "just another job to do" were less energized, with little or no commitment to follow through—investment in developmental training in these instances seldom produces tangible results. You need to define fairly well what the profile of a knowledge champion should be, both in terms of skills and in terms of the softer attributes—this might well require face-to-face discussion.

Look for the compelling early win, and publicize this. Find a project that is already high profile, where the organization knows that learning has occurred, and work with the project members to deliver an early trial of KM processes. Within De Beers, this was !Gariep. The video clips of the key people, recorded during or after the Retrospect, were very powerful marketing tools for the senior management. It was these video clips that really engaged the senior team and secured the KM implementation project.

Make sure you have a dual approach, of building energy at the senior level and at the lower level. This means that you need resources to work at both levels. You also need to provide connections between these two levels so that people in the business will engage both upward and downward within the organization. And this approach also means you need at least two people on the team: one working at a higher level and one working at a lower level.

Build links with other initiatives that are going on at the same time. If there are a lot of initiatives happening in the organization, find a way of coordinating and linking these so that the people in the business see them as complementary and part of a single change rather than two things that need to be addressed separately. In particular, KM needs to work closely with any programs for IT change, especially if these are technology-led.

Ian Corbett is the general manager for intellectual capital within the Operations and Exploration Division of De Beers. He holds a Ph.D. from the University of Cape Town and is based in Hout Bay, near Cape Town, South Africa. Ian developed a Knowledge Management strategy as part of a group-wide strategic review process. His background in placer diamond exploration and mineral resource management led to his interest in organizational learning and systems thinking. His passion is the development of people, and a key area of interest is the role of servant-leaders in building and releasing the potential of high-performing teams.

CHAPTER 11

Knowledge Fuel for Fighting Fires: Knowledge Capture at Ukuvuka, a Four-Year Government, Business, and Community Partnership

By Shanil Haricharan and Sandra Fowkes

BACKGROUND

Against the green slopes of Table Mountain, on an exquisite summer day in Cape Town, South Africa, Sandra Fowkes spoke enthusiastically about her "Ukuvuka" journey with fond memories and some forward thinking. It is the day before the third anniversary (February 2003) of the Ukuvuka Operation Firestop Campaign—an appropriate time for Sandra, the campaign manager, to reflect and reminisce. In the background, the open-plan office is buzzing with final preparation for a high-level anniversary event. Each Ukuvuka anniversary has been carefully orchestrated to reflect a specific aspect of this multifaceted campaign. This year it will be held in Langa, the oldest formal township (suburb) originally created for Black Africans in Cape Town. It will celebrate the campaign's achievements in working in partnership with the City of Cape Town

197

to dramatically reduce the risk of fire to the vulnerable communities living in fire-prone shacks that have sprung up around the township. The shacks house rural people flooding to the city in search of work.

Ukuvuka, meaning "to awaken or rise up" in the local language, isiXhosa, is a campaign started to awaken the citizens of Cape Town, both institutional and individual, to what they can do to significantly reduce the risk of damage and danger from uncontrolled fires in the mountains and in the informal settlements of Cape Town's Cape Peninsula. In addition, the campaign contributes to poverty relief by creating opportunities for employment and training. The campaign is further tasked to create a role model of a government, business, and community partnership that can be replicated in other functional and geographical areas. How the "role model" aspect was to be put into practice was not clearly set out in the otherwise comprehensive business plan, prepared by the initiators of the campaign.

The campaign was born out of the opportunity created by a crisis. Cape Town is one of only two cities in the world with a large national park within its urban fabric. Fire is a necessary part of the ecosystem of the national park, but the natural fires are made very much fiercer and more frequent by the presence of invading alien plants (IAPs), introduced mainly from Australia and Europe. Using the concern generated by a highly visible and dramatic fire that burned on Table Mountain and its surrounding mountain chain for six days in January 2000, government and business contributed resources to support a short-term (four-year) partnership to address the issue of uncontrolled fire.

The cost of the fires was estimated at R30 million (in rand, the currency of South Africa) since they destroyed 8 homes and damaged more than 50 others, and devastated over 8,000 hectares (or 20,000 acres) of the national park and surrounding areas. The estimated cost, R30 million, was nearly double the operational budget for fire and emergency services of the local council in whose area the fire occurred. This amount is also equivalent to the cost of providing 1,500 low-cost homes or one year of employment for 1,500 people working on alien clearing. Another way of looking at the issue is that one-third of R30 million would have removed the invasive plants that fueled the fire from the fire hazard area of the entire Cape Peninsula.

Ukuvuka was modeled on the internationally acclaimed approach to controlling invading alien plants of the Working for Water Program, initiated in 1995 by the national government. It was designed to address the environmental problems of IAPs exacerbated by fire, through labor-intensive methods such that socioeconomic developmental opportunities are created for some of the disadvantaged residents of the city.

The full name of the campaign, the Santam Cape Argus Ukuvuka Operation Firestop Campaign, reflects two of the five sponsors. Santam is a short-term insurance company, and the *Cape Argus* is the daily English-language evening newspaper of the area. The largest sponsor is the City of Cape Town. Two other businesses with commitment to the environment, Nedbank and an international oil company, Total South Africa, are the remaining sponsors.

Sandra reflects that the 10th objective of the campaign, "to be a role model," placed significant demands on the Ukuvuka team to focus on managing and sharing its learning and knowledge. The campaign had a clear strategy, a specific set of deliverables, a timeline of four years, and limited resources. One of the requirements was to make sure that this model could be replicated in other areas. Its aims and objectives are the following.

The Ukuvuka campaign aims to significantly reduce the risk of damage and danger from uncontrolled fire in the Cape Peninsula.

The campaign will achieve its aim through its partner implementing agents—the local authority, the City of Cape Town, and the Cape Peninsula National Park—by working with the land and its plants to

- Control invading alien plants.
- Rehabilitate fire damaged areas.

It will work with communities and individuals to

- Create employment, training, and poverty relief for disadvantaged people.
- Protect the most vulnerable communities from fire.
- Promote cooperation and social cohesion between communities.

It will work with institutions to

- Implement integrated fire management plans.
- Manage the urban–natural interface.

The campaign is supported by

- An accountable administration.
- An effective communications and education program.
- By the end of the campaign, there will be
  Replicable role models.

The campaign actively manages

- Relationships with the various partners—implementing agents, sponsors, and supporters—in order to deliver benefits and returns on investment.

So, how did Knowledge Management (KM) surface at Ukuvuka? "By serendipity and synchronicity," says Sandra with a quizzical smile. In June 2001, Shanil Haricharan, a consultant assisting Ukuvuka with developing a remuneration policy and checking role size against levels of remuneration, made a connection with Sandra through the passionate articulation of his readings and research into KM for his M.B.A. dissertation. Sandra was excited at the potential of the growing "discipline" of KM and saw that it offered a way to give effect to the role model objective. Thus, a knowledge courtship was initiated.

This case study is about knowledge capture at Ukuvuka, in the form of Knowledge Assets, within a partnership arrangement of business, government, and society to deliver on sustainable development objectives.

DRIVERS FOR THE DEVELOPMENT OF THE KNOWLEDGE MANAGEMENT INITIATIVES

Sandra was a key driver in the KM initiatives and in identifying the benefit of harvesting and capturing knowledge at Ukuvuka. Throughout her working life she had been a "reflective practitioner": evaluating, extracting lessons after consulting and training interventions, and then researching and testing ways of improving delivery. She had amused some colleagues by referring to this approach as "prac-ademic." She was therefore keen to look at how to document the exciting things that Ukuvuka was doing and the lessons that the team was learning.

The event that catalyzed the first foray into KM was the impending emigration of the team member who had responsibility for putting the crucial fire management plan for the Cape Peninsula into effect. Sandra did not want his insights and experience to be lost to the campaign. Shanil's indication that there were tested and systematic KM tools for capturing explicit as well as tacit knowledge presented a way of addressing the loss of the team member.

So, in August 2001, the campaign took its first structured steps in the pursuit of Knowledge Management. Shanil had created a draft KM readiness diagnostic tool (see the Knowledge Management Diagnostic Tool section at the end of the chapter) for his M.B.A. dissertation on the Western Cape Provincial Government (the final version of the diagnostic is available on www.hologram.org.za). Sandra was keen for the diagnostic to be tested at Ukuvuka to assess Ukuvuka's knowledge position and its existing intellectual resources. The diagnostic measured the KM processes to get, use, learn, share, assess, and build/sustain knowledge. All 10 team members completed the questionnaire. The outcome of the diagnostic at Ukuvuka is illustrated in Figure 11-1.

Ukuvuka had an overall score of 59%. The Ukuvuka team members' perception of their ability to manage the different knowledge processes, as shown in Figure 11-1, is on the higher end of the continuum when compared with public sector institutions (Haricharan and Moollan, 2001). Ukuvuka's strongest KM process is building and sustaining knowledge—i.e., ensuring that future knowledge-based assets are designed to keep the organization viable and competitive; the weakest process is assessing knowledge—i.e., how to measure what knowledge the organization has and what it requires. The team members' perceptions indicate that greater investment is required across all the KM processes to effectively fulfill the campaign's objective of becoming a "role model." It was realized

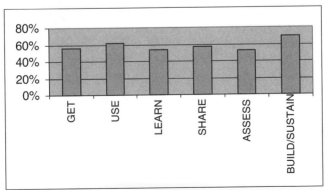

Figure 11-1. Knowledge Management processes

that KM was emergent, not an explicitly developed objective of the campaign, and that Ukuvuka had no formally defined KM program.

Shanil suggested a session with team members to introduce KM concepts, models, and processes.

To prepare for the workshop, Shanil asked Carol Gorelick (visiting faculty on his M.B.A. KM elective course) to lend him the John Henderson video clip (BP case study). Carol's response was that it is not hers to lend, but she would come and present it at the workshop. This was more than Shanil had bargained for (having a KM professional at the session), so he kindly accepted the offer—a true example of knowledge sharing.

What is the Henderson clip, and why did he want to use it? At the BP IT Colloquium (1996), Henderson made a presentation on KM to a skeptical group of BP executives, and he posed the question "What does the U.S. Army know about hurricane cleanup?" as an illustration of the value of KM (see sidebar on page 106). The video gives an impressive account of the steps, with support from the Center for Army Lessons Learned (CALL), that the U.S. Army took within hours in mobilizing its members for hurricane cleanup (not its core business). This triggered the question "What does Ukuvuka know about preventing uncontrolled fires in the Cape Peninsula?" After the campaign is over people will still need to know how to prevent fires and be motivated to do so.

All 10 members of the Ukuvuka team attended the workshop. The concepts of knowledge and Knowledge Management were introduced, the BP case study was presented, and a dialogue was initiated among team members on their understanding of KM and their experiences in managing knowledge at Ukuvuka. This session was a turning point in Ukuvuka's journey as a knowledge-centric organization.

Another event during this period that fueled the flame of KM— call it synchronicity—was Sandra's exposure to "utilization-focused evaluation" at a workshop by Michael Quinn Patton (Patton, 2002). His approach strongly resonated with her experience and context, and provided powerful conceptual models and rich insights from the case studies that he shared. These shaped the monitoring and evaluation of the campaign's delivery of its objectives and thus also contributed to KM. Key elements of the approach to evaluation are to identify the end users of any evaluation, to meet their needs for the insights delivered by the evaluation, and to prepare them to use the products of the evaluation.

It had become clear to Sandra that though the initial assumption of the role model objective (a key driver for KM) was how to replicate the whole program, the campaign had become a knowledge incubator or laboratory for a wide range of initiatives. (It is coincidental that on the front door of the Ukuvuka rented office, in the world-renowned Kirstenbosch Botanical Garden, there is a sign that reads "Laboratory." It now bears an addition and reads "Knowledge Laboratory.") This led to Ukuvuka commissioning Shanil to develop a Knowledge Asset of the lessons emanating from a creative multistakeholder initiative to bring conservation-worthy private land under the management, if not ownership, of the Cape Peninsula National Park. This would contribute to the overall campaign aim by increasing the area that would be managed to remove invading alien plants, thus lessening the fire risk.

The next Knowledge Asset initiative was to document the campaign's experience and share the valuable lessons on how it was learning to function as a multistakeholder partnership. The speed with which the campaign was formed, using the opportunity created by the crisis of the fires, meant that there was a lot of work required to bring the wider staff members of the partners into active engagement with the campaign. The work is ongoing, especially with the sponsors, a number of whom were not clear as to their expectations of the benefits they would derive from their involvement with Ukuvuka.

These two initiatives resulted in the creation of Web-based Knowledge Assets (posted on www. ukuvuka.org.za).

METHODOLOGY, IMPLEMENTATION, AND RESULTS: CREATING KNOWLEDGE ASSETS

Ukuvuka had no explicit KM program couched in any formal conceptual frameworks of the emerging KM "discipline," though KM elements were implicitly located within the role model objective and auditing requirements of the campaign. Sandra recognizes that they have been harvesting their knowledge and disseminating much of it through a variety of explicit means:

- Regular monthly reports to the campaign's governance structures
- The minutes of the diverse elements of the governance structures (the Ukuvuka board, Trust, steering committee, technical committee, and the various ad hoc working groups set up around campaign initiatives)
- The external evaluation reports of aspects of the campaign

- Notes and minutes of the workshops held on diverse topics with campaign partners
- Articles written by team members as well as external journalists
- Presentations to diverse interest groups, conferences, research meetings, seminars and workshops, and campaign events
- Giving effect to the communication and education objectives of the campaign, particularly through the media partner, the *Cape Argus*
- An extensive, informal set of electronic notes taken during the weekly team meetings
- The hardcopy and electronic filing system
- The copious notes that many team members take in their many meetings

KM initiatives can emphasize a collect or a connect strategy. They "collect" information or "connect" people. A full description of these concepts is in Hansen, Nohria, and Tierney's (1999) seminal article "What's Your Strategy for Managing Knowledge?" At Ukuvuka the knowledge tools used to create the knowledge assets were of a "collect" nature. Literature and documents were collected and reviewed, individual reflection sessions and focus groups were held with about 20 stakeholders, the inputs were documented and analyzed, lessons distilled, and a validation process with stakeholders instituted.

For Shanil this was an exciting and intense learning period as he started to move from theory to practice. The latter was more demanding than writing his M.B.A. dissertation. He felt uneasy and questioned whether he was doing it right. He realized that there was no right or wrong way but that you proceed through trial and error. Making sense of people's learning—(which is a complex cognitive process itself) constructed by one individual's mental model and then deconstructed using your own mental model as a lens—was a key realization of the difficulty in extracting tacit knowledge. He also realized the wisdom of management thinkers such as Schein, Nonaka, and Davenport when they say that *Knowledge Management is about people*. It is about interacting with people and collecting the experiences they have gone through, and then documenting it.

The four After Action Review questions were used to gather inputs: What was supposed to happen? What actually happened?

Why were there differences? What can we learn for next time? Some of the interviewees were negative, while others positive and constructive in their criticism. Many people "dump and vent" when asked to reflect. Some take the positive for granted—why talk about that? Sandra and the board were interested in what people were saying. Shanil captured the comments about what should change and what did not work—more than what did work. The initial product was a mixture of lessons, findings, and recommendations.

Four months later, Shanil looked at the lessons report again and used Fannie Calder's (2002) article (presented at the Bali Conference on Sustainable Development) that highlighted the benefits, shortcomings, and issues relating to multistakeholder networks as a framework to extract the Ukuvuka partnership lessons. The learning was that capturing knowledge is an evolutionary process. "Distilling the Lessons from the Ukuvuka Partnership" was presented as the following themes:

- Transparency, inclusivity, developing trust
- Sharing skills and fostering innovation
- Holistic planning and comprehensive analysis
- Joining-up governance
- Strong balancing mechanism
- Leveraging resources
- Ownership and commitment to take action
- Partnership's objectives
- Communications
- Secretariat/management team
- Partnership arrangements and governance

As part of a wider program of auditing and evaluation, a number of other initiatives of the campaign have been used to create knowledge assets. Among these are videos of

- The informal settlement fire mitigation plan that reduced the loss of shack dwellings by over 90% in the first year (1,280 in 2000, 120 in 2001). The Fire and Life Safety Education program piloted the radical shift in a 150-year tradition of fire suppression in the Fire Service to instituting a fire prevention approach that reached over 8,000 primary school children in its first year of operation and showed over 90% retention in key behavior to prevent being vulnerable to fire.

- The High Altitude Alien-Clearing Teams, a program that trained 22 unemployed people in mountaineering and alien plant clearing and deployed them to remove the invader plants that are an ongoing source of seed pollution from the mountain tops in the national park.
- An interactive theater intervention in the informal settlement currently in the middle of the national park, aimed at changing the fire behavior of the 550 residents. Twenty-three fires were reported in the area surrounding the settlement in March 2002. It is anecdotally reported that in March 2003, there has been a dramatic decrease in fires. Further monitoring will establish the actual number of fires.

Ukuvuka wants to be a role model and it is creating knowledge assets, but the issues are for whom and to meet what needs? The immediate users are, first, the three spheres of government—national, provincial, and local—but particularly at the local level, and, second, the "implementing agencies" with the responsibility for managing fire. The needs are to improve service delivery to citizens and to use the limited resources, which include capital, skilled staff, and of course time, as effectively and efficiently as possible. The third group of users are the sponsors who also have needs that can be met, at least in part, through the knowledge assets generated by the campaign.

In a rapidly changing world, business's response is to innovate—e.g., firms such as 3M constantly develop new products. Some 80% of their current products apparently did not exist five years ago. For that level of innovation, a huge investment in research and development (R&D) is required: 3M reputedly spends some 60% of its after-tax profits on R&D.

The level and rate of change also has an impact on governments, but there is little possibility that the public sector can make similar levels of investment in R&D, especially in a developing country with such pressing social justice issues as South Africa. One of the unexpected learnings emerging from the campaign is the potential usefulness of its institutional form for government. A short-term partnership, bringing resources of both the public and private sectors to bear on addressing a specific issue, is a powerful way to meet the need for R&D by government.

The campaign received over half of its funding from government. Having the funds in an institutional form at arm's length from government gave Ukuvuka flexibility to test ways of addressing fire-related problems. It is well known that the public sector is generally risk-averse. The perception of risk frequently threatens willingness to innovate. Sandra reflects that for Ukuvuka, perceived "failure" is a potent way to learn lessons and has given rise to some of the most notable successes of the campaign.

The mind-set of the Ukuvuka team members is certainly not risk-averse. In fact, the short-term nature and the level of the challenge seem to attract a type of personality that relishes the opportunity to throw everything into making a real, positive change to people's lives and the natural environment. The possibility of contributing to ecological integrity at the same time as to social justice is a heady combination!

The outcome is that the successful innovations can be incorporated into the government's operations. Approaches that were less successful stay within Ukuvuka, protecting the partners from any criticism, negative press, or opprobrium. The incorporation of successful initiatives is apparent in many cases, such as the informal settlement fire mitigation plan, which has been extended by the City of Cape Town from the initial 25% of the Joe Slovo area to the whole informal settlement. The Fire and Life Safety initiative has led to a change in the way that the Fire Service is structured. For the first time, there is provision in the organization chart and future budget for 23 Fire and Life Safety officers.

PROBLEMS AND CONCERNS

KM is not a known or proven management tool. KM was not one of the commonly used management tools of the partners in the Ukuvuka campaign. Even though one of the 10 original objectives was "to create a role model," the means to give effect to this objective, in terms of both the approach to be used and the resources (skill and finances), were not set out in the business plan. The amount budgeted for the role model objective was $10,000, or 0.1% of the total budget of the campaign, and there was no explicit responsibility allocated to any of the original job descriptions of the team members.

Competing demands and time pressures exist. Given the short-term nature of the campaign (four years) and the pressure to deliver the main aim of fireproofing the areas that interface between the national park and the city, the role model objective, or the KM focus, was the "Cinderella." Shanil and Carol played the role of "fairy godmother" in using the magic wand of their advocacy and competence to show Ukuvuka the potential of the approach. Shanil's role extended to that of Prince Charming in the work that he did to produce two knowledge assets for the campaign.

Inadequate resources are allocated to KM. The challenge is that as midnight arrives and the coach (an irresistible pun since Shanil was indeed Ukuvuka's KM coach) turns back into a pumpkin, how does Ukuvuka sustain the KM work? Without the resources, especially in-house expertise, to undertake KM and with the work pressure to deliver on the other campaign objectives, it is challenging to sustain the KM work.

As Ukuvuka evaluates the remaining items of its business plan that it still has to deliver and the remaining resources, a case will need to be built for reallocating unused parts of the budget to the role model objective. Undoubtedly, the use of KM will be important in delivering this objective.

LESSONS LEARNED

There are exciting interactions during focus group sessions and classic moments that should be captured using audiovisual media. Technology can make knowledge assets living (like the Henderson clip), to engage and stimulate people.

Knowledge management is a living "discipline"—it is about people, emotions, and mental models.

KM is not about contracting consultants as an event. It must be part of an organization's journey. It needs to be underpinned with understanding of the value of tacit and explicit knowledge. Managers need to think carefully about employees' sensitivity when extracting tacit knowledge in the context of performance management systems and organizational culture. This is especially relevant to HR practitioners who provide performance evaluation support and could help equip managers to handle extracting tacit knowledge.

Organizational culture is critical for KM initiatives to succeed. When organizations put together a Knowledge Management strategy, they should attempt to deal with cultural issues up front as a top priority. The degree to which knowledge sharing is valued within an organization contributes to the level of success of KM initiatives. Hence, senior managers have a crucial role as knowledge champions and ambassadors.

Committing dedicated resources to KM projects is essential. Senior managers will have to prioritize KM activities and commit time and organizational resources that should be aligned with a KM strategy.

Shanil Haricharan is a change leader with diverse professional work experience in the NGO and the public sectors. He started a teaching career in alternative education for learners from disadvantaged communities in Johannesburg, Cape Town, and Maluti (Transkei) between 1986 and 1989. Shanil worked for the Tongaat Child and Family Welfare Society (director), Gauteng Provincial Government Department of Development Planning and Local Government (director), Mercuri Urval in Denmark, and Labat Africa. He held senior consultant positions in the latter two management-consulting firms. Currently, Haricharan is a consultant at Palmer Development Group, in Cape Town, a policy, planning, research, and consulting company specializing in development-related issues primarily in the public sector. He focuses on business strategy, institutional transformation, capacity building, and Knowledge Management.

He has contributed e-newsletter articles on KM in the public sector and e-government as a member of the Horizontal Learning Program for Local Government—HOLOGRAM (www.hologram.org.za)—and is the key driver of the District Municipality Learning Network.

Haricharan has consulted for the Ford Foundation, European Union, Danida, Swedish International Development Agency (SIDA), Independent Development Trust, National Treasury (South Africa), University of Cape Town, and a range of national, provincial, and local governments in South Africa and Namibia. Some of his NGO clients include the Social Housing Foundation, Ukuvuka Firestop Campaign, and the Zanempilo Health Trust. His knowledge and experience emanate from working in a variety of business areas, from strategy, operational, consulting, and academic to research and development.

On completing his high schooling in South Africa, Shanil studied postsecondary science at Wilson College, Bombay. He obtained a B.S. (Life Sciences) degree at the University of the Witwatersrand (1985), a postgraduate Diploma in Adult Education at the University of Natal, Durban (1993), and an M.B.A. at the University of Cape Town (2001). He has completed courses toward an M.S. (Urban & Regional Planning), University of Natal, Durban (1995). He has delivered papers at national and international conferences. His M.B.A. dissertation was titled "An Assessment of the Readiness for Knowledge Management in the Western Cape Department of Economic Affairs, Agriculture, and Tourism."

Sandra Fowkes is currently campaign manager of the Santam Cape Argus Ukuvuka Operation Firestop Campaign, a short-term government–business partnership focused on significantly reducing the risk of damage and danger from fire in the Cape Peninsula. This multifaceted campaign aims, among other things, to link removal of invading alien plants that contribute to the frequency and intensity of fires to poverty alleviation, promotion of social development, and interinstitutional collaboration and cooperation.

Fowkes' previous career as a facilitator and an environmental scientist in the early days of environmental impact assessment in South Africa challenged her to develop skills in managing communication and conflict among the wide range of people who became involved in environmental issues. This led her to become a highly experienced facilitator who has also had to act as a mediator. She has consulted for public, private, and parastatal sector organizations as well as community-based organizations and NGOs throughout southern Africa.

With her husband, John, Sandra has been involved in ecotourism research and consulting in Botswana and KwaZulu. She has facilitated interactions between local communities, conservation agencies, and private sector ecotourism operators. The work in Botswana led her to coauthor the first and second editions of *The Visitors' Guide to Botswana* with her husband, John, and a friend, Mike Main.

Fowkes holds a Bachelor of Science degree in zoology and microbiology from the University of Cape Town, a B.S. Honours degree in botany/microbiology from the University of the Witwatersrand, a Graduate Certificate of Science Education from the University of London, and a Master of Science degree in environmental science from the University of Cape Town.

KNOWLEDGE MANAGEMENT DIAGNOSTIC TOOL

To use the Knowledge Management diagnostic tool, shown in Table 11-1,[1] consider the organization that you are evaluating, and decide to what degree the statement describes your organization. To calculate your score, use the following scale:

- Strong = 3
- Moderate = 2
- Weak = 1

---

[1] Adapted from Bukowitz, W., and Williams, R. *The Knowledge Management Fieldbook*. London, UK: Prentice Hall, 1999.

Table 11-1
Knowledge Management Diagnostic Tool

Knowledge Management Diagnostic	Strong	Moderate	Weak
1. Groups and individuals routinely share information about their expertise.			
2. The electronic and physical places where we store our knowledge are kept up to date.			
3. Training on new systems focuses on how these technologies can be used to improve the quality and efficiency of how people work.			
4. Specific individuals identify, collect, classify, summarize, and disseminate organizational knowledge.			
5. Experts play a role in identifying important information for other users.			
6. The electronic and physical places where we store our knowledge contain the best information available on a wide range of critical topics.			
7. When people are given the task of searching for information they are able to fulfill the request.			
8. The organization has created electronic and paper-based tools that direct people to available resources.			
9. We have established ways for people to document and share information.			
10. We distinguish between information that should be centrally controlled and information that anyone should be free to document and share.			
11. Our reporting relationships do not interfere with people getting the information they need.			
12. Everyone can describe how his or her decisions can affect overall organization performance.			
13. Everyone speaks up if they have an opinion or idea to offer.			

Table 11-1
Continued

Knowledge Management Diagnostic	Strong	Moderate	Weak
14. We give all promising ideas thorough consideration, no matter who they come from.			
15. We make a point of not structuring some of our meetings because it helps us think more creatively about problem solving.			
16. Involving our clients in the process of creating and developing new products and services is a well-established practice in our organization.			
17. People would describe our organization as flexible rather than rigid.			
18. Everyone in our organization can explain the basics about our financials.			
19. We frequently partner with suppliers/sponsors to improve the value we deliver to the client.			
20. We use approaches that people would call playful as part of our problem-solving process.			
21. Before people fix a problem, they consider the overall context in which the problem occurred.			
22. We build models of our decision-making systems to better understand why things happen the way they do.			
23. Teams engage in off-site learning experiences to find better ways of working together.			
24. Reflecting on lessons learned from work experiences is an established practice in our organization.			
25. When people finish projects, they generally take the time to meet with their team and analyze what went wrong and what could have been done better.			
26. Our learning process often includes gathering feedback from customers.			
27. People admit when they fail.			

28. People apply the ideas they developed in past work situations to new ones.
29. Our organization supports group activities that promote mutual learning.
30. We treat disagreement as an opportunity to learn from one another.
31. Dedicated roles, such as knowledge manager or knowledge coordinator, support the knowledge-sharing process.
32. The organization has determined where knowledge sharing across groups will yield the highest mutual benefits.
33. People would say that sharing knowledge does not diminish the individual's value to the organization.
34. We link people across traditional organizational units and functional groups to promote knowledge sharing.
35. Professional moderators and facilitators help people better express what they know so that others can understand it.
36. People have a say in what happens to the ideas and expertise they share with others.
37. Knowledge-sharing behavior is built into the performance appraisal system.
38. Our organization looks for ways to remove barriers to knowledge sharing.
39. People can identify others in the organization who might benefit from their knowledge.
40. The organization has legitimized sharing knowledge by giving people the time to do it.
41. We recognize that knowledge is part of our asset base.
42. Members of the senior management team frequently talk about Knowledge Management when reporting on the state of the organization.
43. The process of measuring knowledge helps us better understand what it is we are trying to manage.
44. We measure our Knowledge Management process and its results.

Table 11-1

Continued

Knowledge Management Diagnostic	Strong	Moderate	Weak
45. We have developed a framework that links Knowledge Management activities to strategic outcomes.			
46. We have a framework that describes how our organization's knowledge-based assets interact with one another to create value.			
47. Senior management assesses what knowledge needs to be developed when it allocates resources.			
48. Assessment of knowledge-based assets is part of our overall organizational performance measurement process.			
49. We rely on a team whose members have valuation, measurement, and operating expertise to assess our Knowledge Management process and its results.			
50. We have mapped the process flow of Knowledge Management activities.			
51. We routinely ask ourselves how we can leverage our knowledge into other areas.			
52. Our IT systems connect us to information sources we need to do our work.			
53. Our IT systems promote the formation of different networks of people.			
54. Our managers include Knowledge Management in their business plans.			
55. Our organization treats people like assets rather than costs.			
56. We find ourselves increasingly teaming up with other organizations in strategic networks or partnerships to bring innovative products/services to our clients.			
57. We view information technology as a tool to help us get our work done.			
58. We strive to retain people who have mission-critical skills.			
59. We have a formal policy that ensures that we share technology and ideas across unit or group borders.			
60. People know when it is not appropriate to share knowledge externally.			

Scoring

The questions are grouped into the following sections:

- Questions 1–10 correspond to the Get process.
- Questions 11–20 correspond to the Use process.
- Questions 21–30 correspond to the Learn process.
- Questions 31–40 correspond to the Contribute process.
- Questions 41–50 correspond to the Assess process.
- Questions 51–60 correspond to the Build process.

The maximum score for each section is 30; you can then work out the percentage score by dividing your score by 30.

REFERENCES

Calder, F. "The Potential for Using the Multi-stakeholder Network Model to Develop and Deliver Partnerships for Implementation for the World Summit on Sustainable Development." Discussion paper. UK: Royal Institute of International Affairs, 2002.

Hansen, M. T., Nohria, N., and Tierney, T. "What's Your Strategy for Managing Knowledge?" *Harvard Business Review*, March–April 1999.

Haricharan, S., and Moollan, R. *KM Readiness in Five Departments of the Western Cape Provincial Government*. M.B.A. dissertation, University of Cape Town, 2001.

Patton, M. Q. *Qualitative Research and Evaluation Methods, Third Edition*. Thousand Oaks, CA, Sage Publications, 2002.

CHAPTER 12

Where Did We Start?
Building Our Own
Knowledge Park at
Old Mutual

By Antonia Gillham

We, the Knowledge Improvement team, work at Old Mutual South Africa, at the southernmost tip of the African continent in a beautiful city called Cape Town. Our city has mountains and seas and claims the richest indigenous plant kingdom in the world. It is therefore not surprising that we talk about our work in terms like *Siyakhula*, which means "We are growing," and embrace a culture of *Ubuntu*, which means working together with people, where you share and support each other, as is the African way.

Old Mutual South Africa is part of Old Mutual PLC, which is an international financial services group whose activities are focused on asset gathering and asset management and which offers a diverse range of financial services in three principal geographies: the United States, the United Kingdom, and South Africa.

In South Africa we are the largest financial services business, started 150 years ago, and we provide life insurance, asset management, banking, and general insurance to our clients. In the United States, we are one of the top 10 fixed annuity businesses; in the UK, we focus on wealth management with Gerrard, our largest UK operation, as one of the leading private client stock brokering businesses in the country.

Being a part of this truly global and competitive group helped us realize that we had to do many things better and faster than anyone

217

else in our industry, and one of the most important of these was learning. So in 2000 we started to focus our energy on designing and implementing the first corporate university in Africa, which today is known as Old Mutual Business School. It was launched in February 2001 and is situated in a spacious, modern building. It teaches over a hundred programs and workshops every year. We are proud of this achievement and rightly so, because the prominence and value that learning is given in the organization has increased substantially. Leadership development has been enhanced through international and national learning partnerships, and the value of learning is being tracked through the implementation of ROI initiatives that measure the impact of learning on the business.

In order to build vigorous and continuous learning in our organization, we developed a sound and believable learning strategy that could create a common language and inspire the various existing business unit heads and learning professionals into throwing their weight behind the business school. Everyone had to believe that better and faster learning would enhance the organization's ability to grow shareholder value and achieve high performance. This we did. Our group learning strategy became a benchmark in South Africa, and our learning model was admired and copied at international conferences.

While all of this was happening, our whole organization was participating in a change and empowerment initiative called Siyakhula, "We are growing," which captured people's hearts and souls.

At the business school too we sang, "Siyakhula, we are growing," and a wave of change swept the organization across all levels. People and teams everywhere debated and explored new ways of working and living, and questioned how we could promote and sustain vigorous, fresh, new growth, and how this never-ending growth could be sustained. We also discussed where it would be most likely to arise, why it would happen, and how. After much thought, debate, and research, the answer became clear: Learning would help us grow, but only if we learned *the right things*. We needed to make absolutely sure that we identified the right knowledge to reach our goals. We had to find it, continuously capture it, grow it, create it, and use it to the best advantage of all.

Yes, you have guessed it, we found Knowledge Management. Without it, we could not learn effectively; in fact, we might even learn the wrong stuff and take the wrong fork in our journey to high performance and growth.

Our learning strategy therefore made space alongside all the good learning practices and objectives for the Center for Learning and Knowledge Management. Learning and Knowledge Management had to sit beside each other and sing in harmony, and we were proud of this because no one else, other than Daimler Chrysler's corporate university, had cottoned on to this important understanding. This we discovered when we attended the European Corporate University summit in London in November 2000 and presented our learning model.

Choosing the Site

And so, it came about that Knowledge Management was born at Old Mutual SA and the first knowledge manager was appointed. Our beautiful new business school would be situated in a garden or park of knowledge, where learning would take place in an environment full of flowers and trees and ponds and rivers, because we felt that is how knowledge would manifest itself in the organization. Knowledge would appear in many forms, some of it fixed and easily seen like large shrubs and trees, some of it blooming only briefly and shedding its blossoms on the way to becoming fruit or forming new buds and new flowers, some of it flowing away in rivers or sinking to the bottom of ponds, where it would be difficult to catch and keep.

We would care for it and teach people to replant it continuously and nurture, fertilize, and prune it for survival. Not only would the business school provide learning opportunities for all, but it would be a place of new knowledge, of continuous learning of the right things, and a place where knowledge would be shared and captured and used and discarded when it is of no use to anyone any longer. In this way too, old knowledge would become compost for the growth of new knowledge.

The Gardener Gets Going

Our new knowledge manager, who we will refer to as our first "knowledge gardener," was filled with enthusiasm. He talked to people and tried to create Knowledge Management networks. He conducted a readiness survey and organized Karl Erik Sveiby, a renowned Knowledge Management practitioner, to give a master class to managers. He visited other South African cities, universities, and companies to find out what they were doing, to discover the best

Knowledge Management teaching and practices, and he organized vendors and consultants to come and display their products and services. The concept of Knowledge Management was presented at our Learning Advisory Board, where senior learning professionals meet to share matters of learning that affect everyone across all the business units, and Knowledge Management workshops were designed and taught, which we called *Get Set Know*. We even demanded from one of our learning partners in London that they teach our executives what Knowledge Management was.

We anticipated a rich and plentiful knowledge harvest from our park that would result in:

- Improved business processes and products at reduced costs
- Increased innovation and speed-to-market
- Reduced duplication of effort
- Minimized trial and error
- Identification and implementation of best practices
- Organization-wide and international perspectives
- Informed employees focused on high performance
- A culture of knowledge sharing

We thought that people would immediately see how valuable this wonderful discipline was, the benefits were so obvious. Surely?

The First Crop Failed

But Knowledge Management was not well received. Most of the people we spoke to or who came to our "Get Set Know" workshops had little or no knowledge of what Knowledge Management was, and those who did, thought that it was a technology-based solution or, worse, a scary thing that someone would foist onto already over-stretched managers and executives. We were appalled and, from our now somewhat lonely and disheartened corner, continued to spread what we thought of as truly good news.

We designed our own Knowledge Management strategy for the business school and even decided to start with the restructuring of our traditional corporate library, known as the Information Resource Center, so that it could become a virtual knowledge resource for the whole organization. It eventually became known as the KnowledgeHub.

Progress was slow, and very few people showed much enthusiasm. Sadly, after a while our knowledge manager left, and a few enthusiasts at the business school offered to take on the function of Knowledge Management caretaker rather apprehensively.

THERE WERE DIVERSE POTTED PLANTS THAT WE DISCOVERED LATER

Had we been better at managing our own knowledge, we would have been less despondent, because while we were despairing, other areas in the organization were making some progress in getting better at identifying and using knowledge. Small, independent initiatives were quietly and almost surreptitiously springing up; databases, knowledge assets, and small communities that shared and learned together had formed, but we were unaware of them at this stage.

THE NEXT BATCH OF SEEDS IS PLANTED

Then, from our somewhat ignorant perspective, things started to look up again. The Siyakhula initiative had identified a number of areas where the organization needed to focus energy, and we were ecstatic to see Knowledge Management on this list. Each area of focus, called a Siyakhula work stream, was allocated a highly competent senior manager, and the business school, which until now had been solely responsible for Knowledge Management, became part of a wider team. Suddenly, we had an interest from the business units rather than being a lone HR-driven function. It was a cause for celebration. We provided the work stream with some excellent research, best-of-breed companies were identified, best practices in organizations from all over the world were documented, a Knowledge Management model was designed and distributed, a survey to test organizational readiness was designed, and a number of people were surveyed. The first group that called itself a community of practice was launched, called the Athenaeum, which consisted of people interested in Knowledge Management, and it held its first meeting. Also, for the first time, we gave a formal presentation on the nature and benefits of Knowledge Management to the executive team.

Finally, it seemed that Knowledge Management was being viewed as a priority. Delighted, we watered our seeds and waited for the seedlings to sprout.

THE SEEDS NEVER GERMINATED; WE EXPERIENCED A SEVERE DROUGHT

Suddenly, everyone involved was absolutely unequivocal about the need for Knowledge Management in the organization. Everyone who was surveyed saw it as a critical need, and large wish lists were presented of many wonderful new ways in which the business would be enhanced. Why then, once again, did we observe with a mixture of puzzlement and sadness that it had all died down again?

Our work stream leader moved on to other, more pressing concerns, and the whole work stream initiative was closed down. Even the community of practice co-coordinator was told to stop the Athenaeum because it was premature. It seemed that once again our precious seeds had fallen on fallow ground and furthermore were hampered by a severe drought.

What had we done wrong, we asked ourselves. Why did clever people who should know better not see the benefits of Knowledge Management?

Once we thought about it, it wasn't hard to figure out.

- *There wasn't enough sunlight.* Knowledge Management, first, is not easy to understand. Many people objected to the idea of "managing" knowledge, saw it as extra work, or believed that they were already doing it.
- *The soil analysis was incorrect.* Those who did know something about it (not much, mind you) tended to think of it as a technology system and wanted to place it into the IT function of the organization, where they would own it and control it.
- *People wanted a garden fence around our park.* The concept of something as fluid as Knowledge Management, which is as much human focused as process and systems focused, was also seen as being far too uncontrollable by some and, worse, a possible threat to the power base of a small group of managers who, mostly unknowingly, excluded others from knowing too much, to ensure their superiority.
- *The planting beds had not been sufficiently planned.* We did not have a strategy for introducing a pilot or two into the organization to demonstrate the benefits of having Knowledge Management; our strategy was mostly focused on the business school.
- *The gardeners tried to be butchers and bakers and candlestick makers, as well as gardeners, all at the same time.* We had not

launched a proper project—the Siyakhula Knowledge Management work stream was an add-on to already busy people's schedules.

- *Our park had no sponsor.* The most important reason for our failure, however, was the fact that we had no real sponsorship. Providing lip service was not enough; we needed active marketing, influencing, and a preparedness to allocate resources.
- *We ignored the potted plants.* We did not make enough effort to discover where Knowledge Management was already happening, who was doing it, and where. We could then have learned from them.
- *Fruit ripened and rotted without being shared.* People were not keen to share their hard-earned knowledge and viewed it as their own personal intellectual capital that ensured them power over those who did not know.

So What Happened Next?

Undaunted, we carefully examined our failed seeds to learn from our mistakes, and then plowed them back into the soil to fertilize our next crop.

This time we prepared the ground thoroughly, dug deep, turned the soil, and left any planting until the soil was ready, fertilized, and watered just right for our new plants to take root in safety. We couldn't fence our park, because this would be contrary to the philosophy of Knowledge Management. Nor could we spread insecticide around—the insects are part of the knowledge sharing. So we still had to be vigilant and tenderly nurture every little seedling with warmth and plenty of encouragement as well as big dollops of admiration when things went well.

This time we received impetus and sponsorship from the group CEO, who wanted to see evidence of Knowledge Management initiatives in the organization, as well as from the head of human resources, who was required to deliver them. In the latter, we finally had real support, and we referred to him as our director of parks and gardens. Since it was spring again, planting could begin in earnest.

A new knowledge manager was appointed (knowledge gardener number two), and we attended a session with people who were viewed as thought leaders to explore how the organization could implement some new and workable Knowledge Management initiatives. This session was run by our "director of parks and gardens"

and had people from across the whole group participating. Awareness was now spreading rapidly. A spring wind was blowing.

Shortly thereafter we wrote a vision document called "Creating
our Knowledge Park," which, written in a lighthearted and easy-
to-read style, quite unlike the usual solemn and jargon-driven
corporate documents we normally read, outlined the benefits of
Knowledge Management. It gave examples of some of the wonderful things Knowledge Management could provide to the organization and how these would enhance cost cutting, productivity,
competitive advantage, and shareholder value and result in all-
around high performance.

This document was well received, and we were given the go-ahead
to launch a project that would identify and implement some Knowledge Management initiatives. Quickly, we embarked on the task of
identifying and scoping the activities and resources that we would
require, in a very high-level and fairly informal way. This was also
when we ditched the term Knowledge Management and adopted our
own name: *Knowledge Improvement.*

Suddenly, no one argued with us anymore about the fact that they
believed that you could not manage knowledge, because it just
doesn't seem right to argue about needing to improve the organization's ability to use knowledge, now does it?

THE YEAR 2003 HAD ARRIVED, AND OUR SPRING WIND HAD GIVEN WAY TO SUMMER WARMTH

At this time, some of us participated in an enormously successful
learning conference, hosted by the business school, which focused on
learning but also had a Knowledge Management component. We
invited Carol Gorelick from New York to come and run a workshop
on Knowledge Management and also consult with the Knowledge-
Hub team on how Knowledge Management might be introduced into
the organization. She inspired us and introduced us to our first Peer
Assist, which consisted of people here in South Africa who were
already involved in Knowledge Management. We also contacted Nick
Milton, who had worked on the BP Knowledge Management team.

GARDENING LESSONS FOR THE TEAM

Learning and Knowledge Improvement still remained for us an
inseparable twosome, and in order to practice what we preached,

our Learning and Knowledge Management manager at the business school set about educating his own team, which would ultimately form the core of the Knowledge Improvement Project team, and used a novel and easy way to do this. Everyone was given chapters from Collison and Parcell's book *"Learning to Fly"*[1] to read, after which they got together to share understanding and identify practical things that they could implement in their own areas. These sessions were enormously effective, and soon we all spoke the same language. Speaking the same language was important because we needed to be able to identify the real seedlings from a huge plethora of weeds.

Choosing the Paths, Ponds, and Park Benches and Building the Garden Shed

After some more discussion with the director of parks and gardens, it was decided that the project would consist of a number of phases and focus on a number of defined areas. Phase 1 would consist of the following:

- A number of databases would be created that would house knowledge required by all—i.e., current projects across the organization, abbreviations and acronyms, functional experts, and all learning events. These were our garden ponds.
- A number of communities of practice would be established, one in HR, one in product development, and one in the area of finance. All of these would eventually become group-wide initiatives and would be our paths.
- The project would also take another project—the implementation of a technology platform, a learning management system for the organization—and combine this into a dual learning and knowledge system. We felt strongly that learning and Knowledge Improvement should sit together in the same system. This would be a very special garden bench.
- The corporate library, now known as the KnowledgeHub, would be placed into the project, to become fully functional as a group-wide knowledge enabler, and the education and marketing around Knowledge Improvement would also be driven by the project. This would be our garden shed.

[1] Collison, C., and Parcell, G. *Learning to Fly: Practical Lessons from One of the World's Leading Knowledge Companies*. Capstone Publishing Inc., 2001.

The Weather Is Hot, So We Forget About Seeds, and Start Planting Shrubs and Trees That Have Already Started Growing

Even though the project had not yet formally started, we launched into what proved to be rather haphazard but enjoyable actions. Perhaps we were acting out of sheer frustration, because for so long we had been unable to reap any fruits from all our sowing, planting, and ground leveling that we did not want to spend too much time planning or scoping; we just wanted to do it and grow it and pick it.

We ran a stakeholder session with human resources staff in order to set up a community of practice for human resources practitioners. We developed presentations and a support pack for anyone else wanting to start a community of practice. The KnowledgeHub launched into action with Green Spade Sessions (we were digging together for knowledge). A Green Spade Session is a one-hour, lunchtime talk or sharing session for people interested in a particular topic.

We also started gathering acronyms and abbreviations across the organization to populate a database called OMSPEAK (Old Mutual Speak) that everyone could access.

We set up a stakeholder meeting and invited all the people who we could discover in the organization who were already involved in or embarking on Knowledge Improvement ventures. The purpose of this meeting was to find out what they were doing so that we could perhaps piggyback onto their initiatives, share our project objectives, and fly a kite in terms of the deliverables we had chosen. Running a Knowledge Café gave everyone a few deliverables to discuss around a table, and then they were asked to join the project, either as a thought leader or as a participant. Fortunately, there was a fair degree of sharing and enthusiasm in the room, and this group formed the core of our new Knowledge Improvement community of practice.

Shaping the Beds Once the Plants Are Already Growing, and Going Back to Seedlings as Well as Shrubs and Trees

Only at this point did we appoint a dedicated project manager who would be our plant nurseryman, and we started to plan and scope the project properly.

Finally, after two years of choosing our original park site—the business school—and starting to till the ground, we are getting a real sense of progress. In fact, we are experiencing the good feeling that we are systematically and responsibly on our way.

A number of subprojects have been established, each with its allocated subproject leader and each with a collection of separate but integrated activities. They are:

- Vision and Strategy of Knowledge Improvement—Across the group
- Management—Providing best practice and measurement
- Communication and Marketing—Of all our Knowledge Improvement initiatives
- Communities of Practice—Providing support through guidance, technology, and passion
- Research and Benchmarking—Of Knowledge Management around the world
- Practices and Processes—That will be documented as they arise in the project
- Technology and Collaboration—For all the initiatives that require it
- Education—Providing learning products and services for all staff in the understanding and best practice of Knowledge Improvement at all levels
- The KnowledgeHub—Providing the organization with a truly efficient knowledge capability that will store, maintain, and distribute critical knowledge linked to the business strategies
- Old Mutual Business School Integration—Our most important pilot site right now

THE KNOWLEDGE PARK IS BECOMING VISIBLE

The site and borders of our park have increased to far beyond the boundaries of the business school, even though Knowledge Improvement is still being driven from here, and the enthusiasm for our various initiatives, especially those that will service the whole group, from our colleagues at the head office in London, has been exciting and inspirational.

We have presented our project to everyone who works at the business school at a team meeting so that everyone knows our latest gardening tips. We even placed some of these tips in the bathrooms, on the back of the doors for everyone to read, under the title "Learning While Doing," which resulted in much learning and laughter.

Everyday, new people in the organization approach us and want to share in the beauty and bounty of our growing park, and we are discovering that our new motto, *Stop Guessing, Start Knowing*, is starting to spread further and further into the organization.

In Our Park We Now Have a Green Pool That Reflects How Knowledge Will Nurture Everything We Do

As part of defining and sharing our understanding of Knowledge Improvement, we have designed our own *very green and cyclical* Knowledge Improvement model (see Figure 12-1). It looks like a deep green pool of ever-moving water and easily allows us to explain to others the benefits and function of Knowledge Improvement at Old Mutual.

Our pool is green because this indicates its richness, growth, and abundance, and green is also our corporate color used in all our marketing material and campaigns.

Our team of passionate gardeners has grown from three to six permanent members, and one day soon, we hope, we will be viewed by

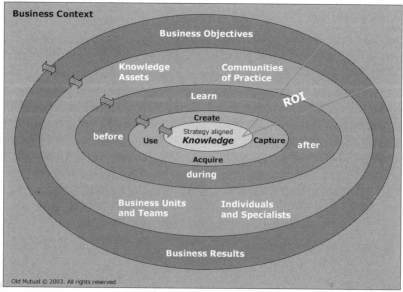

Figure 12-1. The Knowledge Improvement eclipse

others who themselves are starting their implementation of Knowledge Management in their organizations, as a worthy benchmark in Africa and beyond.

Antonia Gillham, who has degrees in both literature and law, is the CEO of Pinoak Consulting, which delivers business solutions in the fields of human resources and learning strategy, and Knowledge Management design and implementation. She has taught and consulted on learning, return on investment for learning, and Knowledge Management to large corporations in the financial services, oil, and mining industries. Gillham is currently consulting with the Old Mutual Business School on Knowledge Management strategies and implementation, and is an active member of the Knowledge Improvement team.

CHAPTER 13

Generating Capabilities in Communities of Practice: The Clarica Story

By Debra Wallace and Hubert Saint-Onge

A pioneer in developing and utilizing its knowledge capital, Clarica Life Insurance Company (now merged with Sun Life Financial) expanded its knowledge strategy with a program to create communities of practice. This case study outlines Clarica's approach for establishing strategic communities in order to generate individual and organizational capabilities. With the Agent Network, a virtual community of independent financial planners and insurance agents from across Canada, Clarica identified a process model to guide further community development.

Communities of practice can play a vital role in any organization, but their greatest value comes when they are leveraged for the strategic capabilities that they generate. A planned approach to community development enabled by a technology infrastructure to support collaboration and learning creates value for the organization, individual community members, and the practice at large.

Background

Clarica Life Insurance Company merged with Sun Life Financial in May 2002. Prior to the merger, each organization had been in business for over a century. Headquartered in Canada, but with an international reach, each company had developed individual

231

strengths in specific markets, offering a range of insurance and wealth management products and services.

In the mid-1990s, Clarica developed an innovative organization-wide knowledge strategy spearheaded by the Strategic Capabilities Unit. With a mandate to generate capabilities at an accelerated rate across the organization, Clarica moved away from a traditional human resources management structure to a model centered around strategic capabilities. Just as organizations have historically tended to focus on products rather than customers, the traditional human resources function tended to focus on its tools (e.g., compensation, training and development, recruitment, staffing) rather than on the capabilities of the employees.

This new organizational unit provided an approach and a supporting structure that positioned knowledge and learning as an integral part of effective business leadership. The model also supported the systematic development of communities of practice, with an emphasis on communities that were directly aligned with strategic imperatives.

The Knowledge Capital Initiative

Clarica's business objective was similar to the primary goal of most corporations: increase earnings and accelerate growth to create shareholder value. Based on that business focus, Clarica launched the Knowledge Capital Initiative in 1996 to generate the individual and organizational capabilities that would allow the corporation to meet current and evolving market challenges (see Figure 13-1). The initiative had five core goals:

- Accelerate the generation of individual and organizational capabilities.
- Develop a culture of self-initiative, shared ownership, and collaboration.
- Renew people management processes in support of building capability and a culture based on self-initiative.
- Harness the power of the corporate technology infrastructure.
- Build a systematic and readily accessible knowledge architecture.

The Knowledge Capital Initiative was designed to accelerate the acquisition of new capabilities that were required not only to serve changing market needs, but to launch new income streams to support

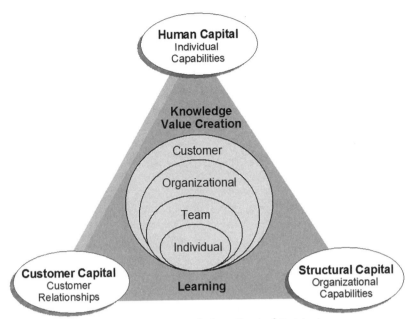

Figure 13-1. Knowledge Capital Initiative

business growth. The belief that these capabilities would create new solutions encouraged the organization to reach beyond its traditional structures. By enhancing individual capability in the organization, the Knowledge Capital Initiative strengthened the organization's ability to acquire and retain critical resources in a highly competitive marketplace.

COMMUNITIES OF PRACTICE

The Knowledge Capital Initiative supported a wide variety of programs, each designed to contribute to the broader knowledge strategy. To manage the work, a new group called the Strategic Capabilities Unit (see Figure 13-2) was formed to serve the organization. It included the more traditional human resources functions (renamed membership services), a team of organizational capability consultants, an individual capabilities consulting practice, the brand team, the e-learning team, and the knowledge team. With this new structure, Clarica was able to collaborate with the various business units in generating the capabilities required to achieve strategic imperatives as well as support an organization-wide infrastructure to support knowledge and learning processes.

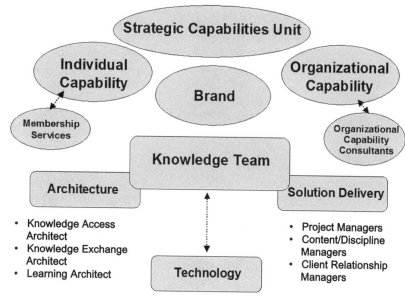

Figure 13-2. Strategic Capabilities Unit

One of the many innovative programs sponsored by the knowledge team was the development of collaborative approaches that leveraged the organization's extensive technology infrastructure. Within that program was the development of a systematic approach to building communities.

People have formed groups to address work-related issues for centuries. The community of practice model is actually an age-old structure existing within modern businesses that was first identified by Jean Lave and Etienne Wenger in their book, *Situated Learning* (1991, 2000). Wenger and a number of other practitioners and consultants have continued to develop the concept of communities of practice as informal networks that bring people together for problem solving, innovation, and learning—through knowledge creation and exchange.

At Clarica, more than 30 active communities of practice were identified, covering a wide spectrum of community types—from informal communities of interest to structured communities of practice. Each community had its own characteristics, coming together on an as-needed or more regular basis to collaborate on finding ways to improve business practices and add to the organization's capabilities. Realizing the importance of these communities, Clarica identified the need to establish a process that would support community building in a systematic, cost-effective way.

A PROJECT MANAGEMENT APPROACH TO COMMUNITY DEVELOPMENT: THE AGENT NETWORK

Seeing the benefits of formally supporting communities, Clarica embarked on a number of initiatives to develop communities. After several failed attempts to establish a community of practice for its independent agents and financial planners, Clarica turned to a more structured project management approach to community design and implementation. The project was sponsored by the vice president of strategic capabilities in partnership with the vice president of sales force operations. The project groundwork was laid by the knowledge team, a group of knowledge architects and consultants, in partnership with the information technology group.

A steering group, consisting of two practicing agents, two members of the sales force development unit, Clarica's knowledge architect, and a dedicated project manager, collaborated on the community's design. To ensure the project's success, time was spent on exploring the nature of communities, understanding the agent environment, and designing a community with maximum value to its members.

The purpose of the community development project was twofold. First, Clarica sought to support the development of a vibrant community of practice for its independent sales agents. Second, a best-practice example would be identified by a process model and an analysis of lessons learned that could be used to create other strategic communities at Clarica.

The first initiative was to establish the Agent Network, a community of practice for 150 Clarica agents from across Canada who represented a wide range of years of experience, areas of product or service expertise, and markets served. The project goals were as follows:

- Create a collaborative "space" to
    - ▽ Support the career growth of developing agents (fewer than five years' experience) to improve career satisfaction, productivity, and retention.
    - ▽ Support the renewal and continued professional development of experienced agents (five or more years' experience)

as a means to move them to their next level of professional potential.

▽ Provide opportunities for agent networking that would lead to increased sales, innovation in the business practice, and professional cohesiveness.

- Leveraging the organization's technology infrastructure, provide an opportunity to increase agents' use of computer technology, especially increasing their awareness of the Internet in support of e-commerce initiatives at Clarica.

- Evaluate the use of a Web-based application for community development.

Given our previous futile attempts to develop a community for our independent agents, we approached this community development project quite differently. In our third attempt, we

- Established a pilot project with cross-functional sponsorship from stakeholders at the executive level.

- Engaged a group of key agents to collaborate on the community design and act as catalysts for community participation.

- Defined the strategic nature of the community: purpose, projected benefits, and alignment with strategic imperatives and business unit priorities.

- Engaged a team of people with specific areas of expertise and obtained input from the larger body of stakeholders.

- Articulated principles of the community approach.

- Laid a foundation of understanding about the nature of communities and how they could contribute to increasing capabilities.

- Provided resources (people, tools, materials) to the community.

- Selectively communicated the pilot project's progress.

- Created a parallel project to identify a process for designing and implementing communities.

In addition to these factors, we had perhaps the most significant advantage—experience! The past two failures, our continued study of communities, and our collaboration with an experienced vendor of community applications had increased our capabilities. In other words, we lived our Knowledge Management strategy—we learned from our experience, utilized our new knowledge, leveraged our architecture and technology infrastructure, and collaborated with our agents.

We made a conscious effort to formalize our processes, documenting our ideas and providing statements of direction. Because there was a dual purpose for developing this community (i.e., a purpose from Clarica's perspective and a purpose from the agents' perspective), we identified objectives for the pilot project from a strategic point of view that complemented the community's purpose. Although these two perspectives were closely aligned, they were nevertheless coming from two directions: bottom up from the agents and top down from the corporate sponsors. But they did converge. While the corporation was looking for increased productivity from the sales force, the agent was looking for increased profitability from his or her own business. Fundamentally, we were both talking about the same thing: increasing the quality of performance.

LEVERAGING TECHNOLOGY TO CREATE A VIRTUAL COMMUNITY OF PRACTICE

Clarica wanted to use the community experience as a way to increase the technological capabilities of the agents, especially their Internet-based skills. They had automated most processes around the sales cycle, and many agents were reasonably comfortable with their laptops. However, the corporate focus on achieving industry-leading e-business capability meant that we needed to increase agents' capabilities to integrate Internet-based tools into their practice and saw participation in the community as one approach to achieving this objective.

Rather than training agents on Web use as an isolated skill, we gave them a Web-based tool as a means of learning from each other. We provided them with a "real life" use of the Internet rather than a set of modules from which they would learn in isolation from their "real work." They learned to use the Web through their use of the community forum. This approach was consistent with our understanding of adult learning principles—that adults learn best in the context of their work, where the learning is practical and the application of new skills is immediate.

The Agent Network (now called the Advisor Network in Sun Life Financial) continues to be a virtual community. The steering group, since its inception in fall 2000, has only met face-to-face once as an entire group. And the community itself continues to utilize a variety of collaborative technologies to support their work—they've not met face-to-face yet!

The Community Development Process: Model, Narrative, and Lessons Learned

After phase 1 of the Agent Network pilot project was evaluated, efforts turned to analyzing the community development approach and identifying a process model. This analysis also included discussions with community development consultants involved in supporting other communities at Clarica, providing a richness of experience that would form the basis of best practice.

We found that developing a community of practice was accomplished in two phases (see Figure 13-3). In phase 1, we established the community's infrastructure in three main steps with the active guidance of a project manager:

1. *Define community project*—The community project is planned: The characteristics of the community are identified (setting the context) and the project is defined.
2. *Establish community components*—The project tasks are identified (often in the form of issues to be resolved), a work plan is developed, and objectives are achieved.
3. *Launch community*—The community is available to the members, enabled by collaborative technology.

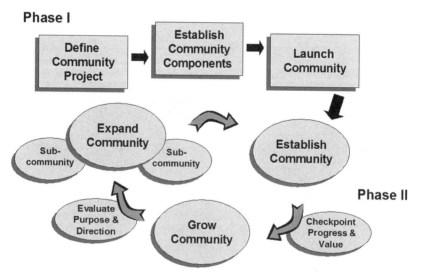

Figure 13-3. Phases of a community of practice

In phase 2, the community itself is now the driver, not the project development as seen in phase 1. During this phase, the community matures in a continuous cycle of development, evaluation, and growth with the aid of a facilitator. This phase is perhaps better described by the key outcomes of each step rather than the actions required.

- *Establish community*—A sense of community is developed through knowledge creation and exchange in member discussions, shared resources, and related activities.
- *Assess progress and value*—The community's value to its members and sponsors and the approach to laying the community's foundation (logistics and infrastructure) are assessed.
- *Grow community*—Directions are identified for increasing the community's value through community building, knowledge creation and sharing, and knowledge navigation approaches.
- *Evaluate purpose and direction*—The growth directions and value propositions are further evaluated, assessing benefits to the community, its members, and its sponsors.
- *Expand community*—New members are added, subgroups and new communities form, and the original community purpose is renewed or revised.

The danger of a process model is that it can appear to be a step-by-step technical manual—a cookbook full of recipes for success—when, in fact, the objective is to highlight key points for consideration, for adapting to individual situations.

To provide a richer description of the Clarica experience, we continue with a narrative that describes the process steps in further detail.

PHASE 1—COMMUNITY DESIGN AND LAUNCH

In Phase 1, we created a preliminary design and planned the launch of the community. Figure 13-4 describes the steps in Phase 1.

Step 1: Design the Community Project

During the first step in the community's development, the context for the community was identified and the nature of the community was proposed. The work was accomplished by a steering group, made up of agents and Clarica staff, with input from project sponsors and other executives responsible for agent activity.

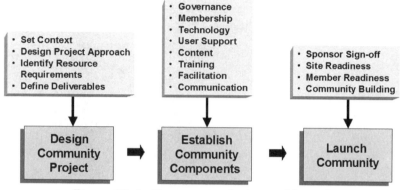

Figure 13-4. Community design and launch

Given that the Agent Network project was the pilot for communities of practice development at Clarica, a significant amount of time was spent in discussing how to position the project for success. Time was also devoted to negotiating the contract with the community application vendor, Communispace Corporation. Key actions included

- Establishing context for community—Understanding the members' environment, their opportunities and issues, and the reaction to the need for and anticipated value of a community.
- Understanding knowledge creation and exchange culture—Identifying existing channels and patterns, barriers, and trust levels.
- Identifying the political environment—Understanding the relationship between the community members and the corporate structure.

Once the context was identified, the project was defined, including the resources that would be required, the infrastructure that would support the community's exchange, and the approach that would guide the process. Key objectives and actions included

- Creating a steering group to guide the community development.
- Hiring a project manager and establishing a project approach, including the roles of the steering group, facilitator, and sponsors; creating working documents; and establishing a corporate liaison/communication approach.
- Identifying the resource network of company personnel needed to implement the community's infrastructure.
- Drafting the project plan with milestones and a time frame.

Step 2: Establish Community Components

During the second step, the project manager prepared to implement the community. Before we "went live" with the community, issues were identified, tasks were completed, and materials were produced to support the members' participation in the community. The network of Clarica staff continued to grow as expertise from across the company was required to complete the long list of project activities. For the Agent Network, it was during this step that the statement "It takes a team to build a community" was coined. This step included eight components:

- *Governance*—Identify the structures needed to guide policy and process development and to make decisions on the community's directions and approaches.
- *Membership*—Establish the selection criteria and process for inviting participation in the pilot community.
- *Infrastructure/community tool*—Select the computer application to support community development and knowledge exchange, and identify technical resources and processes required to implement the application.
- *Technical and user support*—Identify the help desk issues and solutions or approaches needed to ensure access to the community and usability of the application.
- *Content*—Locate the personal data for member profiles, and seed content that would populate the community at launch and during the community development phase.
- *Learning*—Create the materials and resources to familiarize community members with accessing and using the collaborative tool.
- *Facilitation*—Identify the moderator, guide, cheerleader, and traffic cop who would ensure the smooth exchange of ideas; nurture community building; and liase with stakeholders and the application vendor.
- *Communications*—Identify the public relations activities needed to promote the use of the community, and provide information on the status of the community's development to sponsors, senior management, community members, and Clarica employees.

Step 3: Launch the Community

The community members were identified, the application was customized, the training and support resources were distributed, the sponsors signed off on the launch, and the community members waited for the "doors to open." In step 3, the Web-based tool that supports the community's online activity was made available to the members during a facilitated "ramp-up" stage, where members were encouraged to edit their profiles and familiarize themselves with the application's functions.

At this point, the project manager's role diminished and the facilitator's role increased as the community members were "greeted at the door" and the tone for the community was established. Key actions included

- Determining whether the project manager was also the facilitator or they were two different people. In this case, it was the same person, but that isn't always the case, so we tend to distinguish by role, not person.
- Obtaining sign-off from sponsors and steering group members.
- Providing members with log-in and site information.
- Making the site available.
- Beginning facilitation activities: welcoming members, reinforcing use and contributions, starting to gather usage statistics, and encouraging broad participation.

PHASE 2—COMMUNITY IMPLEMENTATION AND GROWTH

In phase 2, the focus was now on developing the community and ensuring that value was established—value that would encourage members to commit time to contribute to the community and that would support the organization's decision to invest in the infrastructure and other resources required to support the community.

Phase 2 also marked the move from the more linear process in phase 1, which was necessary to set the community in motion, to a cyclical process where development, evaluation, and growth interact in a more dynamic fashion (see Figure 13-5).

Step 4: Establish the Community

Attention turned to developing the community. Members became familiar with each other and learned how to share their knowledge in a new environment. Facilitation continued to play a key role in helping members see the benefits of their participation and ensuring

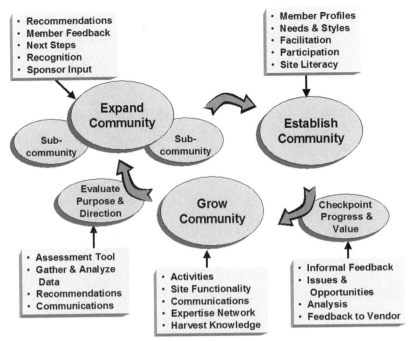

Figure 13-5. Establish the community

that the communication tool was functioning properly. A core group of community members, the "A-List," began to emerge. Key actions included

- Encouraging members to complete profiles and get to know each other.
- Beginning community-building activities: assessing needs, identifying preferences for methods of knowledge exchange, and identifying pockets of expertise.
- Establishing the role and personality of the facilitator.
- Encouraging member contribution to the community.
- Increasing community site literacy.

Step 5: Checkpoint—Assess Community Progress and Value

Shortly after we launched the community, we wanted to ensure that we were heading in the right direction. So we took an informal check on the community's health. Was the community moving ahead? Were barriers beginning to form? Were the conversations productive, supporting the members and moving their business ahead? In other words, how were we doing so far?

Rather than waiting for a postmortem on a serious issue that may result in the failure or death of the community, we established a permanent channel for informal feedback. Approaches included

- Collecting informal comments made in dialogues, sent in e-mails, made in related meetings, etc.
- Consulting the steering group and sponsors on issues and opportunities—soliciting feedback on perceptions as we moved forward.
- Analyzing statistics—establishing a baseline for various participation points.
- Providing feedback to the community software vendor—keeping channels of communication open regarding the status of the application and feedback on member satisfaction.

The checkpoint is a very informal step, but an important one. It helped us "calm down" a bit because the feedback was positive. For the most part, we found that we were on the right track. Members also seemed to appreciate that we were checking in with them rather than just barreling ahead full steam without consulting the broader community.

Step 6: Grow the Community

In this step of the process model, the community's identity began to emerge. The members had established a basic level of trust and were willing to put the necessary effort into making the community "fly." As they became comfortable with the technology that supported the community and readied themselves to test the boundaries of the community, the power of their collaborative problem solving and innovation emerged.

The steering group and community facilitator engaged in a variety of community development activities—moving forward on the recommendations based on the evaluation completed in the previous step.

It was during this phase that the Agent Network faced its first significant hurdle. Senior executives questioned the organization's support of the community. The actions of one member regarding a Clarica policy issue resulted in a perception that the Agent Network was being used to further the personal goals of one member, who had not gathered all the facts. In the end, a public relations effort and support from sponsors addressed the concerns, but the incident highlighted the need for building community on the basis of agreed-upon principles and guidelines. Key actions and objectives included

- Increasing community participation.
- Preparing guidelines regarding governance, participation, and contributing reference items.
- Extending the community activity calendar—further utilizing the community tool.
- Communicating details of the community's successes more broadly.

Step 7: Evaluate Purpose and Direction

A letter of thanks to the founding members of the Agent Network from the project sponsors began with the following:

We thought it was a good idea. We thought you might be interested in trying out some new technology to share ideas. We thought we had a pretty good plan in place to get the ball rolling. . . .

Clarica embarked on developing a community of practice based on a set of assumptions identified by the sponsors and steering group—assumptions that anticipated success. Although informal evaluative comments had been collected throughout the pilot phase, during this step a formal evaluation was completed to test the value proposition to the community membership, measure perceived success, identify areas for improvement, and test the original assumptions. Clarica's marketing research department designed an online survey, administered the survey, and analyzed the survey findings. Its expertise in gathering data from agents was a valuable asset to the evaluation phase. Key actions included

- Designing a survey tool.
- Gathering and analyzing data.
- Preparing recommendations for the next steps.
- Communicating results to sponsors, community members, and Clarica employees.

Step 8: Expand the Community

We started the Agent Network as a pilot project with a select number of members and a desire to test our assumptions about the value of communities as a forum for increasing capabilities linked to strategic imperatives. We also wanted to test the technology to see how we could leverage our infrastructure in partnership with a trusted vendor.

With the formal evaluation completed, we prepared a comprehensive report of our efforts over the previous seven months. Our list of recommendations was discussed with the steering group, and a summary was developed for the sponsors.

During this phase, a "team space" was established for the steering group, an opportunity to build a closer working relationship with this now-expanded group of members and to test another functional layer in the collaborative tool. Key actions included

- Evaluating recommendations and planning for improving approaches.
- Communicating the findings of the report and obtaining feedback from the community.
- Recognizing participation in pilot efforts, within both the community and the organization.
- Reviewing direction with project sponsors.

It's relatively easy to talk about the applied science (the tangible work) of community development—the part that is guided by a project plan with a project manager cracking a whip. It's more difficult to talk about the art of community building in terms of process because, for the most part, community building is dependent on the community itself and its membership, not on a prescribed process. And in attempting to describe what we did, there's a much less clear path for the community implementation and development part of this process model than what we saw in the logistics phase.

On the other hand, the community implementation and growth phase is far more exciting than putting the foundation pieces in place. Everyone gets caught up in the successes of the community. Emotions run high when actions by members or the facilitator jeopardize the value proposition of the community.

Although the process of creating a sense of community and establishing value from community participation may be difficult to explain, the rewards are far greater when the community's ability to advance strategic imperatives is recognized by the members, the people involved in supporting community efforts, and the organization's senior leadership.

LESSONS LEARNED

Clarica's experience with the Agent Network yielded a wealth of new knowledge about corporately supported communities of practice and the use of technology to enable a virtual gathering of expertise across the country. The following points are just the "tip of the iceberg" and highlight some of our key learnings.

- *Purpose*—A corporately sponsored community of practice recognizes that there are multiple purposes at work in the community that change depending on the perspective of the stakeholders: the individual community members, the community as a collective, and the organization. Recognizing that multiple purposes exist and working to ensure that they are complementary increases the trust level between stakeholders, thereby increasing the benefits for all concerned.
- *Technology*—Technology is an enabler, not the focus of community development. Is it the novelty of using a new technology to communicate that drives the success of the community? Does the tool define the community? If the answer is yes to either of these questions, then it is questionable that the community can be sustained. Set expectations as to what the technology can and can't do as an element of the community infrastructure, and focus on the community, not on the technology that supports it.
- *Facilitation*—Facilitation increases the community's ability to innovate. Left on its own, the community would most likely succeed to some degree, but the speed at which it achieves its goals and the extent of the success are increased through facilitation. The facilitator must be aligned with the community, but need not be a content expert. Facilitation competencies (knowledge base, skills, and attitudes) outweigh the need for expertise in the field(s) represented by the community. The facilitation role should be clearly defined, with responsibilities agreed upon by the community.
- *Vulnerability*—Never consider that a corporately supported community is sacrosanct. Unexpected challenges to its value can call into question the organization's support. The community

needs to actively engage in communication with stakeholders to ensure that misunderstandings are avoided and that issues and opportunities are escalated through appropriate liaison channels without breaching the confidentiality of the community or its individual members.

- *Responsible participation*—Negative incidents within the community (such as a breach in confidentiality, misuse of information, or unprofessional conduct) may be indicative of the community's growth and should be used as learning experiences to strengthen the sense of community and further its development. Guidelines for responsible participation can assist in establishing a code of conduct. But these guidelines should be framed as informing a member's decision regarding how he or she will participate, not as a set of rules to police the membership.
- *Process model*—When developing a community of practice, a process model should be situated as a framework, not a cookbook with strict recipes to follow. The process model is there as a guide to identify resources that will be required and point out possible pitfalls. Individual communities have unique characteristics that need to be the center of the development plan approach. The community purpose is the driver of the process, not an outcome of a prescribed process.

CONCLUSION

As a pilot, the Agent Network community of practice development project not only provided a retrospective analysis of what occurred, but also provided the opportunity to propose the next steps for both expanding the Agent Network into subsequent phases and developing other communities at Clarica.

As Sun Life Financial continues to develop its community program (postmerger and postintegration) and realizes the benefits, the process model we identified as a guideline will evolve. Since the model was identified, additional strategic communities have been launched, each with unique characteristics that have enriched our knowledge of how communities emerge and develop.

Benefits of the pilot project were not limited to experiences related to the Agent Network. Using the new process model, Clarica was able to significantly collapse the lead time required to launch additional communities of practice using a variety of collaborative tools.

Although the process model has made a difference in our ability to support sustainable communities, it's really the community model that has made the most significant impact. We've found that communities of practice

- Increase meta-capabilities within individuals and the organization, capabilities like learning and collaborating that generate other capabilities.
- Generate new knowledge assets—increase the knowledge capital of the organization.
- Help shape culture by modeling successful collaborative, knowledge-sharing environments that are motivated within the community, not mandated by the organization.
- Create knowledge networks—connect people and leverage their tacit knowledge, knowledge that could never be systematically codified.
- Promote innovation, increasing the speed at which the organization can meet market demands.
- Make a significant contribution to our competitive advantage through utilizing our wealth of knowledge assets.

In summary, we found that although communities of practice are naturally forming structures that exist already in an organization, they can be purposefully created with some time, attention, and resources devoted to their success. As a key component of an organization-wide knowledge strategy, these cross-generational communities can be leveraged for strategic advantage and may very well be instrumental in moving toward a new organizational structure, positioning it for success in the knowledge era.

Although Clarica's commitment to communities of practice as a significant organizational structure was grounded in its knowledge and learning strategy, Clarica was still at the very early phase of understanding the significance of communities as structures to support the development of knowledge capital. Clarica's recent merger with Sun Life Financial has resulted in changes in leadership, strategic priorities, and organizational structure that may ultimately affect Clarica's original community development direction.

Observing the changes (positive and negative) to Clarica's strategy for developing communities of practice and the value proposition of communities as key structures that contribute to creating a competitive advantage will further the understanding of the role that communities play in generating knowledge capital and enabling knowledge-driven organizations.

As the newly merged company takes shape, communities could play a significant role in shaping the culture, integrating capabilities, identifying knowledge capital, and providing a knowledge and learning platform. Understanding the value of communities of practice as a tool to speed the integration process in a merger environment could benefit the broader business community that experiences continuous change in company ownership and organization.

Communities of practice may be the most significant, tangible example of Knowledge Management at work in an organization. As groups of people are drawn to each other because of a common purpose, they begin to share their existing knowledge, create new knowledge, and apply their collective knowledge to either increase their own capabilities as practitioners or improve their practice. In the end, not only do community members excel in their practice, the wealth of the organization increases as well through the contribution of the community's knowledge capital.

The community development process model improved Clarica's ability to efficiently launch communities aligned with strategic imperatives with the speed and agility required to meet the fast-paced changes of the marketplace. This case study is part of a larger assessment program by the new Knowledge and Learning Team that continues to explore the nature of communities of practice, their importance to the development of knowledge capital, and, now, their contribution to an effective integration process in merged organizations.

Debra Wallace is a consultant of Knowledge and Learning Strategy Development at Sun Life Financial. She is responsible for developing the enterprise-wide knowledge and learning strategy for the newly merged Sun Life Financial and Clarica Life Insurance companies. She consults with business units to ensure alignment with corporate imperatives, technology directions, and industry standards to provide state-of-the-art knowledge sharing and learning solutions that increase individual and organizational capabilities. She coauthored *Leveraging Communities of Practice for Strategic Advantage* with Hubert Saint-Onge. Wallace holds a B.S. from Moorhead State University, an M.Ed. from the University of Manitoba, and a Ph.D. from the University of Toronto.

Hubert Saint-Onge is the CEO of Konverge Digital Solutions. He is a respected advisor to Fortune 500 companies and is widely recognized as a leading practitioner in the field of Knowledge Management. Formerly senior vice president of strategic capabilities at Clarica Life Insurance Company and vice president, Learning Organization and Leadership Development, for the Canadian Imperial Bank of Commerce, Saint-Onge has been lauded in the international community for his innovative thinking and leadership skills. He is currently executive in residence in the Centre for Business, Entrepreneurship and Technology (CBET) at the University of Waterloo. He holds an Honours B.A. and an M.A. in political science with specialization in international economic integration.

REFERENCES

Lave, Jean, and Wenger, Etienne. *Situated Learning: Legitimate Peripheral Participation*. Cambridge, UK: Cambridge University Press. 1991.

Saint-Onge, H., and Wallace, D. *Leveraging Communities of Practice for Strategic Advantage*. Boston, MA: Butterworth-Heinemann, 2003.

Wenger, E. C., and Snyder, W. M. "Communities of Practice: The Organizational Frontier." *Harvard Business Review*, 2000, Vol. 78, No. 1, pp. 139–145.

CHAPTER 14

Building a Membership Firm Through Practice Communities at Arthur Andersen

By Stephen John

As the 1990s started, Arthur Andersen (AA) was enjoying unparalleled growth. The firm's leadership correctly projected a decade of enormous economic opportunity if AA could develop enough partners to service large-client needs. Executives at these organizations insisted on a partner being their primary source of contact with AA. AA formed a task force, which they named AA21, to identify the challenges and suggest solutions for AA to prosper into the 21st century.

AA would need to define and implement a People Strategy that was comparable to its business strategy—i.e., create both a high-performing organization (HPO) and Employer of Choice (EOC) firm. By excelling at both elements (HPO and EOC), the firm would significantly improve its overall strategy execution capability and reap tremendous economic rewards. An EOC culture would enable the firm to build the talent pipeline needed to promote partners sufficiently experienced to interact with senior executives at large client organizations. This EOC culture would have to be strong enough to reverse the trend of new recruits leaving the firm in droves within three years of their joining the firm. New recruits out of the universities were looking for exciting work, which AA provided. However, they were also looking for a firm that would enable them to balance their work and personal life. They were not willing to completely sacrifice their personal life for a partnership opportunity approximately 14 years away.

One key element of having an EOC culture was to create a membership feeling for employees. Practice Communities (PCs) were formed as the core component of building a membership culture. Support and active participation by senior partners would ensure successful deployment of the PCs. A media-based communications campaign also gave tangible support to these PCs. Finally, HR directors and managers were trained to coach and counsel the PC leaders as well as community members. HR also shared lessons learned within their community with other communities. Success was tracked using e-mail "pulses"—i.e., short, focused questions on employee satisfaction within the firm.

As a result of the PC initiative, employees stayed on the job longer because they felt connected to their community. They could surface professional and work/life issues as well as interact with regional leadership and see change occur as a direct result of their community.

AA is gone now—a casualty of the post-Enron world. Rumor has it that at least one audit community continues to connect people with each other and support each other in times of adversity as well as happiness. It's also rumored that some communities have split into smaller communities and continue their community building even though the firm is gone. It seems they have learned both the power of community and the skills and tenacity to have their community endure in the face of incredible negative forces that, by all accounts, should have killed the community when AA died.

Introduction

Arthur Andersen had a lot to celebrate as the 1990s started. It had successfully separated its audit and management consulting practices in 1989 by forming a new business unit—Andersen Consulting—to focus on management consulting services. In addition, the firm was actively engaged in developing a Knowledge Management capability. This capability would mature as the 1990s progressed, and in 1996 a new business unit would be formed, called the Knowledge Enterprise. In the firm's more than 80-year history, there were only three business units: Arthur Andersen, Andersen Consulting, and now, the Knowledge Enterprise. AA was also starting to experience growth and, correctly, projected enormous growth potential throughout the 1990s. The firm's leaders were projecting 15% a year compounded growth rate in revenues. This would bring the firm's total revenues on a yearly basis to approximately \$7 billion by the end of the 1990s. The firm would need approximately 70,000 employees by decade's end to deliver this volume of services across the globe. Several partners, however, saw some clouds forming on the horizon—clouds that they knew could limit the firm's growth. These visionary partners formed a task force (AA21) representing key geographies and practice specialties such as audit, tax, and business consulting services.

This task force sought input from AA partners and employees as well as external thought leaders who were experts in organizational strategy and tactics. The task force posed a straightforward question: The approach of the 21st century will require that organizations significantly improve their strategy formulation and execution capability—what must AA do to meet the strategy execution challenges of the 21st century? In order to minimize internal conflict and politics, the task force contracted with a consulting firm that was world recognized in working with organizations to improve strategy execution capability. This firm, working with the AA21 task force, designed the data collection content and process, collected the data from firm partners and employees, drafted the report to firm management, and researched best practices in and out of AA's industry. It would take almost two years for the task force to complete its work and report its findings to the Board of Partners for Action.

TASK FORCE STRUCTURE AND APPROACH

The AA21 task force was made up of AA partners and employees, the external consulting firm's engagement staff, and, as a sounding board, the AA Human Resources Continuous Improvement Group, which represented key regions and practice areas.

The study designed and conducted by the external consulting organization had two primary objectives: (1) identify and define the current and projected issues facing Arthur Andersen in executing its strategic vision, and (2) define the role of the global, country, and regional human resources functions in supporting the AA strategic vision.

Their Approach

The contracted firm

- Reviewed the firm's strategy and execution documents at the global, country, and regional level.

- Interviewed senior partners representing global, country, and regional service specialties such as audit, tax, and business consulting services.
- Interviewed (through random selection) employees across the previous demographics.
- Designed a questionnaire for the strategy execution study and a separate questionnaire for the human resources study—stratified sampling was chosen to distribute the questionnaire.
- Reviewed the Arthur Andersen Global Best Practices database as well as external databases for best practices in strategy execution and human resources service delivery.

The task force identified several areas of focus for AA to be successful into the 21st century. The focus of this case is restricted to the task force findings around the AA People Strategy and the human resources function that would be needed to support this People Strategy.

Organizational Context

AA was a complex firm with approximately 40,000 employees and over 1,000 partners worldwide. Over the 1990s, these numbers would grow to over 70,000 employees and 2,000 partners. The firm had offices in over 250 countries. AA was organized into geographic regions and, within a region, by practice specialty. The primary practice specialties were audit, tax, and business consulting services. The CEO of the firm was titled managing partner (MP) of the firm. There were MP titles for region heads, office heads, and head of each practice specialty area.

The task force found several major trends that would need leadership action for the firm to reach its strategy execution goals.

- The firm had made significant progress in improving its competence in executing its strategy. Many regions and practice specialties were high performing or in the process of building high-performance organization capability.

  The firm created a set of metrics to assess its progress toward reaching its strategy execution goals. The firm's strategic plan set goals in four areas:
  ▽ Exceeding client expectations
  ▽ Best people and fulfilling work environment
  ▽ Growth and market share
  ▽ Quality risk management

These four "cornerstones" of the strategy were tracked and measured, and reported to all employees on a quarterly basis (see Table 14-1). Results were summarized yearly and communicated to all employees.

Some measures were computed using the automated internal tracking system—e.g., the number of training hours per employee. Some measures were computed by surveying or "pulsing" employees—e.g., how employees rated partners and managers as mentors. All partners and managers, as leaders of the firm, were expected to set stretch improvement goals in all four cornerstones. Their bonuses and promotions were based on reaching and/or exceeding these stretch goals. The task force pointed out that all measures were high-performing organization measures—even those in the best people and fulfilling work environment category focused on performance and not on quality of life for employees. This focus would come later as AA developed a vision for strategic human resources and an implementation plan based on the task force's findings.

- The firm needed to substantially improve its People Strategy or Employer of Choice capability. Some disturbing trends in the people area had been uncovered:

    ▽ New recruits were joining the firm and leaving sooner than in past experience. The average length of service was declining. This presented ongoing service issues with clients as well as in building a pipeline of talent to grow the firm.

    ▽ Large clients wanted partners handling their accounts and advising senior management. There were not enough potential partners in the pipeline, especially if recruits were leaving the firm in record numbers, since AA was known for "home growing" its partners versus recruiting experienced professionals and directly admitting them as partners into the firm.

This case study focuses on the firm's effort to build a People Strategy (EOC) that would be equivalent in capability to its business performance capability. This would ensure a steady stream of talent needed to sustain the firm's economic growth.

THE BOARD OF PARTNERS AGREES ON ACTIONS

Leading a partnership is difficult under the best of circumstances. In times requiring major change to leadership behaviors, the challenge becomes even more pronounced. The AA Board of Partners

Table 14-1
Tracking High-Performance Organizational Goals

Cornerstone	Measurement Area	Time Period	
		1998 Goal	1998 Actual
Exceeding client expectations	• Client satisfaction survey scores • Percent of client sat. surveys with overall score of 5.0 • Percent of client service teams with continuity (retention of employees)		

Best people and fulfilling work environment	• Retention of top performers
	• Percentage of offers accepted by outstanding recruits
	• Timely performance reviews
	• Number of hours of training per employee
	• Employee satisfaction
	  ○ MNY/NE as a place to work compared with other companies
	  ○ The effectiveness of partners and managers as mentors
	  ○ Employees believe their current position provides them with an opportunity to do challenging and interesting work		

Growth and market share

- Growth in fees
- Net fees per partner
- Earnings per unit
- Income as a percentage of fees
- Billings and collection percentage
- Number of global 1,000 clients (highly desirable large organizations)
- Number of local public companies
- Number of local private clients (dot-com boom)
- Timelines and quality of client risk assessment documentation
- Completeness and quality of annual client risk assessment review process

Quality risk management (Note: This internal analysis is aimed at identifying clients or perspective clients who, because of their business practices, may put AA in jeopardy—e.g., being named in a law suit) rose to the challenge. The global leadership team agreed to transform the HR function through reengineering. A strategic and consultative HR function would be needed to assist partners in developing and deploying a high-performance/Employer of Choice People Strategy. All regions and practice specialties would be encouraged to transform their HR function and prepare their practice for building a people-focused firm.

The existing HR structure, shown in Figure 14-1, had a critical HR leadership gap. The regions within AA did not have a partner-

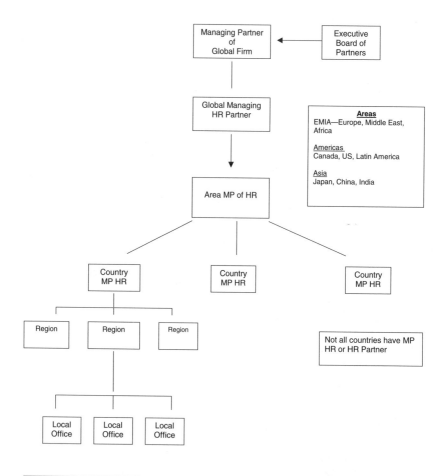

Figure 14-1. Existing HR structure

level HR professional (with the RMP, or regional managing partner) building the EOC strategy with supporting initiatives and processes. Each region and local office within a region was free to handle its own HR issues as it saw fit. Many regions and local offices had people working in HR who did not have training in key HR specialties. The RMP did not have the benefit of a senior HR executive in assessing his region's People Strategy issues and then developing a plan to address those issues. As a result, many people issues were not identified and addressed, which, in turn, caused employees to leave the firm.

When implementing the task force findings, regional managing partners were encouraged to build strategic HR functions by developing local initiatives based on culture and need. The global firm would provide tools, processes, and consulting support to assist regions in developing a short- and long-term transformation plan. Regions would staff locally to use these global supports and to develop local tools, processes, and consulting support to ensure successfully designing and implementing the high-performance organization and Employer of Choice strategy.

THE WORLD-CLASS HR INITIATIVE

We have completed our task force study and are now ready to pilot a strategy that we believe will help us strengthen HR throughout AA. . . . What follows provides you with a substantive overview of what we have learned and where we are headed. . . . World-class HR holds an important key to issues of employee satisfaction, which is directly linked to client satisfaction and to our ability to meet and exceed our growth and profit goals. In short world-class HR links the four cornerstones. (Extract from a memo from *Global HR Managing Partner*, November 1995)

AA found itself at a crossroads. Revenues and profits were soaring. To compete for the best people required to fuel growth, AA must demonstrate its ability to

- Offer outstanding professional opportunities for people with a wide variety of skills.
- Be the Employer of Choice for all demographic groups.
- Operate globally in meeting the needs of its people.

It must achieve this within a context of government regulation and competition for people with firms that are bringing their own HR management into line with business realities.

Arthur Andersen had no possibility of achieving its people-based vision without having in place a solid supporting HR function, because people will drive the firm's future growth.

An extract of the task force's study findings follows.

EXECUTIVE SUMMARY OF STUDY FINDINGS

The current HR function developed out of administrative needs, in an ad hoc fashion, and in a wholly different era of management philosophy and a different external business environment.

Arthur Andersen and the context in which it operates have changed.

- *The firm has changed.* Sources of growth in services are different. Geographic sources of growth have changed. Optimal staffing and other economic models for success have changed. The business can no longer be run by part-time line participation and low-level administrators.
- *The people at AA have changed.* They and the prime potential recruits are much more diverse than in the past. They want more balance between career and personal lives. The prospect of partnership may not be a career goal any longer for many.
- *The business environment has changed.* AA, its clients, and its competitors are more global. Competition for people with a global perspective and the ability to operate across national and cultural boundaries is more keen. Highly qualified people no longer hesitate to leave employers, even ones of long standing.

The gap between the current HR management model and the current operating context is significant. The business unit suffers as a result.

- There is no formal HR strategy, developed with and designed to support business strategy. Relevant HR considerations are not deliberated in tandem with strategic business issues.
- HR issues are not identified and resolved in a systematic fashion.
- AA is not doing an adequate job of retaining the best people.

- Most locations view HR people as administrators only.
- HR people must usually depend on line partners to champion their initiatives and effect their implementation.
- Partners are overburdened with tasks that could be handled by people with specific HR expertise.
- Line personnel, especially partners, do not get the assistance they need to address the HR issues effectively.
- HR capabilities are not adequate for providing the level of service and support suitable to a worldwide, world-class organization, and they are inconsistent from location to location.
- Most HR people do not have the skills or tools they need to provide a high level of professional, value-added service to their "clients" within AA.

None of the requirements for effective competition for the best people can be met with the current structure and mode of managing human resources.

- A strong, credible HR function, serving in a consultative/ strategic rather than merely administrative capacity will remedy these problems. The new role for the HR function is to position HR professionals as "trusted business advisors" to line management.
- People management remains a line management responsibility.

The firm's Board of Partners agreed that a key step in implementing the task force's findings was to fix the HR structure. The Board of Partners approved the new structure, shown in Figure 14-2.

Each region was authorized to formally set up a partner-level HR position for the region and a partner or director of HR position for larger local offices as well. The Board of Partners, however, did not mandate this change but recommended it. Each RMP was free to accept the change or reject it.

Three years had passed since the AA21 task force and the external consulting firm started doing their work. The task force took two years, and internal discussion at the firm's leadership level took another year. The managing partner of the Metro New York and North East Region (MNY/NE—Boston, Hartford, and the Cayman Islands, in addition to the five boroughs of New York City; Stamford, Connecticut; and Roseland, New Jersey) wanted action and not more discussion.

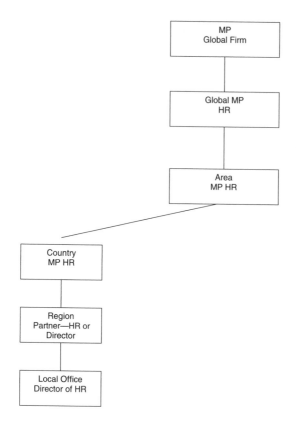

Figure 14-2. World-class HR—proposed HR structure

THE METRO NY/NORTH EAST REGION EXPERIMENT

The MP of MNY/NE was on the AA21 task force and, in the process of going through its work, became a true believer in the HR/People Strategy solution recommended and approved by his fellow members of the Board of Partners.

We are proud of the people we've attracted to our practice [firm] and know we have to do more to help make their experience and professional development at AA more valuable and enjoyable not only to keep them here, but to help move us [AA] and share with us in the next levels of [business] success.

He made the decision in late 1994 to go out of the industry to recruit a partner-level HR executive (HRE) to organize and lead the HR reengineering transformation and to design, develop, and deploy a locally appropriate People Strategy and supporting initiatives. This HRE joined the firm in October 1995. He would be the HR partner responsible for the region as well as the local offices within the region, as recommended by the task force. A critical component of the task force recommendations was to include a senior organizational development consultant to work with the HRE in designing, developing, and deploying regional appropriate initiatives and, as important, to work with the global firm's HR transformation team.

I joined the MNY/NE as the director of HR Planning and Strategy in the summer of 1996. Life would never be the same for me or AA and the MNY/NE region. We started immediately building an HPO/EOC strategy and implementation plan. The MNY/NE region was growing rapidly in new business acquisition and in promoting new partners. The employee pipeline, however, was getting worse. Employee retention rates were falling, and pools of available candidates were shrinking. Accounting graduates were opting to go to investment banks and management consulting firms rather than to audit firms like AA. AA partners had agreed to recruiting and directly admitting partner-level candidates rather than waiting for the pipeline to catch up with the need to field partners for large-client engagements. AA's competitors were also facing a similar crisis and were responding at the local level versus the regional or global firm level. Partnerships are private companies, so the exact nature of their response is unknown. This seemingly straightforward business decision would come back to haunt AA up to and including its Enron experience.

In October 1996, we presented our HR strategy and implementation plan to the RMP and his four partners responsible for the MNY/NE region (see Table 14-2). They approved our work, and we next presented our plan to all MNY/NE region partners—approximately 130 in total. It would take until May 1997 to secure all partners' agreement to our strategy and plan. Although we developed a full spectrum of HR strategies and plans, this case focuses on our using Practice Communities (PC) initiative to build a membership firm

Table 14-2
AA Timeline for Strategic Human Resource Initiatives
MNY/NE Region

July 1996	Formulate HPO/EOC People Strategy
October 1996	Present to RMP and 4 senior partners
May 1997	Announce to MNY/NE region employees HPO/EOC—Bonus for all employees
October 1997	Present Balanced Scorecard Performance Management (BSC) for MNY/NE partners to okay—decision deferred
April 1998	Represent BSC—Approval for immediate implementation May 1998
October 1998	Practice Communities (PC) initiative presented to partners—approved for winter pilot and spring '99 implementation
April 1999	PC pilots evaluated and concept refined—May 1999 started implementation across all practice areas
April 2000	All practice areas have PCs up and running

rather than seeing the firm as a place to get your initial job experience for one to three years and then to move on to your "real" career.

USING PCs TO BUILD A MEMBERSHIP FIRM

A message from the RMP:

As part of the Metro New York People Strategy—to grow and sustain a High Performance Organization and become an Employer of Choice by focusing on people—Practice Communities provide the opportunity for everyone (Partners and Employees together) to develop a sense of purpose and feeling of membership within their Division, their Segment, Metro New York, and the Firm. By focusing on relationships and the work environment, Practice Communities will play a critical role in helping to grow and retain a high performing team.

Each of us in Metro New York must be committed to creating and sustaining our relationships and a work environment that sustains both a high performing and Employer of Choice firm. Practice Communities, successfully implemented, will ensure that Metro New York's "the best place to do great work."

The MNY/NE PC design and deployment strategy called for two parallel tracks to be worked on:

- Design of the PC, which included a working definition of PCs, a detailed implementation plan for PC leaders (all partners in AA), and training for human resources facilitators (AA HR directors and managers)
- A comprehensive communications package, which included a print package for PC leaders and members for reference, and a humorous video starring AA partners and a puppet named "Rodney Rather Not"

Prior to the PC deployment, all MNY/NE partners were briefed on the PC initiative, its goals, structure, process, roles, and, most important, measures for success. PCs would be implemented in phases. The audit practice would start the deployment by piloting six PCs, each having 45 to 50 employees. The pilots would be evaluated, and the concept refined and then deployed across the MNY/NE region. Three critical roles were defined to ensure the success of the PC initiative (see Figure 14-3).

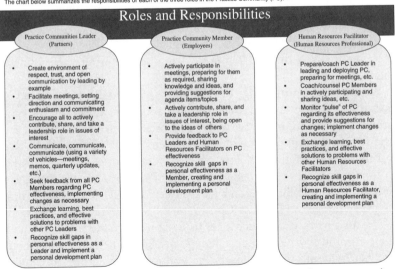

Figure 14-3. *Who is involved in making your practice community a reality?*

Practice Communities will differ across and within divisions with respect to their structure, their objectives, and how they are implemented. While no two Communities will "feel" exactly alike, there are several common key steps (see below) to consider within each Community to successfully implement and sustain the Community.

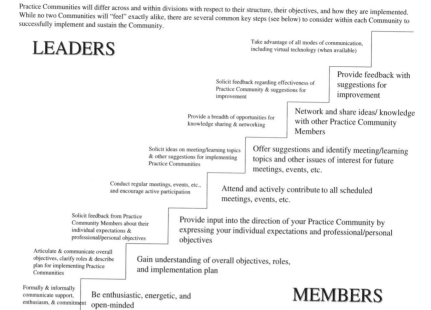

LEADERS

Take advantage of all modes of communication, including virtual technology (when available)

Solicit feedback regarding effectiveness of Practice Community & suggestions for improvement

Provide feedback with suggestions for improvement

Provide a breadth of opportunities for knowledge sharing & networking

Network and share ideas/ knowledge with other Practice Community Members

Solicit ideas on meeting/learning topics & other suggestions for implementing Practice Communities

Offer suggestions and identify meeting/learning topics and other issues of interest for future meetings, events, etc.

Conduct regular meetings, events, etc., and encourage active participation

Attend and actively contribute to all scheduled meetings, events, etc.

Solicit feedback from Practice Community Members about their individual expectations & professional/personal objectives

Provide input into the direction of your Practice Community by expressing your individual expectations and professional/personal objectives

Articulate & communicate overall objectives, clarify roles & describe plan for implementing Practice Communities

Gain understanding of overall objectives, roles, and implementation plan

Formally & informally communicate support, enthusiasm, & commitment

Be enthusiastic, energetic, and open-minded

MEMBERS

Figure 14-4. Key steps to implement and sustain the community

HR facilitators were trained with the PC leaders to organize a start-up meeting utilizing the communications package. The start-up meeting focused on the key steps for implementing their PC (see Figure 14-4).

At the start-up meeting, PC participants decided on frequency of meetings, duration, and location. In addition, they agreed on a process for communicating with each other between meetings, and finally they determined the objectives/focus of their PC. Each PC had a different HR facilitator. The HR facilitators agreed to meet and to keep communities informed of the other PC communities' objectives and activities. Rodney Rather Not (in the rollout video) said it best: "At the core of the Practice Communities is one word—connections. We want everyone at every level to be connected with the people in their community, with their clients, with industry news and trends, and with Arthur Andersen. To be connected, everyone has got to lend a hand. One hand can be strong, but not as strong as two or three, or 30."

Early Wins

Five of the six pilot PCs, from the beginning, immediately connected. The sixth never worked and eventually disbanded. Tax, business consulting services, and shared support such as HR, IT, graphics, and accounting started forming PCs and sought advice from the audit PCs. PCs were generating an enormous amount of positive energy throughout the region. The rest of the firm took notice and started tracking the MNY/NE PCs to see if the concept could be transferred. Ultimately, the global firm did not implement the PC concept. The global firm's leadership governance model was decentralized—i.e., each country's and local office's managing partners were free to adopt, or not, initiatives suggested by the Board of Partners.

Measuring PC Success

Measuring the success of our Practice Communities was critical to the region's receiving the full benefit from deploying the communities. By taking the time in the short term to evaluate how our PCs were doing, we could make the necessary modifications to meet the communities' needs and to maximize their effectiveness and success in the long run.

We collected the PC member's ratings of the following:

- Increased learning on topics of relevance—business development; industry trends, products, and services; best practices; leadership; and human resources issues
- Enhanced feeling by individuals of "connectedness" in a supportive environment
- Greater individual feeling of being self-directed
- Greater understanding by individuals of who they are and how they fit into their segment/division and the firm
- Increased length of service of our colleagues

This data was collected (using short e-mail—pulses) and summarized by the HR directors and managers, shared with the partners, and then shared across all communities. Open and transparent communications was the mantra. An example of a pulse question would be: Rate how effective your Practice Community leader is in establishing an environment of trust and open communication. We used a scale in which 5 meant very effective and 1 meant not effective at

The Service Value Chain—Linking Practice Communities to the Business

Everybody Benefits from Practice Communities

You

Gain
Greater professional
and personal satisfaction
in your work life.

The Firm

Achieves
Higher profits, lower
costs, and increased
retention of our people
and clients.

Our Clients

Receive
World-class service.

Together

*We create more resources and opportunities
for everyone to share in.*

Figure 14-5. The service value chain

all. Our long-term measurement plan called for expanding our measures to the firm and clients along with employee satisfaction measures (see Figure 14-5).

Our plan was to develop a set of measures and corresponding pulse questions aimed at measuring employees' perceptions in the larger firm context (not just PCs) as well as how PCs better enabled us to serve our clients.

LESSONS LEARNED

All organizational initiatives that are designed to improve or reinforce an Employer of Choice People Strategy can provide insight into what's working and what's not in building the culture. PCs are no exception. Following are the primary lessons learned.

Up-front planning for the pilots was insufficient to carry the PCs into full implementation. The PC pilots touched a positive nerve in the firm. The demand for PCs, once the word spread, was too much for the partners (as potential PC leaders) and HR directors and managers to deliver on effectively. In addition, my function was not staffed fully to close the service gap. Planning scenarios for little or lukewarm reception to PCs as well as for the other end of the spectrum—"You can't deliver new PCs fast enough to meet demand" prior to pilot release—would have been helpful.

In a similar vein, *solutions for a PC that was failing to gel were needed*. Our one pilot PC that simply didn't connect was a test for all of us involved in the deployment. In the heat of pilot deployment (in addition to other People Strategy initiatives like the Balanced Scorecard, strategic partner/employee orientation, etc.), we simply didn't have a plan for working through a PC failure in its early formation. We possibly overreacted by closing it down quickly and moving the people to other communities. We never went back to find out what went wrong—too little time, too few people to collect the data, no interest in knowing what went wrong from the partners.

We didn't have sufficient technology resources for PCs to collect their thoughts and actions to relook at later or to share across other PCs. Minutes were taken by hand with no one person responsible in an ongoing role. Our HR facilitators took it upon themselves to meet and connect the PCs across each other. They reported back to their PC what they learned at those meetings. In six months, my team could only attend one such meeting of HR facilitators. Identifying common issues and solutions across PCs would have enabled us to present the partners with a stronger case for change and may have expedited the change around people issues.

On a positive note, as a practicing organizational development professional, I was stunned by the immediate acceptance of the PCs by almost every employee involved. Employees, who at many other times displayed significant apathy toward HR-deployed tools, processes, and programs, couldn't get enough of PC stuff—i.e., community meetings and reporting to the partners action steps needed to "fix" the firm. One member summarized the impact of PCs: "[Before PCs] I could say goodbye to Arthur Andersen, but how could you say goodbye to this group?"

In closing, I must say that the RMP was certainly a catalyst for transforming the MNY/NE region. He was one of the visionary partners who saw the need for AA to significantly change as the 21st century was approaching. Yet, AA was a partnership, with each partner having a vote on things that affected their business. They owned their partnership and were not professional managers of the stockholders' business. The RMP never wavered in his vision and used his power and influence in a positive way to win over his partners—sometimes one partner at a time. This shared vision of the senior leadership certainly contributed to the overall success of PCs as well as the other People Strategy initiatives we designed and deployed. It's as close to working for Jack Welsh of GE as I will ever get.

Jack Welsh is a visionary leader. He sees the need for change and then changes himself first, before asking others to change. He leads by example, which is a key characteristic needed of Practice Community leaders. The RMP was also a visionary leader. He saw the need for AA to get a lot better at the EOC/People Strategy side of business. He changed himself first before asking others to change. He led by example. It was inspiring for me to be part of his leadership team.

EPILOGUE

Why did the MNY/NE partners accept the PC concept so quickly? In reflecting on this, I go back to the AA strategic plan—the Foundation of Our Future—which identified Knowledge Management (KM) as a core competency of the firm. AA was an early adopter of the KM concept. They created the AA Global Best Practices database, which electronically stored their solutions to client issues. Clients frequently sought access to this database, which codified AA's explicit and tacit knowledge. Many top executives and some of the world's leading business entities have utilized this KM service. In early 1997, AA correctly predicted the growth of the Web and created a new business unit for the KM practice. Partners and employees were encouraged to contribute their knowledge to the KM practice and were recognized for doing so. An award-winning Web service was created—Knowledge Space—for codifying internal and external knowledge around key business topics and then connecting client subscribers to the appropriate database. This Web site also connected you to a network of people interested in a specific topic. Knowledge Space then connected you to the Virtual Learning Network, where appropriate e-learning courses were available.

For AA, knowledge creation and sharing was a way of life—supported by the partners and the culture. AA was on a mission to help its clients improve their business performance through knowledge creation and sharing. The firm's leadership was energized over what the next millennium would bring to AA, its partners, employees, and clients. They recognized that people were key to reaching their vision of the firm in the 21st century. They had a plan, and some partners were starting to implement that plan.

AA is gone now, killed in action in the post-Enron world. I often reflect that if PCs had been more prevalent throughout the firm, AA would still be out there doing what it did best—serving clients with technical expertise and integrity. That's the AA that I know.

Stephen John joined Aventis as head of Global Organization Effectiveness in 2001. He is responsible for designing and deploying high-performance organization initiatives across the functions and regions of Aventis.

Dr. John joined Aventis from Brown Brothers Harriman, a Wall Street–based financial service firm, where he was senior vice president of HR Planning and Strategy. He was responsible for designing and deploying a global employee opinion survey and a performance and rewards philosophy and system, and working with senior management on a number of organizational effectiveness initiatives. Steve has also worked with senior leadership at Andersen, UBS Warburg, Marsh & McLennan, and Coopers & Lybrand in designing and deploying high-performance organization strategies. Strategies designed and deployed include talent management including leadership development, creating change leaders throughout the organization, Balanced Scorecard performance management and reward systems, business process reengineering, communities of practice for knowledge creation and sharing, diversity through mentoring, and recruiting for values. Steve has a doctorate in Organizational Leadership and Learning from Columbia University. He has an MBA/CPA, specializing in tax M&A.

ACKNOWLEDGMENTS

I would like to thank James J. Minogue Jr., partner in charge of HR MNY/NE region. Jim recruited me into AA, and together we developed the People Strategy that would move the region into Employer of Choice status. His vision of what AA could be was an inspiration to me. I would also like to thank Dr. Francine Deutsch, who I recruited to work with me in the HR Strategy and Development function. Francine and I created and deployed the PC concept. It was only possible because of her dedication to the work as well as her sense of humor in handling setbacks. Many thanks to Bob Schachat, who encouraged me to write about my experiences. Finally, I would like to acknowledge Carol Gorelick, who introduced me to the wonderful world of Knowledge Management and to communities of practice. Without her coaching, there wouldn't have been any PCs at AA.

CHAPTER 15

Piloting Knowledge Management: Lessons Learned from the Small-Scale Approach to Design and Implementation at ETS

By Felicia DeVincenzi and T. J. Elliott

Starting small is now seen as a wise strategy in Knowledge Management (KM) projects because of both the complexity of the domain and the difficulties encountered in more global approaches, especially related to obtaining returns on investments. When Educational Testing Service (ETS) sought to advance its management of knowledge, it commenced that effort with several KM pilots. This case study reports on the approach to designing, developing, implementing, and evaluating those pilots.

CORPORATE OVERVIEW

Educational Testing Service is the world's largest private educational testing and measurement organization and a leader in educational research. The company is dedicated to serving the needs of individuals, educational institutions, and government bodies in almost 200 countries. ETS develops and administers more than 12 million tests worldwide.

Traditionally, ETS's primary purpose has been the development of tests and other assessment tools to provide information (including test scores and interpretative data) to test takers, educational institutions, and others who require this information. ETS is now poised to broaden its scope beyond the United States measurement space into the worldwide education and training space.

BUSINESS HIGHLIGHTS

While ETS has grown from $400 to $700 million in revenues in the last five years through its expanded services, the more important aspect of this growth is its effect on our mission. Through the pursuit and publication of research that no other organization in the field can match, ETS has opened inquiries into the nature of learning so that individuals can make more successful educational and career transitions throughout their lives.

That same research has led to innovative products and services that more directly connect measurement of knowledge and skills to the promotion of learning and performance. ETS has sought through its myriad activities to support education and professional development for all people worldwide. Therefore, ETS initiatives have helped advance quality and equity in education not just by providing fair and valid summative assessments, but also through formative assessment—by providing helpful information and tools that lead to more effective teaching approaches and help learners understand their strengths and areas for improvement. Our Knowledge Management efforts must serve those aims; the more effective and efficient we are, the more we figure out how to harness what we know to improve our performance, the more we can pursue the research that will change people's lives.

DRIVERS FOR THE DEVELOPMENT OF THE KNOWLEDGE MANAGEMENT PROGRAM OR INITIATIVE

It has been written that all organizations manage knowledge; the question is whether they do so systematically and successfully. What constitutes success might differ slightly from one organization to another. At ETS, with the help of our CIO, Arthur Chisholm, we imagined a goal line of connecting knowledge seekers to knowledge sources, of moving beyond a state in which individuals hold data to one in which groups share information in such a way that the organization as a whole gains stocks of useful knowledge. The specific drivers for pursuing KM in a more deliberate way starting in 2001 were diverse.

Our CEO, Kurt Landgraf, recognized that the innovation we wanted to bring to the pursuit of learning throughout the world would not occur unless our researchers, educators, technologists, and administrators collaborated more effectively. As Landgraf pointed out, ETS is an organization where the main assets "card out" every night—our power is in the knowledge of our people. In part because of this challenge, Landgraf created a new executive position at ETS, Chief Learning Officer, and recruited T. J. Elliott for the post. Elliott was charged with ensuring that learning at ETS be strategically driven, supporting the achievement of ETS's long-range business goals and social mission.

Like other organizations with many baby boomers, we were experiencing the gradual aging of our employee population and the exiting of experts in the field from the organization. At the same time, we needed safeguards for the more anomalous events, such as a key employee winning the Powerball lottery. (It hasn't happened yet, but we're all still buying tickets.)

More specifically, we knew through both anecdotes and the organization chart that there were many people at ETS who worked with similar domains (e.g., test-question construction, marketing of educational services, proposal writing, or project management) who lacked the structures or practices to collaborate seamlessly with each other. We also had some knowledge that their individual or group efforts were not always as successful as we desired. In other words, we possessed some evidence that their management of knowledge would improve their performance.

PLANNING

These drivers led us to form a cross-divisional Knowledge Management Working Group (KMWG) and charge it with examining the problems and opportunities we faced. On the one hand, we had little in the way of existing initiatives or practices that would serve as a platform for cross-divisional efforts, nor was there a KM infrastructure and funding source in place (one area, the Center for Education in Assessment, CEA, was an exception to this condition, with its enormously useful collections of tips and tricks for staff who worked in the test-creation process). On the other hand, we had pressing needs and a mandate to address them from the company's senior leadership.

The KMWG was fortunate in that a specific opportunity emerged. One of the group's members was asked to facilitate the second half of an After Action Review (AAR). The review was done subsequent to a failed response to a governmental request for proposal (RFP). This demand for an AAR allowed the group to begin its first pilot project surrounding the process for responding to proposals at ETS.

THE FIRST WAVE: BEST PRACTICES IN RESPONDING TO RFPs

We began the project with a combined approach, which was achieved through the collection of practices as well as through process mapping. Subject matter experts (SMEs) responding to RFPs were invited to participate in a process mapping session under the sponsorship of our sales vice president, Chuck Cascio. The invitation to them emphasized that the session was about the transfer of the SMEs' expertise and experience to one another. Existing materials were solicited and located. Participants came from each of our divisions, which at that time were named according to program areas: K–12, Graduate and Professional Education, School and College Services, Teaching and Learning, and Chauncey Group International (now Capstar), a for-profit subsidiary that offers assessment to industry and professional associations. Effective responses to proposals require additional technical information from divisions that would support implementation of any eventual contracts. Therefore, we also solicited input and existing process documentation from our Centers of Excellence (IS&T, Operations, Finance, and Research).

We facilitated several meetings during which we collected and mapped the various steps in the RFP response processes within which our meeting participants worked. We discovered certain characteristics of the knowledge at ETS on how to respond to an RFP.

- *It was fragmented.* Few divisions had a single document on process. There were many different documents in many different locations in many different forms.
- *It was largely tacit.* Although some artifacts existed in all divisions, there were gaps in information that could only be filled by personally interviewing another employee. Because

important information was not codified explicitly, there was insufficient succession planning for those who had expertise in the process; it was nearly impossible for someone new to join the process and gain the knowledge needed to work independently.

- *It was contradictory.* Processes were conducted very differently in each program. There was almost no comparison of processes among the programs.
- *It was conflictual.* The program divisions had processes that conflicted with requirements the various Centers of Excellence had in their processes.
- *It was incomplete.* Although one group had a process broken into phases, all set the process as beginning only at RFP issuance and ending at proposal submission without preparation or evaluation (e.g., lessons learned from the After Action Review).

From the meeting notes and artifacts that were shared by participants, a small subset of SMEs prepared a "strawperson" process in the form of bulleted points: a collation of best practices for responding to RFPs. The collation was drawn from many sources within ETS divisions; all of the practices were from existing documents. No new practices were suggested.

To prepare for the next meeting, several SMEs helped us to convert the collated items into tasks. We printed each of them out for placement on the wall of the meeting room, so that the entire group of experts could see this graphic illustration when they entered the room.

Participants came prepared to share at least one lesson learned about RFP response. Using low-tech tools such as butcher paper, placards, tape, and markers in that four-hour session, the participants then created a subsequent rough draft of a process map for responding to RFPs. They broke the process into phases that began before the issuance of a request for proposal, went through the development and submission of a proposal, and ended with an evaluation of the effort—i.e., an After Action Review.

Initial Results

We learned several important lessons from this almost-accidental KM effort. First, the SMEs were the key ingredient, but gathering them together was not easy. We needed to get the most out of the times when we had them together. Most of them were senior staff with many responsibilities and had very busy schedules. A combination of powerful sponsorship and satisfaction of their self-interests was necessary. The latter would come from making sure that they received some gain out of attending sessions, whether it was face-to-face or virtual. The benefits that mattered most to the SMEs were the opportunity to talk about what it was they did with others who cared about the subject and the chance to eliminate or ameliorate what they perceived to be overall organizational obstacles to their work.

Second, the documentation and facilitation of such efforts is time and labor intensive. We were reminded in this project that one should find a way to get the most output with the least effort by having the right technologies available as content emerges. In this case, however, absent a specific budget for KM, our initial efforts required us to beg, borrow, and "liberate" resources. Preplanning of such activities had to be done carefully to ensure that the insights and ideas of invited SMEs were efficiently and accurately captured.

Moreover, achieving a balance between the best technology for capturing information and the one that seems most congenial to participants was critical. The two are likely not the same. For example, Lotus Notes databases or collaborative environments such as Quick-Place might prove most efficient for such projects; however, expecting SMEs to learn how to use them or to find time in their schedules to visit the site to see the notes accumulated that day may be unrealistic. (At ETS, we have a substantial technological infrastructure, but its adoption is irregular among our various divisions.) On the other hand, having scads of paper with multiple markings without the resources to convert the mess into accessible and understandable Knowledge Assets is also useless. At ETS, the right balance is likely to shift, depending on the groups of SMEs and their skill in using collaborative computing tools.

Third, the process mapping was a useful activity for revealing gaps in necessary knowledge for an ad hoc group such as this. Workgroups to construct proposals are by definition cross-divisional. SMEs in Finance, Corporate Contracts, and IT combined with their colleagues in a particular business area—e.g., K–12 testing or professional licensing. Then sales and marketing functions were also added to the mix. We learned from the mapping that individuals possessed some data, information, and knowledge that allowed them to create their part of the proposal. However, by tracking their work along a workflow, we could more easily see the ways in which those decisions might have been delayed or even flawed by a lack of all relevant information at the right time. Effective sharing of certain elements of knowledge, even among the members within the same division, was, in some cases, limited; and yet it was critical for effective decision making.

Throughout this collaboration, related and sometimes redundant initiatives were uncovered. For example, two workflow-type databases were in the design stage, and both supported different segments of response to RFP work; however, the designers and stakeholders for one were not aware of the other effort, and vice versa. Another database with important marketing information informed by the sales and marketing segment of the process was already in the prototype phase. Although it could play a key role in the response to RFP overall strategy, it was not integrated into the other two databases.

Fourth, and most influential to our subsequent KM work, we realized that the place where KM might have the most effect was in the making of decisions. As we roughed out the process map, we identified a number of junctures where people need to make choices of action. Delays at these points are damaging or even fatal to the chances of the resulting proposal. The pilot project confirmed that gathering the knowledge necessary to make the best decisions was an issue. We started to discover artifacts—tools that single divisions employed to help make decisions—that would prove important in our later building of a knowledge asset. As this pilot progressed, a direction for a broader KM strategy emerged: The focus for KM at ETS in the short term should be how to make better decisions.

Decision Making as a KM Focus

The ad hoc groups charged with responding to an RFP would need templates for making their decisions. The initial RFP best-practices effort revealed that disagreement existed among divisions on the proper procedures for response and the data needed to determine go/no-go decisions for continuing to pursue an RFP at various points in the process.

One division divided the response effort into phases; others did not. (In their mapping meeting, the SMEs quickly agreed that the response process was both longer and more involved than any of their individual guides to response creation actually stated.) One division had tools that it used to visualize the overall proposal; others eschewed that approach. The necessary documents to construct a response were in some cases redundant. In other cases, this necessary material was hard to locate and needed to be drawn from a variety of sources, including the minds of experts in some area of the proposal domain. The redundancy of key material was due to one individual not knowing that a colleague had already compiled a knowledge asset relevant to work that they both do. The scarcity of material was due to a lack of knowledge in some cases as to who knows what in each domain of the organization's products. The ad hoc groups needed help to become more effective.

The group proposed that a Web-delivered workflow database that managed the proposal response as it progressed throughout the process, housed boilerplate and project management tools, and archived lessons learned through the AAR was a critical need for the success of the initiative. Since this was one of the three databases at the early design stage at ETS, the group's support of the concept was valuable for making design specifications more concrete and promoting the importance of it to the executive sponsor.

Attending to Small Successes

This pilot also reinforced for us the notion that our efforts should aim to gain small successes. In this we were guided by the cautions of Udai Shekawat,[1] who, writing in the online version of *Knowledge Management* magazine, warned of the "Big Bang" approach. Shekawat notes that large projects take months or years to complete. During that time, changes abound both inside and outside of any work organization. By the time the project is finished, the needs of all involved may have changed dramatically. A staged or pilot project approach would allow our KMWG "to minimize the risk and prove the value in increments before the company increases its investment enterprisewide." Moreover, the practicality of the approach appealed to us. It squared with what Siemens advised from the records of its KM work: Get the knowledge of the organization assembled, and apply it to problems that you face.[2] Our task then was to decide which knowledge-intensive decisions could most benefit from the application of KM efforts.

---

[1] Udai Shekawat, "Five Mistakes CKOs Must Avoid" (2002); available at http://www.destinationkm.com/.
[2] Thomas H. Davenport and Gilbert J. B. Probst, eds., *Knowledge Management Case Book: Siemens Best Practices, Second Edition* (New York: John Wiley & Sons, 2002).

THE SECOND WAVE: THE KNOWLEDGE-INTENSIVE DECISIONS INQUIRY

The KMWG concluded that the next step in KM should focus on discovering what the overall critical decisions were for ETS leadership and the knowledge domains to which they were connected. The RFP best-practice pilot had taught us that decisions were important instances where tacit knowledge is applied. In the response process, there had been explicit go/no-go decision junctures, but discussion revealed that many other, less evident decisions informed those more prominent go/no-go decision points. In this new wave of KM exploration, the pilot experience led us to attend to decisions that were not only the responsibility of an *individual* but also the province of a group. We decided to elicit judgments on this subject from the key people in the organization. In this way, we would be able to uncover the types of knowledge that would best facilitate decision making if they were better generated and transmitted.

Data Gathering

Through a Web-delivered survey, we asked colleagues at ETS who make the most important decisions and who follow the largest business opportunities what they felt they needed to know to operate effectively. Our steps were as follows:

1. Construct a brief e-mail survey on the most critical knowledge-dependent decisions within ETS. (See the survey draft in the following sidebar.) Distribute the survey to the list of ETS directors used in communications by the ETS Office of the President.
2. Analyze data collected from the survey. Extrapolate from responses to conclusions about possible decisions that are critical.
3. Mine data from other interviews carried out for other purposes, such as the construction of our e-business plan, in order to see what decision making or Knowledge Management capacity is mentioned.

The following e-mail communication invited executive directors across the corporation to complete the online survey:

Greetings:

In support of certain Long Range Operating Plan objectives, our group—the Knowledge Management Working Group—is requesting your help. In an initial effort to build a greater and more organized Knowledge Management capability at ETS, we are seeking information from key ETS personnel. Specifically, we want to know your opinion of the most critical decisions made at ETS.

Our premise is that many important decisions are knowledge intensive; the decision maker needs to know certain things in order to select the best possible course of action. However, many of those decisions are not unique. They arise from problems or opportunities that someone at ETS previously has seen in some other form. An individual or group, therefore, can take advantage of existing knowledge—the learning and expertise of another individual or group—if he or she is aware of and has access to that knowledge. Consequently, we are seeking to catalogue the decisions that are most important to the organization in order to determine the knowledge required for them. That determination will allow us to target these decisions for our initial efforts, which in turn will provide the greatest return for our efforts. Your opinions about the most important decisions are vital to this effort. The survey is brief. Please fill out the survey below by _____.

The survey itself specified the criteria for nominating a decision as critical: (1) The decision involves choices of action that, if made incorrectly, would expose ETS to substantial risk or negative consequences, such as loss of money, opportunity, capacity, or assets; and (2) the decision involves choices of action that require large chunks of knowledge or information.

The types of questions in the survey were mostly open ended, although possible categories of decisions were presented to the respondents. Those categories included, but were not limited to, the following:

- Reducing costs
- Pricing products
- Executing projects
- Building business

- Evaluating strategies
- Developing products
- Evaluating people
- Driving revenues

We also asked the respondents to tell us what currently existed to help make these decisions: What are the documents, courses, processes, methods, databases, and business patterns already out there? In other words, what are the knowledge assets? What is their maturity level? Do we possess any measures of these assets?

Of those directors invited to respond, approximately 100 people (over 50%) completed the survey. The resulting nominated decisions were sorted into six categories that ranged from "how to incorporate a new technology for assessment" to "how to crack our largest market opportunity." However, somewhat to our surprise, decisions around whether and how to respond to RFPs showed up in great number. We had not expected the RFP process to have such prominence.

Determining Value and Risk

The KMWG met to consider the data and its implications for the KM approach. All of the top categories were analyzed using a value-matrix exercise. The tool for this was a simple matrix. The two axes of the matrix were (1) the value to the organization that would be provided by aiding effective decision making in a particular domain and (2) the risk of initiating such an effort (i.e., the likelihood of its success). Factors that entered into a consideration of risk were the cost of embarking on such an initiative, the complexity of the decision realm, and the kinds of technologies available for application to that type of decision.

Through discussion, each of the top decision categories was positioned within the matrix. We then focused on the decision categories that fell in the quadrant of the matrix that represented highest value and lowest risk as the most appropriate pilot project (see Figure 15-1). The surprise for us was that the response-to-RFPs process again emerged. This was where individuals on the KMWG judged the best possibility of KM having an impact in the short term.

In a subsequent meeting, with the help of an outside facilitator, Carol Gorelick of SOLUTIONS, we created a project plan for moving forward to support RFP decision making, with an emphasis on the expected short-term return and the resources required. The

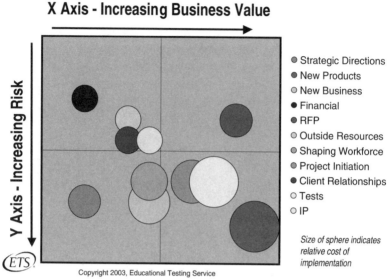

Figure 15-1. Value matrix: implementation risk and value

KMWG had very limited resources with which to pursue this initiative. However, we were able to gather enough resources to build a knowledge asset that would better identify the decisions involved in this pilot domain and aid the more effective and efficient making of decisions in that domain.

The Third Wave: Construction of the Knowledge Asset

We brought the RFP community of SMEs together again to look more specifically at what the tacit decisions were in the phases of the process, what knowledge was needed to make those decisions effectively, and the person or location where the information might be found.

As a follow-up to the initial RFP best-practices work, Felicia DeVincenzi and her staff had distilled the paper-and-pencil maps that the group had created in that first wave of KM activity and constructed a streamlined workflow in responding to an RFP (see Figure 15-2). It was then published in a one-dimensional, flat form on an ETS internal Web site, with companion Web pages, including additional meeting discussion content. In a communication to the SMEs,

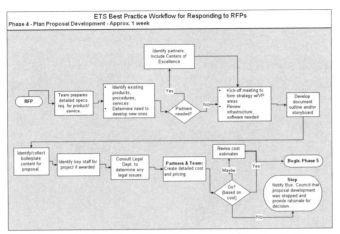

Figure 15-2. Workflow for responding to RPFs

DeVincenzi invited them to critique the map and to suggest improvements and revisions. She noted the goals of this pass at the process mapping.

- Help a viewer (especially an uninitiated viewer) see at a glance the overall process.
- Publish details about tools, regulations, requirements, and people's roles in companion documents.
- Show more clearly how the output of one phase provides input for the following one.
- Show how a go/no-go decision at each phase is informed by different or additional information.
- Show the interdependency and collaborations across the VP areas and the various centers of excellence.
- Emphasize (in the first phase) the criticality of clear business development strategies for an efficient, effective process down the line.

In studying the content from the discussion from the best-practices meeting for the purpose of improving the workflow depiction, DeVincenzi reduced the number of phases (originally 10) to five. Additionally, she was able to organize the content into a more comprehensive process design, including components that go beyond workflow: goals, metrics, people (knowledge, skills, and motivation), parameters (time frame and workflow), organizational structure (organization design and hierarchies), physical space (meeting rooms and location of ad hoc members), and tools.

Several implications emerged that impacted process design. Vice presidents of the business units at ETS function as general managers and set their divisions' business-development targets. The responsibility for business development and its companion goals are therefore dispersed across ETS. If goals for business development are dispersed, it is hard to agree on goals for a common response-to-RFP process; consequently, it is not possible to agree on measurements or metrics for the process. For example, some ad hoc members believed a particular phase in the process should only take two days, while others believed that five days was a reasonable target.

Additionally, a single process owner was needed to manage the process. Temporarily, two members of the best-practices group were identified as the key owners of the process design while clarification was sought on the process owner.

The content of the tools discussion comprised a wish list of functionality for collaborative computing and pointed directly to the need for a Lotus Notes workflow database that would manage the flow of proposal development and house templates, boilerplate, and bios of key resources. Everyone also agreed that the graphic mapping of the process and documentation of process activities and procedures for delivery on the Web should move forward as well.

PROBLEMS/CONCERNS

Several months into the project, although many of the SMEs had argued for the creation of a workflow database that would include the various elements of each RFP and track its development, the business climate had changed. (Approximately six months had passed since the start of the KMWG.) It was deemed unfeasible to pursue that technological tool. The costs of building the database in Lotus Notes and then maintaining it were judged too high. The resources needed to go elsewhere. One of the KMWG members, Teresa Sanchez-Lazer, had guessed at such a reversal in an earlier comment about KM: "It occurred to me that in any business case we build, we will need to be careful to distinguish between *system (software)* development and maintenance versus *process/content* development and maintenance. Although I remain convinced this is a good idea, I think keeping a KM system accurate and stocked with useful content will not be cheap."

We again resorted to a low-tech solution: a meeting of the SMEs as a community of practice (CoP) to reflect on their practice and to keep making revisions to the knowledge asset as a centralized repository of process descriptions, procedures, roles, and contacts. We continued to build on the original one-dimensional Web map, bringing together as much relevant content as we could in order to centralize access. Internal Web sites from various divisions, templates, links to outside sources, people to contact, and personal stories were collected and used to build a multidimensional map describing the process (see Figure 15-3). The original Visio process maps were available as pop-ups within the Web, along with text describing the activities within the process, tools and templates provided by SMEs and other interested parties, related links, and addresses for contacts that carry out specialized tasks within a phase of the process.

The content donated to the site was reviewed by several SMEs. Outdated documents were placed there only when there were no newer content sources available. The authors and the last known revision date for the documents were prominently listed along with a person to contact. Since the multidimensional map has become available, SMEs who were too busy to engage fully at first have sent material for inclusion here and there. Executive Director Robert Kastner was given responsibility for ensuring that the process is followed from a strategic operations perspective. As the Center for

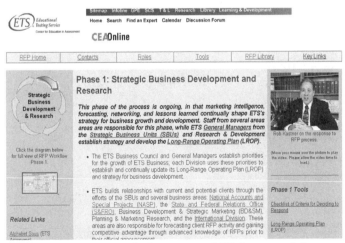

Figure 15-3. Multidimensional Web map of the response-to-RFP process

Education in Assessment receives inquiries about content, we are able to point a colleague to another colleague for more information.

Lessons Learned

The maintenance of the knowledge asset (the multidimensional map) has not been assigned to a group outside the CEA, and DeVincenzi by default has been responsible for its content. The situation is much like when a meeting facilitator is charged with all the action items.

To some extent, this is due to a lack of resources dedicated to supporting the project. However, a less obvious insight that emerged from this pilot explains the current situation with the ownership and maintenance of the site. The work on outputs from the meetings of the best-practices group focused a good deal on the mapping of process and collection of content. Although people were brought together and a sense of community was created, the community itself was not the centerpiece of study and support; rather, a previously nonexistent common process was. Additionally, a single process owner was never fully established, so without executive direction, process improvement is on the slow track.

In retrospect, especially in the case where most knowledge and expertise is tacit, the focus should have been on the people in the community and on the people being considered owners of their knowledge. During one of the SME meetings, as SMEs were trying to identify where important knowledge files were located, the common responses were, "It isn't anywhere. So-and-so has it in her head," and "Nobody can write that down; you have to have the experience to know what to do." Gorelick, working as facilitator, in an aside to DeVincenzi, observed, "Your work can no longer be focused on collecting and codifying content in files and on shared drives. You have to collect the stories of the people."

Seekers and Sharers

As a result of the lessons we learned from the pilot on best practices in responding to RFPs, the learning and development group under Elliott has changed its definition of KM. First, we had narrowed it to be "connecting knowledge seekers with knowledge sources to make better decisions that produce effective action." We had intended the context to be an actionable one that would procure short-term wins for ETS. The light bulb went off one day that many of the people we had to reach were not knowledge seekers. The community believed that they already had all the knowledge they needed. They were not necessarily "seeking" knowledge. For the purposes of a working definition of KM at ETS, we had to alter our description of our colleagues from "knowledge seekers" to "knowledge users." We needed to find out who the people were who could use the knowledge, and convince them that it was worth their while to examine the ways they go about deciding and acting and that this "other knowledge" might actually bring value to their enterprise.

The authors would like to note that this condition of believing one's current stock and variety of knowledge is sufficient is not peculiar to ETS. The work of Argyris and Schon has demonstrated that the default mode of people in organizations is to protect against any information that might disconfirm their existing hypotheses. It might be said that the other side of Seely Brown and Duguid's work is that there is also an antisocial life of information and, consequently, knowledge: People are not necessarily interested in finding out a new way to do things or learning a novel fact, especially if it contradicts their existing view of the world. They may even actively seek to block the exchange of such information.

Leaders may also actively or subconsciously support the hoarding of knowledge. Leading a group of many work experts (relative to groups with nonexperts) may lead to the achievement of higher productivity or gains (as compared to the achievement of those of groups with fewer experts), which leads to greater recognition and, subsequently, a wider and wider span of executive control. From a systems thinking perspective, a "Success to the Successful"[3] dynamic can be in play. Sharing one's knowledge (or the knowledge of one's expert group) can be seen as a way to diminish one's individual expert status, turning the exceptional into the commonplace. If rewards focus on individual, or small group gains, and there are no rewards for sharing knowledge with others and contributing to organization-wide gains, this sort of system can perpetuate. At ETS, where expertise, seniority, and accomplishment are often equated, there needed to be intervening variables to reinforce the importance of knowledge sharing. This year, in fact, leaders have collaborated with Elliott to institute a high-profile performance award, equal to the traditional

---

[3] *The SystemsThinker* (Cambridge: Pegasus Communications, March 1996).

awards given to individually based accomplishments, which will acknowledge the introduction and perpetuation of a best practice across the company.

And because communities of practice often cross divisional and organizational boundaries, this pilot experience reminded us of the extent that politics can impact the Knowledge Management practitioner's efforts to influence a community's work habits and support their work.

There are no politically neutral contexts. Knowledge Management practitioners not only need to be adept at demonstrating the business benefits that sharing knowledge brings to individuals and groups, but they must also be savvy of the political risks involved for members of the community who take steps to change the way they work. One of the SMEs who worked with DeVincenzi to review content of the multidimensional map was concerned that she was spending too much time on the project, would receive no recognition for the effort being expended, and should probably be working instead on her "own" projects, as were the other SMEs.

In his AMA article, "When It Comes to 'Best Practices'—Why Do Smart Organizations Occasionally Do Dumb Things?" Jeffrey Pfeffer (1996) observes, "In organizational politics, as in politics more generally, the benefits of change are more widely dispersed and less certain than the cost of making that change." To support knowledge communities well, KM specialists need to understand the risk from the members' perspectives, considering political and social issues such as who is making which contributions, how a member's status within traditional hierarchies comes into play, and what messages members are receiving (directly and indirectly) from their supervisors and stakeholders. The knowledge practitioner should seek to identify risks for community members ahead of time and consider steps to ameliorate them where possible. If multiple stakeholders appear to have conflicting goals, next steps need to be carefully analyzed.

When Small May Not Really Be Small

Moving forward, we spend more time understanding the context of the potential support initiative and the relationship between this particular effort and those of the larger organization. The group on best practices in response to RFPs was interested as much in a workflow management tool as they were in the multidimensional map (which they did see as valuable as an archive of processes and procedures). The workflow-management database, along with the other database designs they discovered along the way, was considered a separate project, not under the auspices of the KMWG. In fact, though, the workflow database and the multidimensional map together were likely to provide more value to the effectiveness of the community than each would have provided individually. There have been great uses for the multidimensional map as a stand-alone work (e.g., a Six Sigma project used it as a basis for its work, and managers point new staff to it for learning purposes). Nevertheless, the multidimensional map as a stand-alone work is likely bringing less value than it might have if it were complemented by a workflow database.

Since the response-to-RFP pilot, we have been asked to sponsor four other projects from different communities across the organization. Now more mindful of the possibility that a project outside our control could very likely impact the success of our KM projects, we probe more at the start of our projects, with questions such as "To what extent does this initiative stand on its own?" "What does the community use now to accomplish its work?" "What other projects need to be successful in order for this project to be successful?" "Who's running those projects?" "Are they funded?" and "How long is the organization likely to focus on this problem?"

The approach to these new projects has centered more on the communities involved than their work processes (although work process is taken into account and decision points still analyzed and supported). We are working with our colleagues to explore relationships between these new communities and models around communities of practice proposed by Wenger (see "Design Principles for a Community Based Knowledge Initiative," Wenger et al., 2002). Additionally, we are engaging stakeholders in considering measurements for the success of community work (see "Measuring the Impact of Communities," by R. McDermott, Wenger, and Snyder, 2002).

Throughout the effort, we are continually evaluating the relevance of our definition of KM at ETS, the organizational context for KM work, its relationship to what ETS employees value, and the possibilities for helping great things to happen through communities of practice. What we do know is that we have a lot to learn!

Educational Testing Service is a nonprofit company dedicated to serving the needs of individuals, educational institutions and agencies, and governmental bodies in 181 countries. A leader in educational research, ETS develops and annually administers more than

11 million tests worldwide on behalf of clients in education, government, and business. For more information, access the ETS website at www.org.

T.J. Elliott is Associate Vice President of Human Resources and Chief Learning Officer of ETS. He came to ETS as Chief Learning Officer of ETS in February 2002. Prior to joining the nonprofit, that is the world's largest private educational testing and measurement organization, Elliott was, for seven years, Director of Research and Consulting Design for Cavanaugh Leahy & Co, an organizational development consulting firm headquartered in Lawrenceville, New Jersey.

Elliott has designed and implemented leadership, knowledge sharing, and strategy development initiatives for major corporations. His clients included Aventis Pharmaceuticals, Fox News Channel, Mobil Oil, NASA Goddard Space and Flight Center, Verizon Wireless, Pepsi Cola Bottling Group, and Skidmore College. Elliott also served from 1989 to 1994 as Vice President of Longview Associates, a management consulting firm in White Plains, New York. He received his bachelor's and master's degrees from Manhattan College and Nova Southeastern University respectively.

Felicia DeVincenzi is Director of the Center for Education in Assessment, an area in Human Resources that provides leadership for learning and knowledge management support for the company's core competency. The group facilitates communities of practice associated with assessment theory and methodology, as well as providing training and documentation for processes and technologies related to test creation, test publishing, and scoring. The CEA's programs, technology, and document management services are customized for various audiences and specialties across test developers, statistical analysis professionals, and researchers at ETS. At ETS since 1984, DeVincenzi has been active in process analysis, design, and improvement at ETS for several years.

An applied linguist, DeVincenzi has coordinated the design and development of many high-stakes language assessments, as well as teacher certification tests. DeVincenzi led the team that created ETS's first computer-delivered multimedia assessment of listening comprehension. A part of the Test of English as a Foreign Language (TOEFL), the assessment is required by most colleges and universities as one of the entrance criteria for foreign students intending to study in the United States. She has also directed statewide foreign language program assessments in Spanish, French, Italian, German, and Latin.

An alumna of Lehigh University (1978) and Trenton State College (1983), DeVincenzi has taught kindergarten students and doctoral candidates, beginning her career in the Trenton public schools as an ESL teacher and subsequently in programs at Rutgers University and the College of New Jersey, where she taught graduate courses in educational measurement in Mallorca, Spain. At Princeton University, she designed and directed training programs for students working abroad in the Princeton-in-Asia program. She has published teacher resource materials for the assessment of speaking and writing in Spanish, as well as numerous articles and presentations. She remains active in public education by serving as the chairperson for fundraising for the Lawrence Township Education Foundation.

DeVincenzi lives in Lawrenceville with her husband Mario and two teenaged children, James and Elisa.

REFERENCES

Pfeffer, J. "When It Comes to 'Best practices'—Why Do Smart Organizations Occasionally Do Dumb Things?" *Organizational Dynamics*, Vol. 25, No. 1 (Summer 1996), p. 33.

The SystemsThinker. Cambridge, MA: Pegasus Communications, March 1996.

Wenger, E., McDermott, R., and Snyder, W. M. *Cultivating Communities of Practice.* Boston, MA: Harvard Business School Press, 2002.

CHAPTER 16

Knowledge Management at Shell: Innovation and Integration

By Vikas Bhushan

Background

The ability of an organization to learn from and leverage its existing knowledge base and expertise in an efficient and effective way is a distinct competitive advantage. In the business of the exploration and production (EP) of oil and gas resources, which is characterized by very large investments of capital in projects that carry a high degree of inherent risk, this is especially true. Knowledge and experience serve to reduce the level of risk and assist in making well-informed decisions, all of which translates directly into added value. In a company like Shell, with a global staff pool of 90,000 dispersed in over 140 countries, the need to efficiently and effectively share knowledge becomes even more acute. If a large EP company like Shell is able to apply the collective knowledge of its staff where it is needed and in a timely manner, the opportunity exists to leverage this breadth of knowledge on a global scale, leading to competitive advantage.

The focus of this case is on the largest segment of Shell's business, EP, with roughly 40% of the capital employed and 50% of the total fixed assets of the Shell Group.[1] EP is also commonly referred to as the upstream part of the business. The exploration and production

---

[1] 2001 Annual Reports of the Shell Transport and Trading Company and the Royal Dutch Petroleum Company.

of oil and gas is a very expensive and technologically complex business. It is also characterized by a large amount of risk and uncertainty. A decision on where to drill an exploration well must often be based on sparse or highly uncertain information. If a deposit of oil or gas, called a reservoir, is found, then it must be appraised to determine its characteristics and decide whether and how to proceed with development. Finding analogues is a key way of learning from previous experience by accessing the most relevant information.

This case study presents a new approach to identifying analogues systematically through the novel application of an artificial intelligence technique called case-based reasoning (CBR). This approach was developed by two petroleum engineers working at Shell's upstream research and development center in the Netherlands; S. C. Hopkinson initially proposed the approach in a pilot project, and V. Bhushan matured the concept into a robust KM tool deployed globally in Shell's operating units, or OUs (Bhushan and Hopkinson, 2002). During the development of this product, a strong partnership was built between Shell and Everest B.V., a Dutch software consultancy specializing in the development of customized Knowledge Management (KM) solutions. This relationship permitted the early adoption within Shell of leading-edge technology (Automatisering Gids, 2002).

Recently developed artificial intelligence technology incorporating case-based reasoning algorithms within a flexible Java-based architecture has been applied. The result is a Web-based system that permits users in any Shell operating unit to search through thousands of reservoirs in milliseconds to locate reservoir analogues, and then to access additional detailed information about the reservoirs of interest. The application of this tool within Shell to address important business issues will be discussed.

The alignment of the concept behind this tool with certain important high-level business drivers aided in the adoption of the new technology and helped to optimize the value derived from it. Further, the integration with existing Knowledge Management tools accelerated its implementation. These existing tools, which form the backbone of Shell EP's Knowledge Management infrastructure, include global knowledge-sharing networks, global Peer Assists, centers of excellence, and global consultants (see the Company Snapshot sidebar).

Company Snapshot: Shell EP KM Framework
By Kiri Kikis, Knowledge Manager, Shell International
Exploration and Production

The motto "Knowing 'Who' Is as Good as Knowing 'How'"
summarizes the philosophy of the tools Shell has in place to
harvest its learnings. Shell has invested in four initiatives to
apply the best resources to each opportunity at the right time—
regardless of geographic or organizational location. These tools
have been established around the business needs and are
managed on a global level by central teams; they are supported
by subject matter experts from around the globe. Together, these
four initiatives form the backbone of Shell's knowledge-sharing
and Knowledge Management framework. They enable staff to
tap into the right resources at the right time to get their job done.

Global Networks

Global networks are communities supported by Web-based
discussion groups for asking questions, seeking and creating
solutions to problems, imparting knowledge, and sharing successful practices, resulting in time and cost savings. Spanning
the technical disciplines and the globe, the global networks have
over 15,000 members and are growing throughout the exploration and production business and beyond, tapping into the
wealth of knowledge and experience that collectively exists
within the company. The development of the global networks
in many cases has been that of a natural growth; to force
knowledge sharing among the communities is a failing effort,
and effort in developing a knowledge-sharing culture is key to
the success of this tool.

Initially, a skeleton framework for the networks was developed, focusing on wells, subsurface, and surface. Some key
business themes were established, but as the networks grew, the
user community helped define the launch of key new business
areas. For example, much discussion has occurred around the
topic of "thin oil rims," which has led to business success in
this area. As a result, a forum moderator has been established
for thin oil rims, and the forum has been given a greater level
of exposure within the network.

Shell currently harvests 11 global networks: 3 technical
(wells, surface, and subsurface) and 8 cross-business networks

involving the e-business, procurement, EP commercial, venture and project realization, competitive intelligence, benchmarking, knowledge sharing, and gas and power communities.

Global Consultants

Global consultants are nominated experts drawn mainly from Shell's operating units around the world. They are available as in-house consultants to transfer their expertise and to share the benefit of their experiences gained from working in operational environments all over the world. Through an active presence in the relevant global networks, these "gurus" become well known within their technical communities and beyond. Managed by a dedicated New Ways of Working team, a structure and system have been set up to dispatch the correct global consultant to deal with a particular challenge, for a few hours or up to a few weeks, to the designated geographical location.

There are currently 250 global consultants within Shell, whose expertise covers broad-ranging areas including development planning, gas reservoir engineering, production chemistry, regional geology, and many more key business themes. Experience has shown that these global consultants are in constant demand, and their feedback has demonstrated that the work is rewarding.

Centers of Excellence

Centers of Excellence (CoEs) are formally established teams of specialists from various locations around the world with very focused and deep expertise in specific areas relevant to exploration and production. They are tasked with consolidating global expert knowledge in niche areas and then applying it wherever it is needed throughout the global Shell EP business. These CoEs house assets, data, activities, and expertise, and offer know-how to the business. There are 11 CoEs established thus far, providing comprehensive access to assistance in the following specialist discipline areas:

- Underwater activity
- Hazard and risk assessment
- High-pressure and high-temperature operations
- Maintenance strategy and reliability drilling
- Seismic data prestack depth migration

- Offshore structures engineering
- Land seismic data acquisition and processing in desert areas
- Compaction and subsidence
- Petroleum systems modeling
- Groupware IT
- Geographical information systems

Global Peer Assists

A Peer Assist is created by the combination of local and external expertise coming together for a short period to focus on helping and assisting the Shell operating unit to add value to an asset. The Peer Assist team is a combination of operating unit and central office technical, R&D, or service staff who work together in a ring-fenced area, concentrating on the technical and commercial aspects surrounding the asset and looking for ways to make short-term gains that are sustainable in the long term, to increase oil and gas production, and to reduce operating expenses. The operating unit provides the leader of the Peer Assist team. The central office team assists the leader by facilitating the process. Ownership of the Peer Assist process and the report and implementation plan produced as a result of the Peer Assist rests solely with the operating unit.

Setting the Scene for Innovation

The Smart Reservoir Prospector (SRP) is an innovation that was motivated by the realization that there exist significant blockers to the sharing of knowledge and best practices between Shell staff working in different operating units around the world, and sometimes also between different teams within the same OU. These include, for example:

- Time constraints on individuals and the time required to share knowledge with colleagues
- Geographical separation and lack of face-to-face meeting
- A culture or work environment that does not consistently encourage or recognize the value added through knowledge sharing
- Providing insufficient motivation for staff to actively share knowledge

- Security concerns around the dissemination of sensitive information
- Strong and visible management support for knowledge-sharing initiatives

The absence of effective knowledge-sharing tools inhibits staff from gaining access to relevant knowledge when and where it is needed. Within this context, the idea was conceived of a globally accessible knowledge-sharing tool to help facilitate the sharing of reservoir knowledge and best practices.

The SRP is a reservoir knowledge-sharing system with an intelligent "fuzzy logic" search facility. Its main purpose is to locate reservoir analogues in a systematic, reliable, and efficient way. It accomplishes this by applying an artificial intelligence technique called case-based reasoning (CBR) in a unique and innovative way. More traditional hit-or-miss approaches, such as searching through reports or relying on the individual experiences of colleagues, are generally biased toward assessing similarity on a few attributes only and comparing reservoirs on a one-to-one basis. The SRP assesses similarity on the basis of a broad set of attributes and compares multiple reservoirs simultaneously.

There are many reasons for using reservoir analogues at all stages of the hydrocarbon exploration and production cycle. Analogues can be as useful in new, "greenfield" exploration environments—for example, to understand the geological setting or to develop field development options—as in old, "brownfield" acreages—for example, to optimize production plans. Generally, analogues are particularly important when the information available is limited and when the degree of uncertainty is high. In such cases, developing multiple scenarios and benchmarking against prior experience become essential tools in managing the risks and decision making, and access to analogue data is a key enabler.

The identification of reservoir analogues is an important step in planning the development of a new play, particularly when facing difficult technical challenges or when appraisal information is limited. One of the strengths of an EP company with a large and diverse portfolio is its potential to utilize a broad base of knowledge gained from past experience to aid in future development and decision making. A critical enabler in being able to leverage this knowledge effectively is the ability to access relevant information quickly and efficiently. Thus the ability to identify reservoir analogues in a fast, systematic, comprehensive way provides a means of benefiting from breadth and scale of experience. The speed of finding analogues is important when resources are limited and when fast decision making is important—for example, in a bid situation on a new prospect. Further, it is important that a search be repeatable and made in a systematic manner, grounded in a sound methodology. Finally, a comprehensive search helps to ensure that results are not skewed or biased as a result of considering a limited data set.

KM efforts in Shell EP are underpinned by the value in aligning data collection with documented best practices and standards for all user communities throughout the company. Data quality assurance and maintenance of standards are essential for the SRP. Additionally, the SRP is aligned with a number of key business themes in Shell EP: knowledge sharing, applying best practices, and operational excellence.

Knowledge sharing has been identified as an important initiative not only for its potential to add value but also for its direct impact on all aspects of operation, including safety, efficiency, and cost savings. Drawing on previous experience provides an expanded basis to understand the level and nature of risk involved in a project. Analogue data can be used to define and help quantify the degree of uncertainty in key reservoir characteristics, such as the volume of hydrocarbon in place or the reservoir pressure, and to understand possible outcomes and implications of following a particular development strategy. This knowledge can serve to provide confidence when making a decision on entering into a new and technically challenging project, and aid in ascertaining whether a development is feasible both technically and economically.

Capturing and applying best practices and sharing experiences provide a tangible means of using previous successes and failures for future benefit. They are also powerful ways of challenging preconceived notions and mind-sets, and for maintaining an external focus through the development of a culture of being open to adopting practices from elsewhere that prove to be better than locally accepted ones.

As Shell EP strives for operational excellence, analogue data can provide a basis for setting minimum standards and defining targets that are both optimal and realistic. Benchmarking against prior operational performance in other similar environments is one way of developing field development strategies that optimize the production rates of oil and gas and maximize the ultimate recovery from the reservoirs. Further, analogue data can help to define uncertainty ranges and constraints on the values of key parameters in economic and technical scenario modeling used in field development planning, and provide benchmarks against which to validate and interpret model results.

A Unique Approach

The SRP is a unique concept both in its application of CBR and also in the design and architecture of the system itself. The scalable and platform-independent architecture permits the SRP to be easily adapted to the requirements of a globally dispersed and diverse user community within Shell. Further, a component-based architecture permits the system to be expanded.

This concept represents a novel approach to identifying analogues systematically and efficiently. The key lies in characterizing each reservoir by a set of attributes that describe the reservoir and can be used to differentiate it from other reservoirs. A matching technique based on CBR is then applied to search for reservoirs that are similar. A discussion of the concept of CBR can be readily found in the published literature (e.g., Leake, 1996). In essence, CBR is used to adapt known solutions of old problems to help in solving new problems. In the SRP development, we adapted this generic concept to the problem of identifying reservoir analogues. Each "case" in the SRP is a reservoir and is described by a set of reservoir attributes. These attributes are multidisciplinary and include, for example, the geological setting, rock and fluid properties, reservoir production performance characteristics, volumetrics, and a general physical description of the reservoir (lithology, fractures, etc.). The full set of attributes is chosen to provide a full high-level characterization of a reservoir and also to distinguish it from other reservoirs. This method quantifies the degree of similarity and permits users to focus their search on any specified set of reservoir attributes. These characteristics differentiate this method from others currently in use. The result is a Web-based SRP system that permits users in any Shell OU to locate reservoir analogues and then access additional detailed information about the reservoirs of interest.

Search methodologies based on a standard database lookup will only search for matches that exactly meet the search criteria.

A key difference between the SRP and any other such reservoir search system currently available is that the SRP allows users to search for analogues on the basis of matching reservoirs with characteristics that are similar but that do not necessarily match up exactly. This system quantifies the degree of similarity and carries out analogue searches in a systematic and robust way.

The SRP system design is component-based, making use of off-the-shelf components. This approach provides flexibility, scalability, and platform independence to ensure compatibility with the existing IT infrastructure.

Further, it addresses specific concerns and objectives identified as being critical success factors: global accessibility, end-user data updating and ownership, information security, and access limitation to sensitive or restricted data. This distributed system based on generic components also enables the extension of the SRP platform to other (even unrelated) applications.

All routine system maintenance and reservoir attribute customization and data updating are done via a back-end maintenance interface, eliminating the need for calling in programmers each time such changes are required. This has the effect of increasing system flexibility by making feasible the routine adjustment and fine-tuning of system settings. Also, this approach avoids the need to hard-code knowledge and maintains a clear separation among the IT system component, the business knowledge, and the data.

Figure 6-1 illustrates the SRP system architecture. Each component is independent. Further, the search engine itself is Java-based and platform independent, and can be installed on any application server. Multiple instances of the match engine may also be used simultaneously, permitting mirror installations to run locally at locations around the world, speeding up access time. They can each connect to any number of databases of any type that is SQL-based. The user interaction is handled by the Web server and can be customized to specific user communities.

Development Strategy

The SRP was developed through a collaboration with an external software development partner, Everest B.V. The SRP implements

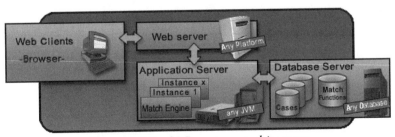

Figure 16-1. SRP system architecture

Everest's Knowledge Framework, which is a suite of components that can be customized to meet the needs of specific customers (see the Technology Snapshot sidebar). It was developed by Everest in parallel with the SRP and was motivated by the lack of any available tool that had sufficient flexibility and could combine multiple representation techniques for knowledge and information into one system. The collaboration with Shell provided Everest with a clear business rationale for their development as well as an early test case for their new technology. Hence mutual benefit was derived from this development collaboration.

The SRP uses a nearest neighbor algorithm to measure the degree of similarity between two reservoirs. This type of algorithm is widely used for CBR applications (Mitchell, 1997; Rich and Knight, 1991). The similarity between any two reservoirs is measured by the SRP as follows:

$$Similarity\,(A,\,B) = \frac{\displaystyle\sum_{i=1}^{n} f_i(A_i,\,B_i) * w_i}{\displaystyle\sum_{i=1}^{n} w_i}$$

A represents the reservoir for which an analogue is being sought; B represents a reservoir in the database; n represents the number of attributes used to describe a reservoir; A_i, B_i represent the attributes that describe reservoirs A and B; f_i is the distance function for the ith attribute (this distance function is appropriately chosen for each reservoir attribute); and w_i defines the weight of each reservoir attribute relative to the other attributes.

Figure 6-2 is an example of a cross-table match function. This is a discrete mapping and is useful for reservoir attributes that have a fixed list of values that are not completely independent of each other. In the case shown here, the attribute is hydrocarbon type, and it can have one of three values: oil, gas, or condensate. When the case value differs from the search value, this table defines the degree of mismatch that is relative to a perfect match. If only a perfect match is desired on any particular attribute, then an exact-match filter can be used.

The similarity between two reservoirs is presented to the user as a scaled percentage score. The match function f_i must be chosen to

	Reservoir A		
	Oil	Condensate	Gas
Reservoir B Oil	1	0.3	0
Condensate	0.3	1	0.7
Gas	0	0.7	1

Figure 16-2. Cross-table match function

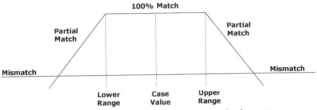

Figure 16-3. Double ramp match function

represent the expected behavior and spread of values of the specific reservoir. These match functions themselves contain information about reservoir descriptions. Thus, a broad knowledge of the geoscience and petroleum engineering disciplines is required in choosing these functions. The match function itself may be any well-defined distribution function or relation appropriate to the attribute. For example, a Gaussian function may be used for the porosity, or a cross-table relationship for the hydrocarbon type (Figure 16-2), or a double ramp function for the in-place hydrocarbon volume (Figure 16-3), or a Boolean function for the presence of fractures.

In a double ramp match function, a perfect match is defined to be within a range around the case value, bounded by a lower range and an upper range. Outside this range, a partial match score is defined, which falls to zero. Beyond a certain range, the score may also be defined to be negative in the case of a mismatch. The ranges may be absolute values or a percentage of the case value.

The selection of both the reservoir attributes and the match functions to be used in searching for analogue reservoirs requires specific technical knowledge. Further, the choice of attributes to use in carrying out an analogue search and the relative weighting of each attribute in the search are functions of the aim of the search and the type of analogue being sought. Therefore, it is essential that the selection of attributes used to match reservoirs and the definition of the match weights remain under user control rather than being hardwired into the system. Figure 16-4 illustrates how a typical analogue using the SRP is carried out. The search criteria can be entered by the user in a number of formats, and the results (i.e., the closest match reservoirs on the basis of the search criteria input by the user) are then displayed along with a quantification of the degree of similarity. Also provided are data summaries for each of the closest match reservoirs and links to additional detailed information about these reservoirs. The user may then focus attention on these reservoirs and decide on the basis of the available information whether any of them are suitable analogues. The system therefore does not tell the user whether a specific reservoir is a good analogue for any other reservoir, because this is highly dependent on the user's input and objectives. Rather, it suggests to the user where best to focus attention on the basis of the search criteria provided. There is no universal definition of what constitutes an analogue; this must be specified by the user through the choice of reservoir attributes and relative weighting used in the search. This ambiguity necessitates the flexibility and user customization inherent in the SRP design.

As shown in Figure 16-4, the user inputs reservoir search criteria in any of three different search modes (one-step, top-down, or full-text), on the basis of which a list of the closest match reservoirs is displayed along with a quantification of the degree of match. The user may then focus attention on any one of these reservoirs and access additional information (reservoir characteristics, development reports, etc.).

A set of rules is used for validation of both input search criteria and reservoir data contained in the SRP, and is implemented through the use of a rule-based inferencing engine, which is a component of Everest's Knowledge Framework. The validation consists of checking that attribute values are within valid ranges and that the data is self-consistent. Also, these rules can be used to add additional knowledge to the search. For example, if the user does not have a measurement available to input for a specific reservoir attribute, but a correlation between this attribute and another one is known for the given reservoir type from prior studies, then the rules can trigger the system to suggest a value (or range) to the user. Hence, in addition to data, prior reservoir knowledge can also be stored and accessed through the use of knowledge-based rules.

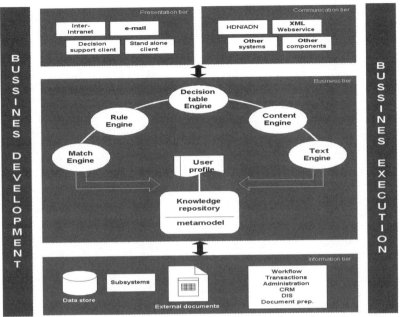

Figure 16-4. SRP information flow in searching for reservoir analogues

Technology Snapshot: The Everest Knowledge Framework

Everest B.V. is a small IT consultancy firm with around 100 staff headquartered in Den Bosch, the Netherlands. IT specializes in developing customized Knowledge Management solutions for its clients. Even though it is still a young company, founded in 1996, it has already established a strong presence in this niche area and currently has many large public and private sector clients. Shell was one of Everest's early clients through their collaborative development work on the Smart Reservoir Prospector project, which has spawned innovation for both parties.

Everest very soon found itself handicapped by the lack of any available IT tool that combines multiple knowledge-based representation techniques with a competitive licensing strategy. This motivated them to develop the Knowledge Framework, which is a suite of IT components that can be integrated into system development to provide specific functionality in a customized knowledge-based solution (Mastop, Lampe, and de Groote, 2002).

The Power of Integration

The Everest Knowledge Framework combines different knowledge representation and search techniques into one suite of Java-based components:

- Case-based reasoning
- Matching
- Rule-based inferencing
- Decision-tree and decision-table inferencing
- Pattern-based natural language processing

This provides the flexibility to tailor make a solution to address the specific requirements of a client in an optimal way, while providing the flexibility to further develop the system to adapt to changing needs without the need to completely overhaul the system.

Versatility Through Innovation

The component-based architecture of the Knowledge Framework enables it to be implemented into virtually any type of IT system development and lends it sufficient flexibility to enable system upgrades and expansion with relative ease. Some key characteristics of the Knowledge Framework are the following:

- It separates program code, business logic, and explicit knowledge.
- It harnesses synergies from a combination of multiple knowledge representation techniques (cases, rules, decision tables) to ensure a highly flexible and maintainable solution.
- It uses an underlying metamodel, common to all the inference engines mentioned earlier, to integrate the different knowledge representation techniques.
- Its portal engine approach separates knowledge, content, and presentation to make a multichannel/multilabel approach possible.

- It is platform independent by making all components Java-based.
- It is easily scalable.
- It has an open architecture (no black boxes).

Figure 16-5 illustrates the concept behind the integration of the components of the Everest Knowledge Framework into system development, which provides an interface between business development and business execution. Information and data from a variety of sources (the "information tier") is fed into a knowledge repository and stored in a particular representation defined by a metamodel. The Knowledge Framework components are used to process this knowledge in accordance with settings in a user profile (the "business tier"). The results are then passed on to the user in any of a variety of formats (the "presentation tier") or alternatively passed on to another system component for further processing (the "communication tier").

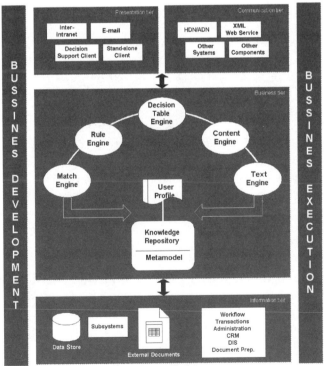

Figure 16-5. Integration of Knowledge Framework components into system development (figure courtesy of Everest B.V.)

Deployment

As is the case with any information technology–based solution, the SRP's effectiveness as a knowledge-sharing tool depends on its embedment and usage within the company. In order to achieve a successful deployment, organizations must have identified the user communities and other key stakeholders whose active participation is essential, and couple it with the existing Knowledge Management framework within the company (see the Company Snapshot sidebar earlier in the chapter).

The latter includes Shell's Subsurface Knowledge Sharing Network (SKS), one of Shell's global networks whose purpose is to enable Shell staff to share their experiences and knowledge with others in a way that saves time, reduces costs, enables faster and better decisions, and creates opportunities. The SKS is a principal vehicle through which staff in Shell have been seeking out reservoir analogues. Although this can be a fruitful method of locating analogues, it is a hit-or-miss approach that is dependent on the availability, ability, and willingness of other forum participants to provide the information in a timely manner. The SRP complements the SKS by addressing these shortcomings and providing a real-time and more comprehensive approach.

A global Peer Assist involves a focused view on a particular asset by a group of experts. One of the first tasks that is typically carried out during a Peer Assist is the gathering of relevant knowledge, prior experience, and best practices. Hence, the SRP plays an integral role by providing a means of identifying and accessing the knowledge being sought. Further, the participants of the Peer Assist play an important role in the validation and entry into the SRP of any new data gathered and in the updating of existing data relating to the asset being focused on.

Once the SRP was developed and tested, five key stages in the deployment of this product were identified.

- Marketing of the SRP. Staff around the world need to be made aware that this tool exists, what purpose it serves, and how they can make use of it. This is accomplished through internal publications, knowledge fairs, and the global networks.
- Embedment into the existing workflow so that staff use the SRP routinely rather than reverting to a more familiar mode of operation.

- Integration and customization of the SRP. Value to the end user is optimized by integration within the existing KM framework. Further, customization of the system is carried out to suit changing user requirements; the system's component-based design flexibility is key in being able to achieve this.
- Development of a user community to provide continuous feedback and shared ownership.
- Maintenance of up-to-date data and best-practice information.

The Way Forward: Integration

The development of the SRP was premised on the implementation of a novel concept to address an identified need for reservoir analogue identification and reservoir knowledge sharing, underpinned by key business drivers and enabled by new technology. The involvement of key customers and end users early in the development process was essential to the success of the project, since it created buy-in, generated a sense of ownership of the product, facilitated product testing and deployment, and created a pilot user community from the start of the project that provided feedback throughout the development phase.

With any new product or new way of working, a fit with the existing work culture within the organization must be determined for effective and continued use. In the case of the SRP, the management team has engaged the various OUs and stakeholders at an early stage of implementation to ensure that their requirements are incorporated into the product, making them a part of the development process. By doing this, the SRP has gained broad management acceptance and buy-in, and facilitated the integration into project workflows.

The next steps for the SRP are continued OU and stakeholder engagement, and further population of the tool with data from internal and external sources to enable access to a broader base of information and experience, increasing its value to the company. As Shell strives for operational excellence as a key part of its business strategy, the alignment of the SRP with key business drivers and integration with the existing KM infrastructure has enabled the SRP to successfully evolve from being a novel concept to being a fully developed and deployed KM tool.

Vikas Bhushan currently works at Shell International's Gas and Power Head Office in London as a senior business analyst in

Corporate Planning and Appraisal. Previously, he worked at Shell Technology Exploration and Production as a Petroleum Engineer, primarily in R&D, with expertise in cased-hole petrophysics and pulsed neutron log interpretation development. He traveled to many of Shell's operating units worldwide to conduct technology transfer and staff training workshops in these areas. He also contributed to a variety of other R&D projects for reservoir characterization and production monitoring. He is an advocate of developing strong research links with universities, having been involved in research projects with a number of universities, including Imperial College in the UK, the Technische Universiteit Delft in the Netherlands, and North Carolina State University in the United States, and was responsible for setting up a joint research project together with the Massachusetts Institute of Technology (MIT) on permeability characterization in fractured reservoirs, which received funding from the U.S. Department of Energy. He is also interested in graduate recruiting, having attended a number of attraction events and conducted candidate interviews. His strong interest in the development of novel KM solutions motivated him to provide the leadership and technical input to drive the development and implementation of the Shell Smart Reservoir Prospector.

Vikas has a broad range of interests in industry and academia. After completing a B.S. Honours degree in mathematics and physics at the University of Toronto, Canada, he went on to complete three master's degrees. He holds an M.S. in theoretical physics at the University of British Colombia in Canada, where he conducted research in the areas of general relativity and dynamical systems theory. He holds an S.M. degree in physical oceanography at MIT in the United States, where he conducted research related to climate studies, specifically in the areas of ocean general circulation modeling and ocean-atmosphere interactions. While at MIT, he contributed to the development and launch of a new Professional Master's degree program in geosystems, which is aimed at educating students for scientific and management careers in the environmental, natural resources, and technical consulting industries. He also holds an M.B.A degree from the Rotterdam School of Management at Erasmus University, the Netherlands, where he completed a thesis on the Employee Value Proposition for new graduate employees in Shell Exploration and Production. During these studies, he developed a strong interest in Knowledge Management and leadership.

Vikas has lived and worked in a number of countries around the world, including the Unites States, Canada, the Netherlands and the

UK. His new focus areas are linked to understanding the business issues (as opposed to technical and operational issues) relating to the oil and gas industry globally.

ACKNOWLEDGMENTS

The authors wish to acknowledge the instrumental early contribution of Chris Hopkinson in the development of the SRP concept, and the development collaboration with Everest B.V., especially Mark Mastop and Michiel Lampe. Thanks are due also to Andrew Barendrecht for useful discussions. Finally, the authors are grateful to Shell for granting permission to publish this article and to Kurt April for providing the opportunity to contribute this article.

REFERENCES

Automatisering Gids, Nr. 41, p. 8, 11 October 2002. Kennis moet bruikbaar zijn.

Bhushan, Vikas, and Hopkinson, Simon Christopher. "A Novel Approach to Identify Reservoir Analogues." *Proceedings of the Society of Petroleum Engineers 13th European Petroleum Conference,* Paper 78338, Aberdeen, United Kingdom, October 29–31, 2002.

Leake, David B. *Case-Based Reasoning.* Cambridge, MA: The MIT Press, 1996.

Mastop, Mark, Lampe, Michiel, and de Groote, Onno. "Knowledge Framework." *Proceedings of the Fourteenth Belgium–Netherlands Artificial Intelligence Conference,* Leuven, Belgium, October 21–22, 2002.

Mitchell, Thomas. *Machine Learning.* New York: McGraw Hill, 1997.

Rich, Elaine, and Knight, Kevin. *Artificial Intelligence.* New York: McGraw-Hill, 1991.

CHAPTER 17

Assessing Readiness to Successfully Implement a Knowledge Management Strategy: Back to Basics at Debswana

By Balisi Bonyongo and Nischal K. Sancho

This case describes Balisi Bonyongo and Nischal Sancho's growing awareness of Knowledge Management (KM) concepts and how they can be applied at Debswana (employer of Balisi Bonyongo). The nucleus of the experience is a research study that fulfilled a partial requirement for Balisi's and Nischal's completion of an M.B.A degree at the Graduate School of Business (GSB) at the University of Cape Town (South Africa). It is an example of applied theory within an action-learning experience.

Debswana knew that the ability to create, capture, share, retain, and use knowledge is increasingly becoming a source of competitive advantage. People within the company recognized a need to develop knowledge systems but did not know if the company was ready and, if so, where to begin. The case study describes the approach that the pair took, under the supervision of Kurt April, to assess Debswana's capabilities, strengths, and weaknesses with respect to the KM processes of creation, capture, storage, sharing, and application of knowledge. KM strategy and implementation plans were developed as a result of the assessment.

CORPORATE OVERVIEW

Debswana is a diamond mining company operating in Botswana, Africa. It is a 50–50 partnership between the government of Botswana and De Beers (the largest diamond mining company in the world). The company is central to the development of Botswana, with its principal product, diamonds, contributing 30% of GDP, 70% of export earnings, and 50% of government revenue. It operates four diamond mines in the country: Jwaneng, Orapa, Letlhakane, and Damtshaa, and the country's only colliery (a coal mine and its connected buildings). Orapa, Letlhakane, and Damtshaa are collectively referred to as OLD Mines.

The company's vision is to become a global benchmark mining company. It developed a strategy that is congruent with this vision. The balanced scorecard (BSC) is used for translating the vision and strategy into reality. The BSC is used at corporate and operational levels. Scorecards have been developed for all levels of employees in the organization and provide a basis on which business, operational, and individual performance are managed. The force behind Debswana's success is its workforce of approximately 6,000. The company employs some of the best-trained and well-educated workers in the country and provides a range of excellent benefits for its employees. It uses leading-edge technology in its mining and diamond extraction processes, producing some 25 million carats annually. This makes Debswana the largest producer of diamonds, by value, in the world.

BACKGROUND

Balisi Bonyongo claims that during his 10 years' experience at Debswana, he witnessed the introduction of major technological advances aimed at improving efficiencies, reducing costs, and improving information flow and management. He was also a member of teams of people who worked on the shop floor and at supervisory, middle, and senior management levels. As part of a professional development program, Balisi, the plant manager, temporarily left Botswana, his family, and job at Debswana to attend a full-time M.B.A. program at the Graduate School of Business at the University of Cape Town. Throughout the course work, Balisi used Debswana as a practice field for his learning. He expected to return to Debswana and assume the role of chief knowledge officer in a business unit.

As part of the Knowledge Management elective at the GSB, Balisi identified several issues that he had experienced and observed as being Knowledge Management related.

First, the organization did not learn from its past mistakes. New projects introducing new ways of doing things went through the same problems that previous ones had experienced.

Second, there were many instances where one part of the organization created a new way of working without being aware that something similar had been done elsewhere in the same operation. This approach introduced inefficiencies in the way the organization utilized its resources.

Overriding these two concerns was the gradual exclusion of mainstream employees who were at the "value-adding face" of the organization, in contributing their knowledge and experiences to the activities and projects being introduced. These employees then had to take over the final product and operate and maintain it to deliver value for the company. This was due to the way business performance was measured—emphasis was on ore tonnage mined and treated through the plant, carats (measure of quantity of diamonds) produced, and costs incurred—but little to no focus on people and other nonfinancial measures. In all business activities, management had focused on the "end product" and not the processes followed to get there. An unintended consequence was a culture that cared very little for how people contributed individually and collectively to the end product.

In addition to his own observations, Balisi felt a need to know why the formal organization wanted to implement a Knowledge Management strategy. He asked the managing director directly and received the following succinct response:

> I believe that the past has not been a good teacher for this organization. We don't seem to be good at learning from past mistakes. I want us to prepare the basis for learning through the utilization of every employee's knowledge, expertise, and experience. I trust that this learning will assist the organization in resolving the rising production costs, inefficient processes, poor safety, and environmental performance, and indeed the downward spiral in motivation of our human resources. This in my view should make us productive and innovative and help us gain sustainable competitive advantage.

Balisi believed that there was support from the top office, and a clear understanding of what would be expected of him. So the first thing he needed to do was develop a KM strategy and implementation plan. He decided to use the opportunity he had as an M.B.A. student to do a formal research study to understand if Debswana (beyond the managing director) was ready to embark on a knowledge program. He thus engaged Nischal Sancho, another M.B.A. student at the GSB, to work with him on the study, using both qualitative (interviews) and quantitative (Web survey) techniques.

The Botswana Knowledge Management Research Project

Why Initiate KM?

Debswana Diamond Company recognized the need to embrace Knowledge Management and potentially embark on implementing a KM strategy in order to achieve its business goals and continue to be Botswana's leading economic growth engine. According to Debswana's deputy managing director, Knowledge Management was necessary for the following reasons:

- *Human capital is a strategic objective.* The Knowledge Assets, especially the human assets, would increasingly become critical to the company's survival in the diamond industry. Debswana's vision was, and still is, to become a global benchmark mining company, and through the balanced scorecard framework, Debswana has elevated the human capital perspective to the top of its strategic objectives.
- *Workforce knowledge and skill retention are critical.* Debswana wanted to capture and retain the knowledge and skills of its workforce. This was necessary, given the uniqueness of the diamond extraction and sorting technologies commissioned during the previous five years. The technological capability was unique because it was developed in-house through the Debswana/De Beers partnership (proprietary technology).
- *Frequent change requires historical information and knowledge.* Debswana operations were subject to major and frequent changes that included expansions and introduction of newly developed technologies. These changes required the use of historical information and knowledge as well as innovations to create new solutions for the company. The capability to access the information and knowledge needed to be created.

- *Industry leadership requires new knowledge and skills to be captured and stored with respect to technology and processes.* The company wanted to create structures and processes that would capture new knowledge and skills as they were developed and acquired by employees, and analyze such skills for immediate application or storage for future use. This would form the basis of Debswana-specific best practice approaches to the diamond business, establishing the company as a leader in the industry with respect to innovative application of technology and processes.

The motivation was clear, but the pair of researchers had some fundamental questions to answer: Was the organization ready to implement a KM strategy? Assuming that Debswana was ready, what was required to realize some, or all, of the benefits associated with a successful KM implementation?

In an attempt to answer these questions as part of their M.B.A. research dissertation, Balisi and Nischal began by reading everything they could find on KM and everything that was appropriate to answering the said questions. This enabled them to become acquainted with both historical, and recent, theory and practice in the general KM field, as well as theories more specifically related to their research questions. They chose a framework (Figure 17-1) developed by Chong, Wilhelmij, and Schmidt (2000) as the foundation of the research project to assess Debswana's organizational "readiness" for implementation of a KM strategy.

The research pair saw the framework as a potential tool for eventually implementing a KM strategy. According to the framework, a business case for Knowledge Management projects should be based on the treatment of knowledge as a system of interconnecting internal capabilities (business enablers) of a company. These include aspects such as social and cultural enablers, leadership and human development tools, compensation schemes, and technological infrastructures, with knowledge representing the understanding of the relationships and interactions between business assets. This helps ensure that knowledge becomes more meaningful in the business context. Chong, Wilhelmij, and Schmidt (2000) conclude that successful organizations should excel in managing the awareness and diffusion of these core competencies. The framework also recognizes two critical aspects for the implementation framework: risk and performance management. Using this framework and other information from their readings, the research pair developed their own frame-

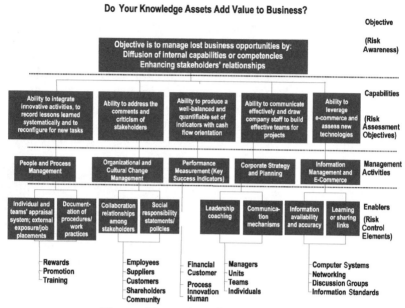

Figure 17-1. The relationship chart

work (Figure 17-2) to gauge the readiness for successful implementation of a KM strategy at Debswana. The framework summarizes the business enablers in defining *readiness* as follows:

- People and Process Management
- Organizational Culture and Structure
- Performance Measurement
- Organizational Strategy and Planning
- Information Management and Technology

Understanding the five categories, or pillars, necessary for a successful Knowledge Management initiative, Balisi and Nischal developed a rigorous research methodology to assess readiness for a KM initiative within Debswana.

THE PROCESS—METHODOLOGY

Phase I: The Interview Process—Asking the Right Questions

In order to assess Debswana's "readiness" to implement a KM strategy according to the framework, Balisi and Nischal conducted

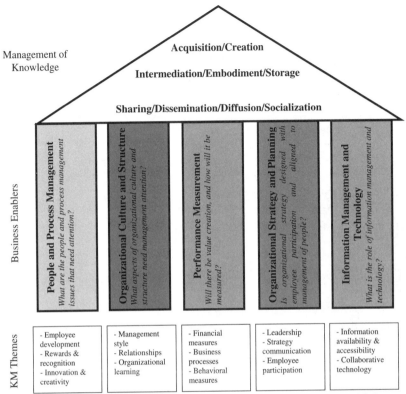

Figure 17-2. Framework to gauge readiness for successful implementation of a Knowledge Management strategy at Debswana

23 semistructured pilot interviews with Debswana's senior management, including executive committee (EXCO) members at the three operations. The interviews sought data and clarity on five main categories (as follows) with 16 open-ended questions, developed in consultation with Kurt April, that made up the entire interview (see Figure A-2 in Appendix A for the questionnaire):

1. Strategic relevance of knowledge and relevance for Debswana's management
2. Knowledge
3. Benefits of KM
4. Barriers and risks to KM
5. Key elements of successful implementation of KM

Interview Questions and Results

The interviewers coded the interview transcripts, categorized the content into themes, and answered the specific questions (using a grounded-theory approach). The questions and a summary of findings follow.

Strategic Knowledge Questions

Question: Do you know what your competitors are doing with respect to the development of knowledge? If yes/no, please elaborate with evidence.

The company Executive Committee (EXCO) members were not aware of competitors' capabilities, outside the De Beers Group activities, with respect to the development of knowledge.

Question: Describe what knowledge assets Debswana has. Any examples?

The company Executive Committee believed that Debswana's Knowledge Assets included intellectual capital, specifically people. The emphasis was on people's knowledge and experiences. Information, they believed, was already stored both in hardcopies and on electronic media.

Question: Who should have prime responsibility for capturing knowledge?

In general, EXCO believed that everyone should be responsible for capturing knowledge through an established process or system. However, it was felt that there should be an appointed driver from EXCO to oversee the process.

Question: Has the company drawn up its knowledge requirement plan for the next 3–5 years?

There was no plan in place. However, the company had begun looking at implementing a KM strategy, and as part of that process, a knowledge requirement plan would be drawn up.

Benefits of KM Question

Question: How will the business benefit by KM implementation?

The Executive Committee members believed that KM implementation would result in productivity improvements through:

- Reduction in mistakes.
- No "reinvention of the wheel."
- Access to best practices within the company and from outside.
- Focusing on value-adding work.

Barriers and Risks to KM Question

Question: What are the barriers to implementation of KM strategies?
The EXCO members saw the key barriers as:

- Silo-type organizational structures.
- Poor employee buy-in due to:
  ▽ Fear of loss of knowledge and therefore power.
  ▽ Increased workload.
  ▽ "Change fatigue."
  ▽ Lack of, or inappropriate, incentives: "What's in it for me?"
  ▽ KM being seen as an initiative that would potentially lead to job losses.
  ▽ Inadequate understanding of where KM adds value, or would add value.
  ▽ Time constraints.

Key Elements of Successful KM Implementation Questions

Question: How is knowledge captured in the organization?
EXCO members believed that knowledge capturing happened in an unstructured way, and saw knowledge capture happening through:

- Reports.
- Project work.
- Ideas and suggestion schemes.
- Electronic knowledge assets.
- Written policies and procedures.

Question: How is knowledge shared in the organization?
EXCO members believed that knowledge sharing took place through:

- Company intranets.
- E-mails.

- Green areas.[1]
- Cross-functional information-sharing sessions.
- Training sessions.
- Presentations.
- Mentoring.

However, they see deficiencies in the way knowledge is shared through these systems.

Question: Does the organization have a culture that motivates employees to acquire and share knowledge? Please elaborate.

In general the EXCO members believed that the culture was not yet conducive to motivating employees to acquire and share knowledge. The key concern raised was that the culture promoted individualism and was seen to be encouraging the "knowledge is power" concept.

Question: What role does organizational culture play in enabling successful implementation of KM?

EXCO members believed that organizational culture played a vital role in enabling successful implementation of KM. They all emphasized the role of management in creating a culture that is supportive to KM. According to EXCO, the culture should:

- Support risk taking and experimentation.
- Support both individual and organizational learning.
- Support sharing of intelligence, knowledge, and wisdom.
- Encourage transparency, and accountability, through open communication.

On a scale of 1–10, where would you rate the current organizational culture's ability to support successful implementation of a KM strategy? How does this affect your framework, plan to implement a KM strategy?

Virtually all of the EXCO members awarded current culture a rating of 5 on a scale of 1–10.

---

[1] Consultative forums where information is shared—the concept of green areas started in Japan, pioneered by Nissan to encourage employees to find solutions to workplace problems and challenges.

Question: What is the role of information technology in enabling successful implementation of KM?

Technology was viewed as an enabler that facilitated capturing, storage, and sharing of information or knowledge. The EXCO members listed examples such as the Internet, e-mail, and bulletin boards as typical technologies in use for the purposes of KM.

Question: What do you believe is an appropriate measure to assess KM implementation?

EXCO members believed that the measurement of KM contribution to the financial performance of the company may not be so obvious, especially in the short term. However, even though the balanced scorecard was never set up to specifically monitor and/or measure KM contribution to the bottom line, EXCO viewed the use of an adapted balanced scorecard approach as an effective way of initially tracking KM implementation.

Phase II: The Survey Process—Asking the Questions

Together with Kurt April, Trevor Wegner (statistics professor at the GSB), and Steven Pieterse (Webmaster at the GSB), Balisi and Nischal designed a 60-question Web-based survey, hosted at the GSB. Since it was not feasible to survey the entire company of 6,000 employees, they consciously subdivided the company to ensure that Debswana's three operations and job grades, described in Table 17-2, were represented in the survey results. The population was subdivided by geography (operation) and job grade or band (see Table 17-1) according to the following criteria:

- Operations: Jwaneng, OLD Mines, and head office
- Patterson grade: C-band, D-band, and E-bands

Population details are presented in Table 17-2.

The structured, quantitative survey was designed to assess the KM business enablers identified in the framework categorized as:

- People and Process Management.
- Organizational Culture and Structure.
- Performance Measurement.
- Organizational Strategy and Planning.
- Information Management and Technology.

Table 17-1
Patterson Grades or Bands Included in the Study (as Defined for Debswana)

E-Upper	Executive management: Formulate corporate and operational strategies (long-term planning).
E-Lower	Provide direction and support in implementation of business plans.
D-Upper	Implement business plans and are involved in short- to medium-term planning.
D-Lower	In general, D-Lower level employees are responsible for implementing operational plans.
C-Upper	This level of employees is responsible for providing supervisory support to shop-floor employees who "do the work," and includes Plant, Maintenance, Pit, Purchasing, and Projects supervisors.
C-Lower	In general employees at this level "do the work." They generally have Ordinary Level (O level) education and have job-specific training. These are skilled workers and include artisans, plant and machine operators, IT assistants, etc.

Table 17-2
Stratified Target Population Details

Grade	OLD Mines	Jwaneng	Head Office	Total
E-band (U&L)	13	10	11	34
D-band (U&L)	160	111	15	286
C-band*	132	92	14	238
Total	305	213	41	558

* Estimates based on the number of graduates, artisans, and operators with at least O-levels.
U or "Upper" implies a higher level of responsibility than L or "Lower" in each band and commands a higher salary.

The survey questions were answered on a typical five-point scale (1 = strongly disagree, 3 = neutral, 5 = strongly agree). The questionnaire was available to employees on the Web, and responses were automatically captured in a Microsoft Excel spreadsheet.

Summary results (Table 17-3) of the questionnaire indicate that the respondents believed that Debswana was ready for a Knowledge

Table 17-3
Business Enablers to Assess Readiness and Questions Below 3

Business Enablers	Mean	Questions Below 3.0
People and Process Management	3.18	6
Organizational Culture and Structure	3.14	5
Performance Measurement	3.36	0
Organizational Strategy and Planning	3.50	1
Information Management and Technology	3.34	3
Overall Readiness	3.30	

Management initiative indicated by business enablers all greater than 3, a normal rating. There were some differences between the categories. Organizational Strategy and Planning was furthest along in preparing for a KM initiative. Performance Measurement and Information Management and Technology were the next highest. The last were People and Process Management and Organizational Culture and Structure.

In order to address potential barriers, the interviewers needed to evaluate the individual questions that indicated actions to be taken to ensure KM implementation success. The responses that indicated a lack of readiness (less than 3.0), it was believed, needed specific attention. These questions are listed in Table 17-4.

The differences between the three geographic operations were also calculated (see Table 17-5). There was only one statistically significant difference between operations—i.e., in the Information Management and Technology criteria. The results indicated that each operation was ready to embark on a Knowledge Management program.

In addition to location, or operation, the data was analyzed by:

- Grade (C-band, D-band, and E-band).
- Length of organizational service in years—less than 3 years, 4–10 years, 11–15 years, and greater than 15 years.
- Length in current position—less than 3 years, 4–10 years, 11–15 years, and greater than 15 years.

These categories could be used to tailor education and training during implementation. Results indicated that the workers and supervisors, C-band respondents, score significantly higher than the

Table 17-4
Individual Questions with Mean Values Significantly Less Than 3

Question No. (Q)	Mean Value	Question
		People and Process Management
1.4	2.37	Encouragement of risk taking.
1.5	2.74	Encouragement of experimentation.
1.6	2.58	Employee promotion linked to acquiring and sharing knowledge.
1.8	2.64	Thinking creatively to solve problems.
1.13	2.81	More team-based rewards than for individual performance.
1.14	2.59	Employee motivation to share knowledge and experiences.
		Organizational Culture and Structure
2.8	2.80	Sharing lessons from experiences is an established practice.
2.9	2.74	People take time to reflect on key issues after projects end.
2.12	2.57	People are encouraged to acknowledge and share their failures.
2.13	2.71	Disagreement is an opportunity to learn.
2.18	2.64	The organization is flexible rather than rigid.
		Organizational Strategy and Planning
4.4	2.80	We sit down at least once annually and decide what information, knowledge, and work practices are relevant going forward.
		Information Management and Technology
5.1	2.81	Sharing knowledge and experiences is possible without IT.
5.5	2.63	Established ways for employees to document and share experiences and learning are well embedded into organizational work routines and used frequently by employees.
5.8	2.62	The intranet is used extensively to share knowledge and experiences.

Table 17-5
Mean Values for Business Enablers Between Operations

Business Enabler	Jwaneng	OLD Mines	Head Office	Company
People and Process Management	3.20	3.17	3.04	3.18
Organizational Culture and Structure	3.16	3.13	3.02	3.14
Performance Measurement	3.37	3.36	3.30	3.36
Organizational Strategy and Planning	3.54	3.48	3.23	3.50
Information Management and Technology	3.42	3.26	3.13	3.34
Overall Readiness	3.34	3.28	3.14	3.30

implementers and middle managers, D-band respondents, for all enablers. They also score significantly higher than the executives, E-band respondents, in terms of Performance Measurement and Information Management and Technology. These differences influence the result of overall readiness. The differences have significant implications for implementation planning since the C-band employees who were ready to participate in a KM program would be hindered without executive and middle management support.

There are no significant differences from an overall readiness perspective between respondents of varying lengths of organizational service. Indications are that respondents who have less than three years' service and those who have greater than 15 years' service believed the organization was more ready than the other two groups—but this result is not statistically significant. On comparison of the business enablers, the only statistically significant result is for Organizational Culture and Structure. Respondents who have greater than 15 years' service scored significantly higher than those who have spent 4 to 10 years at Debswana. This was interpreted as follows:

- Employees with less than 4 years in the company were in a "honeymoon phase"—for them the money is good, and they have not been loaded with significant management responsibilities as yet.

- Employees with 4–10 years in employment were in junior and middle management ranks and were under pressure from the general workforce to address their welfare issues, and from senior management to meet all operational targets—they, on a daily basis, saw the worst part of the organizational culture.

- Employees with more than 15 years were both the architects of the culture and the maintainers of the culture, and as a result of this mind-set had the most to lose. Quite paradoxically though, they were the group that firmly believed that anything was possible and therefore KM, like any other initiative, should be successfully implemented without any real fundamental changes to the way the organization was managed.

There are no significant differences between respondents of varying lengths in their current positions for each of the business enablers as well as for overall readiness.

The Results Summarized

The results of the interviews and quantitative survey gave the research pair confidence that Debswana was ready for Knowledge Management. They labeled and summarized their findings as follows.

Finding 1: Benchmarking

The company EXCO was not aware of what competitors outside the De Beers group of companies were doing with respect to the development of knowledge.

Finding 2: Debswana's Knowledge Assets

The EXCO believes that Debswana's knowledge assets include:

- Intellectual capital, specifically people. The emphasis is on people's knowledge and experiences.
- Information stored both in hard copies and on electronic media.

Finding 3: Responsibility for Knowledge Capture

Everyone should be responsible for capturing knowledge through an established process or system. However, there should be an appointed driver from EXCO to oversee the process.

Finding 4: Knowledge Requirements Plan

Debswana does not have a knowledge requirements plan for the next 3–5 years. However, the company has started looking at implementing a KM strategy, and as part of that process, a knowledge requirement plan will be drawn up.

Finding 5: Benefits of KM

The EXCO members believe that KM implementation will result in productivity improvements through:

- Reduction in mistakes.
- No "reinvention of the wheel."
- Access to best practices within the company and from outside.
- Focusing on value-adding work.

Finding 6: Barriers to KM Implementation

The EXCO members see key barriers as:

- Silo-type organizational structures.
- Poor employee buy-in due to:
  - ▽ Fear of loss of knowledge and therefore power.
  - ▽ Increased workload.
  - ▽ "Change fatigue."
  - ▽ Lack of incentives: "What's in it for me?"
  - ▽ KM being seen as an initiative that would potentially lead to job losses.
  - ▽ Inadequate understanding of where KM adds value.
  - ▽ Time constraints.

EXCO members recognize the importance of organizational culture and performance management as key to KM implementation.

Finding 7: Knowledge Capture Process

EXCO members believe that current knowledge capture happens in unstructured ways. They see knowledge capture happening through:

- Reports.
- Project work.
- Ideas and suggestion schemes.
- Electronic knowledge assets.
- Written policies and procedures.

Finding 8: Knowledge-Sharing Systems

EXCO members believe that knowledge sharing happens through:

- Intranets.
- E-mail.
- "Green areas."
- Cross-functional information-sharing sessions.
- Training sessions.
- Presentations.
- Mentoring.

However, they see these ways as being ineffective or insufficient alone for knowledge sharing.

Finding 9: Culture for Acquisition and Sharing of Knowledge

In general, the EXCO members believe that the culture is not yet conducive to motivating employees to acquire and share knowledge. The key concern raised is that the culture promotes individualism and is seen to be encouraging the "knowledge is power" concept. They, however, point to evidence that the culture is changing for the better and cite the following as examples:

- Ideas and suggestion schemes
- Acceptance of risk taking and experimentation and tolerance of failure

Finding 10: Role of Organizational Culture in KM Implementation

EXCO members believe that organizational culture plays a vital role in enabling successful implementation of KM. They all emphasize the role of management in creating a culture that is supportive to KM, and suggest that the culture should:

- Support risk taking and experimentation.
- Support learning and sharing.
- Encourage transparency through open communication.

Finding 11: Role of IT in Successful Implementation

Technology is viewed as an enabler that facilitates capturing, storage, and sharing of information or knowledge. EXCO members give examples of the Internet, intranets, e-mail, and bulletin boards as typical technologies for use in KM.

Finding 12: KM Assessment

EXCO members believe that measuring the contribution of KM to the financial performance of the company may not be so obvious, especially in the short term. However, they view the use of the balanced scorecard approach as an effective way of tracking KM implementation.

The Primary Research Finding: Debswana Is Ready for a KM Initiative

Overall

Statistically, the overall readiness was greater than 3, and the interviews indicated positive attitudes toward a KM project for Debswana to improve performance. The areas that raised some concern, at the individual question level, relate to People and Process Management and Organizational Culture and Structure (see Table 17.3). These themes summarize significant differences less than 3.0:

- Encouragement of risk taking and experimentation
- Motivation to share knowledge and experiences
- An established practice of sharing experiences
- Encouragement to acknowledge and share failures
- Organizational flexibility

This is consistent with the EXCO members' concern about the organizational culture. Despite their belief that acceptance of risk taking and experimentation and tolerance of failure were increasing, the overall opinion was that they had not increased to an acceptable level. Furthermore, EXCO members considered the lack of appropriate incentives and silo-type organizational structures as barriers to implementation. Another concern identified was that the overall scores for motivation to share knowledge and experiences, as well as organizational flexibility, were significantly lower than 3.0.

The most important theme emphasized the importance of knowledge sharing. Despite Debswana being ready overall and acknowledging the importance of a sharing culture, there was cause for concern in that sharing experiences was currently not an established and embedded practice.

At the Operational Level

All three operations values for readiness were greater than 3.0, indicating that they were ready to embark on a Knowledge Management initiative. Jwaneng was significantly more ready than OLD Mines in terms of Information Management and Technology. This result was driven by the view that more information sharing between departments and operations happened at Jwaneng. Further, the intranet appeared to be used more extensively for sharing knowledge and experiences at Jwaneng than at OLD Mines. An Information Management and Technology usage audit across sites would have been useful in understanding the key differences that affect this result.

Requirements During Implementation—Summary

Table 17-6 summarizes the most important themes associated with each business enabler.

PREPARING FOR IMPLEMENTATION

Having determined that Debswana was ready for successfully implementing a KM strategy, Balisi and Nischal were faced with another level of question: What is the most effective way for Debswana to successfully implement a KM strategy?

To answer this question effectively, they developed a framework to guide implementation: a road map. They used the work of KPMG Consulting (2000) and that of Cheah (2000), of Knowledge

Table 17-6
Important Themes Associated with Business Enablers

Business Enabler	Important Themes
People and Process	Management commitment to employee development
Management	Encouragement of experimentation and of risk taking Motivation of employees
Organizational Culture and Structure	Sharing of knowledge and experiences Learning Organizational flexibility
Performance Measurement	Organizational value of KM must be built into the individual performance management system
Organizational Strategy and Planning	KM implementation to focus on employee participation and best practices Resource allocation by senior management should be dictated by knowledge needs assessment
Information Management and Technology	IT infrastructure and systems as enablers to connect to information requirements IT allowing both ease of relevant access and appropriate security to information and best practices

Management Services (NCS), as foundations to develop their plan for Debswana's KM journey.

PROPOSED CONCEPTUAL IMPLEMENTATION FRAMEWORK—USING A JOURNEY ROAD MAP

The framework assumes that Debswana has an explicit organization-wide business strategy. It recognizes the point that KM strategy should be aligned to this strategy and that planning should precede any form of implementation. The six pillars of the framework represent the business enablers: (1) structure, (2) leadership, (3) culture, (4) people and process management, (5) information technology, and (6) performance management. A "review or audit" pillar is added as a seventh pillar in the framework. The overall purpose of auditing is to be able to justify the return on investment in knowledge assets and to minimize the risk of not having aligned business enablers for achieving business objectives (Chong, Wilhelmij, and Schmidt, 2000). Change management supports all the pillars and represents

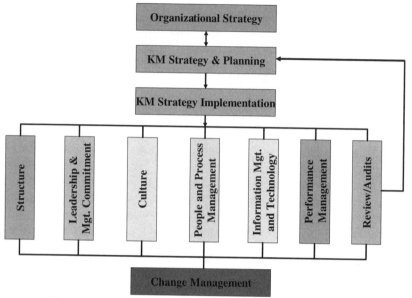

Figure 17-3. Conceptual implementation framework

the foundation on which successful implementation is developed (Figure 17-3). An individual model was developed for each of the business enablers in the framework.

Strategy and Planning Model

Understanding the benefits associated with a KM program helps set priorities for implementation planning. Debswana needs to clearly articulate its Knowledge Management vision to provide direction and a sense of purpose for the workforce. The model in Figure 17-4 is a basis for planning KM implementation in the company.

In the context of this model, Debswana needs to make a business case for implementing KM. In doing so, it should be aware that it is not always easy to link KM value directly to the financial bottom-line results—even though many attempts have been made globally (e.g., Edvinsson, Sveiby, Saint-Onge, Allee, Show Business, Quadrint). Debswana's top management is aware that immediate financial benefits of KM may not be realized.

The model also highlights the need for a KM readiness assessment to be conducted. The research project demonstrated the value of an

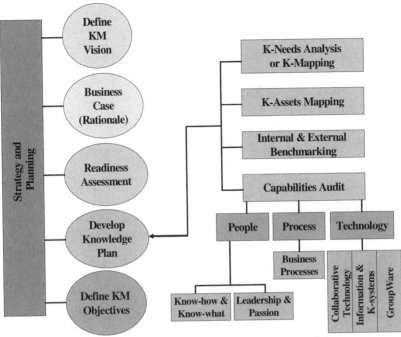

Figure 17-4. Strategy and planning model

assessment to help management to understand the strengths and weaknesses of the business enablers. A strategic planning process is the next obvious step in getting Debswana closer to realizing business benefits from this exercise. Perhaps the most important element of the planning process is the development of a knowledge requirements plan for the company as a whole. Envisaged activities that are part of the process of developing a strategic plan are:

- Knowledge needs analysis or mapping.
- Knowledge assets mapping.
- Internal and external benchmarking. It is important for Debswana to carry out internal benchmarking first, to understand *what the company is good at* with respect to KM processes of capture, storage, access or retrieval, and use. For instance, the OLD Mines may have some highly effective and productive sharing forums. In the internal benchmarking exercise, the characteristics and success factors of these forums will be documented as best practice and dynamically shared with the rest of the organization. External benchmarking should be seen

as an important aspect of planning because it assists management in understanding threats and opportunities that can significantly impact business performance (both from within the sector as well as outside of the obvious sector).

- Capabilities audit. This is an exercise where the company assesses its strengths and weaknesses in the areas of people technologies, process technologies, learning technologies, business technologies, and technological systems and infrastructure. In the context of people, Debswana needs to have a good understanding of the expertise, and individual motivators, of its knowledge workers and where there are located, and prefer to be located (colocated or virtually located), in the organization. Further, the company should identify those people with a passion for, experience in, and a track record in KM, learning, and people management. These are the individuals who could play leading roles in creating conducive local and organization-wide environments for unlocking tacit knowledge. With regard to process, Debswana needs to take stock of its people and performance management processes: employee development, rewards and recognition, decision-making and participation mechanisms. On the technology side, it is essential that the company understand what data, information, intelligence, and Knowledge Management systems it has. These would include the IT infrastructure, databases and data stores, intranets, discussion and bulletin boards, etc.

Once the current capabilities are fully understood, Debswana would then be in a position to articulate a comprehensive knowledge requirements plan. On the basis of this plan, the following questions can be asked: What knowledge is required? Where will the knowledge be sourced and how? Who will source what knowledge?

The answers to these questions should then be addressed through a clear definition of short- and long-term objectives. At this stage, the company would be ready to proceed with the other models in the implementation framework, which addresses the business enablers:

- Implementation structure model
- Leadership and management commitment model
- Organizational culture model
- People and process management model

- Information management and technology model
- Performance management model

CRITICAL CHANGE MANAGEMENT

Implementing a KM strategy in Debswana will bring fundamental change to the way information and knowledge are managed and to the way people communicate, collaborate, and interact to share ideas, insights, and perspectives. Such change may bring fear, anxiety, and uncertainty to employees. In order to avoid potential problems, and to make maximum use of the creative tension such change engenders, Debswana needs an effective change management plan. Figure 17-5 is a proposed change management model, which forms part of the conceptual implementation framework.

Figure 17-5 underscores leadership commitment, a good selling proposition for change, training, piloting, and effective communication as some of the critical success factors required for KM implementation in the company. The following is a summary of the model.

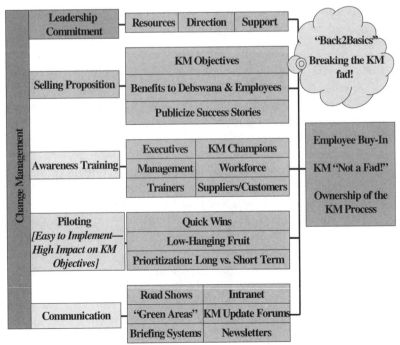

Figure 17-5 Change management model

- Leadership and management teams must fully support the KM initiative through provision of clear direction and human and financial resources. Time and space must also be created for knowledge workers to experiment and take risks and share their knowledge with others.
- A plan to sell KM to all levels of the organization should be articulated. The plan serves as a marketing tool for the initiative and must accordingly create a sense of urgency in the organization. The research pair propose that the plan should sell KM in the form of stories that reflect the culture and diversity of the organization (and the telling of stories should also be used to celebrate early successes, otherwise known as the "low-hanging fruit" successes). Further, to break the thinking that KM may be yet "another passing fad," the KM steering committee and knowledge champions should adopt a slogan that demystifies it. An example of a slogan is "Back to Basics—Using KM—The Implementation Plan."

Balisi summarized the goal: "Let us improve on yesterday, and learn what we don't know, so that we stop repeating previous mistakes and reinventing the wheel." This will be done in three stages.

- Awareness training is essential for successful implementation. Training must initially take place at the executive level of the organization prior to rolling it down to lower levels of the organization. Key suppliers and customers, as well as other stakeholders, must also be made aware of the KM initiative, particularly the role that they will play in it and potential benefits to them (and thus must be asked to be contributors).
- Piloting of KM initiatives is critical and must be seen as a mechanism for developing a convincing case for an organization-wide rollout. A pull strategy should be adopted at this stage—that is, piloting should be targeted at those parts of the business with visible problems and where managers are keen to apply KM methodologies to assist in the faster, more efficient, and cost-effective solving of the problems. The idea is to capitalize on "low-hanging fruit" to gain quick wins that the steering committee and champions can use to sell the KM initiative to the wider group.
- Communication remains the foundation for implementing the strategy, and all existing channels must be used. New commu-

nication channels should be explored and implemented to facilitate buy-in and ownership of the KM process.

In conclusion, an audit or review process (incorporating robust and rigorous measures) is necessary to ensure that the KM initiative is adding, and not destroying, value.

CONCLUSION

Implementation of a KM strategy requires a readiness assessment to help management understand the strengths and weaknesses of the business enablers. Balisi and Nischal developed a useful framework with the following five business enablers to assess organizational readiness for implementation of a KM strategy:

- People and Process Management
- Organizational Culture and Structure
- Performance Measurement
- Organizational Strategy and Planning
- Information Management and Technology

The findings of the research showed that Debswana, as an organization, is ready for implementation of a KM strategy. Results from the primary research survey, however, indicate that there are specific themes in People and Process Management and Organizational Culture and Structure that need attention when an implementation framework is being developed.

In terms of People and Process Management, results show that the levels of risk taking and experimentation, as well as motivation to acquire and share knowledge, are not optimal. EXCO members have also confirmed this during earlier exploratory research interviews.

The major concern in terms of Organizational Culture and Structure is that sharing lessons from experiences and failures is not yet an established practice. EXCO members, who believe that the culture is not yet conducive to motivating employees to acquire and share knowledge, have also confirmed this. Primary research has also revealed that organizational rigidity is an issue. The EXCO considers lack of knowledge-sharing incentives and silo-type organizational structures as barriers to implementation.

The findings also show that each of the three operations is ready for KM implementation. Jwaneng is significantly more ready than

OLD Mines in terms of Information Management and Technology. This result is driven by the view that more information sharing between departments and operations happens at Jwaneng. In addition, the intranet appears to be used more extensively for sharing knowledge and experiences at Jwaneng than at the OLD Mines.

In terms of differences between the employees, C-band employees are of a significantly greater opinion that the organization is ready to implement a KM strategy, when compared with both the D-band and E-band respondents. Further, employees who have greater than 15 years' service believe that the current organizational culture and structure are more conducive to implementation than employees who have spent 4 to 10 years at Desbwana.

The objective for Debswana is to develop a KM system that would ensure effective creation, sharing, and use of knowledge. The proposed framework articulates a broad road map that guides its endeavors to become a knowledge-driven company. The temptation in implementing such a system may be to place high emphasis on technology solutions to drive the process. Although this has advantages, there is danger of being drawn into a "technology trap." Debswana must steer away from this potential detraction and must focus on harnessing the power of human interaction to deliver a sustainable KM capability that will make it a truly global benchmark mining company.

RETURNING TO DEBSWANA

In preparing to return to Debswana after the intense learning experience, Balisi contemplated how he would sell this concept to senior managers. He chose a name for the project, "Back-To-Basics," and developed a selling proposition. His reasons for choosing the name were the following:

- The organization will get back to the employees who feel left out but who do value-adding work everyday. The environment will be created for those employees to contribute what they know. In doing so, these employees will assist in the optimization of processes and systems, thereby adding value and removing non-value-adding activities.
- People will relate to the new name and identify easily with it. This will minimize the charges of KM being labeled a passing fad.

His plan is to kick off the initiative with a KM workshop for senior managers from the three operations. The workshop will introduce the KM framework and strategy. The output of the workshop will be a five-year implementation plan including the following:

- The role of the knowledge leader and his or her team.
- A two-tier strategy focusing on quick wins, especially new interventions in the organizations where application of KM concepts can be demonstrated, and focusing on "mainstream" employees where they add value by getting them involved in the value stream mapping exercises on the business processes. The intention of these exercises will be to initiate conversation among employees on what adds value and what does not, consequently optimizing processes.
- A pull strategy for the implementation process. The team will start working with business units that express a need for and an interest in implementing KM. Once a business unit has shown interest, all aspects of implementation (training, knowledge mapping, identification of opportunity areas, decision milestones, measurement, etc.) will be defined and packaged to meet the expectation of all stakeholders.
- Because of the importance of KM to the organization's business strategy, monthly review meetings between the knowledge manager and senior management (business unit heads) will take place to discuss progress and new initiatives. High-level KM review sessions will be a part of the quarterly review process. Through these forums, the organization's executives will get to know the achievements and implementation challenges faced by the KM team and business units. Most important, they will be given presentations on current actions and the opportunity to endorse future initiatives.

The workshop will end by demonstrating a KM process of "learning after" an event. The learning from the workshop experience will be captured to benefit future workshops, which are planned at the business unit level and will then be cascaded down the organization. We will ask every participant to answer each standardized After Action Review (AAR) question: What was supposed to happen? What actually happened? What were the differences? What would you do differently the next time? What should be sustained, and what should be improved? . . . And the KM initiative at Debswana will be launched.

ADDENDUM

As Balisi returned to Debswana, his personal vision and goal was to generate sufficient conversation in the workplace that would result in a natural tendency by people to want to share their knowledge and experiences, and to get people to understand that they add value to themselves (learn) by sharing what they know with others. He also claimed larger responsibility: "I want to take this philosophy beyond Debswana and be able to practice this passion of mine in the greater society."

Six months later, Balisi had returned to Botswana and assumed a new job at the Debswana head office as divisional metallurgist, with the intention of moving into a very senior position in the company. His intention was to spend 10% of his time on KM issues and to be an advisor to the Debswana KM steering committee. He spoke of his personal intention for KM:

> I am pushing for a new culture throughout the organization that recognizes the value of cross-functional team problem solving. This has taken off via learning-in-action concepts where all projects are now subjected to the process of learning before, After Action Reviews, and Retrospects. Debswana has for many years replicated effort, repeated mistakes, and countless times reinvented the wheel. This is our point of departure in getting people involved in these projects to "talk," to share knowledge. We have defined leading and lagging indicators to assist us in managing the effectiveness of implementing KM projects. There is a lot of enthusiasm among those who have accepted the "KM call."

We have established a Debswana steering committee that oversees KM implementation. A senior executive officer sits on this committee, and a KM coordinator has been appointed at the company level. We are in the process of appointing KM managers at the various Debswana operations who will focus on implementation. We are reviewing the preliminary KM strategy that was drafted in 2002, with a view to positioning KM as *a way of doing things* in Debswana. An electronic directory (K-Exchange) has been developed, and a significant number of our knowledge workers are linked (see Chapter 10, Implementing Knowledge Management within De Beers: The Early Years, for more details).

The next step will be to document functional teams involved in KM projects.

Knowledge Management *is* happening in Debswana.

Balisi Bonyongo is employed by Debswana Diamond Company, a 50–50 partnership between De Beers and the government of Botswana. He graduated from Leeds University in the UK with a First Class Honours degree in mineral engineering in 1992. He began his career with Orapa Mine, one of Debswana's large diamond operations. During the nine years following graduation, Balisi assumed several positions in the company. In 1994, he was tasked with the development of a computer-based system for online monitoring of X-ray diamond sorting machines. The system is now used in all the De Beers operations. In 1996, Balisi was appointed project metallurgist in charge of transforming one of the Debswana diamond processing plants from manual operation to automatic control. The success of this project made him one of the most admired reengineering experts in Debswana. The biggest challenge for Balisi came in 1998 when he was made responsible for the commissioning of a new diamond processing facility at Jwaneng Mine, referred to as the Aquarium Project. The facility, which utilizes state-of-the-art X-ray and laser sorting technology, handles Debswana's total diamond output, amounting to some 26 million carats annually. In 2001, Balisi became the Aquarium's first plant manager. It was on the strength of these achievements that in 2002 Debswana offered Balisi an opportunity to study full-time for an M.B.A. degree at the GSB in Cape Town. On his return, Balisi was transferred to the Debswana head office in Gaborone as divisional metallurgist. His main task was to formulate a Knowledge Management strategy for the company. Balisi has recently been promoted to the position of treatment manager at Jwaneng Mine, the world's richest diamond deposit. He joined the mine's executive committee in August 2003. Balisi is highly respected in Debswana for his leadership abilities, especially in directing business process reengineering initiatives and promoting a "culture of knowledge sharing through collaboration."

Nischal K. Sancho is a South African citizen employed by Caltex Oil South Africa, a downstream operations company in the ChevronTexaco Corporation. Nischal graduated from Natal University, South Africa, with a chemical engineering bachelor's degree in 1994 and completed his M.S. in chemical engineering in 1996. In recognition of outstanding scholastic achievement and excellence, he has been granted membership in the Golden Key International Honour Society. He joined LeverPonds South Africa in 1997, assuming various roles as process engineer in Durban and Boskburg (South Africa), before completing projects and training in Port Sunlight (UK) and Vlaardingen (Holland) in 1999. In 2000, Nischal was appointed regional process development manager for the Unilever Africa Business Group, working primarily on "low-income consumer" projects in West, East, and South East Africa. His success in this role laid the foundation for his being appointed global project leader to assess and develop contract manufacturing options in support of Unilever's "world-class supply chain" strategic thrust in 2001. Nischal completed his M.B.A. full-time, with distinction, in 2002 at the University of Cape Town. His current role at COSA is that of supply chain optimization manager, where he leads all supply chain optimization planning activities across the supply and trading, refining, and marketing business units. He has recently implemented the "street-to-crude" integrated margin methodology to facilitate management decision making.

REFERENCES

Cheah, E. "Knowledge Innovation in Public Service: Knowledge Discovery . . . Let the Journey Begin." Knowledge Management Services—National Computer Systems (NCS) Pte Ltd., http://www.ncs.com.sg/, 2000 (accessed on August 16, 2002).

Chong, C. W., Wilhelmij, P., and Schmidt, R. A. "Where Does Knowledge Management Add Value?" *Journal of Intellectual Capital*, Vol. 1, No. 4, 2000, pp. 366–380.

KPMG Consulting. "The Knowledge Journey: A Business Guide to Knowledge Systems." www.kpmgconsulting.co.uk/research, 2000 (accessed on August 27, 2002).

Readiness Survey for a KM Initiative

By Kurt April

INTRODUCTION

This section introduces a diagnostic tool that management within organizations can administer to every level of employee in their departments, divisions, and business units. The tool is designed as a starting point for management to clarify the readiness of their departments, business units, and divisions for embarking on a Knowledge Management (KM) initiative. If management and their organizations are not clear at the outset about current employees and the human state of affairs (in addition to process and technology) within their departments, divisions, and business units, they will in all likelihood start with an unfocused program or initiative and run the risk of failure. Their energies will be dissipated in broad, and even misdirected, agendas that are not directed toward solving their people and organizational problems in the most efficient and effective manner.

Much of the material that is sold today under the title "Knowledge Management" relates only to the informational base and its accompanying technologies. Therefore, the key focus area of this instrument is the need for understanding some of the systemic barriers to and enablers of Knowledge Management. These factors can make or limit the success of a Knowledge Management initiative in any organization.

The Kukard-April-Pinkham (KAP) diagnostic tool is designed to raise awareness of the potential gaps that exist within departments, divisions, and business units and encourages subsequent action planning and steps on the part of management.

Organizational Lifecycle and Readiness

Ichak Adizes developed the Adizes curve in order to illustrate the changes in organizational culture at different stages of the organizational lifecycle. Figure A-1 illustrates the different stages in the lifecycle of an organization.

Adizes' six stages of the organizational lifecycle can be summarized as follows:

- The *courtship* stage is characterized by entrepreneurial excitement, an external focus, and a focus on innovation, service improvement, and new service development. Organizations in this stage tend to exhibit emergent strategies, rather than fixed strategies, and are flexible and responsive to the environmental forces shaping the organization. There is also a great deal of passion and belief in the organization from staff working in these organizations. This passion, level of excitement, and responsiveness emanate from the precourtship stage (also termed the *infancy* stage, which is the ideas and concept stage).

- The next stage, *adolescence,* sees the organization's expanding service lines (both the number and type of services offered to their customers and the public) in order to get better buy-in from their customers and the public and to deliver on organizational promises in order to meet needs and demands. The focus starts moving away from an external focus to a focus on

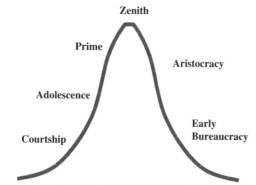

Figure A-1. Adizes' organizational lifecycle stages

internal projects—this stage is characterized by "delivery through projects and services." The strategic vision centers on achieving immediate, visible impacts and results.

- By the *prime* stage, the organization has developed into an efficient and effective organization with a loyal public and citizen base. The organization's image and in particular the image of specific departments, divisions, and business units within the organization are well established. The strategic focus is on developing new services, new work processes, and new departments and divisions within the organization. New communication and marketing strategies are developed during this stage.

- In the *zenith* stage, organizations are at the height of the Adizes curve, and they enjoy the benefits of being an established organization, with a good reputation, and are highly responsive and flexible to the changes in its environment. Systems, processes, and infrastructures are in place, and the strategic focus is on continuous improvement.

- When organizations reach the *aristocracy* stage, they are usually a dominant force. The most notable change is that they are starting to lose their entrepreneurial edge, and complacency starts to set in. Systems start becoming less flexible and responsive, and "red tape" starts strangling creativity and innovation. The organization's strategic focus is on maintaining what it already does, providing services without continuous improvement, and maintaining the status quo, with defensive actions predominating. The organization becomes more and more inwardly focused and less responsive to the environment and its stakeholders.

- This inflexibility is exacerbated in the *early bureaucracy* stage, where the organization is unresponsive to the environment and starts losing sight of its stakeholders' needs as well as its staff needs, with rigid processes predominating. Interactions, systems, and processes become more and more formalized. Senior staff cling to jobs and reinforce their own ways of working (possibly even repeating past successes as a way to address the future), without any desire to reinvent processes, structures, and systems. More and more levels of hierarchy are created, and senior staff grow departmental or divisional "empires" to assert their importance as well as to justify their benefits and salaries.

Adizes recommends that organizations remain in the prime stage. And if they slip forward onto the right side of the Adizes curve, they should try to replicate the environment of the infancy (precourtship) stage in order to return to the left side of the Adizes curve.

This theory is especially applicable to knowledge-intensive organizations because of the flexibility required to interact effectively with the rapidly changing external, local, and global environment. Creativity, innovation, and continuous improvement through learning, in these situations, are the life staff of such organizations' futures. It is important that departments, divisions, and business units continuously (at regular time intervals) make accurate assessments (monitoring) of where they are along the Adizes curve, and adapt their organizational strategies accordingly, making explicit what they want to achieve.

The KAP Organizational Readiness Framework, developed by Julia Kukard, Colin Pinkham, and Kurt April, was designed to evaluate the "people readiness" of an organization for a Knowledge Management initiative and is based on the Adizes curve. The tool is based on the notion of a series of continuums of organizational behavior. These include alignment with organizational strategy, the organizational structure, the processes within an organization, the organization's learning style, learning rewards, etc.

The KAP Organizational Readiness Framework is a diagnostic tool. It is completed by reading the questions along the right-hand side of the table ("questions to be asked to reveal information"). Responses to the questions vary among "good," "bad," "yes," "no," "high," "low," "many," "few," "team," or "individual." A single number ("1")—since only one person completes this diagnostic—is inserted as a response to each question. However, in answering the questions with appropriate responses (as listed earlier), respondents should be aware of where their department or division is along the Adizes curve at that particular time (2-D answer).

An example of a completed diagnostic form is shown in Figure A-2. The resultant scores, together with the knowledge of whether your department, division or business unit is a left-sided or right-sided organization has major implications for *how to proceed further* if you want to maximize, in the shortest time possible, the impact of a Knowledge Management initiative in your department, division, or business unit.

Using the example in Figure A-2, the final totals lead to Table A-1.

KAP Organizational Readiness Framework©
To Evaluate People Management Issues

Areas	Sub-Area	Preference Indicator	Courtship	Adolescence	Prime	Zenith	Aristocracy	Early Bureaucracy	Preference Indicator	Questions to be asked to reveal information
Organizational Alignment	People management aligned with organizational strategy	Good			1				Poor	Do most employees have some understanding of the group organizational strategy (not the department, division or business unit one – but the group-wide strategy)?
	People participation in designing organizational strategy	Yes						1	No	Do most staff get the opportunity to input into the group strategy (not the department, division or business unit one – but the group-wide strategy)?
	HR strategy aligned with departmental, divisional or business unit organizational strategy	Yes				1			No	Are HR objectives in alignment with, and supported by, the existing departmental, divisional or business unit strategy?
	Understanding of departmental or divisional objectives	Yes					1		No	Do staff understand the department's, division's or business unit's objectives?
	Understanding of personal role in achieving organization's objectives	Yes				1			No	Do your staff understand their role in making those objectives manifest themselves in the workplace?
Areas	Sub-Area	Preference Indicator	Courtship	Adolescence	Prime	Zenith	Aristocracy	Early Bureaucracy	Preference Indicator	Questions to be asked to reveal information
Organizational Structure	Hierarchical Organization	Low						1	High	Are there more than four levels of management within your department, business unit or division? Four will indicate a median level, less than four is *low*, and more than four is *high*.

Figure A-2. Sample of completed organizational readiness instrument

Areas	Sub-Area	Preference Indicator	Courtship	Adolescence	Prime	Zenith	Aristocracy	Early Bureaucracy	Preference Indicator	Questions to be asked to reveal information
Bureaucratic Sluggishness	Centralization	Low					1		High	Are the management structures centralized or decentralized? (Highly centralized is *high*, and totally decentralized is *low*.)
	Decision making from the top	High					1		Low	Does the top manager (e.g., MD) have to check all decisions? (If the top manager does have to check all decisions then it is *low*.)
	Devolution of decision making	Yes					1		No	Are staff enabled to make their own decisions for most issues?
	Participation in important decision-making structures	Yes					1		No	Are all staff able to input into the decisions taken by the department, division or business unit?
	Participation in work-related decisions	Yes						1	No	Can staff input into most issues that affect them?
	Risk taking	Yes						1	No	Is risk taking and experimentation encouraged by management?
	Team work	Yes				1			No	Are most projects managed by teams?
	Intradepartmental team work	High					1		Low	Are teams constituted of members from all the main functions, that you work with, within your department, business unit or division?
	Cross-departmental team work	Yes			1				No	Are the teams comprised of members from other departments, divisions or business units?
	Virtual teams in place	Yes		1					No	Are virtual teams (teams that meet electronically, using computers and/or video- or phone conferencing) in place?
	Value of virtual teams	Yes					1		No	Is the business value of virtual teamwork measured and monitored within your business unit, department or division?
	Transparency and customer interaction	Yes					1		No	Are you encouraged to interact with customers?
	Transparency of decisions and documentation	Yes					1		No	Are customers allowed to see your company strategy documents, and able to question your company's decisions and reasons for decisions?

Figure A-2. Continued

Areas	Sub-Area	Preference Indicator	Courtship	Adolescence	Prime	Zenith	Aristocracy	Early Bureaucracy	Preference Indicator	Questions to be asked to reveal information
Staff Rewards and Diversity	Soft incentives	Many	1						Few	How many *nonfinancial* incentives does your department/business unit use (leave, flexible work hours, educare centers, sent on courses not related to work issues, being able to work from home, etc.)?
	Hard incentives	Many						1	Few	What *financial* incentives do your BU/department use (bonuses, 13th checks, overseas trips, investing money on behalf of employee, etc.)?
	Reward basis	Team					1		Indiv.	Are rewards based on team or individual performance, or both? Both would be a median level.
	Staff diversity	High			1				Low	Does the staff mix bear some resemblance to the population mix in the geographic area of your department, division or business unit?
	Staff retention	High					1		Low	Is there a higher than normal turnover of staff (leaving the department, division or business unit, or leaving the industry. Higher turnover is *low*)?
	Marginalization of minority groups?	Low						1	High	Are minority groups (no's within the organization) marginalized within the department, division or business unit?

Areas	Sub-Area	Preference Indicator	Courtship	Adolescence	Prime	Zenith	Aristocracy	Early Bureaucracy	Preference Indicator	Questions to be asked to reveal information
Learning Style	Formal mentorship (business issues)	Yes						1	No	Does formal learning occur through formal mentorship relationships and programs?
	Formal coaching (personal issues)	Yes		1					No	Does personal learning (related to performance) take place through formal coaching programs?
	Formal training	Yes	1						No	Are there formal training opportunities within the organization?
	Regular formal training	High					1		Low	How regular are the formal training opportunities?
	Informal peer assistance	Yes		1					No	Does informal learning occur through peer assistance?

Figure A-2. Continued

Areas	Sub-Area	Preference Indicator	Courtship	Adolescence	Prime	Zenith	Aristocracy	Early Bureaucracy	Preference Indicator	Questions to be asked to reveal information
	Informal dialogue and storytelling	Yes					1		No	Does informal learning take place through informal dialogue and storytelling?
	IT literacy	High						1	Low	What is the level of computer literacy of most people within your department, division or business unit?
	Shared learning	High						1	Low	What is the level to which learning and knowledge is formally shared within your department, division or BU?
Trust, Information, and Commitment	Organizational trust levels	High						1	Low	What is your level of trust with regard to the organization?
	Team trust levels	Yes						1	No	Do you fully trust the team you work with?
	Leadership trust levels	High					1		Low	What is your level of trust, as far as the leadership of the organization (corporate leadership) is concerned?
	Information and trust	Yes		1					No	Do people look to each other for assistance with information?
	Sharing of information	Yes					1		No	Do people, in your department, BU or division, share information freely?
	Senior management commitment to developing other people	High				1			Low	What are the levels of commitment on the part of senior management (departmental, divisional or BU senior management) as far as the development of their employees are concerned?
	Senior management commitment to developing personal people management skills	High	1						Low	What are the levels of commitment by senior management to developing their own people management skills?

Figure A-2. Continued

Table A-1
Example of Summary of Organizational Life Cycle Stages

SPREAD OF RESPONSES—AS IT RELATES TO ORGANIZATIONAL
LIFECYCLE STAGES

Stages	Courtship	Adolescence	Prime	Zenith	Aristocracy	Early Bureaucracy
Total number of responses per stage	1	3	5	5	16	10

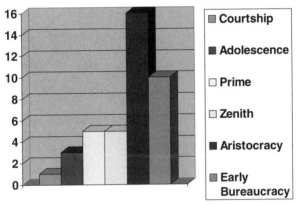

Figure A-3. KM readiness continuum curve

The bar chart in Figure A-3 represents where this organization falls on the Knowledge Management readiness continuum. In this example, it is a right-sided organization, which gives an indication that some fundamental organizational culture, process, and structure changes need to take place before the organization embarks on a Knowledge Management initiative. If the chart is weighted to the left side, an organization is well equipped to establish a Knowledge Management initiative.Table A-2 summarizes the organizational readiness factors for Knowledge Management in left-sided and right-sided organizations.

USING THE DIAGNOSTIC TOOL

Figure A-2 gave a sample of a completed organizational readiness instrument. Figure A-4, which follows, presents the same instrument;

Table A-2
Organizational Readiness Factors for Knowledge Management

	Left-Sided Organizations	Right-Sided Organizations
Factors indicating organizational readiness for a Knowledge Management initiative	• Limited hierarchy • Organizational flexibility • Participatory decision-making structures in place • Focus on teamwork, but also individual responsibility • Cross-functional teams • Majority of staff knowledge workers	• Greater hierarchy • Limited organizational flexibility • Limited participatory decision making • Department-based work as opposed to cross-functional teams • Focus on face-to-face meetings
Planning implications	The organization *can go forward with the knowledge management process* with limited change management interventions.	The *organizational fabric (culture and people processes) need to be addressed* before the knowledge management program can be implemented.

however, it is not filled in. To determine your organization's readiness, you are encouraged to complete the diagnostic tool, using the example in Figure A-2.

After you have completed Figure A-4, you should complete Table A-3. Use the sample summary of organizational lifecycle stage responses presented earlier in Table A-1. Use the resulting data to draw a KM readiness continuum curve to determine whether your department, division, or business unit is a right- or left-sided organization.

Copies of the diagnostic tool should be given to all the employees in your department, division, or business unit to complete anonymously. When they have all returned the completed diagnostic, collate all the results under each of the categories (courtship, adolescence, prime, zenith, aristocracy, and early bureaucracy), reenter the data in Table A-3, and draw a KM readiness continuum curve from the results to determine whether your department, division, or business unit is a right- or left-sided organization.

KAP Organizational Readiness Framework©
To Evaluate People Management Issues

Areas	Sub-Area	Preference Indicator	Courtship	Adolescence	Prime	Zenith	Aristocracy	Early Bureaucracy	Preference Indicator	Questions to be asked to reveal information
Organizational Alignment	People management aligned with organizational strategy	Good							Poor	Do most employees have some understanding of the group organizational strategy (not the department, division or business unit one – but the group-wide strategy)?
	People participation in designing organizational strategy	Yes							No	Do most staff get the opportunity to input into the group strategy (not the department, division or business unit one – but the group-wide strategy)?
	HR strategy aligned with departmental, divisional or business unit organizational strategy	Yes							No	Are HR objectives in alignment with, and supported by, the existing departmental, divisional or business unit strategy?
	Understanding of departmental or divisional objectives	Yes							No	Do staff understand the department's, division's or business unit's objectives?
	Understanding of personal role in achieving organization's objectives	Yes							No	Do your staff understand their role in making those objectives manifest themselves in the workplace?
Areas	Sub-Area	Preference Indicator	Courtship	Adolescence	Prime	Zenith	Aristocracy	Early Bureaucracy	Preference Indicator	Questions to be asked to reveal information
Organizational Structure	Hierarchical Organization	Low							High	Are there more than four levels of management within your department, business unit or division? Four will indicate a median level, less than four is *low*, and more than four is *high*.

Figure A-4. Blank KAP organizational readiness instrument

Areas	Sub-Area	Preference Indicator	Courtship	Adolescence	Prime	Zenith	Aristocracy	Early Bureaucracy	Preference Indicator	Questions to be asked to reveal information
Bureaucratic Sluggishness	Centralization	Low							High	Are the management structures centralized or decentralized? (Highly centralized is *high*, and totally decentralized is *low*.)
	Decision making from the top	High							Low	Does the top manager (e.g., MD) have to check all decisions? (If the top manager does have to check all decisions then it is *low*.)
	Devolution of decision making	Yes							No	Are staff enabled to make their own decisions for most issues?
	Participation in important decision-making structures	Yes							No	Are all staff able to input into the decisions taken by the department, division or business unit?
	Participation in work-related decisions	Yes							No	Can staff input into most issues that affect them?
	Risk taking	Yes							No	Is risk taking and experimentation encouraged by management?
	Team work	Yes							No	Are most projects managed by teams?
	Intradepartmental team work	High							Low	Are teams constituted of members from all the main functions, that you work with, within your department, business unit or division?
	Cross-departmental team work	Yes							No	Are the teams comprised of members from other departments, divisions or business units?
	Virtual teams in place	Yes							No	Are virtual teams (teams that meet electronically, using computers and/or video- or phone conferencing) in place?
	Value of virtual teams	Yes							No	Is the business value of virtual teamwork measured and monitored within your business unit, department or division?
	Transparency and customer interaction	Yes							No	Are you encouraged to interact with customers?
	Transparency of decisions and documentation	Yes							No	Are customers allowed to see your company strategy documents, and able to question your company's decisions and reasons for decisions?

Figure A-4. Continued

Areas	Sub-Area	Preference Indicator	Courtship	Adolescence	Prime	Zenith	Aristocracy	Early Bureaucracy	Preference Indicator	Questions to be asked to reveal information
Staff Rewards and Diversity	Soft incentives	Many							Few	How many *nonfinancial* incentives does your department/business unit use (leave, flexible work hours, educare centers, sent on courses not related to work issues, being able to work from home, etc.)?
	Hard incentives	Many							Few	What *financial* incentives do your BU/ department use (bonuses, 13th checks, overseas trips, investing money on behalf of employee, etc.)?
	Reward basis	Team							Indiv.	Are rewards based on team or individual performance, or both? Both would be a median level.
	Staff diversity	High							Low	Does the staff mix bear some resemblance to the population mix in the geographic area of your department, division or business unit?
	Staff retention	High							Low	Is there a higher than normal turnover of staff (leaving the department, division or business unit, or leaving the industry. Higher turnover is *low*)?
	Marginalization of minority groups?	Low							High	Are minority groups (no's within the organization) marginalized within the department, division or business unit?

Areas	Sub-Area	Preference Indicator	Courtship	Adolescence	Prime	Zenith	Aristocracy	Early Bureaucracy	Preference Indicator	Questions to be asked to reveal information
Learning Style	Formal mentorship (business issues)	Yes							No	Does formal learning occur through formal mentorship relationships and programs?
	Formal coaching (personal issues)	Yes							No	Does personal learning (related to performance) take place through formal coaching programs?
	Formal training	Yes							No	Are there formal training opportunities within the organization?
	Regular formal training	High							Low	How regular are the formal training opportunities?
	Informal peer assistance	Yes							No	Does informal learning occur through peer assistance?

Figure A-4. Continued

	Informal dialogue and storytelling	Yes							No	Does informal learning take place through informal dialogue and storytelling?
	IT literacy	High							Low	What is the level of computer literacy of most people within your department, division or business unit?
	Shared learning	High							Low	What is the level to which learning and knowledge is formally shared within your department, division or BU?

Areas	Sub-Area	Preference Indicator	Courtship	Adolescence	Prime	Zenith	Aristocracy	Early Bureaucracy	Preference Indicator	Questions to be asked to reveal information
Trust, Information, and Commitment	Organizational trust levels	High							Low	What is your level of trust with regard to the organization?
	Team trust levels	Yes							No	Do you fully trust the team you work with?
	Leadership trust levels	High							Low	What is your level of trust, as far as the leadership of the organization (corporate leadership) is concerned?
	Information and trust	Yes							No	Do people look to each other for assistance with information?
	Sharing of information	Yes							No	Do people, in your department, BU or division, share information freely?
	Senior management commitment to developing other people	High							Low	What are the levels of commitment on the part of senior management (departmental, divisional or BU senior management) as far as the development of their employees are concerned?
	Senior management commitment to developing personal people management skills	High							Low	What are the levels of commitment by senior management to developing their own people management skills?

Figure A-4. Continued

Table A-3
Summary of Organizational Life Cycle Stage Responses

SPREAD OF RESPONSES—AS IT RELATES TO ORGANIZATIONAL LIFECYCLE STAGES

Stages	Courtship	Adolescence	Prime	Zenith	Aristocracy	Early Bureaucracy
Total number of responses per stage						

REFERENCES

Adizes, I. *Managing Corporate Lifecycles*. Paramus, NJ: Prentice-Hall, 1999.

Kukard, J., Pinkham, C., and April, K. "Development of a KM Readiness Tool." In-house report of the Graduate School of Business, University of Cape Town, 2000.

Conversational Practices

INTRODUCTION

Appendix B introduces three tools that support conversation, which is a critical skill for knowledge capture, sharing, transfer, and creation: dialogue, Open Space Technology, and the World Café. The three processes are ideally used in face-to-face situations, but they have been adapted and used successfully by virtual workers, teams, and communities.

DIALOGUE

David Bohm labeled "dialogue" as attention to a deeper level of communication and a serious commitment to cooperation (Jaworski, 1996). The word "dialogue" comes from two Greek roots: "dia" and "logos," suggesting "meaning flowing through." This stands in stark contrast to the word "debate," which means to beat down, or even "discussion," which has the same root as "percussion" and "concussion," meaning to break things up. Gerard and Teurfs (1997) state that dialogue consists of four skills and a set of guidelines.

- *Suspending judgment.* Because our way of thinking divides things up and creates what seems like ultimate "truths," it is difficult for us to stay open to alternative views. Our egos become identified with how we think things are. We defend our positions against those of others, and close ourselves off from learning and do harm to our personal relationships. When we "suspend judgment," we see others' points of view, hold our positions lightly, and build a climate of trust and safety. As people learn that they will not be "judged" wrong for having opinions, they feel free to express themselves fully. The atmosphere becomes more open and truthful.

- *Identifying assumptions.* The opinions and judgments we hold are usually based on layers of assumptions, inferences, and generalizations. When we do not look at the underlying belief system behind our judgments, we make decisions that lead to disappointing results. Only when we peel away the assumptions can we see what might be giving us trouble: some incomplete or "incoherent" thought. We can then explore differences, build common ground and consensus, and get to the bottom of misunderstandings.
- *Listening.* The way we listen impacts how well we learn and how effective we are in building quality relationships. We focus on developing our capacity to stay present and open to the meaning arising at both the individual and collective levels. We can learn to listen and perceive at more subtle levels by overcoming typical blocks in our ability to listen attentively and to stay present.
- *Inquiring and reflecting.* Through inquiry and reflection, we dig deeply into matters that concern us and create breakthroughs in our ability to solve problems. By learning how to ask questions that lead to new understanding, we accelerate our collective learning. We gain awareness of our thinking processes and the issues that separate and unite us. By learning how to work with silence, we can identify reactive patterns, generate new ideas, perceive common ground, and gain sensitivity to subtle meanings.

As people gather to dialogue, they commit to a common set of guidelines:

- Listening and speaking without judgment
- Acknowledgment of each speaker
- Respect for differences
- Role and status suspension
- Balancing inquiry and advocacy
- Avoidance of cross talk
- A focus on learning
- Seeking the next level of understanding

- Releasing the need for specific outcomes
- "Speaking when moved"

A great deal of what we call discussion is not deeply serious, in the sense that there are all sorts of things that are nonnegotiable: the undiscussables. No one mentions the undiscussables—they are just there, lying beneath the surface, blocking deep, honest, heart-to-heart communication. Furthermore, we all bring basic assumptions with us—our own mental models or pictures—about how the world operates, our self-interests, etc.

Our basic assumptions are developed from our early childhood days, our life experiences and socialization, our peers and family, our education and reading. We hold these assumptions so deeply that we become identified with them and will defend them with great emotion and energy when they are challenged. Quite often, we do this unconsciously. Jaworski (1996) says, "If there was an opportunity for sustained dialogue over a period of time, we would have coherent movement of thought, not only at the conscious level we all recognize, but even at the tacit level, the unspoken level which cannot be described."

At the next level, we must practice transformationalism, which goes hand in hand with unlearning. This dimension includes attention to releasing human potential and high levels of interaction and alignment. Instead of simply learning to do what we have always done a little better, through transformationalism, dependent initially on individual learning, we must reexamine everything we do. This often means making sense of past experiences and then letting go of some of our existing knowledge and competencies, recognizing that they may prevent us from learning new things. Collaborative inquiry, fostered through dialogue and conversation, forms a bridge between individual learning and the learning organization (Pedler and Aspinwall, 1998).

Adaptive learning is applying the same old concepts or skills in new ways. Generative learning, fundamental to transformationalism—or what Argyris and Schoen (1974, 1996) called "double loop learning," what Bateson (1972) called "deutero-learning," and what Michael (1973) called "learning to learn"—requires the learner to reframe, to develop new concepts and points of view, to cognitively redefine old categories, and to change standards of judgment. Such changes increase the individual's (learner's) capacity to deal with situations in new ways and lay the basis for developing radically new skills. This is a challenging and painful endeavor, and it is through dialogue and conversation—making the implicit explicit—that we come face-to-face with it. When individuals address change in this manner accompanied by a learning effort, then the challenge and pain of examining existing frames is continuous.

Exercising conversation and dialogue, to use Plato's allegory, is akin to encouraging others to come out of the cave and to deal with the true rather than the shadow realities. As Plato pointed out, those who escape from the cave require great skill to persuade others to do the same. The skill of mobilizing others to move to new ground, where they will experience the initial discomfort of new vistas, is what we would like to call transformational learning— seeing the whole by allowing multiple and diverse realities to exist in the same space. Individuals at this level must therefore liberate their colleagues to go beyond the experience base and knowledge base of any one-talent source, to be systems thinkers and optimizers of a living system. For a systems thinker, understanding the network of relationships and investigating the nature of those relationships are primary. The systems thinker understands that to perceive reality is to perceive a certain network of relationships. The systems thinker grasps that different people from different cultures and different walks of life have had different experiences and are themselves living organisms composed of a variety of different networks.

Understanding the implications of this diversity of networks helps us to understand why multiple realities exist. "Stepping back" or "going to a higher viewing point" always provides a different perspective (Beerel, 1998). By seeing the whole, we can better understand how the parts fit together and how the different parts are needed to constitute the whole. To be sensitive to multiple realities is vital in a cross-cultural world, and cross-cultural empathy provides enormous payoffs in dealing with employees, business partners, customers, and competitors. The first step is to acknowledge these new realities through dialogue with other members of the organization. This serves to both communicate and test that these realities exist and that they are perceived correctly. The best teachers have always valued the development of the whole person, but it is now increasingly important in work organizations. This is because of the link between individual personal development and change in the wider system or organization. As Revans (1998) has put it, "Those unable to change themselves cannot change what goes on around them." To make changes at this level requires more than behavioral change. It requires individuals to reframe the situation, to learn new concepts, and to develop new attitudes. In order to develop those capacities, individuals must undergo a learning process that is functionally equivalent to the "organizational learning cycles through learning histories approach" (Nevis et al., 1997), which is used extensively at MIT in the United States.

OPEN SPACE TECHNOLOGY

Harrison Owen (1997) is considered the designer and developer of Open Space Technology, which he considers a collaborative process. It has involved millions of people in 78 countries over 18 years so it has been effective within and across multiple cultures. It is included as a large-scale change tool in organizational development practices. Fundamentally, it encourages conversation as a tool that creates better meetings. For Harrison Owen, "Open Space is a natural laboratory in which to experience and observe superior levels of human performance."

What Is Open Space Technology?

Open Space Technology[1] is one way to enable all kinds of people, in any kind of organization, to create inspired meetings and events. Over the last 15 years, it has also become clear that opening space, as an intentional leadership practice, can create inspired organizations where ordinary people work together to create extraordinary results with regularity.

In Open Space meetings, events, and organizations, participants create and manage their own agenda of parallel working sessions around a central theme of strategic importance, such as What is the strategy, group, organization, or community that all stakeholders can support and work together to create? With groups of 5 to 2,000—working in one-day workshops, three-day conferences, or the regular weekly staff meeting—the common result is a powerful, effective connecting and strengthening of what's already happening in the organization: planning and action, learning and doing, passion and responsibility, participation and performance.

---

[1] Source: Michael Herman at http://www.openspaceworld.org.

When and Why Use Open Space Technology?

Open Space works best when the work to be done is complex, the people and ideas involved are diverse, the passion for resolution (and potential for conflict) are high, and the time to get it done was yesterday. It's been called passion bounded by responsibility, the energy of a good coffee break, intentional self-organization, spirit at work, chaos and creativity, evolution in organization, and a simple, powerful way to get people and organizations moving—when and where it's needed most. And although Open Space is known for its apparent lack of structure and welcoming of surprises, it turns out that the Open Space meeting or organization is actually very structured—but that structure is emergent, literally arising from the people and the work to be done. Thus the structure so perfectly fits to the people and the work at hand that it goes unnoticed in its proper role of supporting (not blocking) best work. And if that is not the case, the people will change it. In fact, the stories and work plans woven in Open Space are generally more complex, more robust, more durable—and can move a great deal faster than expert- or management-driven designs.

What Will Happen?

We never know exactly what will happen when we open the space for people to do their most important work, but we can guarantee these results when any group gets into Open Space.

- All of the issues that are *most* important to the participants will be raised.
- All of the issues raised will be addressed by those participants most qualified and capable of getting something done on each of them.
- In a time as short as one or two days, all of the most important ideas, discussion, data, recommendations, conclusions, questions for further study, and plans for immediate action will be documented in one comprehensive report—finished, printed, and in the hands of participants when they leave.
- When appropriate and time is allowed for it, the total contents of this report document can be focused and prioritized in a matter of a few hours, even with very large groups (1000s).
- After an event, all of these results can be made available to an

entire organization or community within days of the event, so the conversation can invite every stakeholder into implementation—right now.

- *And* results like these can be planned and implemented faster than any other kind of so-called "large-group intervention." It is literally possible to accomplish in days and weeks what some other approaches take months and years to do.

The good news, and the bad news, is that it works. Good news because it gets people and work moving, bad news because that may mean lots of things are going to be different than before. Wanted things can appear, unwanted things disappear, and sometimes vice versa—but that's how life is. In short, then, Open Space brings life back to organizations and organizations back to life.

The Method—Preparation

The following material is adapted from Owen (1997).

1. Issue an open invitation to anyone who is interested in the topic. "Voluntary self-selection is the absolute sine qua non for participation in Open Space." The invitation should be short, simple, and to the point. The objective is to stimulate the imagination of potential participants so that they perceive the pertinence and attractiveness of the issue. Questions are an effective means of creating space for imaginations and ideas to grow. Include logistics in the invitation.
2. Decide on time. One day allows for intense, meaningful, and productive discussion. To create a set of proceedings requires a second day. If the event is scheduled for two and one-half days, it can prioritize issues, converge on related issues, and create action plans. Beyond three days, the law of diminishing returns sets in.
3. Set up the space. Open Space requires one main room large enough for all participants to sit in a circle without crowding. The room should have one free wall that is the community bulletin board, so the ability to tape things on the wall is essential. Breakout areas are also necessary. They can be conversational space and don't have to be formal rooms.
4. Assemble supplies: masking tape, ink markers, flip charts, Post-it notes.
5. Create and post four signs as follows:

The Open Space Theme (from the invitation)

The Four Principles
- Whoever comes are the right people.
- Whatever happens is the only thing that could have happened.
- Whenever it starts is the right time.
- When it's over, it's over.

The One Law
- The Law of Two Feet

Be Prepared to Be Surprised

---

6. Set up the wall where papers will be posted. It must start blank. After the process begins, the wall becomes the agenda; at the beginning it is blank—there is no preplanned agenda.
7. Create and post a schedule and a space and time matrix. This matrix is a place for participants to quickly and easily assign a time and place for their session.

Schedule

First Day
9:00–10:30	Start and Agenda Setting
10:30–12:00	First Session
12:00–1:30	Lunch Available
1:30–3:00	Second Session
3:00–4:30	Third Session
4:30–5:00	Evening News (if only one day, this is closing)

Second Day
9:00–9:30   Morning Announcements
9:30–11:00   First Session
11:00–12:30   Second Session
12:30–2:00   Lunch Available
2:00–3:30   Third Session
3:30–5:00   Fourth Session
5:00–5:30   Evening News (if two days, this is closing)

Third Day
9:00–10:30   Read and Prioritize Issues
10:30–11:00   Compute Results
11:00–12:00   Converge Issues/Develop Actions
12:00–1:00   Lunch Available
1:00–2:00   Action Groups Meet
2:00–3:00   Closing

Space and Time Matrix

Room	10:30–12:00	Lunch	1:30–3:00	3:00–4:30	Evening News
Room 1	Post-it note with: Room 1 10:30–12:00		Post-it note with: Room 1 1:30–3:00	Post-it note with: Room 1 3:00–4:30	
Room 2	Post-it note		Post-it note	Post-it note	
Room 3	Post-it note		Post-it note	Post-it note	
Room 4	Post-it note		Post-it note	Post-it note	
Room 5	Post-it note		Post-it note	Post-it note	

The Event

1. People are assembled in a circle (or concentric circles if the group is large) with a small pile of markers, masking tape, and quarter sheets of flip-chart paper.
2. The opening ceremony moves people as quickly as possible into active, synergistic cocreation. It introduces people to what they are doing, creates an agenda, and begins the work.

- Welcome the group (done by the official sponsor). "Welcome to you all. I know we are going to have a useful time together, and now is the time to get started. Here's Harrison (name of the facilitator)."
- Focus the group. Harrison enters the circle and says, "Welcome to Open Space." He slowly, silently walks around the inside of the circle and invites the participants to trace the circle with their eyes.
- State the theme. Harrison states the theme, purpose, and objective in an evocative or provocative rather than a descriptive or prescriptive way. State any expectations in an upbeat way.
- Describe the process. A brief history of Open Space is given as well as the results achieved. Tell participants that you are going to ask each one who has an issue and is willing to take responsibility for the issue to go to the center of the circle. Write a short title of your issue and your name on a piece of flip-chart paper.
- Create the community bulletin board. Announce your issue and name to the group, and tape the paper to the blank wall. It is OK to not have an issue. The person who took responsibility is the convener of the session and is not necessarily an expert. They choose a time and place for the session. They can choose a Post-it note from the space and time matrix and add it to the flip chart on the blank wall. Once everyone who chooses has created his or her issue page, the village marketplace is opened.
- Open the village marketplace as quickly as possible. Everyone walks around and chooses to sign up for issues that they are interested in. People negotiate to attend sessions of interest; sometimes sessions are combined; some have no people interested and are cancelled.
- Invite people to ask questions (try to limit them—it slows things down).
- Introduce the Four Principles and the One Law as the rules to follow. Explain bumblebees and butterflies. Bumblebees use the law of two feet to flit around, going from group to group. Butterflies never go to a specific group, and create centers of nonaction where silence is OK or a new topic can be explored. Finally, suggest that people should "Be Prepared to Be Surprised."

- Go to work. If computerized proceedings are desired, each person who convened a group is responsible for entering a summary into the computer. The facilitator coordinates production of the final proceedings to be available when the participants leave the Open Space event.
- Use Morning Announcements and Evening News to announce meeting changes and logistics updates. The news adds the opportunity to share experiences of the day and reflect on their meaning.
- A closing session brings everyone together and distribution of final proceedings (if desired) takes place.

The facilitator's role is to create space and time and then to give it all away to the participants. This assumes that the structure is created carefully.

THE WORLD CAFÉ

Juanita Brown and David Isaacs designed this conversational practice to help people discover shared meaning, access collective intelligence, and evolve the future together. The World Café[2] is both a simple methodology and a powerful metaphor for understanding and working with the complex process by which we collectively construct our world. As a metaphor it helps visualize the ever expanding networks of conversation and learning that are at the heart of organizational life. The World Café process has been successfully used all over the world. It has proven to be a way to foster authentic conversation and knowledge sharing among people of varied backgrounds—even if they have never met.

The World Café process implements Humberto Maturana's theory that "We learn, adapt, and bring forth our worlds through the networks of conversation in which we participate" (Brown and Isaacs, 2001). The process fundamentally encourages people to talk together about things they care about and links the essence of the conversation with others in ever widening circles. This process allows participants to notice opportunities for mutual insight, innovation, and action that are already present in the group. World Cafés have been held in many different settings around the globe, with groups of 12 to 1,200 using a few simple practices and principles.

---

[2] Source: The World-Café Take-Out Menu and http://www.theworldcafe.com.

Café Know-How

The key to creating a successful World Café conversation is employing the seven guiding principles, which *when used in combination* foster courageous conversations and collective intelligence.

The seven guiding principles are:

Set the Context
Create Hospitable Space
Explore Questions That Matter
Encourage Everyones Contribution
Cross-Pollinate and Connect Diverse Perspectives
Listen Together for Patterns, Insights, and Deeper Questions
Harvest and Share Collective Discoveries

The World Café process is particularly useful in the following situations:

- To generate input, share knowledge, stimulate innovative thinking, and explore action possibilities around real-life issues and questions
- To engage people—whether they are meeting for the first time or are in established relationships—in authentic conversation
- To conduct in-depth exploration of key strategic challenges or opportunities
- To deepen relationships and mutual ownership of outcomes in an existing group
- To create meaningful interaction between a speaker and the audience
- To engage groups larger than 12 (we've had up to 1,200) in an authentic dialogue process

The Café is less useful when

- You are driving toward an already determined solution or answer.
- You want to convey only one-way information.
- You are making detailed implementation plans.
- You have fewer than 12 people (better to use a more traditional dialogue circle, council, or other approach for fostering authentic conversation).

Clarify the Context

There is an old saying that if you don't know where you are going, any road will get you there. When you have a clear idea of the what and the why of your Café, then the how becomes much easier. Here are a few questions to ask yourself and those helping you plan:

- What is the topic or issue we want to address or explore?
- Who needs to be invited to participate in this conversation?
- Who represents both the conventional and the unconventional wisdom?
- How long do we have for the inquiry?
- What line(s) of inquiry do we want to pursue? What themes are most likely to be meaningful and stimulate creativity?
- What is the best outcome we can envision? How might we design a path toward that outcome?

Hospitable Space

Most meeting places are sterile, cold, and impersonal. Consider choosing warm, inviting environments with natural light and comfortable seating. Honor our long traditions of human hospitality by offering food and refreshments. Hospitable space also means "safe" space—where everyone feels free to offer their best thinking.

Hospitable space begins with the invitation to attend a Café. Include the theme or central question you'll be exploring in your Café in the invitation. State it as an open-ended exploration, not a problem-solving intervention. Use color, hand printing, graphics, and other ways to make it stand out from the deluge of paper and e-messages we all receive. When we ask people where they have had some of their most significant conversations, nearly everyone recalls sitting around a kitchen or dining room table. There is an easy intimacy when gathering at a small table, that most of us immediately recognize. When you walk into a room and see it filled with café tables, you know that you are not in for your usual business meeting.

Creating a Café ambiance is easy and need not be expensive.

- Stagger the tables in a random fashion; don't set them up in straight rows.
- Use plastic red-checked tablecloths.

- Cover these with two sheets of flip chart paper.
- Place a mug or wine glass filled with water-based markers to encourage people to write and draw on the tablecloths.
- Add a small bud vase and a votive candle to complete the table setup.
- Have some soft music playing as people arrive.
- Be sure to have some food and beverages available.

Explore Questions That Matter

Knowledge emerges in response to compelling questions. Find questions that are relevant to the real-life concerns of the group. Powerful questions that "travel well" help attract collective energy, insight, and action as they move throughout a system. Depending on the time frame available and your objectives, your Café may explore a single question or use a progressively deeper line of inquiry through several conversational rounds.

As we have worked with groups over the years, we have asked hundreds of people what makes a powerful question. Several themes have emerged. A powerful question:

- Is simple and clear.
- Is thought provoking.
- Generates energy.
- Focuses inquiry.
- Surfaces assumptions.
- Opens new possibilities.
- Invites deeper reflection.
- Seeks what is useful.

A note about appreciative process. David Cooperrider, an organizational behavior professor at case Western Reserve University, has long championed something he calls "appreciative inquiry." The major premise here is that the questions we ask and the way we ask them will focus us in a particular manner and will greatly affect the outcome of our inquiry. If we ask, "What is wrong and who is to blame?" we set up a certain dynamic of problem solving and blame assigning. Although there may be instances where such an approach is desirable, when it comes to hosting a Café, we have found it much more effective to ask people questions that invite the exploration of possibilities and to connect them with why they care.

One potential pitfall is posing questions that ask about the nature of truth. Philosophers have spent thousands of years arguing the nature of truth, and many of the wars in history have been fought over such questions. We are after "shared meaning," which does not mean that we all share the same perspective on what is true but that each participant has the opportunity to share what is true and meaningful for them. This in turn will allow us all to see our collective situation in a different light, hopefully enlarging our individual views of truth along the way. Our experience has been that questions that focus on "What is useful here?" are more effective at generating engagement on the part of participants and tend to provoke less defensive reactions than questions that focus on "What is true?"

Encourage Everyone's Contribution

People engage deeply when they feel they are contributing their thinking to questions that are important to them. Encourage all participants to contribute to the conversation. As Meg Wheatley (author of *Leadership and the New Science* and credited with establishing a fundamentally new approach to how we think about organizations) says, "Intelligence emerges as a system connects to itself in new and diverse ways." Each participant in the Café represents an aspect of the whole system's diversity, and as each person has the chance to connect in conversation, more of the intelligence inherent in the group becomes accessible.

We have found that on occasion it is helpful to have a "talking object" on the tables. Originally used by numerous indigenous peoples, a talking object can be a stick or stone, a marker or salt-shaker, almost anything, as long as it can be passed among the people at the table. There are two aspects to the talking object. Whoever holds the talking object is the only one empowered to speak. And whoever is not holding it is empowered to listen. For the speaker, the responsibility is to focus on the topic and express as clearly as possible their thoughts about it. For the listeners, the responsibility is to listen to what the speaker is saying with the implicit assumption that the speaker has something wise and important to say. Listen with a willingness to be influenced, listen for where this person is coming from, and appreciate that their perspective, regardless of how divergent from your own, is equally valid and represents a part of the larger picture that none of us can see by ourselves. It is not necessary to use a talking object all the time, but in cases where the topic being explored raises impassioned responses, it can be a very effective way to ensure everyone has the opportunity to contribute, even if they simply choose to hold the talking object and observe a few minutes of silence.

Connect Diverse Perspectives

Ask members to offer their individual perspectives and listen for what is emerging "in the middle of the table." Use the tablecloths and markers to create a "shared visual space" through drawing the emerging ideas. Sometimes the cocreated pictures can really be worth a thousand words in showing the relationships between ideas.

A woman we know once remarked, "The most radical thing you can do is to introduce people to folks they don't know." Make sure that members from the first round each go to *different* tables as the conversational rounds progress. This cross-pollination of ideas often produces surprising results that could not have happened otherwise.

Setting up your Café in conversational rounds and asking people to change tables between rounds allow for a dense web of connections to be woven in a short period of time. Each time you travel to a new table, you are bringing with you the threads of the last round and interweaving them with those brought by other travelers. As the rounds progress, the conversation moves to deeper levels. People who arrived with fixed positions often find that they are more open to new and different ideas.

Our experience shows that it's very useful to ask one person to remain at a table to act as the table host. This person will summarize the conversation of the previous round for the newcomers, ensuring that any important points are available for consideration in the upcoming round.

Listen Together and Notice Patterns

Listening is a gift we give to one another. The quality of our listening is perhaps the most important factor determining the success of a Café. Whole books and courses have been written about how to listen. One of our favorite analogies comes from jazz great Wynton Marsalis, who explains that when jazz musicians get together to jam, whoever is the best listener ends up contributing the most to the music, because they are able to play off of whatever is being offered by the other cats in the band. Café conversations share that jazz element, of inviting each person to express themselves authentically, and those who listen skillfully are able to easily build on what is being shared. Here are a few tips for improving our listening:

- Help folks to notice their tendency to plan their response to what is being said, and inquire internally as to the ways that detracts from both the speaker and the listener.
- Listen as if each person were truly wise and sharing some truth that you may have heard before but do not yet fully grasp.
- Listen with an openness to being influenced by the speaker.
- Listen to support the speaker in fully expressing themselves.
- Listen for deeper questions, patterns, insights, and emerging perspectives.
- Listen for what is not being spoken, along with what is being shared.

Share Collective Discoveries

Conversations held at one table reflect a pattern of wholeness that connects with the conversations at the other tables. The last phase of the Café involves making this pattern of wholeness visible to everyone. To do so, hold a conversation between the individual tables and the whole group. Ask the table groups to spend a few minutes considering what has occurred in their Café rounds that has been most meaningful to them. Distill these down to the essence and then have each table share with the whole group the nuggets that are being discovered at their table. Make sure that you have a way to capture this, either on flip charts or by having each table record them on large Post-it notes or even their tablecloths, which can then be taped to a wall so that everyone can see them. After each table has had a chance to report to the whole group, take a few minutes of silent reflection and consider the following:

- What is emerging here?
- If there were a single voice in the room, what would it be saying?
- What deeper questions are emerging as a result of these conversations?
- Do we notice any patterns, and what do those patterns point to, or how do they inform us?
- What do we now see and know as a result of these conversations?

REFERENCES

Argyris, C., and Schoen, D. A. *Organizational Learning.* Reading, MA: Addison-Wesley, 1974.

———. *Organizational Learning II.* Reading, MA: Addison-Wesley, 1996.

Bateson, G. *Steps to an Ecology of Mind.* New York, NY: Ballantine, 1972.

Beerel, A. *Leadership Through Strategic Planning.* London: International Thomson Business Press, 1998.

Brown, J., and Isaacs, D. The World Café Community (2001). The World Café: Living Knowledge Through Conversations That Matter. *The Systems Thinker,* Pegasus Communications, Vol. 12, No. 5.

Gerard, G., and Teurfs, L. "Dialogue and Transformation." *Executive Excellence,* 1997, Vol. 14, No. 8, p. 16.

Jaworski, J. *Synchronicity: The Inner Path of Leadership.* San Francisco, CA: Berret-Koehler Publishers, Inc., 1996.

Michael, D. N. *On Learning to Plan and Planning to Learn.* San Francisco, CA: Jossey-Bass, 1973.

Nevis, E. C., DiBella, A. J., and Gould, J. M. *Understanding Organizations as Learning Systems.* MIT: The Society for Organizational Learning, 1997.

Owen, H. *Open Space Technology: A Users Guide, Second Edition.* San Francisco, CA: Berrett-Koehler Publishers, Inc., 1997.

Pedler, M. J., and Aspinwall, K. A. *A Concise Guide to the Learning Organization.* London: Lemos & Crane, 1998.

Revans, R. W. *The ABC of Action Learning.* London: Lemos & Crane, 1998.

Wheatley, M. *Leadership and the New Science: Discovering Order in a Chaotic World,* San Francisco, CA: Berrett Koehler Publishers, Inc., 2001.

Knowledge Management Processes

By Paul Whiffen and Nick Milton

INTRODUCTION

This appendix describes some of the learning processes that were developed to implement BP's Knowledge Management System. Peer Assists are processes for "Learning Before" a project or an activity. After Action Reviews (AARs) take place during the activity for "Learning During." Retrospects and Learning Histories are processes for "Learning After" a project or activity, and are concerned with the identification and capture of new organizational knowledge. Knowledge Assets are compilations of Knowledge which has been codified and packaged for the benefit of an end user and described in move detail below. The processes are listed in alphabetical order for easy reference.

AFTER ACTION REVIEWS

How They Work, What to Expect, What to Prepare

The After Action Review is a short, focused meeting for a small team, conducted by the team, and lasting half an hour or less. AARs allow the team to capture useful operational knowledge that is of immediate short-term benefit and that can be plowed back into the next shift or the next day's operation. This allows you to make course corrections during activity based on what you learn. It allows you to address and optimize the way you work as a team, and it allows you to start to build your collective operational knowledge. The process consists of asking four questions:

1. What was supposed to happen in the activity we are reviewing?
2. What actually happened?
3. What were the positive/negative things that contributed to the result?
4. What have we learned from this?

Who to invite—Invite everyone who took part in the event. Make sure everyone is on equal footing—no hierarchy. There should be no spectators—only participants. This may be hard to achieve at first, when you may need facilitation support, but you should transition to this state of "no outsiders." If the facilitator is an outsider, he or she should meet two tests: (1) be a respected practitioner in the processes of the event and (2) be a close observer of the event as it unfolded.

Location and setup—The AAR benefits from being held immediately after the process or action, so the location is likely to be on-site, though away from immediate distractions. A nearby meeting room is fine, with a single table and flip chart. The facilitator must ensure that the meeting is open and that blame is not brought in. He or she must also make sure the process is quick and simple and owned by the participants. The only acceptable climate in an AAR is one of openness and learning. The objective is to fix the problem, not fix the blame. AARs are learning events, not critiques, and emphatically not personal performance evaluation events or even a part of the evaluation process. Nothing kills an AAR program more quickly than using it for evaluation; formal or informal.

Question 1: "What was supposed to happen?"—Look back on the activity or event, and remind yourselves what the main objective was. Ideally, this should be clear, and an objective should have been set before the activity started. Even if there was a clear objective, people may still need to share their understanding and interpretation of what was supposed to happen. If you find out that there was no clear objective up front and that participants had different views of what was supposed to happen, then maybe you have learned something already about the need to set objectives!

Question 2: "What actually happened?"—Here you are looking for the facts about what happened—the ground truth. You can either collect these through discussion or refer to records of the event. If your objectives were clear and measurable ("we need to do X, Y, and Z by the end of the week"), then performance measurement is also easy ("we did X and Y, but not Z, which will not be complete until Tuesday"). Where the objectives are less clear ("we wish to establish credibility with this potential client"), look for facts that support the outcome ("the client said, 'you guys obviously know what you are talking about'").

Question 3: "What were the positive/negative factors?" or "Why was there a difference?"—There are two ways you can ask this question, depending on how clear and measurable the objectives were and how established the work processes are. With clear objectives and established work processes, all the learning comes from differences between planned performance and actual performance. In this case you can ask, "Why was there a difference?" (between planned and actual).

Where work processes may not be so well established, we often found we had learned valuable lessons even if the performance had been as predicted. A different version of question 3 is needed to look at the positive and negative learnings, and we ask, "What were the positive/negative factors? (in delivering the actual outcome). What has gone well? What has not gone so well?" Then we can learn from success as well as failure.

Question 4: "What have we learned"—Questions 3 and 4 generally run together. You can try to keep them separate, but you will find that the team discussion generally runs the two together. Once you have analyzed the root causes of the differences between actual performance and expected performance, you can draw out learnings and recommendations for the future on which to base action plans.

Recording—The AAR will help the individuals become conscious of what they have learned. This in itself is of tremendous benefit, but people will forget over time, so some degree of personal recording can be a good thing. This can be as simple as writing down the learnings in a personal logbook.

Deliverables—Although AAR results are by the team, for the team, some of the learning from the AAR may have wider applicability. This could form much of the basis for the end-of-project Retrospect, for transfer into other teams running similar projects in the future. The AAR facilitators can be charged with recording the lessons to take to the Retrospect. Alternatively, you could introduce some sort of lessons database for storing the lessons so that they can be later packaged into a Knowledge Asset.

HOW TO CREATE A KNOWLEDGE ASSET

A Knowledge Asset is a way of summarizing and storing the lessons from past experience. Knowledge Assets provide a central place where individuals and teams across the organization can pool their knowledge for local and global gain. BP believed that focusing on Knowledge Assets would develop the right behaviors and skills necessary for KM to flourish and expand to a group-wide capability.[1]

The context and histories that make up Knowledge Assets provide a common framework to facilitate reuse of knowledge.

Knowledge Assets can contain:

- Guidelines or checklists, representing the current understanding of best practice.
- Illustrations from past history and experience. These can be stories or quotes to make the guidelines come alive. The stories should be told in the words of the people involved (The "voice of experience").
- Names and contact details of the people who hold the experience.
- Artifacts and records of relevance, such as project plans, examples of solutions, photographs, video clips, etc.
- References such as websites and internal reference documents.

An organization and person needs to "own" a Knowledge Asset. When it is of universal interest, it can be owned by a corporate department or a community of practice. For example, in a major bank, a Knowledge Asset on "how to measure the impact of learning" is managed by the Corporate Education Department and the Measurement Center of Excellence (a community of practice). In other cases, the Knowledge Asset may be owned locally in a single business unit.

Steps or Guidelines for Creating a Knowledge Asset

1. Define the scope of the Knowledge Asset.
    - What will be the subject? What will it cover? It needs to cover a specific—and not too broad—business, activity, or task.
    - What will the content include?
        ▽ What do you need to know to do this activity or task?

---

[1] The material in this section is adapted from British Petroleum's Resource Pack on Knowledge Management, developed by the Group Knowledge Management Team—1998 (as described on page 133).

    ▽ What is the biggest issue facing you?

    ▽ Do you need to know processes, techniques, people, or reasons for doing something, or legal or regulatory requirements?

    ▽ Do you need to know who, what, why and/or how?

- Why are you doing this? What can or will happen if you *do not* capture the knowledge?

2. Make sure a community of practice or business function owns the Knowledge Asset. The community plays several roles:
   - Source of the knowledge
   - Users of knowledge in the future
   - People who ensure the information/knowledge is accurate and up-to-date

3. Collect the existing material:
   - Interviews with key people and teams
   - Important documents and artifacts
   - Retrospects
   - After Action Reviews
   - Learning Histories

4. Describe the context for the Knowledge Asset with:
   - Background
   - Purpose
   - Benefits
   - Relevance

5. Develop general practices describing the activity or task you are addressing.
   - Go through the records of previous work, the Retrospect and AAR outcomes and people's experience, and try to find the common knowledge. Different people will have seen certain approaches work at certain times. Are there general guidelines that you can derive? This is a creative and value-adding step, but it is a challenge. You are taking what may be a mass of material and distilling it to something useful to anyone interested in this function.
   - Develop a checklist for the user of the Knowledge Asset, including the following types of questions:

    ▽ What questions should the user be asking?

    ▽ What information does the user need to gather?

    ▽ What steps does the user need to take?

   - Create the checklist as either a list of questions with answers (like an FAQ) or as recommended steps and actions.

- Add stories, quotes, and examples to the checklist to make it come alive.
- Include a library of related documents and links for users to get more detailed information.
- Include pictures, if applicable.
- Include a list of people who have more knowledge and can be a source of advice to users. Include contact information, a photograph, and a link to a personal Web page for each.

6. Provide information about the Knowledge Asset owner, the person who wrote the practices. Include contact information, a photo, and an e-mail link.
7. Provide the date the Knowledge Asset was created or updated.
8. Validate the content with community members.
   - Does it reflect knowledge and experience?
   - Will it be useful to a new user?
   - Do you have anything to add?
9. Put the Knowledge Asset into an appropriate medium or vehicle for distribution:
   - Corporate Web site
   - Local Web site
10. Launch the Knowledge Asset.
11. Keep it alive and update it.
    - Encourage feedback from users.
    - Ensure there is an active owner.

Note: In BP, trained facilitators created the Knowledge Assets. An outsider's involvement in the analysis and questioning process added value by providing essential objectivity and clarity as well as process expertise.

LEARNING HISTORIES

How They Work, What to Expect, What to Prepare

A Learning History is the knowledge from a major project or other piece of work, compiled through individual interviews with the people involved. A Learning History would be used when the team of Knowledge holders is too big or too busy to schedule a group knowledge capture session, such as a Retrospect. The Learning History approach is time-efficient for the interviewees, who spend an hour being interviewed rather than half a day in a Retrospect. It is less efficient for the interviewers, who, instead of capturing knowledge from, say, a dozen people in a single afternoon, must schedule 12 individual interviews, possibly strung out over the course of a week or more.

A Learning History involves a single interviewer, or a small team, holding free-flowing interviews with key team members and then producing an analysis and synthesis of the results.

Building the team—You need a small, dedicated core team to run the Learning History. A small Learning History covering 10 people or fewer can be handled by a single person, but anything more than this may need two or more people. The team needs interviewing skills and analytical skills, and although they do not need to be experts in the particular knowledge area, they at least have to know the vocabulary and the language. You need some good writers on the team so that the knowledge can be packaged in a readable way. A skilled team can produce a Learning History in a timescale of 1.5–2 man-days per interviewee (therefore, a Learning History based on 20 interviews would take 30–40 man-days, including administration, preparation, analysis, and packaging).

Who to interview—You will probably want to include participants from all levels in the project and all phases. This may be everyone who participated, if the team is small enough. In a larger team, you may not have time to include everybody and will need to interview a representative sample. Make sure you interview the project leader, the core team, internal customers (if appropriate), and representatives from various business entities (departments, refinery units, businesses—whatever makes sense for the story). Ask the project leader and the sponsor to come up with a list of key people to interview.

Location—You need a quiet location where you will not be disturbed. An empty meeting room or a quiet room in the interviewee's home would be ideal. You cannot conduct an interview in an open-plan area. Make sure that the door is closed, that no telephone calls will be put through, and that any noisy fans or air-conditioning units are switched off. If you are making a video of the interview, make sure the lighting is OK.

Recording—The best way to transfer knowledge during the interview process is in the words of the people involved. There is no real substitute for audio recording to make sure these words are captured. Make sure you have a backup, however—either speed-written notes or an alternative form of recording such as video, or even both. Always ask permission before audio recording.

Analysis—The distillation and analysis step consists of extracting the core material from the interviews and presenting it as guidelines for the future. You need to sort out the following:

- The key themes that emerged from the interviews.
- The key recommendations associated with each theme.
- Quotes, stories, and anecdotes to support the recommendations.

This analysis step can be time-consuming and tiring, but there is no shortcut. It may take a full day or two to do the analysis and a further day of cutting and pasting to sort all the material.

Selecting quotes—Select the key quotes from the interview material, the ones that "tell the story" or "give the advice." It can be valuable to have two people do this in parallel. Edit the quotes for grammar, removing the "ums" and "ers" and "actuallys," which are acceptable in speech but do not translate to the written word. Validate these quotes with the interviewees by sending them back to them with a suitable cover letter.

Deriving themes—Sort the quotes into themes. With a single transcript, you can sort the quotes online by cutting and pasting. With many interview transcripts, a good technique is to cut out the quotes with scissors (make sure each quote is attributed first!) and arrange them by topic. Stick them onto flip charts. Start the analysis by identifying the obvious key elements and subthemes. This can add structure to any remaining interviews. Group the quotes by "message" within the themes. Often, several of the quotes will give the same "message." Selecting the messages is another key step, and you need to strike a balance between selecting too many (and ending up with trivia) and selecting too few (and missing value).

Extracting advice or questions—Rephrase the messages as advice for the "knowledge customer," or as questions in a checklist. Some people seem to respond better to a set of questions than they do to a set of rules and procedures. Others will prefer to work according to a rule book. Tailor the approach to the prevailing culture.

Deliverables—The outcome of the Learning History is a Knowledge Asset that includes guidelines for the future (expressed in the words of the interviewees), a history from the project to illustrate the guidelines, the names of people involved for future reference, and the key artifacts.

PEER ASSISTS

How They Work, What to Expect, What to Prepare

A Peer Assist is a process for bringing knowledge into a project, or piece of work, at the outset. It is a meeting where a project team invites a number of people with relevant knowledge and experience, which they bring to bear on the issues of the project. They apply out-of-team knowledge to the team's context. It is one of the easiest and most effective ways of bringing knowledge to the point of need. The Peer Assist involves two teams:

- The host team, or project team, are the ones who need the knowledge and who set up the Peer Assist.
- The visitors, or the visiting team, are the people who have the knowledge and who come to the Peer Assist to help the host team.

A Peer Assist meeting may take anywhere from a few hours to a few days, depending on the scale of the project. It should have clear objectives and deliverables (such as producing a ranked listing of risks and options, or cutting 20% off the project cost, or something similar). During the Assist, the project team will lay out their plans, objectives, issues, opportunities, and challenges, and the visitors will use their knowledge and experience from similar projects to provide recommendations, options, issues, and guidance. The project team is not obliged to act on the recommendations, but use them as valuable input to start the project from a greatly enhanced knowledge base.

Who to invite—The visiting team should consist of people who have recent experience and practical knowledge to share. They should have been involved in similar projects in the past. Choose people with practical knowledge, rather than automatically calling in the head-office specialist. Ask your networks or communities of practice, make use of company "yellow pages" systems, or search your company intranet to find people with experience on a topic. Avoid falling into the trap of "rounding up the usual suspects." Appoint a facilitator. The process may need careful facilitation if it is new to your company culture.

Location—Choose a conference room or off-site facility, where the team members can sit around a single table. This should be quiet and undisturbed. Arrange for flip charts and pens.

Part 1—It is good to kick off the formal part of the Peer Assist with a welcome from the Peer Assist sponsor and an explanation of why the Peer Assist has been called, what its objectives and deliverables are, and why it is important to the business.

Part 2—The second stage is a presentation from the host project team about the history and context behind their project, the current status, their plans and aspirations, and the risks and issues that they see. This section is "what do we know about the context and issues."

Some of this material can also be provided as prereading.

Part 3—Here the visitors can talk through their recent relevant experience to the project team. This can be, at the very least, a reintroduction of the visitors, explaining what background and experience they have that relates to the issues the project team has just presented.

Part 4—The visitors need to develop a good understanding of the details of the issues, the level of understanding, the available data, and the degrees of uncertainty. This is best done through dialogue and possibly one-on-one dialogue between specialists. During this dialogue, the visiting team will be sharing knowledge with the project team as well as gaining a better understanding of the issues in the project. The project team should therefore also be questioning the visitors about their experience and learning, and any insights they can bring to the project. This stage can take up to 50% or more of the Peer Assist.

Part 5—A formal conclusion and feedback session is needed at the end of the Peer Assist, to summarize the outcome of the analysis and present the results. Generally, someone from the visiting team will do this. This is a good opportunity to have the sponsor or manager in the room, to hear the results of the assist. You can follow this session by a presentation from the project team (either a formal presentation or around-the-room comments) on "what have we learned from the visitors" and "what are we going to do about it."

Recording—The peer assist is primarily for the benefit of the project team. Make sure the project team keeps detailed notes, files the presentations and the deliverables, and records the feedback sessions.

Deliverables—The Peer Assist should deliver its stated objectives, which will have been defined by the project team. However, it will also have softer deliverables, and many organizations have found that introducing Peer Assists leads to an increase in openness, the establishment of cross-business linkages and communities, and an increased willingness to learn from others.

RETROSPECTS

How They Work, What to Expect, What to Prepare

The Retrospect is one of the most effective processes for capturing lessons learned from a project team, after the end of a piece of work. With a Retrospect, you can bring out the key knowledge and experience developed by a project team, and capture it for future reuse and the benefit of future projects. By facilitating a dialogue within the whole team, you can bring out the knowledge that comes from the team interactions—knowledge that any one individual may be unaware of but that the team as a whole knows.

Retrospects are face-to-face or videoconference meetings that take place as soon as possible after a project is completed. The duration varies depending on number of people, duration, and complexity of the project. They can be from 30 minutes to an hour for a short, simple project or four or more hours for a 10-person, six-month project. A Retrospect of an alliance between several departments or companies may take two days. A general rule of thumb for working out how long to allow is to multiply the number of people on the team by 30 minutes.

Who to invite—Invite the team who was involved in delivering the project. Include the team leader, all team members, the customer or client for the project, and all other key participants. You cannot really hold a Retrospect with more than about 12 people, so if the extended team exceeds 12, then either invite just the core team, or hold separate Retrospects for subprojects. Appoint an external facilitator.

Location—Choose a conference room or off-site facility where the team members can sit around a single table. This should be quiet and undisturbed. Arrange for flip charts and pens.

Part 1—The retrospect begins by revisiting the objectives, deliverables, and measures of the project. Questions include "What did you set out to do?" "What was the understanding at the start of the project?"

The team leader should prepare a short (15-minute) presentation of the original objectives of the project, referring to original documents such as the terms of reference. It may be a good idea to circulate these prior to the meeting.

Part 2—This part covers "what actually happened." Questions include "What did you achieve?" "Did you get what you wanted?" "Did you meet the deadlines?" "Were satisfaction measures achieved?" "What happened along the way?" In a complex project, the team may wish to construct a timeline or flow chart to determine what actually happened.

The team leader should prepare a short (15-minute) presentation of the final deliverables, including items such as actual vs. budget figures, actual vs. estimated timeline, customer satisfaction surveys, performance data, etc. It may be a good idea to circulate these prior to the meeting.

Part 3—The facilitator then asks the members of the team what went well (in the context of delivering objectives), and they collectively determine why these aspects went well. The success factors should be identified so they can be repeated by this team or other teams. Then, additional questions are addressed: "What could have gone better?" "What were the difficulties?"

No preparation is needed for this section. The facilitator will be pushing throughout for lessons to be turned into specific actionable recommendations for future projects.

Part 4, closeout—The project is given a 1–10 (low to high) numerical rating by each participant in the meeting. This is a numerical rating of the level of personal satisfaction with the project (sometimes two satisfaction ratings are requested—one for the outcome of the project, and one for the project process). This is requested for two reasons—first, as a closure statement for each participant; and second, to ask a final question. If the rating is less than 10, each member is asked, "What would have made it a 10 for you?"

Recording—A considerable amount of knowledge will be shared during the dialogue. This knowledge needs to be captured, and the best way to do this is to record and transcribe the proceedings (or at least part 3 of the proceedings). Audio recording is needed; a tape recorder with table microphones, plenty of batteries, and plenty of spare tapes. Make it clear that no transcripts or copies of the recordings will be published, or used in any way, without the permission of the people involved.

Hard deliverables—The outcome of the retrospect is a Knowledge Asset for the project that includes guidelines for the future, a history from the project to illustrate the guidelines, the names of people involved for future reference, and the key documents that will be useful for future teams.

Soft deliverables—The Retrospect is a process of team reflection and team discussion, which looks to learn from the past in a nonjudgmental way in order to improve the future. Many teams have found that regular Retrospects of projects lead to an increase in openness, an elimination of a blame culture, and an increase in performance focus.

Index

Accenture, 188
Action
  knowledge and, 41–43
  organization levels and,
    46
  patterns of action, 44–45
Action-oriented roles, 74
Action-Reflection
  Subsystem, 30, 31, 32,
    33, 46
Actionable advice, 3
Adaptation
  organizational learning
    and, 44–45
  sensemaking/structuring
    and, 46
  see also Environmental
    Interface Subsystem
After Action Reviews
  British Petroleum, 115,
    125, 129–30, 131, 134
  British Petroleum well
    engineering, 169–70,
    174, 175–76
  De Beers, 184
  Debswana, 345, 346
  Educational Testing
    Service, 278, 279, 282
  Ukuvuka, 204–5
  uses of, 60, 70, 71
Aid Workers Network, 161
Ainger, Steve, 114
Andersen Consulting, 254
Andersen Worldwide, 37
Andriessen, D., 75
April, Kurt, 88, 317, 323,
    327
Argyris, Chris, 27, 291
Arthur Andersen
  assessing progress by,
    256–59

background of, 253–55,
    254–55
  Enron and, 254, 265, 272
  Global Best Practices
    database of, 256, 272
  managing partners for
    clients, 253, 256, 257
  see also Andersen
    Consulting; Knowledge
    Enterprise
Arthur Andersen's AA21
    task force
  approach of, 255–56
  formation/objectives of,
    253, 255–56
  HR findings of, 262–64
  structure of, 255
Arthur Andersen's practice
    communities
  AA Board of Partners
    and, 260–61, 263
  employee retention and,
    253–54, 257, 262
  Employer of Choice
    strategy, 253, 257,
    260–66, 270
  high-performing
    organization and, 253,
    266
  HR initiative, 260–66
  HR initiative at
    MNY/NE, 264–66
  HR structure (previous),
    260–61, 262–63
  as Knowledge Asset,
    49–50
  Knowledge Space (Web
    service), 272
  lessons learned, 270–72
  measuring success by,
    269–70

as membership firm,
    266–69
  MNY/NE experience,
    264–69, 271, 272
  organizational context of,
    256–57
  overview, 253–54, 272
  partner-level HR
    executive, 265
  People Strategy of, 253,
    257, 260–66, 270
  pilots and, 270–71
  roles/responsibilities in,
    267–68
  study findings, 262–64
Assumptions shared,
    59–60

Baird, L., 27
Balanced scorecards
  De Beers, 189
  Debswana, 318
Balfour, Doug, 150, 156
Bangladesh flooding
    disaster, 147–48
Barriers to KM
  cultural issues and, 52,
    53–55, 290–92
  Debswana, 325, 329, 333
  Educational Testing
    Service, 290–92
  knowledge as power, 52,
    53, 222, 223, 291–92,
    333
  Old Mutual, 222–23
  Shell, 301–2
Belbin's team roles, 73, 74
Benefit/cost ratio (BCR), 94
Best practices
  Arthur Andersen, 256,
    272

395

Author Bios

Carol Gorelick co-founded SOLUTIONS for Information & Management Services, a KM consulting firm in 1991 where she pioneered the practice of collaborative learning for performance results. Carol's commitment to drive performance in client organizations through the use of cutting edge learning methods has established good practices in many organizations. She works to bring together the best in people, processes and technology to help individuals, teams and groups improve their results and define their missions.

Carol began her career as an information technology professional. She has been an innovator, introducing personal productivity tools and collaborative technologies in front offices and executive suites. Her success with finding ways to develop and deliver technology solutions for people to be able to participate in work together while being physically and functionally apart has led to the development of knowledge management and education initiatives that enable clients to share skills, experience and knowledge.

Her clients include The Educational Testing Service, Arthur Andersen and Old Mutual (described in this book) as well as First Union National Bank, British Petroleum International, Credit Suisse First Boston, IBM, JPMorgan Chase, Lotus Development Corporation and other innovators in Knowledge Management and Organizational Learning. Carol is a visiting professor at Pace University's MBA program in The Lubin School of Business and at the Graduate School of Business at the University of Cape Town, South Africa where she teaches knowledge management in the MBA and Executive Management programs with co-author Kurt April.

Carol earned a doctorate in organizational learning, collaborative technologies and virtual team building from George Washington University where she worked and studied with the British Petroleum Knowledge Management team and her collaborator and co-author Nick Milton. She lives in New York City.

Nick Milton has unparalleled experience in developing and applying knowledge management for business benefit. He spent two years at the center of the team that made BP the leading KM company in the world, acting as the team Knowledge Manager, developing and implementing BP's knowledge of "how to manage knowledge", and coordinating the BP KM community of practice. Prior to this role he had worked for 5 years as Knowledge Manager for BP Norway.

Since leaving BT in 1999, Nick has been instrumental in developing and delivering KM strategies and implementation plans in a wide range of different organizations, including De Beers (as described in this book), as well as major clients in the mining, broadcasting, manufacturing and energy sectors.

He has a particular interest in capturing and collating knowledge, and has managed major knowledge capture programs, particularly in the area of mergers and acquisitions.

Nick is a widely recognized coach and trainer, and has spoken at many international conferences, such as Unicom, EEMA, EBIC and the IT Directors Forum. Nick holds a Doctor of Philosophy from the University of Wales, is directing training and product development for Knoco ltd, and is based in Somerset, England.

Kurt A. April is the Sainsbury Fellow and Academic Director of the SA-US Centre of Leadership and Public Values, at the Graduate School of Business of the University of Cape Town (UCT). He is also a regular Visiting Professor at Rotterdam School of Management (Erasmus University, The Netherlands), Guest Professor in the Information Management Department (University of Amsterdam, The Netherlands), and Templeton College (Oxford University, UK) where he runs *Leadership, Diversity, Knowledge Management & Computer-Supported Work, Intellectual Capital, Technology & New Work Practices* modules and programmes. Outside of academia, Kurt is Managing Partner of *LICM Consulting*, and Executive Director of *Complex Adaptive Systems*, working with various multinationals and SMEs around the globe, as well as local organisations. Kurt has co-authored 4 books, with two more appearing in 2005.